The British and Peace in Northern

How did the British Government and Civil Service shape the Northern Ireland peace process? What kind of tensions and debates were being played out between the two governments and the various parties in Northern Ireland? Addressing texts, negotiations, dialogues, space, leverage, strategy, ambiguity, interpersonal relations and convergence, this is the first volume to examine how senior British officials and civil servants worked to bring about power-sharing in Northern Ireland. With a unique format featuring self-authored inside accounts and interview testimonies, it considers a spectrum of areas and issues that came into play during the dialogues and negotiations that led to the 1998 Good Friday Agreement and political accommodation in Northern Ireland. This book provides a compelling insight into what actually happened inside the negotiating room and how the British tried to shape the course of negotiations.

GRAHAM SPENCER is Reader in Politics, Conflict and the Media at the University of Portsmouth, Distinguished Senior Research Fellow in the Edward M. Kennedy Institute for Conflict Intervention at the National University of Ireland, Maynooth, and Honorary Senior Research Fellow in the Department of Politics at the University of Liverpool. His books include *From Armed Struggle to Political Struggle: Republican Tradition and Transformation in Northern Ireland* (2015), *Protestant Identity and Peace in Northern Ireland* (2012), *The Media and Peace* (2008), *The State of Loyalism in Northern Ireland* (2008), *Omagh: Voices of Loss* (2005), *Ulster Loyalism after the Good Friday Agreement* (editor with James W. McAuley, 2011) and *Forgiving and Remembering in Northern Ireland* (editor, 2011). He is also a Fellow of the Royal Society of Arts. His research interests include conflict transformation, political negotiation and communication, identities in conflict and reconciliation.

'Principles and rules are intended to provide a thinking man with a frame of reference' — Carl von Clausewitz

'The world of theories is not my world. These are simply the reflections of a practitioner' — Milan Kundera

The British and Peace in Northern Ireland

The Process and Practice of Reaching Agreement

Edited by
Graham Spencer

CAMBRIDGE
UNIVERSITY PRESS

CAMBRIDGE
UNIVERSITY PRESS

University Printing House, Cambridge CB2 8BS, United Kingdom

Cambridge University Press is part of the University of Cambridge.

It furthers the University's mission by disseminating knowledge in the pursuit of education, learning and research at the highest international levels of excellence.

www.cambridge.org
Information on this title: www.cambridge.org/9781107617506

© Cambridge University Press 2015

This publication is in copyright. Subject to statutory exception and to the provisions of relevant collective licensing agreements, no reproduction of any part may take place without the written permission of Cambridge University Press.

First published 2015

Printed in the United States of America by Sheridan Books, Inc.

A catalogue record for this publication is available from the British Library

Library of Congress Cataloguing in Publication data
The British and peace in Northern Ireland : the process and practice of reaching agreement / edited by Graham Spencer.
   pages   cm
ISBN 978-1-107-04287-2 (hardback)
1. Peace-building – Northern Ireland – History.   2. Coalition governments – Northern Ireland.   3. Northern Ireland – Politics and government – 1994–   4. Great Britain – Politics and government – 1997–2007.   I. Spencer, Graham, editor of compilation.
JZ5584.N75B75   2015
941.60824 – dc23   2014032227

ISBN 978-1-107-04287-2 Hardback
ISBN 978-1-107-61750-6 Paperback

Cambridge University Press has no responsibility for the persistence or accuracy of URLs for external or third-party Internet websites referred to in this publication, and does not guarantee that any content on such websites is, or will remain, accurate or appropriate.

For Lynn

Contents

	Notes on contributors	*page* ix
	Acknowledgements	xiii
	Brief chronology of the peace process	xiv
	Abbreviations	xxiii
	Key documents	xxiv
	Introduction	1
1	The terrain of discourse SIR KENNETH BLOOMFIELD	17
2	The Anglo-Irish Agreement: an interview with Sir David Goodall and Lord Armstrong of Ilminster	33
3	The constitutional issue in Irish politics DAVID HILL	55
4	Negotiations and positions: an interview with Sir John Chilcot	79
5	Resolving intercommunal conflict: some enabling factors SIR QUENTIN THOMAS	101
6	Tactics, strategy and space CHRIS MACCABE	120
7	The Joint Declaration and memory DAVID COOKE	147
8	Movement and transition in 1997: Major to Blair SIR JOHN HOLMES	177
9	The challenge of symmetry in dialogue: an interview with Sir Joseph Pilling	201

10	Why was the Good Friday Agreement so hard to implement?: lessons from 'Groundhog Day', 1998–2002 SIR BILL JEFFREY	229
11	Text and context: an interview with William Fittall	252
12	The nature of dialogue: an interview with Sir Jonathan Phillips	277
13	Managing the tensions of difference: an interview with Jonathan Powell	302
	Conclusion	330
	Index	335

Notes on contributors

LORD ROBERT ARMSTRONG was educated at the Dragon School, Oxford, Eton, and then Christ Church, Oxford. He served as the prime minister's personal representative for the Economic Summit from 1978 to 1984, and is also a former secretary to the British Cabinet. He served as principal of the Treasury from 1955 to 1957, and again from 1959 to 1964; as principal private secretary of state to the prime minister from 1970 to 1975; as permanent undersecretary of state from 1977 to 1979; and as head of the Home Civil Service from 1982 to 1988. He was raised to the peerage as Baron Armstrong of Ilminster, of Ashill in the County of Somerset in 1988.

SIR KENNETH BLOOMFIELD KCB, was born in Belfast in 1931, the son of English parents. He was educated at the Royal Belfast Academical Institution and St Peter's College, Oxford, where he read Modern History. On the basis of the Open Competition 1952, he opted to serve in the Northern Ireland Civil Service, where for almost forty years he served as private secretary to three finance ministers, as a cabinet secretary to unionist and power-sharing cabinets, as permanent secretary to local departments, and from 1984 to 1991 as head of the Northern Ireland Civil Service. Thereafter, he has held a wide range of public and other appointments, including authorship of his report *We Will Remember Them* on victims of terrorism. He is a member of the Royal Irish Academy, and the recipient of honorary doctorates from the Open University, the University of Ulster and Queen's Belfast. He is the author of four published books: *Stormont in Crisis*, *A Tragedy of Errors*, *A New Life* and *The BBC at the Watershed*.

SIR JOHN CHILCOT was permanent secretary at the Northern Ireland Office from 1990 until he retired from a career as a senior civil servant at the end of 1997. Since then he has been a (non-party) member or chairman of a number of reviews, inquiries and other bodies, including the Independent Commission on the Voting System (1997–8), the Lord Chancellor's Advisory Council on Public Records and its successor National Archives Council (1999–2004), a review of Royal and VIP security, an inquiry into the PIRA break-in at the Police Service of Northern Ireland (PSNI) Special Branch HQ

Notes on contributors

(2002), and the Review of the Intelligence on Weapons of Mass Destruction by a Committee of Privy Counsellors, chaired by Lord Butler (2004). He was staff counsellor to the Security and Intelligence Agencies (1999–2004) and the National Criminal Intelligence Service (2002–6). He is currently head of the Iraq War Inquiry into the circumstances surrounding the March 2003 invasion of Iraq and its aftermath. He was interviewed three times in London between 2012 and 2013.

DAVID COOKE was a civil servant from 1977 to 2004, based mainly in the Home Office, the Northern Ireland Office and the Cabinet Office. Since then he has been CEO of the British Board of Film Classification under the presidency of Sir Quentin Thomas, who stepped down in 2012. David Cooke was a head of division in the Northern Ireland Office from 1990 to 1993, and then associate political director from 2002 to 2004, working closely with Jonathan Powell and Jonathan Phillips on policy and negotiations as part of the political process at that time.

WILLIAM FITTALL was principal private secretary to Peter Brooke and Patrick Mayhew 1992–3, in charge of the Home Office Counter-Terrorism Division 1993–5, cabinet office chief of the Assessment Staff and a member of the Joint Intelligence Committee 1995–7, Director of the Crime Reduction and Community programmes in the Home Office 1997–2000, and associate political director of the Northern Ireland Office from August 2000 until he left the Civil Service at the end of September 2002 to become the secretary general for the Church of England, where he is still in post. He was interviewed twice in London in 2014.

SIR DAVID GOODALL GCMG was born in 1931 and educated at Ampleforth College and then at Trinity College, Oxford, where he read Classical Mods and Greats. After two years' military service (in Kenya, Aden and Cyprus), he joined the Foreign (now Diplomatic) Service in 1956, serving in Jakarta, Nairobi, Vienna and twice in Bonn. From 1982 to 1984 he was a deputy secretary in the Cabinet Office, and from 1984 to 1987 deputy undersecretary of State in the Foreign and Commonwealth Office. From 1987 to 1991 he was British high commissioner to India. After retirement from the Diplomatic Service, he was chairman of the Leonard Cheshire Foundation (now Leonard Cheshire Disability) from 1995 to 2000; and chairman of the British–Irish Association from 1997 to 2001.

DAVID HILL was head of the Constitutional and Political Division of the Northern Ireland Office from October 1989 to May 1993, and again from December 1995 to February 1999. As such, he was centrally involved in the initiation and management of the Northern Ireland talks process, from its formal inception in January 1990 through to the Belfast Agreement of April

1998, the ensuing referenda and the establishment and first meetings of the new Northern Ireland Assembly. He is one of the very few people to have participated in virtually every meeting of the 'talks about talks', the 'Brooke' and 'Mayhew' talks of 1991 and 1992, and the multiparty talks that ran from June 1996 to April 1998. Apart from advising ministers on the underlying strategy to promote a political settlement and the tactical handling of the talks process, he had lead responsibility within the Northern Ireland Office for constitutional matters.

SIR JOHN HOLMES GCVO, KBE, CMG is the director of the Ditchley Foundation and co-chair of the International Rescue Committee UK. He is the former UN undersecretary-general for Humanitarian Affairs and Emergency Relief coordinator. A career diplomat, he has served the British Government for more than thirty years and has extensive experience on conflict. Having worked on the Lebanon and Middle East peace processes, he was awarded a knighthood in 1998 primarily for his role in the Northern Ireland peace process and the Good Friday Agreement. He served as private secretary (Overseas Affairs) to John Major before becoming principal private secretary to Tony Blair in 1997.

SIR BILL JEFFREY was political director at the Northern Ireland Office from early 1998 until November 2002, following a career spent mainly in the Home Office. He subsequently headed the Immigration and Nationality Directorate of the Home Office, was permanent secretary and Security and Intelligence coordinator at the Cabinet Office at the time of the attacks on London in July 2005, and for the last five years of his service was permanent secretary at the Ministry of Defence.

CHRIS MACCABE began his career as a researcher in the Northern Ireland Cabinet Office. Between 1973 and 1977, he was a private secretary to chief minister of Northern Ireland Brian Faulkner and to several Northern Ireland Office ministers, including the deputy secretary of state. After various appointments, including special assistant to the Chief Constable of the Royal Ulster Constabulary and a director in the Northern Ireland Prison Service, he became head of the Northern Ireland Office's Political Affairs Division at the beginning of 1992. Between 2000 and 2008 he was British joint secretary of the British–Irish Intergovernmental Conference and the political director of the Northern Ireland Office. He is currently a member of the International Verification Commission monitoring the ETA ceasefire.

SIR JONATHAN PHILLIPS worked at Whitehall for some twenty-five years in areas of economic policy before moving to the Northern Ireland Office in 2002, where he became political director. He was then appointed as permanent secretary in 2005, and left the Civil Service in 2010 after devolution of policing and justice powers to the Northern Ireland Executive. He is now warden of Keble College, Oxford. He was interviewed three times in Oxford between 2012 and 2013.

SIR JOSEPH PILLING has served as a member of the Board of Trustees of Macmillan Cancer Relief since December 2005. He previously worked in the Home Office, the Department of Health and the Northern Ireland Office. He was the director general of HM Prison Service in England and Wales, and then permanent secretary of the Northern Ireland Office from 1997 until his retirement in 2005. He was educated at King's College, London, and at Harvard University, and is currently chair of the Church of England Bishops' Review on Human Sexuality. He was interviewed three times in London between 2012 and 2013.

JONATHAN POWELL worked for the BBC and Granada TV before joining the Foreign Office in 1979. He then became a diplomat based at the British Embassy in Washington before joining Tony Blair's 'kitchen cabinet' as chief of staff in 1995; a position he occupied until 2007. Jonathan Powell played a central role in the negotiations leading to the Good Friday Agreement of 1998, and continued as a key player coordinating and managing New Labour policy in Northern Ireland until he left office in 2007. He was interviewed three times, initially in 2009, then in 2012 and 2013.

SIR QUENTIN THOMAS had a Whitehall career in the Home Office, the Northern Ireland Office and the Cabinet Office, where he headed the Constitution Secretariat (1998–9). He served in the Northern Ireland Office as political director (1991–8). He chaired the BBC Governors' Impartiality Review of the BBC's coverage of the Israeli–Palestinian conflict. He was president of the British Board of Film Classification (2002–12).

Acknowledgements

It goes without saying that I want to thank all those who have contributed to this book. Each gave their time and showed great patience in dealing with my requests for further interviews or amendments to chapters. I also want to thank the Centre for Creative and Cultural Research Group at the University of Portsmouth for supporting this project until July 2013, and the many people I have interviewed across Ireland, both north and south, over the years about the peace process. I have always been met with courtesy, respect and consideration by the hundreds I have spoken to and interviewed, and this book is as much a reflection of my relationship with Northern Ireland and the Republic of Ireland as it is anything else. My fascination has always been with the extended interview and the mysteries of interaction that can reveal moments of insight or unknown tension. The interview is ultimately about experience and emotion, and both are essential for understanding relationships and decision-making processes. For those who have shared this with me over the years I am eternally grateful. I would also like to thank *Irish Political Studies* for allowing me to use part of an interview with Jonathan Powell published in 2010. Importantly, I want to thank my very good friends Lincoln Geraghty and Van Norris for the constant hilarity, Sue Harper and Keith Tester for their generosity and advice and Revd Chris Hudson for support and friendship. The book though is dedicated to Lynn Evans who has been an inspiration.

Brief chronology of the peace process

November 1987	The Provisional IRA (PIRA) kills eleven people and injures many more at a Remembrance Sunday service in Enniskillen.
January 1988	Social Democratic and Labour Party (SDLP) leader John Hume meets Sinn Féin leader Gerry Adams.
October 1988	British Government imposes broadcasting ban on Sinn Féin and other groups linked to paramilitaries.
March 1989	Gerry Adams comments on the need for a 'non-armed political movement to work for self-determination'.
November 1989	Northern Ireland secretary Peter Brooke states that the PIRA cannot be militarily defeated and that talks could follow an end to violence.
November 1990	Peter Brooke states that the United Kingdom has 'no selfish strategic or economic interest' in Northern Ireland. Brooke goes on to say that 'It is not the aspiration to a sovereign, united Ireland against which we set our face, but its violent expression.'
March 1991	Talks begin chaired by Peter Brooke. Talks end when the Intergovernmental Conference, which emerged from the Anglo-Irish Agreement, is resumed. The talks focus on Strand 1 only and the process of talks is constructed long the lines of three strands: relations in Northern Ireland, relations between Northern Ireland and the Republic of Ireland and relations between Dublin and London.
February 1992	Sinn Féin publishes the document *Towards a Lasting Peace in Ireland* setting out a political peace strategy.
May 1992	Strand 2 talks chaired by Patrick Mayhew on North–South relations are launched in Dublin and last until November. The Ulster Unionist Party (UUP) attends but the Democratic Unionist Party (DUP) does not.

Brief chronology of the peace process

April 1993	John Hume and Gerry Adams make a joint statement about the Irish people as a whole requiring a right to self-determination. The statement is made after Gerry Adams is seen visiting the home of John Hume in Derry.
October 1993	Ten people are killed when a PIRA bomb explodes in a fish shop on the loyalist Shankill Road.
November 1993	Secret communications between the PIRA and London are revealed.
December 1993	Downing Street Declaration is released stating that Irish unity would require the 'double consent' support of majorities in both parts of Ireland and that no constitutional change would occur without the consent of the majority of the people of Northern Ireland.
January 1994	President Clinton agrees a visa for Gerry Adams to visit the United States.
June 1994	Loyalists kill six Catholic men at a bar in Loughlinisland, Co. Down.
August 1994	The PIRA announces 'a complete cessation of military activities'.
September 1994	The British Government lifts the broadcasting ban on Sinn Féin.
October 1994	The Combined Loyalist Command (an umbrella body for the Ulster Volunteer Force and the Ulster Defence Association) announces a ceasefire.
February 1995	British and Irish governments release the Frameworks Document.
March 1995	Northern Ireland secretary Patrick Mayhew reveals a three-point plan to try to remove PIRA weapons in advance of talks, making decommissioning a key condition for reaching agreement.
May 1995	Sinn Féin meet British Government minister Michael Ancram after exploratory dialogue with senior officials.
July 1995	Drumcree parade becomes flashpoint of the marching season after members of the Orange Order are prevented from marching through a nationalist area.
November 1995	President Clinton visits Northern Ireland.
January 1996	The *Mitchell Report* is published. It canvasses for elections to round table talks and stresses a commitment to non-violence as a basis for participation.
February 1996	The PIRA ends its ceasefire with a bomb in Canary Wharf, London, killing two. Sinn Féin is excluded from talks.

May 1996	Elections take place do decide participants at talks. Sinn Fein gets 15.5 per cent of the votes but does not take part having not made the necessary commitment to non-violence. The PIRA ceasefire is not renewed. Talks take place in Castle Buildings, Belfast and are chaired by senator George Mitchell.
June 1996	The PIRA plants a bomb in Manchester city centre.
July 1996	Drumcree creates a stand-off, but police allow marchers to complete route. This is followed by major rioting.
April 1997	The PIRA creates hoax bomb alerts in the United Kingdom, targeting motorways and the Grand National horse race.
May 1997	Tony Blair is elected as British prime minister.
July 1997	The PIRA announces a renewal of its ceasefire after the British Government resumes contacts with Sinn Féin.
August 1997	Independent International Commission on Decommissioning (IICD) is established to oversee decommissioning of paramilitary weapons.
September 1997	Unionists, including the DUP, boycott talks because of the decision to allow Sinn Féin re-entry. Sinn Féin sign up to the *Mitchell Principles.*
October 1997	Gerry Adams meets Tony Blair.
January 1998	Northern Ireland secretary Mo Mowlam visits loyalist inmates in the Maze prison to convince them to continue supporting the peace process.
January 1998	Tony Blair announces the Bloody Sunday Inquiry.
April 1998	The Good Friday Agreement (GFA) is reached. The DUP opposes the Agreement.
April 1998	The PIRA announces there will be no decommissioning.
May 1998	'Dissident' republicans opposed to the Agreement and the Sinn Féin strategy form the Real IRA.
May 1998	A referendum to gauge support for the Agreement produces a 71 per cent 'for' vote in Northern Ireland, although there is a large 'no' vote from unionists.
June 1998	Elections to the Northern Ireland Assembly lead to the UUP and the SDLP being elected as the biggest parties.
July 1998	Drumcree stand-off leads to widespread violence.
August 1998	Real IRA bombing in Omagh kills twenty-nine people and unborn twins.
September 1998	President Clinton visits Northern Ireland to try to bolster the peace process.

September 1998	Gerry Adams and UUP leader David Trimble lead first talks between unionists and republicans for seventy-five years.
September 1998	Early prisoner releases made possible by the GFA take place.
September 1998	Demolition of security installations and checkpoints takes place under the auspices of 'confidence-building' measures and demilitarisation.
October 1998	David Trimble and John Hume receive the Nobel Peace Prize.
February 1999	Disagreement between the parties over decommissioning continues to hamper power-sharing.
April 1999	Sinn Féin states that PIRA decommissioning cannot take place before the Assembly is up and running.
July 1999	Attempts to nominate ministers for the Assembly fail as the UUP rejects Sinn Féin's inability to deliver PIRA decommissioning.
September 1999	*Patten Report* is released recommending root-and-branch reform of policing. Recommendations include changes to the name, badges and symbols used by police and the setting up of a Policing Board, which would be 'community-led'. Patten also recommends a 50:50 recruitment of Catholics and Protestants to the police service.
November 1999	Sinn Féin agrees to talk with the IICD on decommissioning.
November 1999	Assembly meets and nominates ministers as power-sharing commences.
February 2000	Northern Ireland secretary Peter Mandelson suspends the Assembly because of no progress on decommissioning.
March 2000	Bloody Sunday Inquiry begins in Londonderry.
May 2000	The PIRA announces it will open some arms dumps for inspection. This corresponds with a proposed sequence of events to facilitate a return to power-sharing, but is also linked to a PIRA commitment to decommission. Any PIRA action on weapons to run parallel with movement on policing reform and demilitarisation. For republicans this would create the 'context' within which arms would be 'completely and verifiably put beyond use'.
May 2000	Unionists agree a return to the Assembly on the understanding that arms would be dealt with parallel to the Assembly being up and running.

June 2000	The IICD confirm that they have inspected some PIRA arms dumps and that arms could not be removed without detection.
September 2000	'Dissidents' attack MI6 headquarters in London.
March 2001	'Dissidents' plant a car bomb outside the BBC in London.
May 2001	The slow progress on decommissioning leads to growing tensions within the UUP, and David Trimble threatens to resign as first minister one month after the forthcoming elections if decommissioning is not dealt with.
June 2001	The DUP, under leader Revd Ian Paisley, becomes the dominant unionist party at the elections, and Sinn Féin overtake the SDLP to be the largest nationalist party.
July 2001	David Trimble stands down as leader of the UUP to create a six-week negotiating space.
August 2001	The IICD announces that the PIRA has a plan to put arms 'beyond use'.
August 2001	Assembly is suspended for twenty-four hours. The effect of this is to allow the parties another six weeks to agree who would be first minister and deputy first minister (by 22 September 2001).
August 2001	Three men arrested in Colombia are accused of being in the PIRA and training Marxist rebels. The PIRA announces that it is withdrawing its plan to put weapons beyond use.
September 2001	Clashes and violence occur in Belfast between loyalists and republicans outside Holy Cross Girls' Primary School.
September 2001	Suspension of the Assembly because of slow progress leads to another six-week hiatus (until 3 November 2001) to give the parties more time to reach agreement and elect a first and deputy first minister.
October 2001	The IICD announces that it has witnessed a first act of PIRA decommissioning.
November 2001	Initial deadline of 3 November for the election of first and deputy first minister passes, with Northern Ireland secretary John Reid proposing 5 November as another deadline.
November 2001	Royal Ulster Constabulary (RUC) renamed the Police Service of Northern Ireland.
March 2002	Suspected PIRA involvement in break-in at Castlereagh police headquarters.

October 2002	Police raid Sinn Féin Stormont offices on suspicion that the PIRA is running a spying operation and search for evidence of republican intelligence-gathering.
October 2002	Devolution is suspended and power-sharing collapses amid allegations over continuing PIRA activity.
October 2002	Tony Blair makes a keynote speech on 'acts of completion' at Belfast Harbour, telling the PIRA that it cannot be 'half in, half out' of the process.
April 2003	London and Dublin propose a way forward through the Joint Declaration document.
May 2003	The Joint Declaration is released. Assembly elections are postponed.
September 2003	Independent Monitoring Commission (IMC) is given the role of examining the dismantling of paramilitary structures and the transition to stable democratic institutions.
October 2003	Moves are initiated to choreograph a return to power-sharing based on positive verification of PIRA decommissioning. However, an IICD statement on a third act of PIRA decommissioning is seen as not sufficiently transparent by David Trimble and a return to power-sharing is postponed.
November 2003	DUP and Sinn Féin emerge from Assembly elections as dominant parties, but Paisley refuses to sit in a government until the PIRA has disarmed.
March 2004	Substantive talks between the Irish and British governments and the parties fail to bring about a breakthrough.
September 2004	Talks at Leeds Castle. Sinn Féin name two independent clergy witnesses who will verify decommissioning (Revd Harold Good and Father Alec Reid). The DUP want visual proof of decommissioning, which is rejected by Sinn Féin.
December 2004	A record £26.5 million is stolen from the Northern Bank in Belfast. Security chiefs point towards the PIRA as being responsible, and believe the money is to be a 'retirement fund' for PIRA personnel as well as used for election funding.
January 2005	Robert McCartney is murdered by PIRA men outside a pub in Belfast. McCartney's sisters launch a campaign for justice that leads to international pressure for the PIRA to be brought to an end.
February 2005	The PIRA withdraws an offer to complete the decommissioning of weapons.

March 2005	American pressure on the PIRA to disarm intensifies following McCartney's murder.
September 2005	The IICD announces that it is satisfied that the PIRA has decommissioned all arms.
January 2006	Proposed legislation to allow around 150 'On-the-Run' republican fugitives – accused of paramilitary crimes before 1998 – to return to Northern Ireland is widely rejected by the parties.
April 2006	Tony Blair and Irish taoiseach Bertie Ahern unveil blueprint for restoring devolution, confirming that the Assembly will be reformed on 15 May, with the parties given six weeks to elect an Executive. A fall-back position is that if this fails a further twelve weeks will be given to get a multiparty government up and running or salaries will be stopped.
May 2006	Assembly operates for the first time since its suspension in 2002.
June 2006	The two governments restate that 24 November is the last chance for devolution to be restored.
October 2006	The IMC announce that some of the PIRA's most important structures have been dismantled.
October 2006	DUP leader Revd Ian Paisley takes part in formal talks with Catholic Archbishop Sean Brady and deems conversations to be 'helpful and constructive'.
October 2006	Three days of intensive multiparty talks designed to restore devolution take place at St Andrews, Scotland. May 2008 is called for as the deadline for the transference of policing and justice affairs from London. St Andrews Agreement ratified.
December 2006	The Sinn Féin Executive meets to discuss backing the police service.
January 2007	Sinn Féin members vote to support policing in Northern Ireland
January 2007	Assembly elections are confirmed for 7 March and a transitional Assembly at Stormont is dissolved to allow this to take place.
March 2007	Assembly elections return DUP as the largest party with thirty-six seats, with Sinn Féin taking twenty-eight, the UUP taking eighteen, the SDLP sixteen and the Alliance Party seven.

March 2007	Devolved government is restored in Northern Ireland after DUP and Sinn Féin leaders hold breakthrough meeting.
May 2007	The DUP's Revd Ian Paisley is sworn in as first minister and Sinn Féin's Martin McGuinness is sworn in as deputy first minister.
October 2007	The Executive agree a new legislative programme with a ten-year investment strategy.
July 2008	Slow progress on policing and justice brings the Assembly to a standstill.
November 2008	Executive meetings resumed after a DUP–Sinn Féin agreement is reached on the process for devolving authority for policing and justice.
March 2009	British soldiers and a policeman are killed by 'dissident' republicans. Both the DUP and Sinn Féin condemn the killings.
June 2009	Ulster Volunteer Force decommissions weapons.
December 2009	Legislation passed by the Assembly to pave the way for the transfer of policing and justice powers to Northern Ireland.
January 2010	British and Irish governments meet Northern Ireland parties to finalise steps for the devolution of authority over policing and justice.
January 2010	Ulster Defence Association and Irish National Liberation Army decommission weapons.
February 2010	The IICD stands down.
February 2010	Ten days of negotiations lead to the Hillsborough Agreement with Sinn Féin and the DUP finally agreeing a deal on the devolution of authority over policing and justice. A deadline of 12 April 2010 is set for devolution.
March 2010	The Assembly formally recognises the Hillsborough Agreement.
April 2010	Authority for policing and justice is devolved with David Ford of the Alliance Party elected as justice minister.
April 2011	Police Service of Northern Ireland (PSNI) officer Ronan Kerr killed by 'dissident' republicans.
May 2011	Queen Elizabeth II makes state visit to Ireland.
June 2012	Queen Elizabeth II on visit to Northern Ireland shakes hands with Sinn Féin's Martin McGuinness.
July 2012	Extensive rioting in Ardoyne, Belfast, following rival Protestant and Catholic parades.

November 2012	Prison officer David Black is killed by a 'dissident' republican group claiming to be the 'new IRA'.
December 2012	Decision taken by Belfast City Council to move Union flag from flying permanently over Belfast City Hall to designated days sparks protests and riots by loyalists which continue throughout 2013.
July 2013	Formation of the Panel of Parties in the Northern Ireland Executive with ambassador Richard Haass as chair and Meghan L. O'Sullivan as vice chair to initiate consensual recommendations on parades, protests, flags, symbols, emblems and related matters, and the past.
December 2013	Haass and O'Sullivan produce proposed agreement, which is accepted by nationalists and republicans but rejected by unionists.
May 2014	Sinn Féin president Gerry Adams is arrested, questioned and detained for four days by police in Antrim, Northern Ireland over the abduction, murder and disappearance of Jean McConville in 1972 and for membership of the PIRA. He is released without charge.

Abbreviations

AP	Alliance Party
CLMC	Combined Loyalist Military Command
DFA	Department of Foreign Affairs, Ireland
DUP	Democratic Unionist Party
EC	European Community
FCO	Foreign and Commonwealth Office
IICD	Independent International Commission on Decommissioning
IMC	Independent Monitoring Commission
INLA	Irish National Liberation Army
IRSP	Irish Republican Socialist Party
LVF	Loyalist Volunteer Force
MoD	Ministry of Defence
NICS	Northern Ireland Civil Service
NIO	Northern Ireland Office
OTRs	'On-the-Runs'
PAB	Political Affairs Belfast
PIRA	Provisional IRA
PSNI	Police Service of Northern Ireland
PUP	Progressive Unionist Party
RIRA	Real IRA
RUC	Royal Ulster Constabulary
SDLP	Social Democratic and Labour Party
UDA	Ulster Defence Association
UDP	Ulster Democratic Party
UKUP	UK Unionist Party
UPRG	Ulster Political Research Group
UUP	Ulster Unionist Party

Key documents

Sunningdale Agreement 1973 (SA)
Anglo-Irish Agreement 1985 (AIA)
Downing Street Declaration 1993 (DSD)
Frameworks Document 1995
Good Friday Agreement 1998 (GFA)
Joint Declaration 2003 (JD)
St Andrews Agreement 2006 (SAA)
Hillsborough Agreement 2010

Introduction

This book is a collection of experiences and perceptions by senior British officials about their role in the Northern Ireland peace process. It does not take account of the long history of British association with Ireland and Northern Ireland, which has been extensively researched and analysed already. Nor does it contextualise the peace process within the historical tensions and difficulties that have bedevilled the British–Irish relationship since the seventeenth century (Foster 1988; Jackson 2003; Bew 2007). Equally, it does not seek to view the recent phase of British–Irish relations as a continuum of decision-making that led to the separation of Northern Ireland from the Irish Republic in the 1920s, and relate that to the subsequent violence and conflict that persisted up until the end of the twentieth century (Patterson 2006; Fanning 2013; Townshend 2013). Rather this is a work that examines the end of the modern period of conflict in Northern Ireland (which began in the late 1960s and became more popularly known as the Troubles) through inside accounts of British Government officials working at the centre of what became known as the 'peace process'.

Analysis of efforts to develop peace in Northern Ireland often attributes the inception of the peace process to dialogues between Sinn Féin president Gerry Adams and the Social Democratic and Labour Party's (SDLP) former leader John Hume in the late 1980s. However, attempts to forge peace have a longer timeline and some historical context is called for. The foundations of an attempt to bring about an end to conflict in Northern Ireland can be most obviously seen in the Sunningdale Agreement (SA) of 1973 (the SDLP's Seamus Mallon later famously described the Good Friday Agreement (GFA) of 1998 as 'Sunningdale for slow learners'), negotiated between the British and Irish governments with the direct involvement of the Northern Ireland parties, and, since then, the Anglo-Irish Agreement (AIA) of 1985, negotiated between the British and Irish governments without the direct involvement of the Northern Ireland parties. The demise of the power-sharing Executive that evolved from Sunningdale, which, had it succeeded, would have averted a further twenty-five years of conflict, was stymied at one level by a lack of clarity about the extent of Irish influence and what a Council of Ireland (established at the Sunningdale Conference and consisting of a council of ministers and a consultative assembly with equal numbers of representatives from Northern Ireland and Ireland in the Council assisting in the development of 'executive and harmonising functions and a consultative role', and equal numbers of representatives from both jurisdictions in the Assembly having 'advisory and review functions' (Bew and Gillespie 1999: 73)), set up under the Agreement, would mean for Irish involvement in Northern Ireland's affairs. As Bew observed, this lack of clarity 'succeeded in inflating nationalist aspirations, while at the same time raising loyalist fears of the Council as a means of forcing them into a united Ireland' (Bew 2007: 512). Not surprisingly, given this ambiguity, the SDLP saw the Agreement as an opportunity to develop institutions that would support the transition to a united Ireland (as one of its founder members, Paddy Devlin, put it, the context provided by the Council of Ireland 'would create and sustain an evolutionary process' supportive of the transition to Irish unity (quoted in Bew 2007: 512)), confirming unionist and loyalist fears about the diminution of Northern Ireland in the process. As an indication of differences in understanding about what Sunningdale could achieve, former Northern Ireland prime minister Brian Faulkner, who became chief executive of the power-sharing arrangement, in his account of the period recalls particular concern about the SDLP's use of the word 'identification', sensing that its motivation was not just to bring supporters along, but to facilitate Irish unification 'in practice' (Faulkner 1978: 229). The failure of the Agreement led to both the British and Irish governments 'isolating and insulating themselves against the repercussions' of the fallout, and so entrenched the likelihood of conflict for the long term (Craig 2010: 191).

Although the SA stipulated the key principle of consent (in paragraph 5 it stated: 'The present status of Northern Ireland is that it is part of the United Kingdom. If in the future the majority of the people of Northern Ireland should indicate a wish to become part of a united Ireland, the British Government would support that wish.'), it was largely opposed by unionists from its inception. British prime minister Edward Heath did little to help Faulkner, resisting his objection to Irish involvement in the formation of a new police authority (Bew and Gillespie 1999: 74) and contributing to the impression that Faulkner was unable to prevent nationalists from gaining further influence and control (Bew 2007: 512). For Faulkner, Sunningdale did not last because 'the loose ends of the threads' of the Agreement precipitated confusion that was seized upon by unionist opposition and used to galvanise 'Paisley and his cohorts into new militancy' (Faulkner 1978: 226). Faulkner's later admission that Sunningdale had left many things as 'unfinished business' also intimated that the Agreement had provided too much latitude (as Faulkner saw it) 'to amend, alter and generally interfere with the negotiations' (*ibid.*: 244), creating a lack of concision about what the outcome of those negotiations would mean. Although the Executive itself had understood the nature of decision-making and why compromise was important, among party representatives and members outside the Executive there was a lack of understanding about 'why their leaders were drifting away from the straight course of party dogma' (Bloomfield 1994: 199).

But, even though the ambiguity of Sunningdale contributed to its demise (unlike the later GFA, which depended on it), it is clear that it was the scale of unionist and loyalist resistance that ultimately made the Executive untenable. Just after the Agreement was announced a Fianna Fáil minister, Kevin Boland, took to the Dublin courts to protest that Articles 2 and 3 of the Irish Constitution, which claim Northern Ireland as part of Ireland, were not compatible with the Sunningdale recognition of Northern Ireland's status. This challenge created problems for the Dublin Government, who, in response, claimed that the Agreement was not inconsistent with the Irish claim and that Northern Ireland was not outside Irish jurisdiction, confirming to unionists that the Agreement would offer the Irish a route to unification, a fear that dogged the Agreement constantly (Faulkner 1978: 246–7). And, while the Executive was striving to build a shared politics, with Protestants and Catholics working as a coalition to deliver political and social change, this aspiration was being pursued within a context of continuing violence in Northern Ireland that further divided the communities (Faulkner 1978: 240). Moreover, the general election of February 1974, which effectively functioned as a referendum on the Executive, exacerbated unionist dissent against power-sharing, with the result that eleven of the twelve House of Commons seats were won by those who opposed the Executive. The election had come too soon for those in the Executive who felt that the advantages of accommodation had not been given long enough to show success (Devlin 1993: 252; Bloomfield 1994: 198). Although the election result did not finish the SA at that point, it did augment unionist and loyalist reaction and so provided them 'with the mandate they needed to support their actions aimed at ending power-sharing and, more importantly, stopping the Council of Ireland' (Bew and Gillespie 1999: 82).

Against the background of a newly elected Labour Government, under Harold Wilson, anger fermented into support for an Ulster Workers' Council strike from 15 May, leading to power cuts and factory closures. The strike resulted in the end of the Executive on 29 May, the day after the strike ended, proving to nationalists that unionists did not want to share power after all and encouraging nationalist leaders to look more to the Irish rather than to the British for any future settlement (*ibid.*: 91). In the words of SDLP politician Paddy Devlin, what the short life of the Executive had shown was 'the necessity that it would have to be incorporated as a mandatory principle in any future formula to create peace and political stability' (Devlin 1993: 250). The SA was also to provide a lesson that was heeded in the GFA of 1998, namely, the 'need for inclusion and the need for public demonstration of support for such an agreement' (Tonge 2008: 58) (both of which were shaped through a much longer build-up to the GFA, and because attitudes around armed conflict had changed).

For Devlin, as direct rule was imposed from London, the election result ended the 'goodwill we were rapidly generating' (*ibid.*: 252), and its collapse was used by the Provisional Irish Republican Army (PIRA) to stress how the Irish Government had capitulated to the British and a 'fascist victory' (Rees 1985: 88). Northern Ireland secretary Merlyn Rees was to later note how power-sharing had not been able to work in a climate of civil unrest perpetuated by unionist–loyalist resistance, on the one hand, alongside an intensifying PIRA bombing campaign, on the other (*ibid.*: 89). But, for Rees, the failure of Sunningdale was ostensibly down to Dublin and London, who 'had ignored the reality of the situation in the North of Ireland and especially the lack of support there for the Faulkner Unionists' (*ibid.*: 90). A 'reality' that Rees saw as evidence of a dogged and trenchant 'Ulster nationalism' (*ibid.*: 91).

The deterioration of relations in Northern Ireland led Wilson to contemplate a British withdrawal, in which all British funding would be ended within five years, but it was clear that such a decision, if taken, would reinforce Protestant control and make the possibility of civil war highly likely (Bew 2007: 517). It was this doomsday scenario that discouraged rather than encouraged pursuit of the withdrawal plan and led to Northern Ireland being returned to direct rule (*ibid.*: 518). According to Craig, what lay behind Wilson's consideration of withdrawal was the belief that Northern Ireland should move towards unification with Ireland because Protestants would 'realise their true interests lay in rapprochement and possible reunion with Dublin' (Craig 2010: 182). Wilson also believed that a PIRA bombing campaign in Britain in 1974 would mean there was public sympathy for withdrawal, thereby helping to vindicate such a move. However, the outcome of Wilson's approach to Northern Ireland after Sunningdale, rather than withdrawal, was to commit to a process of 'Ulsterisation' where the conflict would be contained as much as possible in Northern Ireland by security and military means, designed to criminalise the conflict in an attempt to sap the violence of political legitimacy and public support. The impact of this strategy was to make a political solution to the Northern Ireland problem a remote possibility; indeed, it served to exacerbate the conditions of conflict. At one level, the SA and Executive had demonstrated that 'structures of settlement' could be found, but, at another level, that without sufficient public and cross-party consensus there was no 'means with which it could be implemented' (*ibid.*: 195).

The intense conflict, social unrest and political polarisation that led to the collapse of Sunningdale had shifted by the mid- to late 1980s as the futility of conflict became increasingly evident to both republicans and the British (if not openly admitted). The civil rights protests of the late 1960s and early 1970s were transformed and undermined by the explosion of violence that occurred after Bloody Sunday in January 1972, when the PIRA dramatically expanded in response to the British Parachute Regiment killing thirteen unarmed civil rights protestors (a further man died shortly after, with dozens wounded). Within six months, a secret meeting had taken place between the PIRA leadership and Northern Ireland secretary Willie Whitelaw in London, but had failed miserably. Whitelaw was later to write: 'The meeting was a non-event. The PIRA leaders simply made impossible demands which I told them the British Government would never concede. They were in fact still in a mood of defiance and determination to carry on' (quoted in Bew and Gillespie 1999: 54). The meeting, which was followed within two weeks, on 21 July, by one of the most violent days of the Troubles (known as Bloody Friday), nevertheless revealed the value of contact between the British and the PIRA, which was sporadically used throughout the Troubles (and known as 'the link') and enabled avenues of dialogue to be maintained that would later lead to the emergence of the 'peace process' in the late 1980s (O'Dochartaigh 2011; Taylor 2011: 1–48; Huband 2013: 42–55).

Spiralling conflict made the possibility of ending it a distant prospect until after the hunger strikes in 1981, when ten republicans (Bobby Sands being the most popularised and mythologised of the strikers (Spencer 2015)) starved themselves to death in protest at being treated as criminals rather than as political prisoners and because of poor prison conditions (Beresford 1987). Although the conventional explanation of this period is that British Prime Minister Margaret Thatcher showed intransigence towards ending the strikes and allowed men to die, this dominant portrayal has since been challenged both by individual republicans (O'Rawe 2005) and in recently released government papers (Hennessey 2013) that confirm an offer made to the Sinn Féin leadership, which was held back from the hunger strikers to enable Sinn Féin to capitalise politically on widespread Catholic and republican anger, media attention and growing international pressure, all of which Sinn Féin sought to exploit. The hunger strikes created a political platform for republicans, and Sands was elected as MP for Fermanagh/South Tyrone in March 1981, two months before his death, demonstrating a groundswell of support that the Sinn Féin leadership sought to use in order to transform republicanism from a military movement into a political one.

The AIA of 1985 was an attempt by the Irish and the British governments to neutralise the growing popularity of Sinn Féin by responding to the wide concerns of democratic nationalism. By enabling conditions that would help nationalist politics to gain support, the British and Irish believed that this would arrest Sinn Féin's rise, which was closely aligned with the actions of the PIRA. The message of Sinn Féin's political progress was one of violence gaining political credibility, to the detriment of democratic politics, and the Agreement was designed to counter and reverse this development. Importantly, the Agreement adhered to the principle of consent, as in Sunningdale, where any change to the status of Northern Ireland could come about only if the majority living there agreed to it. It also continued with the Irish Government playing a 'consultative' role in Northern Ireland, but with a more specific focus on security and justice (lacking in Sunningdale). The path to the AIA is explored in Chapter 2, where the background to the Agreement is outlined, and then followed by interviews with the two leading British officials who negotiated on behalf of the Thatcher Government at that time: Sir David Goodall and Lord (Robert) Armstrong. This period offers a point of focus for understanding how the seeds of a peace process grew and how the endgame of talks and negotiations developed, but, interestingly, more because of the perceived disadvantages created by the AIA rather than any perceived advantages.

The transition from military republicanism to political republicanism is extensively explored in a number of fine studies (O'Brien 1995; De Breadun 2001; Mallie and McKittrick 2001; Taylor 2001; English 2003; Moloney 2002), which provide detailed background on the emergence of the peace process and how it took shape both indirectly and directly from the late 1980s, resulting in the Downing Street Declaration (DSD) of 1993 and a PIRA ceasefire in August 1994, before the GFA of 1998, which formalised the structures and processes needed to consolidate peace and power-sharing that were fully secured by 2010. There are also numerous excellent academic overviews of this period (Hennessey 2000; Dixon 2001; Bourke 2003; Cochrane 2013), as well as journalistic accounts (Mallie and McKittrick; 2001; Taylor 2001; Godson 2004; Millar 2009), and a raft of material from Irish and British government ministers and officials (from the Irish Government, Finlay 1998; Delaney 2001; Ahern 2009; Reynolds 2009, and from the British Government, Major 1999; Mowlam 2002; Blair 2010; Campbell 2013, and, by far the most comprehensive account, Powell 2008). Other valuable contributions are made by representatives of the various parties in Northern Ireland, and the American role is highlighted by senator George Mitchell's narration of chairing the negotiations (McMichael 1999; Mitchell 1999; Adams 2003; Farren 2010). All these portrayals give necessary context and highlight the range of complexities and difficulties in working to secure a peace settlement.

However, what many of these contributions lack is an expansive analysis of the work carried out by senior civil servants throughout the period. Though a number of the above studies make reference to such individuals, there is no comprehensive or detailed picture of the roles played by civil servants at different times, or how those roles intersected with the political process across a period that included successive governments and changing political demands and expectations. It was very much the work of civil servants within both the British and Irish governments that gave substance to negotiations by distilling complex issues of difference into a point of common focus. To understand what that work entailed and how civil servants created interlocking approaches to what at times appeared to be irreconcilable oppositions is what this book is about. The success of the peace process was not just the result of efforts by political leaders like Albert Reynolds, John Major, Bertie Ahern and Tony Blair (vitally important though they all were), but was achieved through the skills of those working in the background on text and dialogue that would create what one senior civil servant referred to as 'zones of convergence'. The challenges faced by British officials in reaching the GFA (which similarly applied the consent principle from both the SA and the AIA) to secure power-sharing and subsequent areas that required further attention after Good Friday (notably on matters of decommissioning, policing and justice) inform the discussions that follow.

Although most of the chapters in this book provide material that supports historical examination of how the dynamics of peace in Northern Ireland emerged and developed, it is clear that the book is less an historical overview (although Chapters 1 and 2 provide historical accounts of efforts to achieve peace before the peace process) and more an analysis of experiences and practical responses within the peace process from 1990 until formal agreements on power-sharing and policing and justice in 2010. The SA is an indication of the longevity of attempts to bring about peace in Northern Ireland, but it was the development of a highly formalised process of political engagement from 1990 onwards that did so (even if that process may be seen as an extension of Sunningdale and, to a much lesser extent and for different reasons, the AIA), and the contributors to this book (far from the entire team) indicate the scale of attention and effort needed to make that process work.

Structure and content of the book

The structure of the book adheres to a composition of individually written chapters and extended interviews. This combination offers a considered development of specific areas alongside elaboration of more general contextual factors that affected interpersonal relations, and the dynamics and tensions of the peace process. What links the two approaches is that, in this instance, they are both drawn from experience and recollections that indicate how problems were worked through and overcome at textual, performative and practical levels. The extended interview offers a different insight into the work of British peace politics. The spontaneity of the interview elicits articulations and memories that are not worked through in the same way as the drafted chapter. Verbal responses work in a less concise (even if articulate) way, partly because the interview is a work in progress, shaped by questions, but not ultimately restrained by those questions. In my view, questions should be about releasing comment rather than capturing it, thus allowing the interview to be a relatively free-flowing exchange that both converges and diverges on points of interest and concern. All the interviews for this book were semi-structured in format and most of the respondents were interviewed at least twice.

The structure of the interview itself does not follow the same linearity as the written chapter. It moves, jumps about, settles on some points and skates across others, and in doing so it is a reflection of the patterns of conversation, where response and counter-response play off each other. It should be noted that one of the intentions when conducting the interviews was to ask respondents some similar questions about areas that have long fascinated me, and to look for consistencies and differences of perception in response. What were the Sinn Féin negotiators like and how did they compare with unionists and others? How is it possible to maintain principle whilst advocating pragmatism? Were some better at dealing with ambiguity than others? How did movement occur and how was leverage applied? What is the relationship with the interpersonal setting of the negotiating room and translating the outcome of that experience to text? Is personality as important as policy? Was the peace process a metaphorical as well as a literal project? How essential was creativity? Was the peace process a moral as well as a political exercise? How central was strategy in comparison with tactics? And so on. Such questions fascinate because they move analysis away from literature-induced argument and interrogation back into the remembered heat of the negotiation setting and, in that sense, help to build a picture of what things were like inside the room in a way that much academic work fails to do.

What is of particular fascination, perhaps, is that the interview is often mysterious and unpredictable in terms of where it leads and what comes out of it. Attitudes and recollections shift, but what is being emphasised by the respondent is more often than not a matter of importance to them and is revealing because of that. The interview may be constrained by the parameters of set questions, but, in this instance, those questions were largely open and functioned more as a focus for conversation rather than as a mechanical form of measurement. Persuasion is as much a performative process as it is a practical one, and the interview material seeks to quarry this largely uncharted area in negotiations. Behind the questions and responses is a narrative about behaviour in its complexity and how that behaviour informed the intentions of peace-building. Therefore, not only is this book about the key moments within a process that required those such as the contributors here (along with the Irish, the political parties and many others too) to work tirelessly to reach an agreement, it is also a testimony to the importance of human relations, political imagination and the tortuous road of moral introspection when seeking to draw proponents of violence into accepting the argument for ending that violence through the dynamics of talk and text. The connection between these two areas is obvious enough. The concision of the text is a result of the fluid, explorative, responsive forms of conversation and talk that preceded it. But what happens in the transition from one to the other in this multilayered and changeable world of negotiations, and how does the static formality of text reflect the intentions

Introduction 9

of movement that gave rise to it? From the perspectives of British officials that is what this book sets out to examine.

In Chapter 1, Sir Kenneth Bloomfield, a Northern Ireland cabinet secretary to three unionist prime ministers at Stormont in the 1960s, and a senior adviser to three secretaries of state in the 1980s, gives a personal account of his role in the construction of certain key documents and speeches in Northern Ireland from the 1960s to the formative stages of the peace process. In this examination, he compares the quest throughout this period with the metaphor of scaling Mount Everest, viewing some early initiatives as developments to explore unfamiliar terrain rather than examples of a credible movement towards the summit. He discusses the nature of his own involvement in developing ideas, or in blending the ideas of others in effective terminology, while reminding the reader how swiftly and brutally events on the ground could overtake or undermine a promising political development. It is in this setting that Bloomfield discusses the impact of the early efforts of Terence O'Neill to improve 'community relations'; the belated proposals by Brian Faulkner to breathe new life into an expiring Stormont system; the milestone revelation in Whitelaw's Green Paper of 'power-sharing and an Irish dimension' as key elements in any political settlement; and the timely impact of the Whitbread speech made by Peter Brooke, with its renunciation of any 'selfish strategic or economic interest' in Britain's involvement with Northern Ireland. The chapter reveals the crucial interaction between the right and duty of ministers to decide, and the duty of civil servants to offer advice as well as respond to orders. Bloomfield makes it clear that, whatever the skill needed to draft effective and telling words, the true credit must rest with the politicians willing to give effect to them. Moreover, as he reminds us, the long search for peace and stability required the brave deeds of very many as well as the well-chosen words of a few.

In Chapter 2, Sir David Goodall and Lord Armstrong of Ilminster, who were key negotiators for the British Government on the AIA, discuss the development of interpersonal relations with the Irish and indicate how the Agreement led (if not directly or as intended) to the GFA of 1998. The chapter, which consists of a combined interview with both Goodall and Armstrong, elaborates on the security concerns of the Thatcher Government and the political concerns of the Irish about Sinn Féin's political advancement, and how both these positions were managed to shape dialogue and a joint approach to addressing the Northern Ireland problem. Both interviewees provide an inside picture of the dynamics and tactics used at the time of the AIA (which was to set out the parameters for a deliberative and coherent plan to help end conflict in Northern Ireland), and discuss how it provided a context for political accommodation, as well as creating the mechanisms for addressing and confronting the rise of republicanism.

The 'constitutional issue' has historically been highly contentious in Northern Ireland and Irish politics. Chapter 3, by David Hill, briefly sets the scene for this by examining the reasons why the constitutional issue is of such significance to unionists, nationalists and republicans, and charts the evolution of attitudes in the Irish Republic towards the constitutional status of Northern Ireland: through the Treaty, the Irish Civil War and the emergence of the 'constitutional claim' in the Irish Constitution of 1937, to the tradition of 'verbal republicanism'. It will then show how the various formulations of 'the constitutional claim' and 'the constitutional guarantee' evolved during the talks process and ultimately allowed all the different perspectives on the constitutional issue to be accommodated within the concept – endorsed and validated by a 'double referendum', held on both sides of the border on the same day – that the achievement of a united Ireland would require the support of majorities in both parts of Ireland.

In Chapter 4, an extended interview with Sir John Chilcot outlines the management direction taken by the British team in negotiations, and considers the development of trust and relationships both within the team and with others as part of the peace process. Chilcot also highlights the importance of using leverage and argument within the negotiation setting and talks about using creative possibilities when coming up against perceived intransigence and obstruction. During the later stages of the peace process, Tony Blair spoke about the need to go *through* rather than *around* problems and concerns. Here, Chilcot will talk about both these directions, and offers an insightful picture of negotiation strategy operating at macro- and micro-levels. He also talks about interim positions and long-term positions, as well as the interconnections that existed between these two points of focus, and how they were each used to try to pressure the respective parties into movement and eventual agreement.

Chapter 5 discusses some features characteristic of intercommunal conflict and disputes involving minorities within states. They typically involve, for example, differences in a mix of ethnic, racial, linguistic religious and/or cultural characteristics, are often long-standing, complex and difficult, and involve contrasting accounts of reality because of differing historical narratives. They also commonly involve a profound sense of injustice, with differing grievances on each side, often accompanied by formal rituals of remembrance and celebration. Sir Quentin Thomas differentiates, for analytical purposes, between 'incumbents', ready to defend the status quo, and 'challengers', who seek a new arrangement, such as secession. He considers the differing options and objectives of the incumbents and the challengers and what distinguishes them. In particular, the incumbents seek, by repression or co-option, to reconcile the challengers to the current dispensation, or some modification of it, whereas the challengers seek to demonstrate that, without change, it is not viable. The chapter then identifies, against that background, five preconditions to the achievement of a settlement bringing the conflict, or at least its violent manifestations, to an end. First, the continuation of the conflict must impose such costs as to constitute a significant incentive to find a settlement on each of the main parties to it. Secondly, none of the key players must believe that their best chance of securing their objectives lies in continuing the conflict. Thirdly, the grievances or penalties that underpin the conflict must be capable of remedy, at least to an acceptable level and without conflicting with other players' interests so as to sustain the conflict or to create a new one. Fourthly, there must be some expectation by each party to the conflict that the other parties will, as part of the process, accept the prospective deal or can be brought to do so, for example, by external pressure or shifts in the views of their own supporters. Finally, there must be a viable process, involving all the main players and enjoying their confidence, to manage the negotiation of a settlement and its implementation. The chapter considers the Northern Ireland peace process in the period leading to the GFA in terms of these preconditions, suggesting that such enabling factors existed. It then seeks, in contrast, to assess whether such conditions exist in other conflict scenarios, such as in the Israeli–Palestinian situation.

In Chapter 6, Chris Maccabe highlights some of the practical steps that were taken to promote the British and Irish governments' shared objective of inclusiveness in the peace/political process as it began to gather pace. At the beginning of this phase, between 1990 and 1992, persuading the 'constitutional' parties to engage in formal and informal dialogue (with each other and both governments) was paramount. This persuasion included confidential dialogue between officials and members of the constitutional parties, particularly the unionist parties, ranging from grass-roots supporters, party officers and district councillors to MPs and other senior figures. It also involved dialogue with 'opinion formers', including church leaders, community activists, and business and trade union figures. At the same time, it was recognised (at least by the governments) that, ultimately, a comprehensive, durable agreement would not be achieved without the active participation of the representatives of militant republicanism (principally Sinn Féin) and militant loyalism (principally the Progressive Unionist Party (PUP) and the Ulster Democratic Party (UDP)). The chapter looks at how this reality was addressed through direct and indirect dialogue, and how ultimately, following paramilitary ceasefires, these groups were able to take their place at the conference table as equal partners. Finally, it considers how, after the 1998 GFA and consequent devolution, dialogue with representatives of the residual (and small but dangerous) republican and loyalist paramilitary groups that had not been represented at the talks was established and maintained. And how the representatives of the PUP and UDP, who had garnered little electoral advantage in the resultant elections, were encouraged to maintain their ceasefires and develop mechanisms that would allow them to put their creativity and energy at the disposal of their communities.

The role of text was crucial to the success of the peace process. In Chapter 7, David Cooke reflects on the drafting of text, and places this activity in the wider contexts of Civil Service culture, the implications of text for negotiations as part of the political process and the problems of framing. These areas are explored by way of considering individual passages of text, issues of packaging, structure, inclusion and omission. The primary focus of the chapter is on the origins, production and consequences of the Joint Declaration (JD) of 2003, which Cooke worked on as associate political director. There is a lead-up to this through an account of earlier drafting tasks, including briefing for meetings of the Anglo-Irish Intergovernmental Conference, the exchange of messages between the British Government and PIRA, and the DSD. A key aspect of the JD was the focus it provided for what a number of the civil servants understood as 'single-text negotiation', and the significance of this is discussed at various stages in the life cycle of the political process. Related to this was the need to consider the implications that the single-text approach could, and did, have for the style and content of ensuing negotiations. Evolving texts such as the JD have no single author, but a multiplicity of contributors approaching the task from different perspectives. Here, Cooke provides analysis of the dynamics of such a process, as well as team contribution to drafting and amending such documents. A British official would not be 'freelancing', but operating under political direction, and Cooke gives detail of how this accountability worked in practice.

The transition between governments during the peace process highlights, on the one hand, differences in approach, but, on the other, consistencies in policy and aspiration. In Chapter 8, Sir John Holmes looks at the transition between John Major's and Tony Blair's respective governments, and addresses the problem of managing consistency and difference in the attempt to reach a political settlement. Each of the two governments took a varying approach to peace and negotiations in Northern Ireland, whilst adhering to a consistent policy direction in getting agreement. What emergent issues and tensions did this create, and how did the different approaches contrast as well as complement each other when dealing with dialogue and the elusive goal of power-sharing? Such questions are explored along with a detailed examination of the 'push and pull' of relations and exchanges that occurred in the build-up to the GFA of 1998.

In Chapter 9, Sir Joseph Pilling talks about his work and role as permanent secretary in the Northern Ireland Office (NIO), and the challenge of facilitating dialogue between parties. Pilling provides insights into how the British sought to build and maintain symmetrical dialogue through a range of strategic means, and how both formal and informal dialogue were used to construct a consensus of agreed differences on ending violence and producing a settlement. In this wide-ranging interview, Pilling also comments on the relation between principle and pragmatism in negotiations, as well as how pressures were used and dealt with in order to forge movement and shape positions. Importantly, Pilling refers to a range of examples to illustrate how negotiations worked (and didn't work), as well as how spaces were opened and closed down to increase or decrease leverage on the parties. Further, this interview indicates how nuance, tone and intent influenced relations between the two governments and the political parties in the attempt to reach an accommodation.

The success of the peace process did not end with the GFA. Rather, the Agreement produced a context within which parties could agree to disagree. Why was the Agreement so difficult to implement in full? In Chapter 10, Sir Bill Jeffrey addresses this question and explains why the 1998 Agreement proved to be so elusive. In particular, Jeffrey focuses on the period from spring 1998 to late 2002, during which the author was political director at the NIO. Answers to the question of why the Agreement was so hard to implement, depending on one's standpoint, can be found, Jeffrey argues, in the failure of the PIRA to decommission weapons and the failure of the Ulster Unionist Party (UUP) leadership to sell the Agreement more enthusiastically to the unionist people. Jeffrey argues that the second of these was scarcely realistic, given the temperament of the UUP's natural supporters, their limited enthusiasm for the Agreement even in the heady days after it was concluded, and the 'front-loading' of issues that were painful for unionists; most notably prisoner releases and (as the impasse continued through the *Patten Report* and its aftermath) police reform. The chapter describes Sinn Féin's negotiating approach over the period, and speculates about the extent to which it was driven by the prospect of securing greater concessions from the British Government, or by deep reluctance on the part of the republican leadership to act on weapons, or (more probably) by a combination of the two. Jeffrey interrogates the contention that the leadership consciously held back its most convincing moves until the Democratic Unionist Party (DUP) were involved in the negotiations. Jeffrey also looks at some of the events that surrounded the *Mitchell Review* and the subsequent suspension of the institutions in 2000, as well as the growth in trust between British and Irish officials over the period (subject to the setback in relations to which that first suspension led) and the impact of 9/11 on the dynamics of the process. The chapter ends by offering reflection on the role of UK civil servants in support of ministers (including a succession of secretaries of state) across the period, and considers the extent to which fear of 'moral hazard' and distaste for 'moral equivalence' shaped unionist attitudes and responses.

William Fittall acted as principal private secretary to Peter Brooke and Patrick Mayhew in 1992–3, before returning to Northern Ireland as associate political director of the NIO from 2000 to 2002. In Chapter 11, he elaborates on the problems associated with the search for meaning in text that seeks to bridge communal differences, and compares the formative stages of the peace process, where text laid foundations, with the advanced stages, when the struggle to make devolved practices and institutions work in Northern Ireland intensified around a narrowing terrain of key areas and issues. He indicates how documents and texts were structured within specific contexts to support concepts and principles, and how both converged to facilitate dialogue between the British and Irish governments and the political parties in Northern Ireland. Fittall talks about the functions of text in relation to changing political conditions, as well as how text was used to determine positions and shape the context of political movement.

In an extended interview, Sir Jonathan Phillips talks about the role of dialogue and contacts that he experienced between 2005 and 2010, in his role as permanent secretary of the NIO, when the contentious issues of decommissioning and policing and justice in Northern Ireland were being addressed. Using these concerns as a context and backdrop for talking about how dialogue both shaped and facilitated concrete outcomes, Phillips' interview in Chapter 12 indicates the shift from ambiguity to detail as the parties were pulled closer to agreement. It provides a vital contribution to understanding the importance of momentum in a peace process, and presents a detailed explanation of the trajectory of dialogue as the parties moved closer and closer to final positions in relation to power-sharing.

Finally, Chapter 13 is a wide-ranging interview with Tony Blair's chief of staff, Jonathan Powell, who offers an inside picture of trying to manage the relationships and problems that affected the development of negotiations and dialogue leading towards the GFA. The chapter, which draws from interview material published in the journal *Irish Political Studies* (Spencer 2010), includes extended and unpublished material on the tensions of peace drawn from further interviews conducted with Powell in 2012 and 2013. In the interview, Powell traverses areas such as ambiguity, choreography, intergroup relations, personal contacts and trust, and provides a complex overview of the key factors that came into play during negotiations and in reaching agreement. In particular, Powell gives a detailed image of republican participation in the peace process, and creates a compelling and informative account of how the tension of relations was managed to bring peace negotiations to a successful conclusion. He also points towards the importance of intensity and momentum in keeping a peace process alive. Overall, this interview offers a range of important insights and lessons for those seeking a fuller understanding of the issues and concerns that emerged in the struggle to achieve peace in Northern Ireland.

The principle of consent is integral to democratic politics, and its emphasis in Sunningdale was carried into the GFA of 1998. The failure of the Executive in 1973 was partly to do with problems of textual interpretation but, as said, much more to do with unionist and loyalist animosity that would not entertain the idea of power-sharing. By the early 1990s, that animosity was changing into the realisation that power-sharing was the only hope of bringing conflict to an end. The circumstances and structures of that arrangement would still be seriously contested and disputed, but the management of those contestations and disputations was now taking place within a context about what power-sharing would look like. Opposition over the conflict was now re-focused on how to end it, and so required movement away from easy and outright condemnations of right and wrong to conceptual and semantic exchanges about peace-building. The importance of ambiguity as part of this process was paramount. Finding forms of words that would enable each political party to insist that its interests were being represented was vital for keeping those parties engaged. Unlike 1973, when the prospect of power-sharing was anathema for most unionists, by the early 1990s the gathering public perception was that the conflict had inflicted heavy costs with no chance of overall success, and that it was now incumbent on politicians to acknowledge that fact and work to address it. What is clear is that those political parties would need a 'third point' of focus to do this, and this was supplied by the British and Irish governments who produced most, if not all, of the significant documentation and policy direction. In providing this role the tensions between the Northern Ireland parties became reoriented towards the two governments, who would provide guidance and containment of key areas. Inside accounts of how the British did this and what problems they encountered along the way inform the discussions that follow.

References

Adams, G. (2003). *Hope and History*. Dingle: Brandon.
Ahern. B. (2009). *Bertie Ahern: The Autobiography*. London: Hutchinson.
Beresford, D. (1987). *Ten Dead Men*. London: HarperCollins.
Bew, P. (2007). *Ireland: The Politics of Enmity 1789–2006*. Oxford University Press.
Bew, P. and Gillespie, G. (1999). *Northern Ireland: A Chronology of the Troubles 1968–1999*. Dublin: Gill & Macmillan.
Blair, T. (2010). *Tony Blair: A Journey*. London: Hutchinson.
Bloomfield, K. (1994). *Stormont in Crisis*. Belfast: Blackstaff Press.
Bourke, R. (2003). *Peace in Ireland*. London: Pimlico.
Campbell, A. (2013). *The Irish Diaries 1994–2003*. Dublin: Lilliput Press.
Cochrane, F. (2013). *Northern Ireland: A Reluctant Peace*. London: Yale University Press.
Craig, A. (2010). *Crisis of Confidence*. Dublin: Irish Academic Press.
De Breadun, D. (2001). *The Far Side of Revenge*. Cork: Collins Press.
Delaney, E. (2001). *An Accidental Diplomat*. Dublin: New Island Books.
Devlin, P. (1993). *Straight Left*. Belfast: Blackstaff Press.
Dixon, P. (2001). *Northern Ireland: The Politics of War and Peace*. Basingstoke: Palgrave Macmillan.
English, R. (2003). *Armed Struggle: The History of the IRA*. London: Macmillan.

Fanning, R. (2013). *Fatal Path*. London: Faber.
Farren, S. (2010). *The SDLP*. Dublin: Four Courts Press.
Faulkner, B. (1978). *Memoirs of a Statesman*. London: Weidenfeld & Nicolson.
Finlay, F. (1998). *Snakes and Ladders*. Dublin: New Island Books.
Foster, R. F. (1988). *Modern Ireland 1600–1972*. London: Allen Lane.
Godson, D. (2004). *Himself Alone: David Trimble and the Ordeal of Unionism*. London: HarperCollins.
Hennessey, T. (2000). *The Northern Ireland Peace Process*. Dublin: Gill & Macmillan.
    (2013) *Hunger Strike*. Dublin: Irish Academic Press.
Huband, M. (2013). *Trading Secrets*. London: I. B. Tauris.
Jackson, A. (2003). *Home Rule*. Oxford University Press.
Major, J. (1999). *John Major: The Autobiography*. London: HarperCollins.
Mallie, E. and McKittrick, D. (2001). *Endgame in Ireland*. London: Hodder & Stoughton.
McMichael, G. (1999). *Ulster Voice*. Boulder, CO: Roberts Rinehart.
Millar, F. (2009). *Northern Ireland: A Triumph of Politics*. Dublin: Irish Academic Press.
Mitchell, G. (1999). *Making Peace*. London: Heineman.
Moloney, E. (2002). *A Secret History of the IRA*. London: Penguin.
Mowlam, M. (2002). *Momentum*. London: Hodder & Stoughton.
O'Brien, B. (1995). *The Long War*. Dublin: O'Brien Press.
O'Dochartaigh, N. (2011). 'The role of an intermediary in back-channel negotiation: evidence from the Brendan Duddy papers', *Dynamics of Asymmetric Conflict* 4(3): 214–25.
O'Rawe, R. (2005). *Blanketmen*. Dublin: New Island Books.
Patterson, H. (2006). *Ireland since 1939*. Dublin: Penguin Ireland.
Powell, J. (2008). *Great Hatred, Little Room*. London: Bodley Head.
Rees, M. (1985). *Northern Ireland*. London: Methuen.
Reynolds, A. (2009). *Albert Reynolds: My Autobiography*. London: Transworld Ireland.
Spencer, G. (2010). 'Managing a peace process: an interview with Jonathan Powell', *Irish Political Studies* 25(3): 437–55.
    (2015). *From Armed Struggle to Political Struggle: Republican Tradition and Transformation in Northern Ireland*. London: Bloomsbury.
Taylor, P. (2001). *Brits*. London: Bloomsbury.
    (2011). *Talking to Terrorists*. London: Harper.
Tonge, J. (2008). 'From Sunningdale to the Good Friday Agreement: creating devolved government in Northern Ireland', *Contemporary British History* 12(3): 39–60.
Townshend, C. (2013). *The Republic*. London: Allen Lane.

1   The terrain of discourse

Sir Kenneth Bloomfield

When I think of the Northern Ireland peace process I am often reminded of the costly efforts to ascend Mount Everest, the loftiest summit in the world. We all remember and honour Hillary and Tenzing, but, of course, their expedition was far from the first to tackle with courage that dangerous and challenging task. Each successive expedition was able to learn something from the costly failure of its predecessors. Too many gallant mountaineers earned their place in the Sisyphus club of mountaineering. But, in mountaineering at least, there is a finite summit. Politics can present a different type of challenge, and how many 'summit conferences' have wrestled with the same problem?

I wish, too, to reflect on a different aspect of the process. Politicians speak to Parliament or the public. Governments publish Green Papers to stimulate discussion or White Papers to declare new policy. But it is no secret that such documents do not necessarily flow entirely from the pens of the responsible politicians. Some of these, of course, have the flair of effective presentation. I think of those such as Chris Patten, whose public utterances bore the imprint of his own polished composition and delivery. However, the general public has little understanding of the multiple and disparate pressures of ministerial life. The reality is that others often suggest words for their spoken or written pronouncements. This is far from meaning that these anonymous draftsmen *own* the ideas as well as the words in which they are expressed. The speechwriter or policy draftsman seeks to know and understand the policies and objectives of his principal. He must become used to amendment, evisceration or outright rejection of his efforts. In the far-off days of the Stormont Government we would minute our ministerial chiefs. With the introduction of direct rule and the arrival of William Whitelaw, the Northern Ireland Civil Service (NICS) had to adopt the new terminology of the 'submission'. Often, an important document would go through draft after draft, with the ultimately approved document no more than a distant relative of the first effort. Without naming names, I recall one minister who was so pernickety about marginalia that the process seemed endless, but without much useful change to the essential substance. In C. P. Snow's novel, *Corridors of Power* (1964), the narrator, the fictional civil servant Lewis Eliot, reflects on these arcane mysteries:

I did not need reminding, having drafted enough of them, how much speeches mattered – to parliamentary bosses, to any kind of tycoon. Draft after draft; the search for the supreme, the impossible, the more than Flaubertian perfection: the scrutiny for any phrase that said more than it ought to say, so that each speech at the end was bound, by the law of official inexplicitness, to be more porridge-like than when it started out in its first draft... To [the permanent secretaries in the book] it was part of the job, which they took with their usual patience, their usual lack of egotism; when a minister crossed out their sharp, clear English and went in for literary composition of his own, they gave a wintry smile and let it stand.

When I joined the NICS the approach to drafting was distinctly hierarchical in character. As a raw new assistant principal (on the lowest rung of the administrative class), I would sometimes lay some written effort of mine before my assistant secretary (to be viewed from my base camp as a most elevated member of the mandarinate). Even if the task was no more challenging than to seek his signature to some statutory instrument, the charming old-school Tom McCrea (invariably wearing the tie of Trinity College, Dublin) would repeatedly emphasise the pressing need to insert a comma following his signature, and for a conclusive and authoritative full stop after the printed title 'Assistant Secretary' on the line below. If, however, I was seeking his approval for some brief burst of prose (perhaps a draft reply to a Parliamentary Question), I could be sure that his pen would be poised for amendment before he had read the first word, let alone the first line of it.

As one ascended the hierarchy there was an increasing possibility that some of one's work would ultimately reach a ministerial desk (albeit probably much altered and amended in transit through intermediate layers of the bureaucracy). In a small service, a middle-ranking official might become the acknowledged expert in some small corner of his minister's brief. However, a most significant step would be appointment to a ministerial Private Office. In this capacity one would become the pipeline through which would flow the communications between ministers and departmental officials, and acquire an insight into discussions taking place at Cabinet level.

For me, then, the most significant step in my early career was my appointment in January 1956, at twenty-five years of age, to be private secretary to the Northern Ireland minister of finance, at that moment the lawyer-politician Brian Maginess QC. It would prove to be a turbulent year in the political history of the province. Maginess, distinctly to the liberal left of the governing Ulster Unionist Party (UUP), could see that – although notionally second in the order of precedence after the prime minister – he was most unlikely to succeed when Lord Brookeborough, prime minister since 1943, finally stepped down. Reverting to a legal career he accepted in the first instance the post of attorney general. Another lawyer, George B. Hanna moved to the finance portfolio, but he too would leave for a place on the County Court bench before the year was out. Thus, in Captain O'Neill, as he was then known, I acquired my third different ministerial chief within a single calendar year.

As a private secretary one was constantly 'farming out' issues to those deemed most knowledgeable about the topic in question. In practice, though, ministers were often invited to speak on behalf of government to a range of organisations and functions not directly related to the responsibilities of the department. If the private secretary had established himself as capable of stringing a few decently chosen words together, the minister might ask him to draft a few words tailored to the specific occasion. This could be a surprisingly hazardous responsibility. I recall that, relatively early in my service to Maginess, university librarians from across the United Kingdom were to hold their annual conference in Belfast, and the minister was invited to deliver the speech of welcome at the conference dinner, to be held in the Great Hall of Queen's University. Pleased and flattered to be asked by Maginess to draft a speech for him, I scanned the list of attendees, noticing in particular the expected presence of the librarians from the universities of Edinburgh, Glasgow, St Andrews and Aberdeen. Included in my draft, generously endorsed by the minister, were some words designed to offer a courteous bow to our Scots neighbours. My text emphasised the unifying power of good literature: 'Why, even in the Soviet Union they enjoy the poetry of Rabbie Burns.' The evening of the dinner arrived and I heard my ministerial boss doing ample justice to my carefully crafted text, until Maginess came to the passage aimed at our Scots friends: 'Why, even in the Soviet Union they enjoy the poetry of Rabbie Burns', before pausing to go on, 'and surely that proves they're barbarians if nothing else does.' It had never occurred to me that there could be any risk of a minister attempting a joke.

At all events, my Civil Service bosses and our ministerial chiefs became aware that I had a certain facility with words. I would contribute a few phrases to the Budget Statement of 1956, and draft replies to those Parliamentary Questions not obviously directed to some particular division of the department. But it was the arrival on the scene of Terence O'Neill that brought about a step change in my involvement. He and his experienced and knowledgeable permanent secretary, Sir Douglas Harkness, did not see eye to eye or hit it off, and I found myself treated more and more as a confidant rather than as a dogsbody or bag carrier. This could be a perilous and embarrassing state of affairs, and I did my utmost to remind O'Neill where he should look for advice on important matters affecting the department. Long before he acquired the highest office, I could see that O'Neill's methods and approach were more presidential than prime ministerial. When I read about of the conduct of Tony Blair as prime minister, I sense something curiously familiar.

One has to appreciate that at this time the UUP, effortlessly in power for so long, had nothing even marginally resembling a Conservative Central Office or research department. Indeed the UUP, it seemed to me, was hardly a party in the UK sense at all. Local baronies paid little attention to advice or attempted guidance from Glengall Street (the location of the party's headquarters). A leading minister could not turn to this source for useful briefing or well-drafted policy pronouncements. If he or she had a flair for drafting and delivery, they could and did fend for themselves. Terence O'Neill, albeit replete with good intentions, had no such flair. So it was that I was drawn inexorably into the arcane craft of speech drafting. At first, O'Neill would show me his own overnight efforts, often pretty terse, and I would diffidently suggest some modest amendments and additions. Over time the original guidance would shrink to small proportions.

From 1960 to 1963, I was based in New York, as deputy director of the British Development Office and the principal Ministry of Commerce representative in North America, promoting industrial investment. I would now and then meet O'Neill on one side of the Atlantic or the other. While he was no longer my ministerial chief, I continued to keep a close interest in financial and economic developments in Northern Ireland. Towards the end of my time in the US, the focus of opinion in Northern Ireland was on the *Hall Report*, a high-level examination of Ulster's economic problems and prospects that offered little ground for optimism. Goaded by this negativism, I sat down in a motel in Detroit, Michigan (appropriately in the area known as Bloomfield Hills), and wrote in a kind of intellectual frenzy on numerous pages of a yellow lined American legal pad, an appeal to Northern Ireland opinion on the merits of self-help. I posted the draft speech from Detroit to O'Neill at Stormont, which he delivered in the parliamentary constituency of Pottinger in Belfast in what became known as the 'Pottinger speech'. Notably, it won the enthusiastic support of the influential Jack Sayers, editor of the *Belfast Telegraph*, and some months later O'Neill became well placed to succeed Brookeborough when at long last he vacated the premiership.

I would very happily have completed my term in New York, welcomed an extension, and might well have pursued a long-term career in American business where I had already received one tempting offer. But an invitation to serve a newly appointed prime minister, even in a tiny subordinate jurisdiction, was impossible to resist, and so, in April 1963, I returned to the Cabinet Office at Stormont Castle, where I would serve O'Neill and his Cabinet, first as assistant and then as deputy secretary to the Cabinet. Over a period of six years I would formulate most of the policy pronouncements of the prime minister. These included, I might add, successive Queen's Speeches, introducing the government's programme at the beginning of each new session. Americans are often puzzled to learn that while the Queen delivers her 'Gracious Speech' at Westminster, she does not write a single sentence of it. At Stormont, the monarch not only did not write the speech, but did not deliver it either. The latter chore fell to the governor of Northern Ireland, in full pomp and regalia.

I recall that when O'Neill had completed five years of his premiership, we of his 'kitchen cabinet' entertained him at a local restaurant. To mark the occasion, I composed a 'spoof' Queen's Speech, of which I remember only one item: 'My ministers will bring before you measures for the better marketing of eggs. These will be laid before you in due course.' It was fortunate we had the opportunity to laugh together before Northern Ireland entered its 'vale of tears'.

In the US, the identity of presidential speechwriters has for many years been in the public domain. Everyone knows, and indeed knew at the time, that most of the words so memorably pronounced by Jack Kennedy came from the pen of Ted Sorensen. Increasingly, it became common knowledge that British prime ministers too hired expert speechwriters to ensure the proper political tone in major speeches. Yet many of the draftsmen and women of important declarations by government remain anonymous members of the Civil Service. Those of us who, from time to time, worked on statements, pronouncements or other documents of particular significance experienced over time a wide range of relationships with our political masters. Sometimes a 'line to take' would be laid down in more or less specific terms and the person drafting the speech would do no more and no less than clothe the underlying concept with appropriate verbal apparel. Such a line might be laid down in a written instruction, in a one-to-one encounter between minister and draftsperson, or in the setting of a wider attended meeting. Not surprisingly, the mode of approach often reflected the ministerial personality. Thus, O'Neill, as prime minister, was more comfortable with his official advisers than with ministerial colleagues, particularly those he regarded as potential rivals.

This characteristic was underlined and exemplified by O'Neill's approach to the encounter with Irish taoiseach Seán Lemass. He had concluded (and probably rightly) that no such meeting would take place if he opened up the possibility to his Cabinet. Predecessors had adhered rigidly to the line 'no meeting in the absence of full constitutional recognition', and the outcome of a Cabinet discussion might well have been halfway between 'never, never, never' and 'a good idea at the right time, but not now'. Anxious as he was to limit the parameters of the meeting, O'Neill did not want any prior discussion outside the Cabinet Office trio of Sir Cecil Bateman, James Malley and myself. He thought it wise to have a brief and cautious communiqué prepared in advance, and, rather than dictate something to an office secretary, I fell back on the secretarial skills of my wife, Elizabeth, who had before our marriage worked in O'Neill's Private Office in Finance. So it is that in Tom Garvin's comprehensive biography *Judging Lemass* (2009) one can see a picture of the brief statement hammered out on our home typewriter:

We have today discussed matters in which there may prove to be a degree of common interest, and have agreed to explore further what specific measures may be possible or desirable by way of practical consultation and cooperation. Our talks, which did not touch upon constitutional or political questions, have been conducted in a most cordial way, and we look forward to a further discussion in Dublin.

It was never likely to rival Lincoln's 1863 Gettysburg Address (containing the famous line 'government of the people, by the people, for the people'), but the disclaimer of 'constitutional or political questions' was designed to offer some shelter from suspicious unionist critics. One often hears the expression 'constructive ambiguity'. A prime example was de Gaulle's 'assurance' to the 'pieds noirs' in Algeria with the phrase 'Je vous ai compris'. Auditors thought it implied sympathy and understanding. In reality, it could best be translated into American English as 'I've figured you out'. The O'Neill–Lemass encounter had, of course, been profoundly political and constitutional, whatever the disclaimer.

To return, though, to the circumstances in which one could find oneself working on a speech or statement of potential significance and, as I have explained, the responsible politician may well have indicated in greater or lesser detail, perhaps in written form or across a conference table, a line to take. But this was by no means always the case. In time, the wordsmith would build up a sense of his political master's underlying philosophy and approach. With such accumulated knowledge and understanding, he or she might well over time acquire the confidence to say 'Here is something that I hope you will agree needs saying, and here are some words you might think of using in saying it.' Very often such thoughts would never reach the minister. The Civil Service is hierarchical, and under direct rule I would not hesitate to bombard successive permanent undersecretaries of state with suggestions that the secretary of state might usefully and productively say this or that. Many of these, almost certainly deservedly, would fall by the wayside. I never resented this and, on the whole, I think it is better to have too many ideas than too few. I may say that I was far from unique in this excess of enthusiasm. I worked over the years with a middle-ranking Northern Ireland Office (NIO) official who was replete with views, ideas and self-confidence, and by no means restrained from displaying these qualities in the presence of his official superiors. I recall vividly a long drawn-out and important meeting in London, chaired in his office by a very senior official from another department, and involving several participants of elevated status. Unusually, we were meeting on a Saturday morning. As lunchtime approached, my rather self-confident colleague proclaimed 'We seem to have made good progress. Shall we resume at two o'clock?' Our host replied, 'You are, of course, welcome to use my room', reaching for his hat on the hat stand, 'but I will be at the Kempton Park racecourse.'

So, then, we have the draft in response to specific guidance, and the draft prepared in the confident knowledge of a minister's policy objectives.

Between 1974, when the short-lived power-sharing Executive collapsed, and late 1984, when I became head of the NICS, I was primarily concerned with the day-to-day delivery of public services, particularly in the environmental and economic spheres. Nevertheless, the NIO would draw me from time to time into discussions on political issues, and I would offer views through the permanent undersecretary or my predecessor Ewart Bell. However, from late 1984 until my retirement, working to successive secretaries of state, Douglas Hurd, Tom King and Peter Brooke, I became a member of the inner Cabinet of the NIO. In *Stormont in Crisis* (Bloomfield 1994), I observed how I had expected the post of head of the NICS to be the 'real' job and the role of second permanent undersecretary, essentially honorific. I came to reverse that view. Each Northern Ireland department had its own perfectly competent permanent secretary, and on this front I could concentrate on issues crossing departmental boundaries or that required concerted joined up action. On the other hand, successive secretaries of state and their permanent undersecretaries acknowledged the value of harnessing local knowledge and long experience to the task of activating a convincing peace process en route to a stable political settlement.

Subsequent Northern Ireland prime ministers, James Chichester-Clark and Brian Faulkner, were more collegial in their approach. The elements of Faulkner's fiftieth anniversary speech had been hammered out in Cabinet, but it fell to me to clothe these concepts with the words used on that occasion, at the crucial turning point, as it proved to be, between the hope of developing consensus and the harsh reality of a fatally fractured polity. The initial reception of any words, however well chosen, can be misleading. Harsh political reality, as in the aftermath of O'Neill's 'Crossroads' speech, can all too swiftly impose itself. The dismissal of Craig was seen as a willingness to confront the hard-liners. The split in the UUP was now in the open, and it was in this context that O'Neill decided to make the 'Crossroads' speech, taken from its opening phrase 'Ulster stands at the crossroads'. My copy of O'Neill's collected speeches, *Ulster at the Crossroads* (O'Neill 1969), bears the inscription 'From the author of the title to the author', and, indeed, that challenging opening phrase was added by O'Neill when he arrived at the BBC for the broadcast. The immediate reaction was overwhelmingly positive, yet O'Neill would resign, a deeply disillusioned man, in April 1969. There were several causes of this abrupt decline. When the Easter Rising occurred in Dublin in 1916, the leaders of this abortive rebellion represented only a modest minority. It was the brutality of the executions that turned so many home rulers into republicans. In a strange parallel, the ultras led by Bernadette Devlin and others were also a force on the fringe until the marchers at Burntollet were assaulted, afforded no convincing police protection, and criticised by O'Neill without adequate recognition of the brutality of the attack upon them. But reading the 'Crossroads' speech today I can acknowledge two weaknesses or defects in it. It offered no specific further measure of reform within the existing majoritarian system, and no better deal than greater fairness within a state in which unionism would continue to hold all ultimate power.

I return to the analogy of reaching for the summit. It deserves to be remembered that from the 1960s on, efforts were being made to move towards a more fair and just society in Northern Ireland. As I have explained, during a good deal of the time from 1963, I worked relatively close to the centre of political power and as a senior member of the cabinet secretariat from that year until the introduction of direct rule in 1972. As well as this I was part of Whitelaw's 'kitchen cabinet' until late 1973, cabinet secretary to the power-sharing Executive in the early months of 1974, departmental permanent secretary from 1975 until 1984 where I was often involved in the 'Whither Northern Ireland?' debate and from 1984 until my retirement in 1991 as head of the NICS and second permanent under secretary of the NIO working to successive secretaries of state in Douglas Hurd, Tom King and Peter Brooke. From this background I have reflected upon those speeches and documents to which I made some contribution, as well as expeditions up the mountain of consensus that got beyond base camp, but not to any ultimate destination.

The late 1960s was a crucial period and a significant turning point in the history of Northern Ireland. A tide of youthful protest about perceived inequality swept the world. At Westminster a convention of not debating issues devolved to Northern Ireland was swept away. The popularity of Gerry Fitt was a major influence in the Labour Party, and no one could have predicted that he would end his political career with immense enjoyment in the House of Lords. In my own experience, he was impossible to dislike. At Stormont Castle, Terence O'Neill confronted a rising storm. Many argue that he was not a convinced reformer, but rather a realist who appreciated, as some of his colleagues certainly did not, that if reforms to the unionist-dominated state were not offered domestically, there would be the humiliation of imposition by the sovereign power. In my opinion, and I knew him as well as anyone outside his immediate family, he accepted the case for community equity, but knew how difficult it would be to drive it through a divided party. In the forefront of nationalist demands there were such issues as voting rights in local government and the allocation of public housing, but the unionist ultras were persuaded from the beginning that the real objective was to destroy the whole structure of single-party rule. The five-point reform declaration of November 1968 was regarded by senior nationalist politicians as essentially a statement on account. Those five points sought to address the replacement of the Londonderry corporation by an appointed development commission, to get local councils to adopt a 'points system' in the allocation of local housing, to enable certain provisions of the Special Powers Act (1922) to be repealed, to create the appointment of an ombudsman and to take into account universal suffrage at local government elections.

During the tenure of O'Neill's successor, James Chichester-Clark, attention turned to the question of how a minority incapable of forming a government might nevertheless be afforded a more worthwhile place in the democratic institutions of Northern Ireland. A group of officials had canvassed the possibility of establishing an influential system of functional committees in Parliament, and, at one stage, I was dispatched to Westminster, alongside a member of the government, John Dobson, to assess how the committee system was developing at Westminster. We talked, I remember, to a senior Labour figure, Fred Peart, and to Selwyn Lloyd for the Conservatives. After a career in high Cabinet office, Lloyd had been dropped by Harold Macmillan in the 'night of the long knives' (13 July 1962). He saw us, I recall, in one of those small cubby-holes used by backbenchers. I reflected on the hurly-burly of a life in politics when not long afterwards Lloyd became speaker of the House of Commons and the tenant of palatial accommodation. I also had a memorable discussion with the clerk of the House of Commons, Sir Kenneth Bradshaw, who invited me, a total stranger, to lunch at the Garrick Club. When I arrived, he was deep in conversation with a florid-faced man who looked slightly familiar. 'You know Kingsley Amis, I'm sure,' said my host. 'Let's have some large gins,' said the distinguished novelist. By then, Amis seemed to have moved somewhere to the right of Oswald Mosley. 'My idea of paradise', he offered, 'would be the sound of a bloody trade unionist being shot every other minute.'

At all events the official group came forward with proposals that were not acted on until Brian Faulkner succeeded Chichester-Clark as prime minister. The fiftieth anniversary of the state opening of the first Northern Ireland Parliament by King George V in 1921 was on 22 June 1971, and the new prime minister wished to use the debate in reply to the Queen's Speech as a setting for a wide-ranging speech designed to break the political impasse. I had continued to play the Sorensen role (as I stated earlier, Sorensen was recognised as the principal speechwriter of President Kennedy), and devoted much time and thought to this occasion. In a lengthy and detailed speech, Faulkner coupled the proposal for minority participation in influential parliamentary committees with a proposal that all parties in the Northern Ireland Parliament should participate in comprehensive but informal exploratory discussions about the future of Northern Ireland and its politics. He added the caveat:

While those parties with a policy of seeking constitutional change would not be expected in any way to derogate from that policy, the discussions could not be expected to make headway unless conducted in terms of the existing constitutional framework – that is to say, Northern Ireland as part of the United Kingdom, with its own Government and Parliament.

In *Stormont in Crisis*, I observe that, 'Not for the last time, those in favour of a united Ireland were being asked to distinguish between aspiration and current reality.' At the time, the inclusion of this caveat did not deter opposition parties from involvement in an initial meeting on 7 July, or the issue after it of a moderately encouraging agreed statement: 'Nothing of this sort involving private and completely frank exchanges has been attempted before. We all think it worthwhile to continue this experiment in patient discussion and intend to meet again for further talks.' After this hopeful start things moved very rapidly in the opposite direction. The Army shot two rioters in Derry, John Hume demanded a public inquiry, and when this was not conceded the opposition parties withdrew from the Stormont Parliament. It may well be that, even though minority parties had participated in the abortive interparty talks, Hume, as a long-term strategist, had set his sights on a degree of change well beyond the ability of any Stormont government to deliver.

The next throw of the dice would be the publication of a wide-ranging consultative document, *The Future Development of the Parliament and Government of Northern Ireland*. Once again I was deeply involved in its preparation. For the first time a government of Northern Ireland would concede that, 'It is a fact that Northern Ireland has not, in the course of fifty years, been able to develop that high degree of stability and general acceptance which characterises the British democratic system.' The functional committee proposals were repeated, a possible movement to the single transferable vote as a basis for elections was canvassed, and it was accepted that 'it would be highly desirable to promote a situation in which members of both religious communities who accept unreservedly the principles set out in paragraph 36 above could take a part in the executive Government of the country'. Paragraph 36 of the consultative paper was, then, the heart of the matter. It listed three points on which it would not compromise. Two of these, the preservation of the processes of democratic government and the need for firm resistance to methods of violence or coercion, were unlikely to be a problem. The remaining point was 'the maintenance of Northern Ireland as an integral part of the United Kingdom in accordance with the statutory guarantee of the Ireland Act, 1949'. The document explicitly ruled out compulsory power-sharing of the nature that was to feature later, and in which Faulkner would be joined in office by Fitt, Hume and others. Looking back on it now, the cardinal point of paragraph 36 was wide open to misunderstanding. It could too easily be construed as a willingness to share power with nationalists only if they became unionists. The true intention was to reinforce the centrality of the 'consent principle', an issue set to rest only many years later with amendments to the 'claim of right' expressed in the Irish Constitution.

The last efforts of a Stormont government to stabilise the situation were to be recorded in a final White Paper issued on 24 March 1972 as direct rule was about to be introduced. It recorded a continuing opposition to entrenched 'power-sharing', but revealed a willingness to work towards a constitutional 'new deal' in Ireland, under which the right to self-determination would be recognised, but where there would be cooperation in the suppression of illegal organisations, including the concept of a 'common law enforcement' to facilitate the return of fugitive offenders, and a joint Irish Intergovernmental Council to enhance cooperation, particularly in the social and economic spheres.

When William Whitelaw arrived on the scene as the first secretary of state, members of the NICS were nervous about their future. On the British side, there had been some degree of apprehension as to how the NICS would react to such changed political circumstances. In Whitehall itself, officers had been well used to changes in political direction following a general election. Although this 1972 change of direction was the first in Northern Ireland, there was never any question of failure to respond constructively to this unprecedented development, nor, to their everlasting credit, did Faulkner and his colleagues show any surprise or resentment about loyal service to those lawfully appointed ministers who had supplanted him. Whitelaw and his shrewd and sardonic permanent secretary, Sir William Neild, were wise and generous enough to appreciate that officials could make a valuable contribution to the search for a more widely acceptable polity. Permanent secretaries in the NICS, serving as a Future Policy Group, were encouraged to explore and present future options, while the head of the service, Sir David Holden, the outgoing cabinet secretary, Sir Harold Black, and I were embodied in Whitelaw's team of advisers.

In September 1972, all the Northern Ireland political parties were invited to a conference in Darlington to seek common ground. It was not an encouraging sign that the Social Democratic and Labour Party (SDLP), at that time still the major party of nationalism, declined to attend. As the members of the NIO team prepared to go, it was suggested that I might begin to give some thought to a discussion paper that would identify issues and examine alternatives. I spent the weekend in London, in a flat of my aunt's, and wrote in a passion an entire first draft. It would, of course, be modified en route to finality, but the basic structure and argument survived. Normally, government documents produced to promote discussion are described as Green Papers, and, indeed, are published within green covers. Perhaps unduly conscious of the dichotomy in Ireland between 'the Orange and the Green', the document titled *The Future of Northern Ireland: A Paper for Discussion* appeared in virginal white, a faintly comic decision since the unionist government of Northern Ireland's own discussion document the previous year had worn the traditional green raiment. Very large numbers of the 1972 Paper were published and circulated, and gratifyingly the eminent historian Lord Blake wrote to the NIO to welcome it as 'one of the great State Papers of the Twentieth Century'. Like so many other initiatives, these efforts would be overtaken by events. But the 1972 Paper brought to the forefront the two elements that would dominate discussion over the years ahead and would underpin the outcome of the Good Friday Agreement (GFA) and the St Andrews Agreement (SAA), that is to say, power-sharing and an 'Irish dimension'. It spoke of:

> measures to secure the acceptance, in both Northern Ireland and in the Republic, of the present status of Northern Ireland, and of the possibility – which would have to be compatible with the principle of consent – of subsequent change in that status; to make possible effective consultation and cooperation in Ireland for the benefit of North and South alike; and to provide a firm basis for concerted governmental and community action against those terrorist organisations that represent a threat to free democratic institutions in Ireland as a whole.

From this platform colleagues in the NIO would move forward to legislation providing for a form of power-sharing, to be introduced following agreements at the Sunningdale Conference. Unhappily, this initially promising structure would be short-lived as the Ulster Workers' Council Strike succeeded in creating conditions in which the Executive received quite inadequate backing from the forces of the state.

The new Labour administration turned to the device of a constitutional convention, in which the elected representatives of the people of Northern Ireland would themselves seek to agree on a mutually acceptable form of devolved government, under the chairmanship of the Lord Chief Justice, Lord Lowry. In spite of his best efforts, and the services of two of the finest minds from the NICS, John Oliver and Maurice Hayes, the convention could not reach the necessary consensus. At least the White Paper proposing the convention afforded me the opportunity, as the secretary to the all too short-lived Executive, to offer to posterity, for inclusion in the Paper, the opportunity to recognise this first attempt to cross the great divide of local politics. In plain terms, I wrote:

> The Ulster Workers' Council in association with the paramilitary organisations brought down the Executive, which, in a spirit of partnership, had undertaken the tasks of government in Northern Ireland since January 1. In the political history of these islands, few men had ever undertaken a more arduous yet honourable task, with a full awareness of the political and even personal dangers to which they were exposing themselves. What they attempted to do was undoubtedly distorted and misrepresented and they found it difficult to establish themselves and their policies against a background of continuing violence... Yet, if the Executive failed, the men who served in it did not fail. They disproved for ever the idea that it is not possible for Protestant and Roman Catholic to work together for the good of Northern Ireland and its people.

From 1975 until 1984, I held a succession of posts as a departmental permanent secretary, directing most of my time towards serving the several ministers dealing first with environmental and then with economic matters. I was not totally isolated from the ongoing search for a political settlement and the restoration of public order. From time to time the NIO would draw me into the exploration of 'what if?' alternatives, often alongside Maurice Hayes, whose distinctive perspective was invaluable. Nevertheless, there was a step change in my involvement with my appointment in late 1984 as head of the NICS and second permanent undersecretary at the NIO. Initially, I thought the first of these roles would be substantive and the second titular. Over time I would revise that view. Northern Ireland departments were led by competent permanent secretaries, and it was seldom wise to second-guess them on their own territory. My role in this sphere would be coordination rather than direction. In the wider area of political development, successive secretaries of state and permanent undersecretaries could see the benefit of incorporating an experienced local official into the inner think tank of the administration. There was to be, nevertheless, one significant 'exclusion zone', and at the highest level it was decided that only members of the Home and Diplomatic services could be party to the processes leading ultimately to the Anglo-Irish Agreement (AIA).

There are two issues here. Was the Agreement, as its negotiators would claim, a necessary and indeed vital step on the road towards a comprehensive settlement? Certainly, Garret FitzGerald looked to it as a means to inhibit the rise of Sinn Féin and to persuade unionism to prefer power-sharing to an absence from the new 'top table' of the Intergovernmental Conference. Of course, power-sharing ultimately returned, but only after further bloody years and the inexorable rise of Sinn Féin. Was it sensible not merely to exclude political unionism from the process, but to regard membership of the NICS as a disability? Perhaps my exclusion, wounding as it was at the time, did me a favour, since the first breach in the total boycott of the NIO by unionists came from a contact with me. I doubt if my presence would have made much practical difference to the outcome, where even cautionary noises from senior NIO officials were likely to be characterised as 'going native' by the grand viziers of the Cabinet and Foreign offices. It was, though, ironic to revisit the published results of the Open Competition of 1952 for graduate entry into the Civil and Diplomatic services. The list of the successful included Douglas Hurd, Robert Andrew and Kenneth Bloomfield.

At the ministerial level, Douglas Hurd was deeply involved in the negotiations leading to the AIA of 1985. I had known well, over a good many years, the officials involved on the Irish side, such as Dermot Nally, and had the utmost respect for their abilities. Since the central issue was a search for peace and stability in Northern Ireland, it could be argued that the negotiating process would have benefited from the participation of the second-ranking official in the NIO (albeit a 'native'), not least because of the pronounced imbalance at political level. While the British side regarded the process as a bilateral negotiation between the two sovereign powers, it could be taken for granted that Dublin would take soundings from the SDLP in general, and from

John Hume in particular. It was galling to realise, after the event, that one had been deliberately excluded. However, while I have, in writing since then, expressed a residual resentment, on mature reflection I tend to the view that I was well out of it. The Cabinet and Foreign offices were bound to be the heavy hitters on the British side, with cautionary words even from the NIO to Whitehall officials likely to be discounted as a symptom of 'going native'. Moreover, in a strange sense, my exclusion secured my future usefulness, even if that was not its rationale. Garret FitzGerald's memoir *All in a Life* (1991) reminds me of his hope that the Agreement would arrest the alarming rise of Sinn Féin and persuade unionists to accept power-sharing as the only means to abstract Northern Ireland domestic affairs from the purview of the Intergovernmental Conference. Of course, it did nothing of the kind. After a brief dip, Sinn Féin's electoral support forged ahead, and far from embracing devolution as an escape route, unionism broke off all contact with government. However, as it was widely known that I had not been involved in the Agreement process, the first feelers of potential re-engagement were extended to me by members of the UUP, leading in time to a series of exchanges between myself and the permanent undersecretary Robert Andrew, and thereafter John Blelloch, on the one side, and Ian Paisley and James Molyneaux, on the other.

Hurd's successors, Tom King and Peter Brooke, were prepared to incorporate me into the top team of the NIO. At first, we would sit in various more or less comfortable chairs around the Stormont Castle office, until King installed a round table at which knights and others could be comfortable. The introduction of videoconferencing made a huge difference to the conduct of business. The secretary of state would normally spend part of the week in London, for Cabinet, Cabinet committee or parliamentary business and part in Belfast. By these means we could all join in 'morning prayers' for a pretty free-wheeling address of the current agenda as well as the problems of the day. It is an ironic fact that, during one videoconference between bomb-torn Belfast and generally peaceful London, those of us in the Belfast studio witnessed our colleagues on the other side of the Irish Sea abruptly vacating their premises. It was the day on which a PIRA device was projected into the garden of 10 Downing Street. The business would sometimes include consideration of the launch of a new initiative. This might involve anything from the mere kernel of an idea to a detailed schema or even a full draft.

The 'Whitbread' speech (where, in 1990, Brooke made his now famous 'no selfish strategic or economic interest' statement) fell into this last category. What was important in the launch of an initiative of this kind is what I might describe as a 'sense of ripeness'. One would not put pen to paper in the absence of sound grounds for believing such an approach could be timely and productive. Of course, each major political interest would wish to present such a démarche as leaning in its own direction. One would even see the insertion by some of non-existent commas into the published version, to promote the idea that the speech represented a total disclaimer of any continuing interest in Northern Ireland. As far as I was concerned, in drafting the speech, it was important to state what the British interest *was* as well as what it *was not*. The message was about what the role was, rather than about what it was misrepresented as being. In essence, it was to stand behind the consent principle, which left the ultimate destiny of Northern Ireland in the hands and votes of its own people. I had reflected on a fortuitous conversation with John Hume in a shared taxi ride on the issue of selfish strategic and economic interest, although I did not at that time appreciate the extent and significance of his dialogue with Sinn Féin's Gerry Adams. But I had long felt that progress in our complex relationships would demand dropping the 'claim of right' embodied in the Irish Constitution. Other statements in whose preparation I had played some part had been, to re-visit the mountaineering analogy, attempts to move towards the summit, but fated to return to base. Whitbread did not make the top, but reached a camp from which, over time, a successful effort could be made.

Too often in the past, people like Enoch Powell had fantasised about the strategic importance of Northern Ireland for Britain's security. In my mind at least, the positive message was that Britain would stand by the determination of the franchise as a means of assuring Northern Ireland's right to decide its future. As I wrote the words, I recalled the absurdity of the parallel status declarations embodied in the Sunningdale Agreement, and the devaluation of well-meant assurances by the Irish Supreme Court's identification of a 'constitutional imperative'. I profoundly believed that the abandonment of the territorial claim inherent in Articles 2 and 3 of the Irish Constitution would have to form part of any comprehensive peace process, and so, after many years, it has turned out to be. On the 'parallel declarations', it should also be recalled that the 1937 (de Valera) Constitution had incorporated Articles 2 and 3 in what was regarded by unionists as a 'claim of right' to Northern Ireland. Faulkner pressed this issue at Sunningdale, where Conor Cruise O'Brien favoured abolition in principle, but warned that this would require a referendum, which he felt certain would fail. At the end, Article 5 of the Sunningdale 'Agreed Communiqué' was to take the bizarre form of two pillars. To the left, the Irish pillar read: 'The Irish Government fully accepted and solemnly declared that there would be no change in the status of Northern Ireland until a majority of the people of Northern Ireland desired a change in that status.' On the right pillar: 'The British Government declared that it was, and would remain, their policy to support the wishes of the majority of the people of Northern Ireland. The present status of Northern Ireland is that it is part of the United Kingdom. If in the future the majority of the people of Northern Ireland should indicate a wish to become part of a united Ireland the British Government would support that wish.' The differences here were subtle, but the significant point was that the Republic, unlike the United Kingdom, had a written constitution, which retained the 'claim of right' unless and until amended.

Politicians and those officials who supported them over those testing years would do well to acknowledge all that was done and suffered by others. If statements and documents succeeded or failed in full public gaze, the prospects of ultimate success rested also on the broad shoulders of many courageous and wise people, such as Brendan Duddy in Derry or Michael Oatley who, in the secret world, laboured bravely and, for a long time, unacknowledged. And as I became involved from 1997 in work to bring succour to victims of our struggle, I would meet so many who had risked life and limb. There are sometimes chill winds at the summit we ultimately reached, but at least we can envisage the possible and aspire to the best. On a possible note to end we might ask, do speeches matter? My response to that is to suggest, not of themselves, no. They are simply the means of declaring actual or potential changes of policy. But, of course, public messages, available to the wider world, are not close to being the whole story. I am in no doubt that, over these testing years, many private messages, some of which may never be revealed, passed between the principal players, but the extent to which those messages changed minds and directions is for those principal players to determine and for historians to continue to interrogate.

References

Bloomfield, K. (1994). *Stormont in Crisis*. Belfast: Blackstaff Press.
FitzGerald, G. (1991). *All in a Life*. Dublin: Gill & Macmillan.
Garvin, T. (2009). *Judging Lemass*. Dublin: Royal Irish Academy.
O'Neill, T. (1969). *Ulster at the Crossroads*. London: Faber & Faber.
Snow, C. P. (1964). *Corridors of Power*. London: Macmillan.

2 The Anglo-Irish Agreement: an interview with Sir David Goodall and Lord Armstrong of Ilminster

Background

The Anglo-Irish Agreement (AIA), negotiated and signed by the British and Irish governments on 15 November 1985, has been viewed as a moment of history that 'ushered in an era of direct rule with a green tinge', and, because of this, 'sent a shudder of horror through the unionist community' (Bew and Gillespie 1999: 190–1). The preamble to the Agreement emphasised collaboration and cooperation between Ireland and the United Kingdom in the context of the European Union, which required the two governments to work as 'neighbours and partners'. That cooperation was directed, in particular, at the need to try to reduce division and 'achieve lasting peace and stability'. Significantly, the Agreement stressed a requirement to reconcile the rights of the different traditions 'represented, on the one hand, by those who wish for no change in the present status of Northern Ireland and, on the other hand, by those who aspire to a sovereign united Ireland achieved by peaceful means and through agreement'. Adhering to an approach already expressed in the Sunningdale Agreement (SA), Article 1 of the Agreement underlined that any change in the status of Northern Ireland could come about only with the consent of the majority of people who lived there. It affirmed that since the majority wished for no change in that status, Northern Ireland would remain part of the United Kingdom. But (and this would provoke the fear of unionists) 'if in the future a majority of the people of Northern Ireland clearly wish for and formally consent to the establishment of a united Ireland' the two governments 'will introduce and support in the respective Parliaments legislation to give effect to that wish'. The framework used to facilitate this possibility, and allow the Irish a consultative role in Northern Ireland's affairs, would take the form of an Intergovernmental Conference, set up to deal with political, security and legal matters, the administration of justice and the promotion of cross-border cooperation.

For Irish taoiseach Garret FitzGerald, who endorsed the Agreement, the motivation for negotiation was influenced by the rise of the Provisional IRA (PIRA) following the hunger strikes; a situation that FitzGerald believed had been made worse by its bad handling by the British Government. For FitzGerald, ignoring or rejecting the chance to 'combine some kind of "Irish dimension"' as part of a devolution policy 'would have contributed further to a possibly disastrous radicalization of Northern nationalist opinion and an erosion of the Social Democratic and Labour Party in favour of Sinn Féin'. The very real fear for FitzGerald was that if the PIRA gained traction and became the dominant voice of nationalist representation, 'it might be emboldened to raise the threshold of violence to the point of risking outright civil war in the North' (FitzGerald 1994: 191–2) (a possibility that, it must be said, looked highly unlikely even before the Agreement was signed (*ibid.*: 202)). Although Sinn Féin had acquired only 10 per cent of the vote in Northern Ireland by 1982, this was enough for FitzGerald to move with 'urgency about securing arrangements that would reduce the alienation of a large part of the nationalist minority from the institutions of Northern Ireland', arguing that the way to address this problem was through joint authority (*ibid.*: 193). In advance of negotiations, and to shape a context that favoured moves in that direction, FitzGerald set up the New Ireland Forum, designed to allow unionist opinion to be expressed more directly to those in the Republic. FitzGerald's aim through the Forum was twofold. First, to try to set out principles that would underscore movement towards peace and stability in Northern Ireland in order to 'provide a common basis upon which the Irish and British governments could proceed in relation to negotiations'; and, secondly, to articulate the possibility of 'joint sovereignty or joint authority' as a means to try to open negotiations and explore 'other possible models' of authoritative influence in Northern Ireland (*ibid.*: 194).

Significantly, in 1983, FitzGerald made a '"deniable" approach' to Margaret Thatcher, expressing a 'willingness' on the part of the Irish 'to assist in defusing nationalist alienation' by way of 'direct involvement in the security process in Northern Ireland, should this commend itself to the British government' (*ibid.*: 195). By 1983, the Irish were also considering, in conversation with John Hume of the Social Democratic and Labour Party (SDLP), using the area of security as a means to develop an Irish dimension within Northern Ireland, and conceptualised this in relation to a strategic shift in emphasis from '"not Brits out, but Irish in"' (Bowman 2013).

At a summit in November 1983, FitzGerald explained the purpose of the New Ireland Forum to Thatcher, and seemed to have caught the prime minister's interest, although official discussions on joint authority did not take place until May 1984. The British did not reject outright a proposal by the Irish on joint authority and, for FitzGerald, this was because they were more interested in exploring the concept in relation to security than politics (FitzGerald 1994: 196). In general, though, the Thatcher Government reacted negatively to any suggestion that authority in Northern Ireland should be diluted to the advantage of the Irish. Of more interest would be a joint body to explore in a coordinated way security-related areas supported by a joint secretariat in Belfast with ministers from both governments chairing such a body. From FitzGerald's point of view, the British preoccupation with security matters did little to help an Irish desire to address the alienation of the nationalist community in Northern Ireland and to confront rising support for the PIRA (*ibid.*: 198). Nor was this helped by regular leaking of the negotiations to the press, which intensified pressure on the British not to make concessions to the Irish and further angered unionists. However, for FitzGerald, the aim was not to '"downface" the unionists', as the media portrayals inferred, but rather 'to weaken support for the IRA by reducing the alienation of the nationalist minority in Northern Ireland and to stabilise the position in that area by creating conditions in which this minority would identify with the system of authority there as it had not previously been able to do' (*ibid.*: 201).

In his account of the path towards the Agreement, titled 'Edging towards Peace' (2010) (along with his Irish counterpart Michael Lillis), Sir David Goodall, one of the key negotiators for the British Government, highlights a number of influences that shaped British reaction. He notes, for example, that 'alienation' was a concept that Thatcher found difficult to relate to, sensing, in her mind, Marxist underpinnings (even if also acknowledging the need to take this 'very seriously' (Bowman 2013)). Thatcher, according to Goodall, thought 'that successive Irish Governments were less than wholehearted in combating IRA terrorism, insufficiently vigorous in preventing terrorists from using Southern territory as a safe haven, and disposed to put obstacles in the way of cross-border cooperation between British and Irish security forces'. As Goodall suggests, the options for resolving the Northern Ireland problem by 'integrating Northern Ireland fully into the United Kingdom's administrative structure', or by trying to address the concerns of nationalists in the context of confirming the Union, or by ploughing on with direct rule whilst seeking to defeat terrorism in the hope that 'some form of devolved government' might be restored, appeared to be the only ones available, with the last of these most likely. Interestingly, Goodall indicates that the Irish appeared to have considered what they wanted from negotiations more clearly than the British, framing their negotiating positions to converge strongly with Irish proposals. His intimation is that although the British would not accept Irish involvement in matters of British sovereignty and authority, for the Irish it was believed that 'outright acceptance of the Union would be a price worth paying for measures which, by addressing Northern nationalists' concerns, would end their alienation from the institutions of the state in the North and demonstrate that constitutional – i.e. non-violent – nationalism could achieve more for nationalists than Sinn Féin and the IRA' (Goodall 2010). Goodall notes how, on 7 November 1983, FitzGerald pitched his 'basic equation' idea to Thatcher at Chequers of 'outright Irish endorsement of the Union and closer security cooperation in return for an Irish role in the government and administration of justice in the North'. Since Thatcher had rejected the suggestion of joint sovereignty, FitzGerald argued for joint authority instead. And although Thatcher found this prospect similarly unacceptable, FitzGerald made the case for recognising the common ground that had been established and which would provide a basis for further proposals to be discussed. What followed, Goodall recollects, was 'a long series of probing operations in which the two sides jointly tested the relative weight which each of the two elements in the "basic equation" could be made to bear and discussed ways of putting the elements into mutually acceptable language', with the British trying to restrict the role of the Irish to security matters. As Goodall put it, 'the British wanted a visible and effective Irish commitment to joint anti-terrorist operations' (*ibid.*).

For the Irish, joint counter-terrorism initiatives pointed towards a need for closer political cooperation and responsibility, and FitzGerald was not convinced that joint authority would amount to a diminution of British sovereignty, as Thatcher believed. To partly assuage this concern, the Irish Government's role in the North, the British suggested, might over time morph into '"a devolved administration"', which could support a sharing of power between nationalists and unionists, but such a transition was mistakenly interpreted by the Irish, according to Goodall, as 'making *any* Irish involvement in the North conditional on the prior establishment of a power-sharing administration' (*ibid.*).

For Goodall, the outcome of the negotiations was a compromise, where the Irish did not get the joint authority sought, but '"consultative" structures', which underpinned the development of 'mutual confidence' that laid the ground for positive relations leading to the Good Friday Agreement (GFA) of 1998 (*ibid.*). Unlike the SA of 1973, which failed because of the unwillingness of unionists to support it, Goodall contends that the AIA happened because both the British and Irish governments were committed to it happening. That the Agreement amounted to Irish recognition of British sovereignty over the North, where there could be no pressure to absorb the North into a united Ireland against the wishes of the majority there, meant that it solidified the principle of consent and a consultative/harmonisation role for the Irish as emphasised at Sunningdale. This would later become the context for negotiations leading to the GFA of 1998.

In Margaret Thatcher's memoirs, *The Downing Street Years*, she makes it clear that the political ramifications of the AIA were seen primarily in terms of their impact on security (which she viewed as 'intertwined') (Thatcher 1993: 385). Her suspicion of Irish motives throughout negotiations is also evident, so when the Irish amended Articles 2 and 3 of the constitutional claim to Irish unity, from a legal claim to an 'aspiration', the effect of this was to make her 'more pessimistic and suspicious' (*ibid.*: 399). However, against this discomfort she continued to negotiate, supporting the compromise of a consultative role and successfully getting the Irish to publicly state that there would be no change to the status of Northern Ireland without a majority there deciding that this would be the case. Though her resistance to any Irish desire for a united Ireland, or a confederation of two states or joint authority, was demonstrable with her famous 'out, out, out' speech in November 1984, this nevertheless could not fully disguise her aspiration to reach agreement. Indeed, in a joint communiqué released (separately and slightly in advance of the Irish) on 19 November, when this dismissive remark was made (causing some consternation to FitzGerald, but also made just over a month after the Brighton bomb when the PIRA killed five people and injured more than thirty at the Conservative Party Conference in Brighton), the message was also reiterated that 'The identities of both the majority and minority communities in Northern Ireland should be recognised and respected and reflected in the structures and processes of Northern Ireland in ways acceptable to both communities' (Bew and Gillespie 1999: 185). However, despite her attempts to pre-empt and assuage unionist anxiety about the Irish role with the 'out, out, out' performance, Thatcher underestimated the extent of hostility from unionists towards the Agreement and the subsequent fallout from it (Thatcher 1993: 402); a problem which, in her view, was made worse by FitzGerald 'exaggerating the powers which the Irish had obtained' through the Agreement (*ibid.*: 404). Interestingly, for the Irish, the Agreement did not halt the appeal and rise of Sinn Féin, and for the British it did little to improve security arrangements with the Irish (*ibid.*: 404–5).

The signing of the Agreement demonstrated that the management of the Northern Ireland problem undisputedly required the involvement of both the British and the Irish, but that this joint role also signalled potentially contradictory messages about the future status of Northern Ireland, with the consent principle indicating the possibility of constitutional change that allowed for nationalist objectives to be pursued, but, inevitably, which unionists viewed as to their detriment (Arthur 1993: 224). For Arthur, the Agreement had shown innovation on the Northern Ireland problem 'by moving it from a sphere of responsibility to that of a functioning regime' (*ibid.*: 225), meaning that cooperation and harmonisation between the governments created new arrangements and networks of organisation that would, over time, render boundaries and territorial claims less vital for either the British or the Irish. The possibility of change, which the Agreement had created, incited a range of unionist contentions about integration, on the one hand, and devolution, on the other (Aughey 1989: 96), with both constrained by widespread hostility towards Dublin (an advertisement carried across sections of the press in Northern Ireland at this time stated 'a Dublin Role means a Dublin Rule'). Although the SDLP reaction was more positive in seeing the Agreement as an 'opportunity' for political progress and Sinn Féin saw it as 'formal recognition of the partition of Ireland' (quoted in Ellis Owen 1994: 37), perhaps ironically it was the possibility for nationalism to play a stronger role in Northern Ireland that also encouraged Sinn Féin to move increasingly towards politics and eventually distance itself from the imperatives of armed struggle. Clearly, FitzGerald's aim to neutralise Sinn Féin was based on trying to halt growing support for the PIRA rather than assisting the development of republican politics and the end of armed struggle, which came after the GFA. But the context created by the AIA may have made it harder for republicans to sustain violence over the long term given the environment it created for nationalist politics to build a stronger role in Northern Ireland, and, because of this, provide the conditions that led to dialogue between nationalism and republicanism and the emergence of the peace process. In that the SDLP was able to make the case that the Agreement had changed circumstances which could only advantage nationalism, so the justification for violence was likely to lose appeal and even though it took some time for the PIRA to relinquish violence, the focus had incrementally shifted to internal politics as the problem (with unionism) rather than external politics as the problem (with the British). For unionists, as Mallie and McKittrick observed, the AIA 'was a victory for constitutional nationalism, and constitutional nationalism agreed with them', and it 'represented, in fact, an unprecedented new partnership between London and Dublin', which sowed seeds for the peace process (Mallie and McKittrick 2001: 60).

Interview

The answers ascribed to Sir David Goodall and Lord Armstrong in this chapter were given in interviews with each of them separately, and are brought together here for record of convenience and with their consent. The record is in no sense a discussion between them, and the interviews were conducted in London. The background and conclusion that accompany this interview were written by the editor with no involvement from the interviewees.

GS: Can you give me the background to British involvement with the Irish at the time of the AIA?

RA: It all started after the election of 1983 when Mrs Thatcher came back as prime minister for her second term. She won a majority of a hundred seats in that election, and she came back into office with a feeling that there were two outstanding matters which had been left unresolved from her previous administration, and one was Hong Kong and the other was Northern Ireland. On Northern Ireland, she came into office in 1979 with a strongly pro-unionist bent which she inherited from Airey Neave, but she had become disenchanted with the unionists in her first administration, and in 1982 she and James Prior introduced a programme called 'rolling devolution' which went nowhere. So she felt that this was unfinished business. Also Northern Ireland was costing lives and a great deal of resources. Because 'rolling devolution' had got us nowhere, Mrs Thatcher thought she would explore what could be done in relation to the Irish dimension, but she was also moved to do this because Charles Haughey had ceased to be taoiseach. She became disenchanted with Charlie Haughey because of the attitude he and the Irish Government had taken on the Falklands affair, and I don't think we'd have got anywhere if Mr Haughey had remained in office. But there was an election in the Republic, as a result of which FitzGerald had come into office with a position where he could look forward to several years before he had to face another election. So at that time we had a prime minister in England in London and a taoiseach in Dublin, both of whom were reasonably secure and could look ahead to some means of ameliorating, if not resolving, the problems of Northern Ireland. The Irish were interested in opening conversations and this was discussed in London. The issue of security was really uppermost in everybody's mind, particularly Mrs Thatcher's, and the security of the border was a central consideration. I had conceived of the possibility that instead of having a line for the border we might have a five-mile strip of land either side of the border into which the security forces of either country could enter when in pursuit of terrorists. So the British security people could go five miles into Irish territory and the Irish security forces could go five miles into British territory. And I was sent to talk to the government secretary in Dublin about this idea, which lasted for about five minutes. We would have been prepared to see Irish troops or Irish police coming into the territory of Northern Ireland, but the thought of British troops coming across the border into the Republic was more than they could take. For them that was just not possible. But it was clear that they were interested in talking, so we decided to seek and institute negotiations to see if there was any basis for an agreement without any transfer of sovereignty. We wanted to explore whether there was any way in which you could have some kind of arrangement whereby the interests of the nationalists might be better represented in government without them necessarily being in it, and Mrs Thatcher agreed that we should pursue these possibilities with the Irish on this. Mrs Thatcher didn't want the negotiations to be run by the Foreign Office or by the Northern Ireland Office (NIO), so she asked me to take over the leadership of them. Then things could be kept and run very clearly under her hand or direction. I went over to Dublin early 1984, which was when I first talked with Dermot Nally, the government secretary (equivalent of cabinet secretary) in Dublin, and out of that came this negotiating process where David Goodall, myself and, later on, Robert Andrew from the NIO were the negotiating team on the British side, and Dermot Nally, Michael Lewis and Sean Donlon, who was the permanent secretary to the Ministry of Foreign Affairs, were on the Irish side, with an important role played by Noel Dorr who was the Irish ambassador in London. We met regularly, probably every two or three weeks for the next eighteen months, out of which came the Anglo-Irish Agreement.

DG: I always felt that British–Irish relations were a bit of a tragic mess, but also so close culturally and historically. Personally, I didn't have any professional involvement in this at all, but I was seconded into the Cabinet Office where I was second to Sir Robert Armstrong, cabinet secretary on overseas and defence matters. The British were in the middle of the Falklands War and that was our main preoccupation. At the end of that war there was a dinner and afterwards Margaret Thatcher invited me up for a drink. Where the conversation turned to Ireland, I said I thought it was a tragedy that the only place in the world where British soldiers' lives were lost in anger was in the United Kingdom, in Northern Ireland. We had a conversation about it and she said reflectively that if re-elected she would like to 'do something about Ireland' and I remembered that. In the following year, Garret FitzGerald became taoiseach, but previous to that British–Irish relations had gone into cold storage because of comments by Charlie Haughey over the Falklands War. When Garret came into office, Margaret Thatcher was re-elected with a big majority, so both were looking at five years in charge of their respective governments and this was a window of opportunity for doing something about Anglo-Irish relations. There had been Anglo-Irish talks before where committees had been set up to look at various aspects of the British–Irish relationship, but that had come to a halt as a result of this disagreement over the Falklands. When Garret came into office he sent Dermot Nally across to London with the idea of trying to revive talks which had previously been conducted on the basis of an Anglo-Irish Government Conference, but which, as said, had gone sour under Haughey. The suggestion was that talks should be revived and that we should try to move on in small ways culturally through developing links etc. And it was agreed that it would be overseen by this Anglo-Irish Intergovernmental Conference, which was simply a grand name for the two leaders meeting at a summit every six months or so. The Irish nominated Michael Lillis, who was in charge of Anglo-Irish relations in the Irish Ministry of Foreign Affairs at the time, but was also a close personal friend of Garret FitzGerald and the chief architect of operations on the Irish side. The question then arose of who was going to be the equivalent on the British side, and it was decided that this should be the second senior foreign affairs official in the Cabinet Office, but not in the Foreign Office or the NIO, which was me.

GS: Was it the Irish that initially made the approach?

DG: Yes it was, but they were proposing to re-animate what had been agreed two years earlier, which had never actually got off the ground. We had a meeting in Dublin with quite a number of other ministries represented and at that meeting I met Michael Lillis. He invited me to go for a walk with him along the canal in Dublin. It was made clear that Garret FitzGerald was very worried about the situation. He thought that it was sliding towards Sinn Féin becoming the leading nationalist party in Northern Ireland and he saw that as threatening the stability of the whole of Ireland. On that basis, he thought that we should make a serious attempt at trying to get an agreed settlement and that if that was possible, on the Irish side, it would be possible to amend Articles 2 and 3 of the Irish Constitution in exchange for the Garda taking part in operations in Northern Ireland (which for us was unthinkable). It was reasonable to assume that Michael Lillis was speaking on behalf of the taoiseach. As a result of those talks there was a meeting of the British–Irish Association in Oxford, which Michael Lillis also came to and again we had another long talk about the situation. I reported this back to Robert Armstrong who took it to the prime minister. The disposition in London and in the NIO was to say they had never heard of this and they didn't think that Michael Lillis was reliable.

RA: There had been rather desultory discussions started by Charles Haughey, where machinery had been set up for an Anglo-Irish Conference and this had really not taken off. It had not been abolished or disowned, it just didn't happen. The breakdown of relationships over the hunger strikes and over the Falklands meant that this machinery effectively fell into disuse. But the Irish were deeply worried about Sinn Féin and their possible influence on domestic politics in the Republic and that was a key factor for them to address.

GS: Was there a text about this at the very early stage, or was it just dialogue?

DG: Initially, there was no text other than exchanges about meetings and about concerns related to interdepartmental committees on cultural matters. We went over to Dublin together and then there was a meeting between Margaret Thatcher and Garret FitzGerald, and she said that she didn't want there to be secret talks. It was important for her that she was able to say that there were no secret talks going on. She was pretty sceptical about the whole thing and the Irish went away rather disappointed, but actually, after they left, we all sat down at Chequers and discussed what happened, and she directed that a study should be made of the situation and what possible negotiation might be worth for the Irish. The thinking was mainly oriented towards improved security. On that basis, Robert Armstrong and I went off to Dublin with proposals that we put to the Irish.

GS: What were the parameters for these negotiations?

RA: We discussed each stage as we went along with our principals, and the Irish officials would have discussed it with FitzGerald just as I and David Goodall would have discussed it with the prime minister and her colleagues.

The issue was how to build on the Sunningdale process when there had been the Council of Ireland. It was not thought that this could be revived, but it was seen as necessary to give the Irish Government a means whereby they could represent the interests of the Catholics and the nationalists in the North. Of course, the question was what price they would pay. We should have been happy to see some modifications to Articles 2 and 3 of the Irish Constitution, but, in the end, the price that we were prepared to pay was not big enough to enable FitzGerald to do that and to get over the obstructions that would allow for the Constitution to be changed. We wanted a commitment to security from the republican threat, but we were also looking for some possible means whereby the Irish Government could contribute to the formulation of policy within Northern Ireland without transferring sovereignty. We wanted to get a commitment from both sides that there should be no change in the constitutional status of Northern Ireland except with the will of the majority of the people in Northern Ireland. That was the first clause in the Agreement that they were prepared to give and that was quite a big offer on their part, because the Irish Constitution is committed to the unification of Ireland, so no change in the status of Northern Ireland except by the will of the majority in Northern Ireland was a big move for them.

DG: I think the nature of the dialogues considerably surprised them, and because the prime minister said she didn't want secret talks they weren't prepared. They thought that they would have to wait until they had concluded their own internal assessment of this problem (the New Ireland Forum) and that nothing would happen until they'd finished that. So they were taken aback to receive British proposals. From then on there were regular meetings. They said they were in effect taken by surprise, and that there was too much emphasis on security and there had been no chance for considering the possibility of amending Articles 2 and 3. So it was all quite tricky from their point of view. But they responded to what they didn't like and that was what initiated a real negotiation.

RA: Mrs Thatcher would not have accepted anything that appeared to compromise the sovereignty of the British in Northern Ireland, so anything that would seem to do that was out as far as she was concerned. Garret FitzGerald had set up the New Ireland Forum, which had a look at three possible relationships between Britain and Ireland over the North. As far as Margaret Thatcher was concerned, any one of these three areas would have compromised sovereignty so we had to find some means whereby the Irish could be involved in discussions of affairs in Northern Ireland, and able to bring the interests of the Catholics and nationalists to bear on those discussions, without compromising British sovereignty.

GS: When they responded did they do so with a piece of text, or was it a verbal response initially?

DG: Around February/March 1985 they sent us quite a large note, which caused Mrs Thatcher considerable offence because she didn't like the tone of it. We replied to it immediately before the meeting and the prime minister agreed a more temperate reply than I thought she would have. She and Garret FitzGerald then had a meeting and negotiations carried on.

GS: Can you summarise how Irish thinking compared with British thinking?

RA: When it came to text and language, I did a lot of the drafting and Noel Dorr on the Irish side had a similar role. We were both talking the same language really, and because of this I think that we saw this as the opportunity for profound change in the relationship between Britain and Ireland. You must remember that this was a relationship that had been run on mutual suspicion, even hostility since 1922, and, of course, before that. The relationship between the two governments was not good or close and they tended to deal with issues through megaphone diplomacy or columns in newspapers, which didn't contribute to good relations. I think one of the purposes we had was to create some means whereby there was clearer and greater trust between the two governments, so that when difficulties arose the first response was not to turn to the media but to talk, and on the whole I think we succeeded in doing that. The process developed a kind of mutual trust and confidence, which bore fruit in subsequent agreements. There was a greater readiness to talk between the two governments and to discuss problems before they became public issues. Clearly, we were not going to get an agreement unless it was acceptable to both sides and that was the main object of the exercise, to find not just language but ideas that commended themselves to both sides. Getting the ideas and the language right was crucial for this and we argued about it endlessly. There was an agreement on having some kind of joint Anglo-Irish body, but it was disputed as to whether it should be called a committee or not and this, to indicate the differences, means something different in Irish. A committee is something very local and is more reflective of parishes, so it's not a very grand word in Irish political life. Understandably, they wanted something more because of that.

GS: How much freedom or slack did you have in these dialogues and how much of it was steered and reined in by the prime minister?

DG: At the start only Robert and I were on the British side, but then after the second meeting between the prime minister and the taoiseach the Northern Ireland permanent secretary became part of the team and the Irish ambassador in London, who was Noel Dorr. We had this small group of officials where the two cabinet secretaries would report to their principals and get authority to carry on to the next round of meetings. It had been agreed that these meetings would take place under the umbrella title of the Anglo-Irish Intergovernmental Conference, which were six-monthly meetings between the prime minister and the taoiseach.

GS: Why was the Agreement constructed in the order it was?

RA: It was constructed in the order it was because it needed to start with the statement that there would be no change in the status of Northern Ireland except by the will of the majority of the people there. It was important to us that the Irish Government sign up to that, but it was also important to the Irish Government that we should sign up to the possibility of change if the majority wished it. And both of those were new. In a sense, we had previously said in various forums that we had contemplated the possibility of change by the will of the people of Northern Ireland, but it was the first time that that had been enshrined in a formal treaty, an agreement between the two governments, the two countries. And to get that up front in the document was clearly very important to both of us and the rest mostly followed from that.

GS: The document almost starts from a position of trust then?

RA: It's established in a position of trust, but, of course, it was a great change because since 1922 Northern Ireland had been part of the United Kingdom not part of the Republic of Ireland, and we wanted to keep it that way, not just because that was what the majority of the people wanted, but for our own strategic reasons. We didn't want the Irish Government controlling that channel between Belfast and the ports in the North. That was very important, in the First World War and again in the Second World War. Historically, there was a great deal of concern about the possibility that territory under the control of the Irish Republic might be used by our enemies in a world war. And on the Irish side the memory that Ireland had been, if you like, a colony until 1801 and then part of the United Kingdom made them feel very much subordinate, not independent. Perhaps, almost for the first time, they were persuaded that we were not trying to re-establish an old relationship, but that we were looking for a new one between two sovereign and independent countries.

GS: I understand the whole thing from start to finish was tied up roughly in eighteen months. That indicates good relations does it not?

DG: The thing was done at two levels. The prime minister and the taoiseach met roughly every six months and they also had bilateral meetings at European Community (EC) summits. But the detailed negotiations carried on within this very small group of officials, and we got to know one another very well. I think that the confidence that developed between us was crucial in making the eventual Agreement possible; no two ways about it. I mean we got to know one another pretty well and we trusted one another pretty well and could be very frank with one another too. In that sense, it was a classic negotiation.

GS: Can you give me any idea of how you actually determined what was going to be in the Agreement, in terms of the final draft?

RA: It was a process where at each stage we discussed things with our Irish counterparts, then we came back and discussed them with our principals in London, and they went back and discussed it with their principals in Dublin. So we were constantly working at the contents and the words. I can't remember at what point we first had a complete draft, but you explore the ideas and then you explore the language in which the ideas are going to be expressed, and when you're getting somewhere, to some kind of agreement with your counterparts and your principals, then you come to the point where you begin to formulate a draft text.

GS: So did you spend months just talking to each other in a process of development? Was it a kind of debating and then a formalisation of what had been debated?

RA: I put forward this idea about the border strip, which Garret FitzGerald was clear wouldn't run. But we were then able to discuss ideas and try them out on each other. We were meeting every fortnight to do this. Mrs Thatcher kept very careful control of it at every stage and so did they. We would talk to our colleagues in Dublin and then go back to Mrs Thatcher and Geoffrey Howe and Douglas Hurd and we would say how we got on, suggest what the next stage was and what the difficulties were, where there seemed to be possibilities of progress and obstruction. We would then make proposals and seek agreement as to what we would say at the next stage. So in a sense we were negotiating two ways, first, with the people in Dublin and, secondly, with the prime minister and her colleagues. It was always businesslike and it was never confrontational. If they suggested something that we couldn't take and didn't believe we could get agreement on we would explore something else.

GS: Did you go in with well-worked-out positions beforehand, or was it exploratory?

DG: In the sense of positions being exploratory yes, but we did have specific proposals. As I said, one proposal derived from Mrs Thatcher's preoccupation with improving cross-border security. She believed that, for better or worse, the Irish were half-hearted about anti-terrorism security and she didn't really believe in their good faith, even if she did believe in Garret FitzGerald's good faith. We concentrated on different parts of the problem at different meetings, but generally we had specific proposals. The Irish had come up with the idea at the very start of the Garda operating across border territory and that idea didn't particularly appeal much to Mrs Thatcher. Our counter-proposal was that if that was going to happen, then the RUC should be able to operate with the Garda on Irish territory and they didn't like the idea of that either.

GS: Was there a real belief that you would get peace out of this, or was it a containment document?

DG: On the British side there were the two considerations, one to get a better security accommodation across the border, and the other to deal with the question of Articles 2 and 3, which, at that time, seemed to loom very large in the hostility of the unionists. As the negotiations proceeded, it became much clearer that to enable Garret FitzGerald to carry his own people to amend Articles 2 and 3 we should have to pay a much bigger political price in terms of Irish involvement in the North than we were prepared, or able, to pay. So the amendment of Articles 2 and 3 gradually receded as a British objective. It was never given up, even if in practice we had come to realise that just wasn't going to happen. The ministerial perception was that you had to do something rather than nothing with Northern Ireland, and what you could do was set about evolving ideas in these negotiations. An important objective for the Irish was being able to demonstrate to the non-republican nationalists that non-violent patriotism could achieve results. That you didn't have to have terrorism and that if this could be conveyed it would take the wind out of Sinn Féin's sails.

GS: You mentioned that for Garret FitzGerald the main concern was the rise of political Sinn Féin. Was that a concern for Margaret Thatcher as well or, for her, was it ostensibly a security issue?

DG: It was of concern to her and she saw it very much as a security issue. I think she thought, we probably all thought, that Garret was somewhat exaggerating the dangers of Sinn Féin. But you must remember that the time this process began the British had run out of ideas on what to do in Northern Ireland. They had tried all kinds of things, including a collaborative administration, but there was a kind of stalemate in which Sinn Féin or the PIRA seemed to be making progress. So there was a strong feeling that something had to be done. I do not think that anybody was under any illusions once we got going that this was going to solve the problem once and for all, but we thought it would strengthen the hand of the non-violent nationalists and help to shape a good atmosphere between the two governments. Because it involved the Irish consultatively in the business of governing Northern Ireland, it promoted much better confidence and collaboration between the two governments than had existed since 1923. Looking back on it, it's not what the Agreement actually achieved at the time that proved significant, but what it led to.

GS: Did you envisage the hostility of the unionists to the document?

DG: How to carry the unionists with us was a worry because we knew the Irish side was consulting the nationalists very closely. But we simply could not do that with the unionists because they had firmly rejected any form of collaboration with Dublin, and if they had been taken into the government's confidence about the negotiations there wouldn't have been any. In my view, that was the great weakness on our side, which was that we couldn't carry the unionists with us.

GS: Did the negotiations come close to breaking down at any point?

RA: Well there was one terrible moment when there had been a meeting between Mrs Thatcher and Garret FitzGerald at Chequers around November 1984. Business appeared to have gone reasonably well and they came back to London and each gave a press conference. But when Mrs Thatcher was asked about the proposals that had emerged in the New Irish Forum she discarded each with an 'out, out, out' dismissal, and she did it with characteristic aplomb. Unfortunately, the Irish Government were not represented at that press conference, so when FitzGerald gave his press conference and was faced with this response he was caught unawares and had not been able to prepare about how to deal with it. I remember thinking that that was probably curtains for the negotiations, but FitzGerald was too big for that. Mrs Thatcher didn't mind people knowing that she felt strongly about something, but he may have found it rather a setback that she expressed herself with such vigour, which FitzGerald would not have expected. My guess is he might have expected her to have expressed it more diplomatically. He certainly wouldn't have expected her to agree to any of his propositions and she would have made that clear to him, but the dismissive response was taken as a slap in the face. I was afraid at the time that he would feel this had done so much damage politically that he couldn't go on. But, by that stage, they both wanted negotiations to reach an agreement and, at that point, the final Agreement required only a relatively small move to conclude. You could argue that if the SA had not been wrecked we could have been in 1974 where we did not get to until after the Belfast Agreement in 1998. Arguably, the Sunningdale process tried to do too much, but I think that if Edward Heath had won the election in February 1974, which took place two or three months after the SA, he would have been committed to make the SA stick and we might have saved ourselves twenty years of misery. Wilson who came in in March 1974 with a minority government, knowing he was going to have another election within six months, was not prepared to commit in the same way, whereas I think if Heath had been there that failure might not have happened. Mrs Thatcher offered Molyneaux a privy councillor's briefing, but, I think on Enoch Powell's advice, Molyneaux refused. One could understand why because if he had accepted it he would have been muzzled, but the result of that was the unionists were never officially informed about what we were doing.

GS: Did you discuss in advance what you were going to do in the face of a hostile reaction?

RA: We tried to assess whether we should have a repetition of what happened after Sunningdale, or, whether it was something which would be made to stick because the difference between Sunningdale and the AIA was that the AIA did not require any cooperation from the unionists, it could come into effect without their say so, which the SA could not have done. I remember one of the key things was what the reaction would be in the US after we had finalised the Agreement but before it was actually signed. I went over to Washington with Sean Donlon from Dublin to talk to some of the Irish supporters there and to make sure that they would support it, which they did. They supported it not only with words, but with setting up a fund to promote economic development in Northern Ireland.

GS: Can you talk about the processes of dealing with language and interpretative differences?

DG: The key issue was that the eventual Agreement would allow the role of the Irish Government to be more consultative than it had been, even though it was not consultative enough for them. So, the Agreement allows for a consultative role, but it does not actually say so in those terms. We made it clear all we could offer them was a consultative role. They said that was not really good enough, but they acquiesced in it. Of course, this sort of thing can be fatal, but it is also inevitable with an agreement of that kind that there are going to be things that the two sides interpret differently. I think the Irish accepted that it was consensually meant to be a consultative role, not an administrative role.

GS : How much persuasion did you have to apply to Margaret Thatcher in order to get her to agree to what you were doing?

DG: Well she left us to do it, but she was certainly not accommodating. She was very torn about the whole thing really, and her head and her heart were pulling her two different ways. There were days when she reacted against the whole thing and we thought it is no good, she is going to call everything off. But then there were days when it became apparent that she knew she needed an agreement.

GS: So you are dealing with ambiguity in some way and Mrs Thatcher does not like it. How then do you reach firm agreement?

DG: We did not say it was constructive ambiguity. There were various points in the negotiations when she came very close to breaking them off. But to my surprise, she kept it going. Every now and then she would get fed up with the way she thought the Irish were behaving, but she never quite broke it off. She needed an agreement that would improve security between the British and the Irish, and she wanted an agreement because of that.

GS: What does clear thinking mean in negotiations like this?

RA: It is a matter of thinking straight and a matter of ensuring that the words you use express with absolute clarity what you want them to express. Unless there are times when you have a deliberate ambiguity, as in the first clause of an agreement, where here it stated that there would be no change in the status of Northern Ireland without the majority of the people there deciding so. We originally had the words 'constitutional status', but the Irish representatives felt that the word 'constitutional' would get them into trouble in relation to their own constitution, so we dropped that word. I was under very clear instructions from the prime minister that there was to be nothing that even looked like surrender of sovereignty, or a sharing of sovereignty, and that the sovereignty of Westminster in Northern Ireland had to be maintained. Equally, on the other side, everybody wanted some kind of progress in the relationship between the two governments, Northern Ireland and the East–West and North–South connections. But not compromising on sovereignty was the core issue.

GS: Was Margaret Thatcher pleased with the final Agreement?

DG: No, I do not think so. But she defended it and she recognised that it was the best outcome from her point of view, even if she didn't like it. She endorsed and defended it. It was a very difficult thing for her because she was both a very publicly declared and emotional unionist herself, and when she had said earlier that Northern Ireland was as British as Finchley she meant it. All the time she was in touch with Enoch Powell, for whom she had respect, and with her parliamentary private secretary, Ian Gow, who was very anti-Agreement and very strongly unionist. He was very close to her personally and so she had all that to overcome, and when they had the meeting when the Agreement was signed Gow resigned because he disagreed so strongly with it. She also had people like Enoch Powell breathing down her neck, so she had a real struggle between her heart and her head over it.

GS: How did you decide the amount of text for the final document?

RA: Different bits of the Agreement would have been discussed and the text would have changed as we went along. I would not say that we had a document that was constantly being revised, but we did have bits of it that were constantly being revised and that others would have looked at. The Irish lawyers and their attorney general were bought in on their side and we bought in people from the

Home Office, along with lawyers. You cannot have a draft treaty without the lawyers being let loose on it.

GS: From what you are saying it appears that the process of negotiation was relatively smooth. Is that the case?

DG: That was not how it seemed at the time. It had its tremendous interruptions. The 'out, out, out' response, for example, was unpredictable and had unintended repercussions. But there were also breakthroughs where, for instance, we did not think that it would be possible to get the Irish to amend Articles 2 and 3 of their Constitution, but early on in the negotiations they seemed ready to contemplate it.

GS: Why was Mrs Thatcher so determined to avoid compromise? What was that stance about?

DG: It was her vehemence of it and that was her style. The Irish had had this internal review, the New Ireland Forum, which had come up with proposals that she had actually already told Garret were not acceptable. So there was a big internal problem for the Irish, and Haughey was accusing the Irish of selling out to the British and that was all part of the background to it. She was making the case in her usual style, creating the impression that everything the Irish wanted should be rejected out of hand. But that was not actually what she was saying, and that was certainly not what she intended. She was dismayed by the effect some of her reactions had on Garret and she was actually concerned about that and him.

GS: You mentioned that you suspected that the unionists would go berserk once they saw the document, but was there any assessment or consideration of the way nationalists, and particularly republicans, would react to the document?

DG: We knew that the unionists would be deeply opposed to it and we expected a hostile unionist reaction. We certainly worried about the nationalists and we wanted to have them on side, after all, one of the purposes was to help the nationalists, which, initially, I think it certainly did, and they were pleased with it. It was a proviso that if the nationalists and the unionists could agree on a shared system of government, a lot of the provisions for Irish involvement in the North would lapse. This was intended precisely as an inducement to the parties to look at collaborative government, which they have now got of course.

GS: Was the Agreement a success or failure because Sinn Féin did develop politically and the PIRA carried on its campaign until the early 1990s?

DG: I do not think you can talk in simple terms like that. I think the achievement of the Agreement was, first of all, an agreement between the British and Irish governments about the future shape of the administration of Northern Ireland.

Secondly, and very importantly, it involved Ireland in the administration of the North, admittedly consultatively, but it brought them into the business of governing Northern Ireland and that created a much closer relationship between Dublin and London. So they had to cooperate, instead of making speeches at one another over the Irish Sea and they actually had to work together. Out of that developed a remarkable degree of mutual confidence between the British and Irish governments, which would have been impossible without the Agreement.

GS: Did you discuss extensively with your colleagues about how to present the Agreement when it was concluded, and how you were going to sell it?

DG: We certainly negotiated the communiqué, because with a treaty text that the two governments signed there was quite a complicated negotiation about what the communiqué would say. There was a rehearsal on the day the Agreement was to be signed, when we were all at Hillsborough and the prime minister and the taoiseach were given a certain amount of coaching about how to deal with questions.

RA: A lot of care went into the immediate PR. The Agreement was signed ceremoniously at Hillsborough in November 1985, and great preparations were made for that in terms of working out what questions were likely to arise and how they should be answered. But it was not very long before FitzGerald left office and Haughey was back in, and then Mrs Thatcher was overtaken by things like the Westland and Spycatcher affairs. It was the first time the Irish Government had, in effect, said that they could not do this except with the agreement of the people in Northern Ireland, and that had not been said before. It was not in the Irish Constitution, so this was for them a very solemn moment and both sides had moved to get there. We had moved to get there because we were actually preparing to contemplate that at some stage a majority of people in Northern Ireland, who wanted a united Ireland or a reunion with the Irish Republic, could have that, but that that would not happen unless the majority wanted it.

GS: Was there any talk of a peace process at that point in 1985?

RA: Various arrangements were laid down in the Agreement for a process of consultation whereby the representatives of the Irish Government in Maryfield, Belfast, would be involved in a consultative arrangement with the people in Northern Ireland. But it was not a peace process, which emerged from later developments. It is also important to bear in mind that the British and the Irish both joined the European Community at the same time in 1973, and I think that had a bearing on it because we were both members of the EC and so they were not subordinate to us. They were separate and they were independent. Of course, the relationship between Britain and Ireland is very close geographically, historically and so on, but the independence of Ireland from Britain was certainly confirmed by the fact that Ireland became a member of the European Community at the same time as we did. There was a separate set of negotiations, and Ireland had even its own currency, the Punt, and your own currency is a distinct aspect of national identity. The Irish also had their own system of justice and, looking back on it, for the first time with Mrs Thatcher it was clear that there was no desire at all for Ireland to go back to being part of the United Kingdom. She totally accepted that the Irish Republic was separate, sovereign and independent, and that was never in question. In a sense, the most important achievement of the Agreement was that it removed distrust.

GS: What impact, if any, did events like the Brighton bomb in October 1984 have on the talks?

RA: It did not affect Margaret Thatcher's commitment to the talks at all, because she thought that it vindicated the political process. It demonstrated the inadequacy of republican violence to achieve anything too. There were certainly people who thought that with the continuing violence the British would eventually get fed up with it and give in, and Harold Wilson came somewhere near saying that in 1974, but was persuaded that to withdraw from Northern Ireland and to take the Army out of it would have precipitated a civil war leading to a great loss of life. So he was persuaded against doing that.

Conclusion

The AIA did contribute to an engagement on the political question of Northern Ireland, but not because of positive repercussions. The political talks and negotiations that emerged in 1990 and led to the peace process that followed were triggered more by unionists trying to 'negotiate away' the AIA and its perceived negative impact on the Union (as David Hill points out in the next chapter). In the eyes of many, the AIA reinforced a 'political paralysis' that could be dealt with realistically only if the unionists could be convinced that their best interest lay in trying to negotiate a better relationship with the Irish Republic, and that talks and democracy were needed to try to confront Sinn Féin and defeat violent republicanism. The argument that if unionists engaged in dialogue the British could help them edge towards something that might be more acceptable, namely a 'broadly-based Agreement', proved to be an important factor in shifting the political climate from what was highly divisive after the Agreement. Unionist animosity towards the Agreement and the perception that it amounted to a signing away of the Union (Bew and Gillespie 1999: 192) resulted in a key document being produced by a unionist task force of UUP and DUP representatives in 1987 called *An End to Drift*. The document was a response to over 200,000 people who marched as part of a 'No' to the Agreement protest at City Hall, Belfast, on 23 November 1985, and to the by-election results of January 1986 where some 418,230 electors endorsed a campaign of resistance to the Agreement (*ibid.*: 197). *An End to Drift* argued the need to address the dangers of 'an endless process of compromise and concession', and stressed that if there were no attempt to confront the Agreement sooner rather than later, then its influence 'will in all probability prove immovable'. Interestingly, and importantly, the document made the case for unionists to enter into negotiations in order to 'give hope to a community dangerously immune to disappointment and defeat'; reinforcing that negotiation 'need not be the precursor to "sell out" or "betrayal"'. On that basis, the task force invited support 'for an alternative to and replacement of the Anglo-Irish Agreement, and the commencement of "without prejudice" discussions with Her Majesty's Government thereto'. Although offering no detail, the document concluded: 'In advance of any negotiation we feel it must be made plain that failure to arrive at consensus would leave the unionist leadership no alternative but to seek an entirely new base for Northern Ireland *outside* the present constitutional context.'

It was this refusal to accept the AIA and the problems that a devolutionary process might create that influenced Northern Ireland secretary Peter Brooke's keynote speech to local business people in Bangor, Co. Down, on 9 January 1990, in which he recognised that the purpose of a devolutionary process by unionists was to make the AIA unworkable. Brooke also saw that more powers devolved to Stormont 'would be one very positive means of leeching power out of the Anglo-Irish Agreement and away from Dublin' (Bloomfield 1998: 23). Using the AIA as a basis to initiate talks was the main aim of Brooke's speech in which he stated: 'Any agreement between the constitutional political parties on new arrangements for exercising political power in Northern Ireland would have substantial implications for the Anglo-Irish Agreement, and both governments would... be bound to consider these implications seriously and sympathetically.' Brooke went on to state that the AIA would be used 'sensitively in the interests of bringing about talks' in recognition of the need to 'negotiate an alternative' (*ibid.*: 23–4). It was the search for this 'alternative' that created the dynamic towards the peace process that followed.

References

Arthur, P. (1993). 'The Anglo-Irish Agreement: a device for territorial management', in D. Keogh and M. H. Haltzel (eds), *Northern Ireland and the Politics of Reconciliation*. Cambridge University Press, pp. 208–25.
Aughey, A. (1989). *Under Siege*. Belfast: Blackstaff Press.
Bew, P. and Gillespie, G. (1999). *Northern Ireland: A Chronology of the Troubles 1968–1999*. Dublin: Gill & Macmillan.
Bloomfield, D. (1998). *Political Dialogue in Northern Ireland*. Basingstoke: Macmillan.

Bowman, J. (2013). 'FitzGerald approved overtures to Thatcher on joint sovereignty', *The Irish Times*, 28 December.

Ellis Owen, A. (1994). *The Anglo-Irish Agreement: The First Three Years*. University of Cardiff Press.

FitzGerald, G. (1993). 'The origins and rationale of the Anglo-Irish Agreement of 1985', in D. Keogh and M. H. Haltzel (eds), *Northern Ireland and the Politics of Reconciliation*. Cambridge University Press, pp. 189–202.

Goodall, D. and Lillis, M. (2010). 'Edging towards Peace', *Dublin Review of Books*, Issue 16, Winter.

Mallie, E. and McKittrick, D. (2001). *Endgame in Ireland*. London: Hodder & Stoughton.

Thatcher, M. (1993). *The Downing Street Years*. London: HarperCollins.

3   The constitutional issue in Irish politics

David Hill

As I write (January 2014), the talks between the parties on the Northern Ireland Executive, chaired by the former US diplomat Richard Haass, have petered out without reaching any conclusion. Among the issues on the agenda are the extent to which various parades should be subject to a code of conduct intended to reduce the risk that they might inflame intercommunal tension; and the circumstances in which the Union flag may be flown over the City Hall in Belfast. On both issues it seems that unionist negotiators have been unable to secure an outcome that would satisfy the loyalist community. Only last year there was extensive rioting in parts of Belfast in protest at the decision by Belfast City Council to limit the flying of the Union flag over City Hall to those ceremonial days on which it is typically flown on public buildings throughout the rest of the UK. Those protests may appear to be about something either arcane or purely symbolic, but in reality they reflect a deep underlying anxiety within the loyalist community about the security of their position as citizens of the UK.

That anxiety, in turn, is one element of a broader feeling among many loyalists that the unionist community 'lost out' all along the line in the negotiation of the Belfast Agreement (BA), that republicans conversely gained, and that the overall outcome must therefore have weakened the prospects for Northern Ireland remaining a part of the UK – which is, after all, the defining objective of the whole unionist community. For as long as this analysis remains unchallenged it will continue to be difficult to secure what might otherwise appear to be a sensible accommodation between the two parts of the community in Northern Ireland on difficult issues such as the management of parades and the display of flags and emblems. This brief analysis will examine the constitutional issue in Northern Ireland and Irish politics over the period since partition, and show how it was eventually resolved as part of the 'talks process'. In doing so, it will demonstrate that – in respect of this crucial element of the BA – it was actually the unionist view that largely prevailed and the republican position that had to shift furthest. We begin with an analysis of different perspectives on the constitutional issue and how they evolved over the period 1920–80.

The nationalist perspective

The constitutional issue in Northern Ireland and Irish politics had its origins in the circumstances in which Ireland was partitioned in the early years of the twentieth century. The traditional nationalist view was that Ireland should have been treated as a single political entity, reflecting its geographical unity and, to some extent, its constitutional history. On this basis, the views of a majority of the people of the whole island, as expressed in Sinn Féin's success in winning a majority of the seats in Ireland at the UK general election in December 1918 should have led to Home Rule/dominion status/independence for the whole of Ireland. Against this background, partition was viewed as a cynically divisive attempt by Britain (inspired by strategic and financial considerations) to retain control of Northern Ireland. The creation of an artificial unionist majority in Northern Ireland was seen to be the cause of unfairness and discrimination within Northern Ireland, and the grant of a veto against Irish unity to the Northern Ireland majority as an unfair obstacle to constructive political dialogue about Irish unity. The more extreme 'republican' perspective was that the authority of the First Dáil had passed by apostolic succession via the IRA Army Council to (ultimately) the Provisional IRA Army Council, which was therefore the legitimate government of the whole island and had a mandate (conferred by the last all-Ireland election of 1918) to wage war against the partitionist governments in both parts of Ireland.

Leaving that aside, partition cast a long shadow over the political life of both parts of Ireland in the years following 1920. Within Northern Ireland the development of 'normal' politics came to be inhibited by the constitutional issue, which impelled unionists in particular to subsume any policy differences they may have had with each other on social and economic issues within a broad policy of support for the Union. In the South, although the Irish Civil War triggered by the treaty negotiated in 1921 was almost wholly fought on other issues (primarily the role of the Crown and British Empire in what became the Irish Free State), partition led directly to the founding of the two main political parties in the Republic, who traditionally took different approaches to the issue: Fianna Fáil, led by de Valera, vigorously opposed partition; and Fine Gael took the mantle of the 'pro-treaty' forces in being willing to accept partition, while continuing to work for Irish unity by peaceful means and standing up for the interests of the minority community in Northern Ireland.

The result of the Irish Civil War was, of course, defeat for the IRA and victory for those who supported the terms of the treaty and accepted the creation of the Irish Free State. In 1925, the Free State Government formally accepted partition in a treaty signed with representatives of the United Kingdom and Northern Ireland governments. However, the policy adopted by Fianna Fáil when it returned to power was based on dismantling the settlement of the 1920s, and this led eventually to the drafting of the Irish Constitution of

1937, which asserted (Article 2: 'the constitutional claim') that 'the national territory consists of the whole island of Ireland, its islands and the territorial sea'. Article 3 limited the application of laws passed by Dáil Éireann to the territory of the former Irish Free State 'pending the reintegration of the national territory, and without prejudice to the right of the Parliament and Government established by this constitution to exercise jurisdiction over the whole territory'.

Set alongside this qualified assertion of Irish unity and the right of Dáil Éireann to govern the whole island, support grew throughout the Irish polity for the view, articulated by the Irish 'revisionist' school of history, that partition was not after all an evil imposed on Ireland by the British, but rather something that stemmed from pre-existing irreconcilable differences between those who lived on the island of Ireland, and probably represented the least awful alternative at the time. Certainly, by the early 1970s, as the Social Democratic and Labour Party (SDLP) demonstrated its readiness to participate in devolved government in Northern Ireland and both Fine Gael and the Irish Labour Party demonstrated their readiness to accept that the future constitutional status of Northern Ireland should depend on the views of those who lived there, this view became increasingly prevalent within Irish political discourse and the views reflected in Articles 2 and 3 of the Irish Constitution were dismissed as mere 'verbal republicanism'.

The British perspective

The UK Government of 1920 saw partition as a temporary arrangement. The Government of Ireland Act 1920 incorporated provision for the establishment of a Council of Ireland to facilitate cooperation between the northern and southern parliaments and as a focus for joint action in relevant areas, and to provide a framework for working towards Irish unity. However, the political and military reaction in Ireland prevented any of this coming into effect.

The 1925 Treaty gave the Northern parliament the right to opt out of the new Irish Free State, which right was duly exercised; and when the time came to acknowledge and accommodate Ireland's wish to be a sovereign independent state outside the Commonwealth, this philosophy of allowing the constitutional status of Northern Ireland to be determined by the Northern Ireland Parliament (a point on which successive unionist governments had sought formal assurances from the UK Government) was enshrined in the Ireland Act 1949. After the fall of Stormont in 1972 the principle was re-cast, following an amendment moved by Dr Paisley, in section 1 of the Northern Ireland Constitution Act 1973, which affirmed that Northern Ireland was a part of the United Kingdom and ('the constitutional guarantee') should not cease to be so 'without the consent of *the majority of the people* of Northern Ireland voting in a poll held for these purposes' (added emphasis).

In practice, successive elections and opinion polls showed a settled majority in Northern Ireland in favour of maintaining the Union. Parties supporting this viewpoint regularly secured a comfortable majority of the vote in elections. In the 1973 Border poll some 58 per cent of the total electorate (and an overwhelming majority of those who voted – the minority community largely abstained) voted to retain the Union and in opposition to Irish unity. The British Government was also conscious that many votes cast for the Alliance Party (AP) (which supported the Union) came from members of the minority community in Northern Ireland and that there was other evidence, such as opinion polls, demonstrating that a large proportion of the minority community was not actively in favour of immediate Irish unity. Certainly, throughout the author's twenty-six years in the Northern Ireland Office (NIO), from the mid-1970s onwards, the settled view was that on the basis of the constitutional guarantee Northern Ireland was likely to remain a part of the UK for the foreseeable future.

The unionist perspective

From 1920 onwards, the constitutional issue dominated the political thinking of the unionist community in Northern Ireland and its representatives. There was a wide range of factors that may help to explain this:

- *Security*: A central unionist concern – particularly during the various Troubles – was that the conditional nature of Northern Ireland's status as a part of the UK gave republican terrorists some grounds for believing that they could be successful in persuading the UK Government to drop the 'constitutional guarantee' and detach Northern Ireland from the rest of the UK in defiance of the wishes of the majority of the people who live there. The argument was made that if the guarantee were unambiguously supported and acknowledged by all concerned (or, better still, if it were replaced by a completely unconditional assurance that Northern Ireland would always remain a part of the UK) republican terrorists would be forced to accept that their objectives were unobtainable and would declare a ceasefire.

- *Fear of being dominated by an alien culture in a united Ireland*: Unionists pointed to the significant decline in the numbers of Protestants in the Republic since 1920 as evidence that Protestant values would be attacked and undermined in a unitary state where the majority had a fundamentally different ethos. This was not just a matter of the extent to which specifically Roman Catholic moral teaching was reflected in the laws, education and constitution of the Republic – after all, many Protestants in Northern Ireland held similarly conservative views on issues like divorce and abortion. It was more an anxiety that the traditional Protestant emphasis on the primacy of

personal conscience would be lost in constitutional and statutory provisions and, therefore, that in any area of personal and family life the interests of their community could be overborne.
- *Economics*: Throughout the twentieth century the economies of the two parts of Ireland were not interdependent or complementary, and cross-border trade remained a very low proportion of GDP in Northern Ireland and the Republic. There may be some scope to expand this, but certainly throughout the twentieth century there was no economic incentive for unionists to consider Irish unity favourably (and taoiseach Jack Lynch's ambition to 'turn the Orangemen green with envy' did not gain much traction). Indeed, the size of the subvention that Northern Ireland receives from the UK Exchequer remains a significant economic disincentive to Irish unity, since the Irish state is unlikely to be able to match this in the foreseeable future.
- *A strong positive commitment to the UK*: There are strong family, social and cultural (including sporting links) between Northern Ireland and the rest of the UK. Northern Ireland shares significant historical experiences (especially the First and Second World Wars) with the rest of the UK, and common economic concerns. A sense that Northern Ireland has for centuries been a part of the wider polity that is now the UK; common educational experiences and social values; and exposure to national media over many decades also strengthened unionists' perception of themselves as British. At a rhetorical level, many unionist politicians express passionate support for the liberal pluralist ethos of the UK and for the institutions of the British state, notably the Queen. There are also frequent commemorations of episodes in the Glorious Revolution of 1688/9 and of events, such as the battle of the Somme, that underline the contribution that Northern Ireland has made to the UK, though some seem strident and driven by defensive motives.

However, whatever the strength of *their* commitment to the Union, unionists as a community have always felt uniquely vulnerable. They are a minority within Ireland and a tiny minority within what has often been an unsympathetic UK, and with very little support worldwide. Their nightmare, certainly during the height of the Troubles, was that the British Government, supported by world (and mainland British) opinion, egged on by the Irish Government and the nationalist community in Northern Ireland and driven by a desire to avoid republican terrorist attacks, especially on mainland UK targets, would seek to coerce them into a united Ireland without their freely given consent. They remained very conscious of how close the Union had come to being broken in the early part of the twentieth century and continued to feel that the constitutional status of the province was under direct and immediate threat. Throughout the twentieth century this coloured their attitude to a whole range of political issues. For example:

- The difference of view among unionists over 'devolution' versus 'integration' arose mainly from a difference of view over which form of government would most effectively protect the constitutional status of Northern Ireland. The purist approach (expressed most clearly by Enoch Powell, but reminiscent also of Carson's resistance to Home Rule) was that a policy of integration with the rest of the UK would underline and reinforce Northern Ireland's constitutional status, whereas pro-devolutionists argued that only by getting their hands on the levers of power could unionists ensure that they were in a position to head off unwelcome constitutional developments. In this context, the constitutional debate in Scotland from the 1970s onwards, and the eventual devolution of powers to Scotland and Wales after 1997, made it easier for unionists in Northern Ireland to support devolution, because Northern Ireland was not thereby being singled out for special treatment.
- Proposals for 'sharing power' with representatives of the minority community in Northern Ireland were often interpreted as opening the door to Irish unity, either by conceding an indirect role for the Dublin Government or by enabling nationalists to prepare the ground for Irish unity and generally weakening unionists' grip on their own destiny.
- Cooperation between the two parts of Ireland or joint activity, especially if this were to involve institutional arrangements, was opposed for the same reason, although this opposition was much reduced if genuine economic advantages could be demonstrated.

One major source of unionist insecurity was that no Irish Government since 1937 had been able unequivocally to accept that Northern Ireland was a part of the UK or to endorse the principle that a majority *in Northern Ireland* should be able to determine its constitutional future. A case had been taken against the Irish Government in the Irish Supreme Court for accepting and solemnly declaring, in the 1973 Sunningdale Agreement (SA), 'that there could be no change in the status of Northern Ireland until a majority of the people of Northern Ireland desired a change in that status'. This was alleged to be incompatible with Articles 2 and 3 of the Irish Constitution. The case was dismissed, but only on a technicality. And whatever more moderate views might be held by the SDLP, Fine Gael and the Irish Labour Party, Fianna Fáil, especially under Charles Haughey (leader 1979–92 and taoiseach in 1979–81, 1982 and 1987–92), consistently refused to accept in principle that Northern Ireland was an appropriate unit for self-determination. Mr Haughey frequently described Northern Ireland as 'a failed political entity'.

The 1980s: shifts and changes

Unionists were therefore naturally anxious when, during his first spell as taoiseach, Mr Haughey began a round of 'teapot diplomacy' with Mrs Thatcher.

Ultimately their meetings did not appear to lead to anything. However, the communiqué issued after the Dublin Summit of December 1980 did initiate a small, but ultimately significant, evolution in the formal position of both governments in respect of the constitutional issue. The main focus of attention after the Summit was the commitment by the two governments to initiate a series of joint studies into 'the totality of relationships' between the UK and the Republic, a development that the unionists treated with great suspicion.

More significantly, for the purposes of this chapter, the communiqué also incorporated a joint acknowledgement that Irish unity 'would only come about with the consent of a majority of the people of Northern Ireland', and a joint commitment that if in the future a majority of the people of Northern Ireland were formally to consent to the establishment of a united Ireland both governments 'would introduce and support legislation in their respective Parliaments to give effect to that wish'.

At the time, this was challenged on both sides of the Irish Sea. The NIO (not at that stage as directly engaged with handling relationships with the Republic of Ireland as it would later become) remonstrated with the Foreign and Commonwealth Office (FCO) for moving beyond the simplicity of the constitutional guarantee, and beyond the line taken in the SA (see above). Asserting that the consent of a majority of the people of Northern Ireland should be a minimum condition for Irish unity was one thing. Accepting that such a majority would be a necessary *and sufficient* basis for introducing legislation to give effect to Irish unity was a significant change of policy that had not been debated and agreed. It also put the British Government in the illogical position of requiring that any new political institutions within Northern Ireland should have broad support across both main parts of the community, whilst appearing to accept that Northern Ireland's status as a part of the UK (a matter of even greater significance) could be settled on the basis of a simple majority vote.

The proposition was one that could not realistically be delivered in practice and would be likely to create major tensions as any 'tipping point' approached. I remember talking to one of the founding members of the SDLP in the mid-1980s about whether he thought a natural majority in favour of Irish unity would ever emerge in Northern Ireland. He described this as 'the Rabbit Theory of Irish unity', and commented that while he would continue to take pleasure in seeking to bring it about he did not want to be around at the point when it happened. Quite apart from the risk that paramilitary organisations would seek to accelerate or delay the achievement of a simple (potentially tiny) majority in favour of Irish unity, his point was that it was difficult to conceive of a practical basis on which the British Government could enforce, or the Irish Government could agree to, the achievement of a united Ireland in the teeth of opposition from a million unionists. If Irish unity were ever to come about, it would need to have the broad support of both main political traditions in Ireland. These reservations were expressed, but not pursued particularly vigorously. No one in the NIO anticipated that a position taken in a communiqué after a relatively low-key prime ministerial meeting would assume such significance in the future.

Meanwhile, in the Dáil, Mr Haughey was challenged by Neil Blaney TD on the grounds that his acceptance that Irish unity would come about only with the consent of a majority of the people of Northern Ireland was inconsistent with Articles 2 and 3 of the Irish Constitution. Mr Haughey's reply was somehow typical of his style; he argued that the use of the word 'would' meant that the phrase was an acceptance of political reality, not a concession of principle. This had all the hallmarks of a Haughey 'stroke'; it suggested that through a devious use of words he had secured a real concession from the British Government without conceding anything of substance in return. However, in the short term attention moved elsewhere. The positive tone of the Thatcher/Haughey summits of 1980 rapidly dissipated during 1981 in the welter of the hunger strikes, and the programme of joint studies made little progress. Mr Haughey briefly lost power in 1981 and, following the extraordinary events of his second premiership (in 1982), a Fine Gael/Irish Labour Party Coalition Government took office, led by Dr Garret FitzGerald. He embarked on a range of initiatives to address unionist concerns in the hope of bringing about a rapprochement between the two main political traditions in Ireland and opening the door to 'normal' politics within Northern Ireland. His 'constitutional crusade' to remove various theocratic provisions from the Irish Constitution and legal framework was seen to backfire when the outcome of the necessary referendums was effectively to entrench the original provisions.

The New Ireland Forum, set up by Dr FitzGerald with the active support of the SDLP Leader, John Hume, fared little better. It was billed as an opportunity to create a positive consensus across the spectrum of constitutional nationalism in support of a vision for a 'New' and inclusive Ireland that might appeal to unionists. Evidence from unionist spokespersons was welcomed, and observers were promised a constructive outcome in the form of a set of 'principles' that could provide the basis for a dialogue with unionism. In the event, constrained by its desire to produce consensus among the main constitutional nationalist parties in Ireland, the New Ireland Forum conspicuously failed to address the central constitutional issue, and eventually produced an ambiguous reference to the need for 'the political arrangements for a new and sovereign Ireland . . . to be freely negotiated and agreed by the people of the North and by the people of the South'. The failure of the New Ireland Forum to achieve a platform for constructive dialogue with unionism was underlined immediately after its publication when Mr Haughey told the post-Forum press conference that Fianna Fáil would only support one of the three 'illustrative models' for a

New Ireland, that is, Irish unity. Mrs Thatcher was equally clear in saying that all three models were 'out'.

The Anglo-Irish Agreement and its impact

In an effort to move on from this apparent nadir in Anglo-Irish relations, the two prime ministers set up small teams (on the British side, mainly involving the Cabinet Office and the FCO) to negotiate what became the Anglo-Irish Agreement (AIA) of November 1985. I, and many others in the NIO, read it with a sense of shock and anger. Section 1 of the Agreement, dealing with the constitutional issues, repeated the casuistic language of the 1982 Thatcher/Haughey summit communiqué in affirming that Irish unity 'would' come about only with the consent of a majority of the people of Northern Ireland, and reaffirmed and formalised the joint commitment to legislate to bring Irish unity about if ever a majority in Northern Ireland did formally consent to that. The use of a formula that had been invented, and defended, by Mr Haughey did at least mean that this part of the Agreement was proof against criticism from that quarter. Apart from reiterating that constitutional formula, the Agreement appeared to be based on a bogus 'parallelism': that the Irish Government should have a formal role (and a visible presence in Northern Ireland) in representing the interests of the minority community in Northern Ireland, to 'balance' a perceived role for the British Government in protecting the interests of the unionist community. If that was the logic, it was fatally flawed because the British Government had a duty to serve the interests of all parts of the community in Northern Ireland. There were principled resignations on both sides of the Irish Sea in protest at the terms of the Agreement. Viscount Cranbourne resigned from the British Government and senator Mary Robinson, a constitutional lawyer and subsequently the first female president of the Irish Republic, resigned from the Irish Labour Party.

Ultimately the AIA had a significant positive impact on the political situation in Northern Ireland – but not in the way that its authors appear to have expected. For many in the NIO, the AIA illustrated several weaknesses in the two governments' respective approaches. Above all, it illustrated the danger of leaving negotiations in the hands of the well-meaning but ill-informed. The British negotiators, for example, clearly believed that Article 1 of the AIA represented a breakthrough in securing formal Irish commitment to the principle that any change in the constitutional status of Northern Ireland would require the consent of a majority of the people who lived there. However, they completely failed to appreciate that the wording used was identical to a formula that had been justified to the Dáil by taoiseach Charles Haughey a few years previously, is no more than a recognition of political reality and therefore not inconsistent with the 'constitutional claim' in Articles 2 and 3 of the Irish Constitution.

There were similar failings of understanding by the Irish officials, who put significant weight on a part of the Agreement that committed the two governments to discuss the introduction of three-judge courts in Northern Ireland in place of the 'Diplock' courts used to try scheduled (i.e., terrorist-type) offences there. It was easy to demonstrate that this would have *reduced* the rights of those charged with scheduled offences (e.g., by removing their ability to appeal on grounds of fact – by reference to the written judgment handed down by the single judge in a Diplock court), but it took quite a while for that message to be received at a political level.

Another issue was the failure of both sets of negotiators to understand and appreciate the unionist position. On the British side, the negotiations were conducted without engaging unionist politicians, or even those in the NIO who could have told them the likely unionist reaction. The Irish Department of Foreign Affairs (DFA) had 'travellers' whose role it was to visit Northern Ireland and engage with different groups, including a range of unionists; but those they met were not fully representative of the whole spectrum of unionist/loyalist opinion. Certainly, the scale and vigour of the unionist reaction to the creation of a 'consultative' role for the Irish Government in relation to Northern Ireland seemed to come as a surprise to both sets of negotiators.

The British negotiators were also clearly hampered by the narrowness of the scope within which they were allowed to negotiate. Reflecting the prime minister's wishes, their primary focus seems to have been on improving cross-border security cooperation, including securing a commitment from the Irish Government to facilitate and speed up the extradition of suspected terrorists. Whilst the Irish secured a role for themselves in relation to Northern Ireland that they believed would strengthen constitutional nationalism, there was no apparent recognition on the British side of the wider need to improve relationships between unionism and nationalism more generally.

Finally, there was the implicit assumption that in negotiating the Agreement and operating the Intergovernmental Conference the two governments would be acting on behalf of their respective 'clients' in Northern Ireland. That may have been true of the Irish Government, but could not be true for the British Government, which had a duty towards *all* the citizens of Northern Ireland and could not properly act on behalf of only part of the community. This left an asymmetry in the operation of the Agreement, which unionists sensed and which left them feeling even more exposed and aggrieved.

Either way, the unionist reaction to the Agreement was pretty extreme. There was a monster demonstration – probably attended by over 400,000 people – highlighting the extent of unionist antipathy to the Agreement, the 'Ulster Says No' campaign, the withdrawal from any contact with British ministers and the resignations of the unionist MPs in order to trigger a set of by-elections as a quasi-referendum on the Agreement – although it backfired somewhat because it resulted in a victory for Seamus Mallon of the SDLP in the constituency of Newry and Mourne. There were also initiatives that came closer to the category of political violence: the army of men waving gun licences; Peter Robinson's 'invasion' of Clontibret; the attempt on the 'day of action' (3 March 1986) to bring Northern Ireland to a standstill. Gradually, however, the realisation dawned in the unionist community that the Royal Ulster Constabulary (despite the pressures placed on many of its officers) was standing firm in defence of the Agreement and that their efforts to 'smash' the Agreement were not going to be successful. For a community with a long tradition of functional political violence – going back to 1912 and demonstrated more recently by the Ulster Workers' Council strike of 1974 – this was a salutary lesson. Ultimately, in 1987, the Joint Unionist Task Force published an analysis called *An End to Drift*, effectively making the case that as the unionist community had not been successful in forcing the abrogation of the Agreement, it would be necessary to enter a process of dialogue and negotiation to achieve that objective. The Agreement had at least led the unionist community to realise that simply saying 'no' was an inadequate strategy. To that extent, it may perhaps have been a necessary step on the road to a political settlement.

In the short term, however, there was no very obvious opportunity to move things forward. While Dr FitzGerald's Fine Gael/Labour Coalition Government might have wanted to encourage devolution within Northern Ireland, that was not an objective of Charles Haughey's Fianna Fáil/Progressive Democrat Government after it took power in 1987. Meanwhile, in Northern Ireland, the unionist boycott of British ministers was still in force and any prospect of dialogue between unionists and the SDLP had been dealt a blow by the SDLP's decision to engage in talks with Sinn Féin.

Regrouping and repositioning

By 1989, however, the NIO had concluded that the time was right to launch a further attempt to secure a political settlement in Northern Ireland. The department was in a strong position to do that because, by 1989, key roles in both London and Belfast were filled by people who were either Northern Ireland born and bred or who had extensive experience of working in the NIO. Many had in fact joined the NIO in the mid- to late 1970s and were now reaching senior positions, previously often held by people on relatively short-term secondments from other government departments. This cadre knew and trusted each other and had a good range of shared experience, including – very importantly – experience on the 'security' side of the office, dealing with security policy, security operations, policing, prisons and other functions that had given them a real understanding of the terrorist organisations and of the understandable visceral reactions that terrorism can give rise to.

By 1989, and in the years following, the key posts in the NIO responsible for advising or reporting on 'political' issues were held by members of this group, including myself, Peter Bell, Brian Blackwell, John McConnell, Chris Maccabe, Ken Lindsay, Jonathan Stephens and David Brooker. At the top of the office, Ian Burns, Joe Pilling and John Chilcot all had extensive prior experience of Northern Ireland. We also had excellent working relationships with senior colleagues in the Northern Ireland Civil Service, particularly Ken Bloomfield (albeit towards the end of his career at that point) and then his successor David Fell, and David Watkins. Other key players, while initially 'new' to Northern Ireland affairs, were exceptionally able, quickly grasped the essence of the issues and made major contributions: these included Quentin Thomas, David Cooke and HM Ambassador in Dublin, Sir Nicholas Fenn. Certainly, from 1989 onwards, the NIO had a very powerful and capable team of officers in key roles, and that was a major factor in its ability to initiate and steer the Northern Ireland talks process to a successful conclusion. In doing so, we sought to learn lessons not only from the weaknesses of the Agreement, but from the whole series of failed political initiatives over the period since 1974.

An early move was to secure the NIO's position as the acknowledged lead department in Whitehall in respect of the search for a political settlement in Northern Ireland. Mrs Thatcher and the cabinet secretary were persuaded to agree to the establishment of a Cabinet Official Committee on Northern Ireland (to coordinate advice to relevant ministers), and, unusually, that this should be chaired by the NIO political director, rather than anyone from the Cabinet Office. The NIO also provided the Secretariat. This turned out to be the dying days of traditional Cabinet government, but the Committee held several meetings and we gradually secured the acquiescence of the other members (senior officials from the Cabinet Office, FCO, Ministry of Defence and Home Office) in the NIO leadership of the whole agenda. One of the mistakes of the process of negotiating the Agreement would not be repeated.

More generally, the broad analysis on which we proceeded was that:
- the political tensions between the two main parts of the community in Northern Ireland and between the two main political traditions in Ireland had found expression in terrorism, intercommunal violence, and mutual fear and distrust;
- the failure thus far of constitutional politics to resolve those tensions had given greater credibility to extremists and gunmen on both sides of the community;
- ultimately, the best way to resolve the intercommunal tensions in Northern Ireland would be to secure a functioning political accommodation between the two main parts of the community, expressed in devolved institutions that had broad support across the whole community;
- that, in turn, would require a resolution of the tensions between the two main political traditions in Ireland, such that they could work constructively together for their mutual benefit;

- the achievement of these objectives would require significant compromise – on all sides – and no politicians could be expected to 'sell' such an outcome to their communities, or operate the resulting institutions, unless they had been directly involved in striking those compromises;
- direct contact between the Northern Ireland parties and between the unionist parties and the Irish Government was in any event highly desirable in order to raise levels of mutual understanding and to begin to develop the mutual trust that would be required to achieve a successful overall outcome;
- the way forward, therefore, was to put in place a *process* of dialogue involving all the relevant political actors, rather than seeking to set out options in a White Paper or negotiate something between the two governments.

A further insight was that any talks process would need to have a broad agenda and involve the Irish Government as well as the Northern Ireland political parties. Not everyone should, or would, need to be involved in every aspect of the talks – hence, the 'three strands' with their different cast lists – but there was no realistic prospect of dealing with one set of issues in isolation. The breadth of the agenda (which, of course, grew further as the talks progressed) also increased the chance of finding negotiating gains in one area to offset 'losses' in another, so we hoped it would increase the prospects of success in the long run. And everyone was protected by the (actually inevitable) 'rule' that nothing could be agreed until everything was agreed.

It may be worth emphasising at this point that in launching the talks process there was no expectation that it would engage Sinn Féin (or the loyalist political parties) or lead directly to the ceasefires and a comprehensive 'peace settlement'. The objective, rather, was to counter alienation and disenchantment with constitutional politics – on both sides of the community in Northern Ireland – by providing a vehicle for the constitutional political parties and the two governments to explore the scope for a fair and equitable political settlement. It was anticipated that any measure of success would re-kindle confidence in constitutional politics, secure a local political input to decisions about tackling Northern Ireland's distinctive needs, give both parts of the community more of a 'stake' in society, and reduce the level of latent support (again on both sides of the community) for unconstitutional activity. It was hoped that a widely acceptable political settlement would create a context in which it would become easier to take tough direct action against republican and loyalist terrorist organisations in Northern Ireland, and that a political settlement endorsed and supported by the Irish Government would also lead to enhanced cross-border security cooperation. It was therefore with these relatively modest aspirations in mind that NIO officials advised the newly appointed secretary of state for Northern Ireland Peter Brooke in September 1989 that the time was right to administer a 'nudge' to the political process in Northern Ireland.

An initial hurdle to overcome was Mrs Thatcher's strong reluctance to allow the Irish Government any role in relation to the political situation in Northern

Ireland; her priority in Anglo-Irish affairs was to enhance security cooperation, and she did not wish to upset the unionists again as she had with the Agreement. However, the unionist 'preconditions' for engaging in any talks process included a requirement that the operation of the Agreement should be 'suspended' – something that could not be achieved by the British Government acting alone – and that provided a sufficient rationale to persuade Mrs Thatcher to sanction opening discussions with the Irish Government. So the Agreement had one final value in helping to create the circumstances in which a broader and more inclusive dialogue could begin.

The Agreement was a traumatic shock for unionists because they interpreted it as evidence that the Conservative Government had joined 'the enemies of Ulster' in working towards the achievement of Irish unity. Subsequent reiteration of the constitutional guarantee hardly reassured them, and the operation of the Anglo-Irish Secretariat in Belfast and the regular meetings between the secretary of state for Northern Ireland and the Irish foreign minister under the aegis of the Anglo-Irish Conference brought into being by the Agreement was a constant affront. We will, of course, never know what use Dr FitzGerald and his coalition partners would have made of the Irish Government's role under the Agreement, because by the time the Agreement had bedded in they had lost power to Mr Haughey's third administration. It is possible that Fine Gael and the Irish Labour Party would at least have sought to use the Agreement to promote improved political dialogue within Northern Ireland. But the Fianna Fáil Government used it to actively criticise and challenge security arrangements and the legal system in Northern Ireland, in ways that were bound to irritate and alarm the whole unionist community. Ultimately, however, the failure of unionist efforts to break the Agreement forced a number of leaders to the conclusion that unionists would need to 'negotiate' the AIA away, making them receptive to the announcement in January 1990 by secretary of state Peter Brooke of his intention to initiate a talks process that could lead to a broad political settlement.

Meanwhile, with political dialogue among the constitutional political parties in the deep freeze, the SDLP had opened a dialogue with Sinn Féin. Several meetings were held during 1988, and one very significant theme related to the constitutional issue and the basis on which the future constitutional status of Northern Ireland should be determined. In essence, the SDLP leadership argued that if Sinn Féin were correct in believing that it should be for the people of Ireland as a whole to decide their constitutional future, then the people of Ireland as a whole also had the right to determine *how* that decision should be made. The outcome of the discussions was not made public at the time, but it ultimately led to the conclusion that any resolution of the constitutional issue would need to be validated by referendums held simultaneously in both parts of Ireland in order to create a philosophical basis for the republican movement to accept something short of its purist position.

The Northern Ireland talks process: the early stages, 1990–2

By late 1989, in the absence of any of the promised security benefits arising from the AIA and in the face of continued unionist intransigence, Mrs Thatcher was happy to authorise Peter Brooke to initiate a talks process that would address the whole range of relationships affecting the political stalemate in Northern Ireland. That is:

- relationships within Northern Ireland and the need for widely acceptable political institutions there;
- relationships between the two parts of Ireland and the need for institutions that would enable the constructive pursuit of common interests and acknowledge the Irish identity of the minority community in Northern Ireland; and
- the relationship between the two governments and the need to consider 'a new and more broadly based' Agreement between the two governments, and address the Irish 'constitutional claim'.

The third set of issues was very significant for unionists and helped to persuade them to explore the possibility of political dialogue. Developments during 1990 reinforced both the significance of 'the Irish Constitutional claim' and the unionists' hope of securing the repeal of Articles 2 and 3 of the Irish Constitution.

In a mischievous attempt to subvert the Agreement, two unionists, the brothers McGimpsey, had introduced a case against the Irish Government in the Irish Supreme Court arguing that the Agreement was incompatible with Articles 2 and 3 of the Irish Constitution. The case was rejected in early 1990 on the basis of some highly ingenious arguments, but most attention focused on the court's view that Articles 2 and 3 laid a 'constitutional imperative' on the Irish Government to seek to bring about 'the reintegration of the national territory' (by peaceful means). This finding reinforced unionist concerns about the Agreement as a vehicle for achieving Irish unity, and the coincidence of an Irish Supreme Court refusal to extradite some suspected terrorists to Northern Ireland enabled unionists to allege that this 'constitutional imperative' encouraged republican terrorism and inhibited the Irish courts in dealing with terrorists.

What was particularly interesting, however, was the public and political reaction within the Republic. There was substantial editorial and public support for a unilateral revision of Articles 2 and 3 to reflect an aspiration to ultimate Irish unity on the basis of the consent of the people of Northern Ireland. Senator Mary Robinson proposed wording to this effect. In a Dáil debate in December 1990 on a Workers' Party Bill to amend Articles 2 and 3 there was strong support for the amendment in principle from all parties except Fianna Fáil. The vote was lost, however, (even though all the parties combined could have outvoted Fianna Fáil) because Fianna Fáil's coalition partners, the Progressive Democrats, supported it in opposing the Bill on the grounds that they did not favour 'divisive and counter-productive' single issue referenda on the Constitution. Nevertheless, during the debate, Mr Haughey went further than he had ever done before in referring to the AIA in terms that were a public affirmation of the Irish Government's commitment to Article 1 and the need for the consent of a majority of the people of Northern Ireland to any change in its status. He also repeated that Articles 2 and 3 would be on the table in any political talks on the lines then being proposed. Those developments were an important factor in unionist attitudes to the talks process. They sensed that it provided an opportunity to secure an amendment of Articles 2 and 3, and therefore a clear acknowledgement of Northern Ireland's present status and an endorsement of the constitutional guarantee, but realists among them accepted that the Irish Government was only likely to be able to secure support for the necessary constitutional amendment in the context of a comprehensive political accommodation.

However, while the 'talks about talks' – involving the two governments and the four main constitutional political parties in Northern Ireland – dragged on into 1991, another series of indirect and unacknowledged exchanges involving the republican movement, the two governments and various intermediaries was also beginning to have an impact. The British Government was consistently clear that there could be no formal dialogue with Sinn Féin on political and constitutional issues unless and until the Provisional IRA (PIRA) had declared a ceasefire and demonstrated a commitment to exclusively peaceful methods; but it was equally ready to clarify its position on key issues if that would help the republican movement to reach the momentous decision to turn away from violence. That was the context for an important speech made by Peter Brooke in November 1990 on the nature of the British presence in Northern Ireland. In a wide-ranging and carefully argued speech (given to the Annual Dinner of the Association of Canned Food Importers and Distributors!) he explained that 'the British presence' was more than just the presence of British troops on the streets of Northern Ireland or UK ministers at Stormont, and that it rested on the fact that a substantial majority of the population of Northern Ireland wished to remain within the UK. He emphasised that the British Government itself had 'no selfish strategic or economic interest' in Northern Ireland remaining within the UK, and was content to abide by the wishes of the people of Northern Ireland regarding their constitutional future. He had previously made clear his personal hope that the Union between Great Britain and Northern Ireland would continue, and had drawn attention to the political reality that – on the basis of the constitutional guarantee – Northern Ireland was likely to remain a part of the UK for the foreseeable future. But, by emphasising the principle of self-determination and denying any strategic or economic imperative on the British Government to maintain the Union, he provided an important line of argument for those within the republican movement who were seeking to create the circumstances in which it might switch from terrorism to exclusively democratic methods.

The interparty talks (between the British Government and the four main constitutional political parties in Northern Ireland) finally got under way in April 1991 and ran until early July. A further round of talks commenced on 27 April 1992 (immediately after the UK general election) and ran until November, with important sessions taking place in London (at the point where the Irish Government joined the process on the launch of 'Strand 2' of the negotiations) and subsequently in Dublin. By that point the Irish Government had accepted that, in the context of a comprehensive political settlement, it 'could' propose the withdrawal of the constitutional claim in Articles 2 and 3 of the Irish Constitution. Pressed by the Ulster Unionist delegates (the DUP had ultimately found it impossible to attend the session in Dublin), Irish foreign minister David Andrews – in what was widely billed as a deliberate slip of the tongue – confirmed that in the right circumstances the Irish Government 'would' propose the amendment of Articles 2 and 3 of the Irish Constitution, before hastily 'correcting' his position back to 'could'.

Many other issues had, of course, been discussed during the 1992 talks, and when they ended there was a general sense that an overall accommodation – including the amendment of Articles 2 and 3 of the Irish Constitution – was on the cards.

The Downing Street Declaration

All this clearly added to the pressure on the republican movement to find a way in from the cold before a settlement was reached over their heads. It was clear that the republican movement had been following the talks process closely, since there were no republican terrorist attacks during the two months of the 1991 talks or the seven months of the 1992 talks (although the level of fatalities from terrorist attacks in the rest of the year more than made up for that). It also became clear that the new taoiseach Albert Reynolds and the SDLP did not wish to resume the talks process without every effort being made to engage Sinn Féin. Attention, therefore, turned to the creation of a context in which the republican movement could be persuaded to implement and observe a ceasefire as a first step towards their involvement in future rounds of talks. In that endeavour, the British Government's formal position on the constitutional issue as set out in Article 1 of the AIA, whatever its illogicalities and inconsistencies, became a crucial factor. The republican movement sought a reaffirmation that the two governments would legislate to bring about Irish unity as soon as there was a simple majority in favour of Irish unity within Northern Ireland, and a formal reiteration of the key elements of Peter Brooke's 'British presence' speech.

The two governments spent a year negotiating a text that would provide a framework for a resumption of the talks process on a basis that would enable Sinn Féin participation, whilst not losing the unionists. Among other things, this required them to reiterate the position reflected in Article 1 of the AIA while balancing that with a formal commitment by both governments to the principle of 'the constitutional guarantee', and a commitment from the Irish Government that it would (in the context of a comprehensive political settlement) propose the amendment of Articles 2 and 3 of the Irish Constitution. This text became the Downing Street Declaration (DSD) of 15 December 1993, which was – on several levels – a critical document in the Northern Ireland talks process. On the constitutional issue, the key breakthrough (dimly foreshadowed in the conclusions of the New Ireland Forum) was the elaboration of a doctrine that cleverly brought together 'the right of national self-determination' of the people of Ireland and the 'constitutional guarantee' that the achievement of Irish unity would require the consent of a majority of the people of Northern Ireland. For its part the British Government agreed 'that it is for the people of the island of Ireland alone, by agreement between the two parts respectively, to exercise their right to self-determination on the basis of consent, freely and concurrently given, North and South, to bring about a united Ireland, if that is their wish', and 'reaffirm[ed] as a binding obligation that they will, for their part, introduce the necessary legislation to give effect to this'.

The Irish Government, in a complementary paragraph of the Declaration, accepted that 'it would be wrong to attempt to impose a united Ireland in the absence of the freely given consent of the majority of the people of Northern Ireland ... [and] ... that the democratic right of self-determination by the people of Ireland as a whole must be achieved and exercised with and subject to the agreement and consent of a majority of the people of Northern Ireland'. The commitment to legislate to bring about Irish unity on the basis of majority consent in both parts of Ireland was helpfully set within a broader acknowledgement by the taoiseach 'that stability and well-being will not be found under any political system which is refused allegiance or rejected on grounds of identity by a significant majority of those governed by it', and a reference to his 'hope that over time a meeting of hearts and minds will develop, which will bring the people of Ireland together'.

There is much else within the DSD that acknowledged the fears and aspirations of both main traditions in Ireland. The taoiseach, for example, said he would

> examine with his colleagues any elements in the democratic life and organisation of the Irish State that can be represented to the Irish Government in the course of political dialogue as a real and substantial threat to [the unionist community's] way of life and ethos, or that can be represented as not being fully compliant with a modern democratic and pluralist society, and undertakes to examine any possible ways of removing such obstacles.

Importantly, he also 'acknowledge[d] the presence in the Constitution of the Republic of elements which are deeply resented by Northern unionists, but which at the same time reflect hopes and ideals which lie deep in the hearts of many Irish men and women North and South', and went on to say that 'the time has come to consider together how best the hopes and identities of all can be expressed in more balanced ways, which no longer engender division and the lack of trust to which he ha[d] referred'. He then formally confirmed that, 'in the event of an overall settlement, the Irish Government will, as part of a balanced constitutional accommodation, put forward and support proposals for change in the Irish Constitution which would fully reflect the principle of consent in Northern Ireland'.

The vehicle for achieving such an overall settlement was identified as being 'a process of political dialogue', 'building on the progress already made in the talks process'. The DSD reiterated the two governments' view that 'the achievement of peace must involve a permanent end to the use of, or support for, paramilitary violence', and confirmed that 'in these circumstances, democratically mandated parties which establish a commitment to exclusively peaceful methods and which have shown that they abide by the democratic process, are free to participate fully in democratic politics and to join in dialogue in due course between the two governments and the political parties on the way ahead'. Ultimately, the PIRA Army Council declared a ceasefire in August 1994 (and the loyalist paramilitary groups some months later), and formal dialogue with British Government officials commenced with a view to establishing their commitment to exclusively peaceful methods.

Unionists were naturally opposed to Sinn Féin participation in the talks process and sought to apply a range of 'preconditions' to any such participation, including a requirement for the prior decommissioning of PIRA weaponry – a position initially supported by the British Government. The unionists also argued that they had no electoral mandate to participate in negotiations alongside Sinn Féin, and that it was also important to demonstrate that Sinn Féin's participation in any talks and its weight in those talks were related solely to its electoral mandate. For these reasons they wanted participation in any further round of talks to be based on an election, something that was initially rejected by the Irish Government. This combination of constraints led to a prolonged logjam in the talks process, which was ultimately broken – oddly enough – by the breakdown of the PIRA ceasefire. In the turmoil that followed the Docklands bombing of 9 February 1996, the Irish Government accepted that there should be 'elections to the negotiations', and the British Government moved away from its previous position on decommissioning to requiring the reinstatement of the PIRA ceasefire and a demonstrable commitment to exclusively peaceful methods as the price for Sinn Féin participation in any future talks.

The multiparty negotiations, 1996–8

The stage was therefore set for the multiparty negotiations, which ran from the 'entry to negotiations' elections of 1996 through to Good Friday 1998.

The electoral system designed for those elections achieved its objectives in creating an electoral mandate for ten political parties in Northern Ireland to participate in the talks – including the two small loyalist parties the Progressive Unionist Party (PUP) and the Ulster Democratic Party (UDP), 'Labour', the Northern Ireland Women's Coalition and Robert McCartney's UK Unionist Party, as well as the Ulster Unionist Party (UUP), SDLP, Democratic Unionist Party (DUP), Sinn Féin and the AP. Sinn Féin was, of course, excluded from participation because of the absence of a PIRA ceasefire and, after a tense opening session, attended by taoiseach Bertie Ahern and British prime minister John Major, senator George Mitchell was duly installed as the independent chairman and the talks got under way. The initial focus was on a range of essentially procedural matters: what should be the basis for taking decisions in the talks process? What issues needed to be addressed and how should the agenda be set and the talks structured? There was inevitably a degree of shadow-boxing during this period, as unionists sought to make progress – especially in establishing a mechanism to oversee the decommissioning of terrorist arsenals – before there was any risk of Sinn Féin joining the talks, and the Irish Government and SDLP sought to avoid positions being established that would make it difficult for Sinn Féin to join at a later point. However, the decisions reached during this period provided a solid foundation for the future.

The notion that decisions should be taken by 'sufficient consensus', for example, was elaborated into a rule that any decision would require the support of:

- both governments;
- parties representing (on the basis of the votes they secured in the 1996 elections) majorities in each of the unionist and the nationalist communities in Northern Ireland; and
- a majority of the ten political parties represented at the talks.

This enabled progress to be made without Sinn Féin present (because the SDLP had secured a majority of the nationalist vote in the 1996 elections), and it meant that that DUP did not have a veto (because the UUP and the PUP and UDP between them had secured a majority of the unionist vote in those elections). That actually gave the DUP the luxury of being able to vote against certain things without preventing progress, something they consciously did on a number of occasions. This period of the talks also saw the elaboration of the procedural basis of the talks, including agreement on agendas for the three existing 'strands' of the negotiations and on the addition of new work streams related to decommissioning, policing/'demilitarisation' and equalities issue. Throughout this period the Labour Party at Westminster maintained a statesmanlike position of supporting the British Government's approach – not giving anyone grounds for thinking that delay (until after the forthcoming UK general election) would help matters.

After the election, however, the new Labour Government was in a position to force the pace in the talks process. Careful choreography of Mo Mowlam's first few days in office gave a new sense of optimism and urgency to the talks. A double murder by the PIRA led to a clear riposte from Tony Blair (in his first speech as prime minister outside London) that challenged the republican movement to re-establish the ceasefire and join the talks process or 'the train would leave the station' without them. The ceasefire was reinstated and after a suitable interval Sinn Féin were admitted to the talks. The UUP, the DUP and the two loyalist parties withdrew, but ultimately the UUP and the two loyalist parties rejoined – initially to challenge Sinn Féin's commitment to exclusively peaceful methods, but subsequently to participate in the various strands and work streams of negotiation.

There were further ups and downs in the talks process. At different times both Sinn Féin and the loyalist UDP were excluded from the talks for periods of time when the PIRA and Ulster Defence Association (UDA, the paramilitary wing of the UDP), respectively, were perceived to have broken their ceasefires. Some strands and work streams made more progress than others. Strand 1 (the development of new political institutions for Northern Ireland) actually received very little attention up to virtually the last minute because the main parties were not really ready to engage until they had achieved their objectives in the other strands of their negotiations.

For the unionists, the key issues were those being dealt with in 'Strand 3': the negotiations between the British and Irish governments (with regular reports to the independent chairman and other participants) on the future institutional relationship between the two governments, including the constitutional issue. The outcome of that strand is clearly set out in the BA, reached on Good Friday 1998, and largely mirrors the 'constitutional' elements of the DSD. It was agreed that:

- the right to self-determination of the people of Ireland as a whole could be exercised only on the basis of majority consent in both parts of Ireland;
- section 1 of the Northern Ireland Constitution Act 1997 should be amended to incorporate a commitment to legislate to bring about a united Ireland if ever there were majority support for that in Northern Ireland, and the Government of Ireland Act 1920 should be repealed;
- Articles 2 and 3 of the Irish Constitution should be amended to reflect the concept that the achievement of Irish unity would require the consent of majorities in both parts of Ireland; and

- the AIA should be 'superseded' by a more broadly based British–Irish Agreement, which would not focus exclusively on Northern Ireland, and the remit of the Anglo-Irish Secretariat similarly widened.

Elsewhere, it was agreed that the whole Agreement should be presented to the electorates in both parts of Ireland, on the same day, for validation in a 'double referendum', thus trumping the outcome of the previous all-Ireland election (of 1918).

There was much in the Agreement that unionists were uncomfortable with, but on the key constitutional issues they had secured their major negotiating objectives: a formal commitment by both governments and by all parties to the principle that Irish unity could not, and should not, be achieved without the consent of a majority of the people of Northern Ireland; the rewording of Articles 2 and 3 of the Irish Constitution to reflect that principle; and the 'scrapping' of the AIA. Sinn Féin, conversely, found much of the constitutional and political provisions of the Agreement difficult to deal with. Apart from having to accept that Irish unity could be achieved only with the consent of a majority of the people of Northern Ireland, they also had to overturn their previous objection to participating in 'partitionist' political institutions within Northern Ireland. Ultimately, on Good Friday itself, Sinn Féin abstained in the final vote on the draft Agreement, but under the rules of 'sufficient consensus' the Agreement was approved despite the DUP's absence and Sinn Féin's abstention. Subsequently, Sinn Féin convened a special party convention to secure the necessary support for acquiescing in such a significant adjustment of their historic position on political and constitutional issues. They naturally used the occasion to highlight their negotiating successes in other areas – prisoner releases, the 'demilitarisation' commitments, the promise of a review of policing and new equalities measures – and the necessary changes to their formal positions were duly voted through. Ultimately, the Agreement was, of course, endorsed by both parliaments and passed by large majorities in both parts of Ireland, crystallising and validating the new constitutional settlement.

Conclusion

Throughout the various sessions of interparty dialogue that constituted the Northern Ireland 'talks process', there was only one occasion when unionists and nationalists directly debated the formula at the heart of the constitutional guarantee. This was in late June 1991 when the Brooke talks, having been bedevilled by procedural issues for the first few weeks, finally moved into an intense period of round-table political discussion between the four participating political parties – the UUP, DUP, AP and SDLP. Seamus Mallon subsequently referred to these discussions – the first formal round-table talks between the political parties in Northern Ireland on political matters since the mid-1970s – as 'golden moments', which held out the promise of further progress in future. In one evening session a member of the UUP delegation – it might have been Reg Empey – posed the question of why the constitutional status of Northern Ireland should be determined on the basis of a simple majority vote in a Border poll, when potentially less significant issues such as the nature of any new political institutions for Northern Ireland needed to have 'broad support across both main parts of the community'. The response he got from the SDLP delegation was that they would be happy to talk further about that. However, that dialogue was never picked up.

On the unionist side, as described above, attention focused on the removal of Articles 2 and 3 of the Irish Constitution; and the formalisation (in the DSD) of the two governments' commitment to support legislation to bring about Irish unity if ever a majority in Northern Ireland expressed support for that seemed to leave little room for manoeuvre on that front. However, it has always seemed to me that this is unfinished business and that – in time – a sounder and more honest understanding of the constitutional position could be reached in which all sides would accept the reality and the principle that Irish unity could, and should, be brought about only on the basis of a reasonable degree of consensus within Northern Ireland. However, even without that further refinement, the constitutional elements of the BA represented solid gains for the unionist and loyalist participants. Flag-waving loyalists on the streets during the 'marching season' may not fully appreciate those gains, but on the key constitutional issues:

- the 'constitutional guarantee' (that Northern Ireland will not cease to be a part of the UK without the consent of the majority of the people who live there) has been re-affirmed, endorsed by referendums in both parts of Ireland and is now formally reflected in relevant statutory provisions in both the UK and the Republic of Ireland;
- conversely the 'constitutional claim' in Article 2 of the 1937 Irish Constitution (that Northern Ireland was *de jure* part of a united Ireland) has been repealed and replaced with an aspiration to Irish unity and an acknowledgement that for this to come about there will need to be majorities in favour in both parts of Ireland; and
- the republican movement's claim to have inherited the mantle of the First Dáil on the basis of the outcome of the 1918 general election in Ireland has been finally undermined through the mechanism of the double referendum of 22 May 1998.

These are significant gains for unionism. Taken together, they mean that – unless there is an unexpected change of heart by a significant number of unionists – Northern Ireland will remain part of the UK for the foreseeable future. Unionists and loyalists ought to take comfort from that and be more confident as a community; and that confidence should make it easier to deal with some of the difficult symbolic and legacy issues that still trouble Northern Ireland society.

The BA also brought further practical benefits, including:

- Political institutions in Northern Ireland that provide a fair and appropriate voice for all parts of the community; and machinery for dialogue and constructive cooperation between both parts of Ireland and between the UK and the Republic. Everyone has democratic channels through which legitimate interests and grievances can be pursued, and the decision-making arrangements mean that all parts of the community have influence in proportion to their electoral support. Institutions with these characteristics may sometimes be painfully slow in achieving consensus on any given issue, but they should ultimately produce fairer outcomes and generate support and loyalty across the whole community and provide the foundation for long-term political stability that will benefit everyone.
- A very significant reduction in the nature and scale of Northern Ireland-related terrorist activity. This has already lasted (since the ceasefires of 1994) for twenty years, and while Northern Ireland is not yet free of security threats these are an order of magnitude lower than the threat to normal life that existed before 1994.
- A major 'peace dividend' in the form of a surge in inward investment and economic development in the years following the BA. Northern Ireland's GDP more than doubled in the twelve years after the BA. Not all parts of the community have benefited to the same extent and the recent recession has obviously had a negative impact, but in general Northern Ireland is significantly more prosperous than it would have been without the BA, and that again is good for everyone.

Peace, political stability, economic development, clarity about the current constitutional status of Northern Ireland and the circumstances in which it might change and institutions that ensure equitable treatment for all and respect the different identities of the two main parts of the community in Northern Ireland all represent solid gains for all parts of the community in Northern Ireland, but particularly for the unionist community.

4   Negotiations and positions: an interview with Sir John Chilcot

Interview

GS: What did your job involve?

JC: I started work in Northern Ireland in the mid-1960s as a young official in the Home Office. Roy Jenkins was Home Secretary and I was his junior private secretary, and I was involved in Northern Ireland from there. By about 1967 things began to change significantly. I was called back at very short notice by Jim Callaghan, who had succeeded Roy after devaluation at the Treasury. He said he wanted contingency plans drawn up in a hurry for Northern Ireland just in case we had to intervene, and he courageously went there to face the situation and that left a very deep mark on me. I did not go back to the subject matter of Northern Ireland until 1990, but I spent a lot of years in between dealing with areas such as policing and security, and was very alert to the terrorist dimension. I followed at a distance what was going on with Willie Whitelaw and then Merlyn Rees, and in 1977–8 I became Merlyn Rees' principal private secretary when he was home secretary. Despite Roy Mason's secretaryship in Northern Ireland, where nothing shifted, or was not allowed to be seen to shift, I got more and more personally interested in the problem and when I was offered the job of permanent secretary in 1990, I jumped at it. On my very first night I was woken in the small hours with the news that a series of proxy bombs had killed a number of soldiers, and had to deal with the dilemma of whether to stay there or go back to London to handle the political flak from Parliament. So it was a baptism of fire in that sense. It was also apparent to me then that leadership in symbolic terms was very important when it came to Northern Ireland and how to respond to what was going on there.

GS: What do you mean by symbolic leadership?

JC: Where one is communicating with a set of audiences by one's own action or inaction through words or lack of words. And in Northern Ireland, where there are a million and a half people, the cut-through on political messaging is very quick. There you are certainly right up against direct human contact and relationships. I remember one leader of the Ulster Unionist Party (UUP) telling me that he did not want all this 'leadership stuff' after direct rule. He went on to say that the unionists had to be given real problems to deal with and not symbolic ones, and that would involve dealing with mundane political decision-making on things like repairing pot-holes. I learned quickly that Northern Ireland was not just about being engaged in a war, or struggle or a negotiation around sets of words, but required being engaged with all kinds of human communication at different levels that worked in relation to trust, hate, love and other emotions.

GS: Can you tell me when you first heard of 'the link' and what you knew about it?

JC: What was clear from the outset was that there was a chain of communication. It had been on and off over many years with different characters playing different parts in the chain. It was evident, even when I took over in Peter Brooke's time, that Tom King had his means of indirect communication, serviced in my time essentially by the security service and by well-wishers on both sides. But the question was always are you hearing direct from the mouth of the speaker, or are you hearing interpreted words or words that another party in the chain wished had been spoken and was then playing back?

GS: In that situation is it better when there are only two or three people in the chain rather than, say, six or seven? Does a smaller number make trust more credible?

JC: I think the essential feature of trust is who are they and what is their 'track record'? This is more important than the number of links in the chain. By the time I came on the scene at the beginning of the 1990s, we were reasonably confident that what was coming through was what was being sent. But, of course, there would always be entrepreneurs somewhere in that short chain. Entrepreneurs in the best sense, who wished to encourage, promote and bring about a connection between the two sides, where what you said to one side you said to the other, and how you relayed that information from side to side.

GS: What about the distinction to be made between reality and perception?

JC: That relied much more on third-party observer-style intelligence assessment on the toings and froings of communication. How far are these guys in control of their situation? What is their understanding of our political position and our government, and what do they think and how is the Ard Fheis going to go? These were the key considerations and informed much of our approach.

GS: Were you taken by surprise by Peter Brooke's statement on 'no selfish strategic or economic interest'?

JC: Not in the slightest. I cannot remember the etymology of it, but we wanted to get across something with the collapse of the Soviet Union and the end of the Cold War that there was no strategic dimension anymore and to confront the PIRA idea that this still had some kind of basis. That it was no longer about policing the eastern Atlantic and the Soviet submarine routes around Derry. So the message was that we do not have a selfish or strategic interest and if we had one before, which might have been right or wrong, it was not there any longer, so please understand this. That was the point of the speech and it was carefully thought about.

GS: Was the 'no selfish strategic or economic interest' speech of Brooke really John Hume's speech?

JC: I do not think it was. As I said, it was a useful message to convey to the Provisionals that we did not want to hang on to Northern Ireland for strategic reasons. We formed the impression that that was what they thought, and we wanted to displace that thought by lifting their understanding to the level of geopolitical strategy.

GS: Was there any contemplation of putting the word 'political' in there too?

JC: No, definitely not. Peter Brooke is an amazingly subtle-minded but straightforward politician, and he would have wanted to distance party, local or national politics from the realities of the process.

GS: Where he delivered the speech is interesting. Why at the British Association of Canned Food Importers and Distributors at the Whitbread Restaurant in London?

JC: We just chose an occasion. It was not a case of thinking let's sit back eighteen months and find a future occasion. It was much more about here is something we want to say and get across, so find a moment and find a way. I suspect this political speech was more thought about than many or most. Although we tried to stir up something, I am not sure we succeeded. Did the message get through? I have never known whether it changed the calculus in the minds of the PIRA or not. One hears that it made a difference, but this was never really confirmed.

GS: Can you give me a brief overview of what was happening at the time that Peter Brooke made the 'Whitbread' speech, because, as we know, it had been preceded by Brooke's 'one hundred days in office' speech when he said that it was difficult to envisage a military defeat of the PIRA?

JC: There were several speeches made of course, but the famous one, as you indicate, was the 'no strategic' statement and the debate subsequently about whether there should have been a comma between each of the areas.

As permanent secretary you are looking at other people's contributions and either editing or steering, or saying a speech is fine to go through. But the purpose of speeches, such as those made by Brooke, should be seen as part of a process along with interpretative communication through back channels. The leadership on the republican side would have understood the intended significance of that, although whether they believed it or not is another thing.

GS: Was there a different sense of interpretation on words and messages on the Irish side?

JC: Not in the singular, but in the multiple-plural there was a huge difference in terms of tone, colour and feel.

GS: On the question of trust, is it made easier when talking directly or better when a piece of text is on the table?

JC: It is a good question. The first answer is that trust lies between people, but then there was a cultural distinction, even if in a sense they also complemented each other. Between the Irish written culture and the British bureaucratic culture, both rely very much on the choice of word, the syllable, even the tense and mood, and they can speak to each other in a way that, for example, you cannot with the Americans because they do not get it, and perhaps we do not get what they say in that way either.

GS: What do they not get?

JC: Nuance and subtlety, the 'but' after the 'yes', the 'no' but the 'maybe', all of that.

GS: Can you elaborate further about the distinction between the British and the Irish in that regard?

JC: Like it or loathe it you can deal bureaucrat to bureaucrat with the Irish official system on fully comprehending terms. We may not agree, of course, but you both know what you are saying and the importance of language, and that a thing said and signed off is a thing undertaken; it is an obligation. I think the two political communities in Northern Ireland are quite different in that regard, but I think the two official communities were very close, partly because of common heritage, but also because of a different set of streams coming together and merging.

GS: Irish officials I have interviewed mention how class in Ireland is not as prominent as it is in England. Did this difference prove a factor in how you both worked together, with one more hierarchical than the other? Did this influence in any discernible way the logic of dialogue or the means of rationalisation and reasoning?

JC: I have dealt with the French, the Germans, the Japanese and the Americans, but with the Irish, even though there was by no means an identity of interest, there was an identity of understanding that you did not find elsewhere and that I do not think has anything to do with class. I think it has a lot to do with education. The British mandarin system certainly was then and still is much more independent-minded of party political interest than the necessity of senior Irish officialdom, where there is having, declaring and owing an allegiance to the ruling party.

GS: How does bureaucracy work, and how do continuous checks and balances shape the bureaucratic process?

JC: In the case of the Northern Ireland Office (NIO), in the early to middle 1990s, the key players would have been Quentin Thomas, Jonathan Stephens, David Cooke and David Hill. We would all have been uncomfortable if we had strayed outside our shared moral boundaries in giving politically alert and sophisticated advice, and that was the main constraining factor.

GS: Were those moral boundaries tightly discussed or felt?

JC: They are felt and known. They do not need to be explicit.

GS: Can you recall a time when you tested that boundary?

JC: Not with Peter Brooke or Patrick Mayhew, no. I do not know whether my predecessors had it tested in earlier times, but, frankly, I did not have to find that out. I worked with Peter Brooke, Patrick Mayhew and Mo Mowlam, all of whom had genuine moral integrity and independence of mind, so it was easy in a way and it was not tested. I thought that my Irish counterparts at times had much more difficulty, although less with Albert Reynolds, but it was pretty difficult at other times.

GS: Some Irish officials have talked about getting 'the deal' done. How much emphasis was there on process and how much on reaching the deal as quickly as possible?

JC: There is not a distinction between the deal and the process. Rather it is the endpoint and what that entails. I do not think that there was a fag paper between us and the Irish civil servants on this. The Irish Department of Foreign Affairs had a very strong dogmatic inheritance to its culture and in that sense is much more like the British Home Office, which is about just keeping the thing dampened down, making sure justice is being served and limiting the number of people being killed. At the end of the day, the deal was, if you like, a reconciliation reached by curving routes and different starting and end points.

GS: Was your reading of what reconciliation might mean different from the Irish reading?

JC: I really have no idea. My own version is that it will take five, if not ten, generations to achieve (if it is achievable) genuine cultural mutual assimilation and coming together, but that does not matter providing the conditions on the ground of living and life are acceptable to both communities.

GS: But how can the endpoint be envisaged or known?

JC: Well what about the English Civil War [laughs]? You do not set those endpoints as political goals, so to that extent the process dominates ultimate ends. On the other hand, you have to powerfully articulate and have clear intermediate goals.

GS: Process is surely more important than end result, because if you get to that end result and it is collapsing then process is the only thing that can keep it going?

JC: It is very good this one and, as I said before, to use Peter Brooke's metaphor, at difficult moments it was wise to 'park up' and see how things were changing around you. We could not change the conditions on the road which is about process. People might think it is surely about goals and aspiration, etc., which it is, but ultimately it is the process that matters. It is like the doctor keeping the patient alive when he is in near-critical condition.

GS: Even knowing when to 'park up' takes considerable understanding and knowledge of everything moving around you at the point?

JC: Yes, it does, and also I would say real political insight and judgement. How much can you affect the people who say come on get going or we are not going anywhere, and that if you cannot move, just crash? Managing that as a politician in high office with a contentious political situation between London, Dublin and Belfast takes consummate political skill.

GS: If you take Canary Wharf where some might have wanted it called off and others wanted to keep it going, how did you judge the tension between those positions?

JC: At that time tension was considerable, but we knew why it was done and we managed to prevail over anyone who wanted to make a knee-jerk response.

GS: How did you determine the response, and how long you should leave it before responding?

JC: Or leave it politically as well? Where I think we had the advantage over our Irish counterparts in managing this whole thing was we had London and Belfast, so we had to manage the unionists as well as the governing interests in London. But the Irish had to do it all from Dublin and looking into the black North, where they represented in a minor way with the Irish Secretariat. So we had this double interpretation and, even in those early days, videoconferencing in real time which was very secure. So you could actually bat this back and forth and play it and game it, and address 'what ifs' and make a reasoned risk assessment. I do not think that was as possible from Dublin.

GS: Was videoconferencing productive or as useful as face to face?

JC: You cannot substitute one for the other because a huge difference was that quite a lot of double travel went on from the British side. You would find yourself in Belfast and something horrible would happen in the curve and blips, so you would fly back to London, but you have seen it and felt it and analysed it from a Belfast perspective with the unionists and the republicans and the Social Democratic and Labour Party (SDLP). And when you go to London you can look at it from the Westminster and London political perspective, and we had staff from both sides doing the same job so we had some convergence. We had the Belfast security policy people and the London security policy people talking about it all the time, and that double cross-bearing was of great importance in levelling and balancing the judgements that we had to make from moment to moment.

GS: Were the Irish working in a similar vein?

JC: I do not think the Irish Embassy in London was a significant player, nor was our embassy in Dublin actually. The real dialogues took place in Dublin, Belfast and London, and that relationship was where the dynamic really lay.

GS: What difference did the Americans make?

JC: I think quite a lot of difference on the republican front and a bit on the nationalist front in relation to Hume etc. I really do not know how much influence, if any, the Americans had in Dublin. Our assessment would not have been that different from the Irish assessment. The US consulate general was in Belfast, but I never felt that it was particularly influential in turning the tide of things.

GS: When republican veteran Joe Cahill was allowed a visa to go to the United States, what impact did that decision have?

JC: It was politically awkward for John Major, but it was not significant over the longer term. The Americans had their own domestic politics to worry about and manage, and, of course, after 9/11 they reversed 180 degrees, but that was a later moment. I remember having to go and give evidence in a federal court in San Francisco against a PIRA man, and the American State Department, the FBI, etc., were absolutely at one with us. There was just a bit of congressional politics going on and fundraising in Boston. Although it is a very unfair estimation, if you were to ask whether the Americans were more important than the Germans, I would have to answer yes.

GS: When you write a piece of text are you thinking of Adams and Trimble talking? Are you imagining how people will behave when you draft text?

JC: Yes, absolutely. Of course, they have got their own politics and constituencies to manage, and one must take into account what words mean to them. So the problem is one of how can you make those words congruent with what the same words will mean to a quite different constituency, and you try to draft across the difference. That is part of the craft.

GS: How does that craft shift and change as the process goes along?

JC: Because it is so long ago I am prone to forgetfulness and oversimplification, but essentially, to hold the unionist interest because ultimately they are the majority in the Northern limited constituency. But alongside that to gather in the 'greens' through the constructive, but ultimately self-destructive, constitutional nationalism and bring in as best you could all but the wilder fringes of republicanism.

GS: Can you give me an example of text doing that?

JC: It is in the ultimate documentation of the process. It is signalling. How do you say we have no selfish strategic or economic interest to nationalism and republicanism and yet reassure unionism that it does not mean you are selling them out? It is as much that as the legalities, which ultimately matter very greatly, I do agree.

GS: What did your job consist of on a daily basis as regards text and meeting people and facilitating dialogue?

JC: Right at the end of the process, coming to its culmination, you are very much all there in a similar space exchanging text on paper and informally in corridors and assessing whether these words will work and the limitations of what we can say. But if you go back three years it was quite different. It was about not distant exchanges, but an accumulation of occasional and formal exchanges, with more informal conversation through time as much governed by events on the ground. That was certainly so in the early to mid-1990s compared with the late 1990s. During the late 1980s, however, the response was almost all in relation to events on the ground.

GS: Much of the literature points to the emergence of the peace process from 1988 and the Hume–Adams dialogues, but what do you think significantly changed from 1972 in terms of where people ended up?

JC: If you take a tragic view of life, very little. However, people age, learn, mature, ripen and situations become easier or harder. There were five or six key people on unionist, nationalist and republican sides who proved remarkable and that, it seems to me, was very much indicative of an evolution of change and adaptation. In making political intelligence assessments we also had to consider how reliable and predictable this was in the Irish context. This also proved helpful.

GS: Can you remember any predictions that turned out to be wrong?

JC: No. We would look with great interest and care at the outcome of each Ard Fheis, to see if the leaderships were still in command and consider what their room was for manoeuvre. And that never really went wrong in my time.

GS: Did you strategically place statements in the public sphere in advance of each Ard Fheis in order to facilitate movement?

JC: If the opportunity arose we would have, but I do not think it really happened quite like that. The idea that because Adams was going into a difficult Ard Fheis and might lose the next generation was somehow a reason to give him a sop was not how it worked. We were assessing whether the key figures could still control events on the ground, as well as looking at those who might be in the ascendancy and might create problems for the leadership more generally.

GS: Would you say in 1996–7 that republican leaders were thinking about sharing power with the Democratic Unionist Party (DUP)? That even then they were thinking way down the road?

JC: Yes, the ultimate deal was between the DUP and Sinn Féin. It may have been seen as politically extreme at that time, but in terms of depth of difference and the need to reconcile that difference that was certainly the deal to seal.

GS: Were you thinking about pushing the moderates outward to expose the extremes, or was it more about bringing the extremes into the middle?

JC: I think it started like that in the late 1980s, but there was a dawning realisation, which I think I had as early as anyone, that John Hume was ready to sacrifice the SDLP and the nationalist interest because the ultimate deal had to be the bigger one.

GS: When did you recognise that?

JC: I could not put a note to it, but it became apparent as the UUP declined in power and influence over the unionist majority, and as Hume and Mallon started to lose control and split and factionalise. Whether the DUP saw that very early as well, I do not know.

GS: Did John Major face a number in his ranks that were keener to see the PIRA defeated?

JC: I think there was a short-term perception on the right side of British politics that the PIRA could be beaten, but there was little advantage in that perception. I think that kind of thinking may have been more prevalent in the mid- to late

1980s after the hunger strikes, but that was also true on the other side of the political divide. However, as time went on the possibility and expectation of military victory certainly lost appeal.

GS: Is party political thinking different from political thinking?

JC: Yes, and who you are surrounded by in office or in high opposition office. Purely political thinkers are looking for advantage at the next event, occasion, election and that is your main pressure in office.

GS: Today, you have Sinn Féin leaders saying protagonists have to face up to some of the things they did during the conflict. This would have been unthinkable in 1993/4. The question is how does that fit in with the next stage?

JC: You just have to wait it out. Truth and reconciliation is fine, but you cannot set if off with a bang. This will take generations, but what you have to do is have a framework of institutions and processes that enable that slow reconciliation and acceptance to take place.

GS: Principle or pragmatism, which is more important?

JC: It is a bit flip, but a fair balance. You must adhere to principle and never abandon it. But you must not allow it to dominate completely the realities of a particular situation, and if you do you may find yourself bringing about the unwarranted death of innocent civilians.

GS: But when you say it cannot be allowed to dominate a situation you seem to be into the realms of potentially undermining the principle, so how do you gauge where that is?

JC: I do not agree with that proposition. I do think that ultimately it boils down to judgement about human affairs, informed and infused by principle and integrity and as much transparency as you can manage, but also by as much discretion as you can manage too. This is what judges and magistrates do every day of the week. It is very difficult, but you cannot set one above the other.

GS: On the relationship between ambiguity and clarity, it is apparent that in a situation of this sort you start off ambiguously to get people to engage, but that ultimately a judgement has to be made about when to move that ambiguity into clarity.

JC: You are right in the sense that both British and Irish cultures go for certainty, but from different perspectives. The Irish legal system stems ultimately from a tribal system with authority from the top. The British comes from the common law system, which is ultimately a group of people living in the same area making judgements about who is honest and who is not. They are two very different things, but they do come together as well.

GS: In the peace process you worked across the three strands. Were there advantages in having those three strands, beyond legislative reasons? For example, if you were not making progress on one could you move to another, make progress and then move back to the initial strand?

JC: I think there was immense advantage to the outcomes, as far as we got intermediate outcomes anyway, from the mutual education that goes on between the strands because you learn from each of them. Each party learns from dealing with others by way of the different strands. If one were to ask whether the strands were numerous enough, or political enough or influential enough for a better outcome, then I do not know. But it was immensely advantageous to have a three-stranded approach where three party interests could be reconciled.

GS: Metaphors like 'peace train' have been used in ways that, presumably, would have had next to no impact on a piece of paper. So to what extent was the peace process a metaphorical process as well as a literal one?

JC: Can I start with a cultural observation, which is that one of the things that the British and Irish Civil Service has in common is a tradition in the English language that tends to the metaphorical. Why is that? It is because it actually helps to manage the political dimension since it is more flexible and elastic, more imaginative and suggestive. When you come to drafting the instructions for a piece of legislation, for the outcome of that imaginative policy, you have to crystallise it right down to hard-edged, non-metaphorical language and concepts. And it goes back to what you were talking about much earlier in that there is an arc that starts with a lot of ambiguity and metaphor and flowery language, but gradually, if it succeeds, comes to quite hard sharp points and so to a different kind of language. I think there is a different kind of risk here and the temptation for politicians is to go for the inspirational metaphor at the wrong moment, when it is too late.

GS: But the metaphor and the strategy combine, so if you are thinking strategically about 'drawing the lobster into the pot', which is another one I have heard, that is a different way of dealing with people is it not?

JC: From being a caravan on the road parking temporarily because you want to go on and on, yes it is, but, as said, our American friends do not do metaphor a lot, as neither do the Australians or the Canadians. But with the Irish we both do a lot of it, and I think for a purpose. It is not just a shared cultural education, it does serve a purpose.

GS: On the point of talks there were proximity talks, talks about talks, substantive talks, inclusive talks, multilateral talks, bilateral talks, talks which were business-like and frank, and so on. But was there any strategic difference at work across these various kinds of talks?

JC: I think these are sort of easements in terms of coming into the process and discussion, and they wear out after a bit so you have to find a new one. I have no knowledge at all of the Middle East peace process and I do not know whether the Israeli Foreign Service talk in metaphors to the Americans because the State Department on the whole do not do a lot of that, but I think it does have important uses, even if they are primarily illustrative, because there is also an indication of intent at work there.

GS: One gets the impression from Adams' memoirs that the republicans, without wanting to show it, were a bit scared of the British and that they would get caught up in word games. That it was going to become a philosophical exercise.

JC: That is slightly surprising because they were very deft and sophisticated, and there was a sharing of language. Frankly, I think we were pretty much able throughout to rely on their ability to control the PIRA and we were not wrong on that. Were they scared of getting entangled in a tricky web of British deception? Well, I have never forgotten that moment when Adams, talking about decommissioning with his head in his hands, said something like 'That is a really tricky political problem', because that was a sharing moment. That was not about getting enmeshed by us, but a sign that we all had to find a way through.

GS: One Irish official said to me that the problem with decommissioning was you could do nothing with it because you could not disagree with it.

JC: No, that is right. It was more difficult for them than us actually. I think it was politically difficult for us, but for them it was a matter of real principle because they were facing possible insurgent civil war, whilst we were facing a terrorist threat that we could 'sit on' for as long as it took.

GS: So it was a more precarious situation for the Irish?

JC: I do agree that there was more threat in there, but I do not think precarious politically as it turned out. Sinn Féin was not able to recruit the disadvantaged working-class areas of Dublin. But while they saw that as an existential threat, for us it was not. It was more something to cope and deal with and take a bit of pain and spend a bit of blood and treasure on. But without getting the security right it would have been difficult to do anything.

GS: When you talked to unionists did they give you the historical preamble like republicans?

JC: No, not really. They do not have the same narrative, but more a position on any situation. And they have the perception that they are the majority who are entitled, but have been let down and betrayed. Within the Orange Order there is a longer narrative, but it is a mythical one.

GS: So, would it be fair to suggest that republicans saw the peace process in terms of a narrative whilst unionists saw it more in terms of positions?

JC: That is a tremendously attractive suggestion in a persuasive sense. I am going back to the trial in the federal court in California for a PIRA extradition hearing for which I was the chief witness for the British. There the opening case for the defence by an American lawyer was asking if it was true that in the twelfth or thirteenth century the Protestant British dominating military power invaded a peaceful Catholic Ireland. The sense of a long narrative was there in the briefing sheet presumably.

GS: Some republicans could compartmentalise violence from any Catholic influence, but it is unlikely you would get such compartmentalisation in the unionist community. It seems unlikely they would have supported the contradictory position of the Armalite and the ballot box.

JC: That is right. The distinction between unionist parties, including the DUP, and waving the firearms certificates is that these are legal and the loyalists are scoundrels. There is also that great competition between the decent working class and the others in unionism. This is far less evident on the other side because they are all victims to some degree. Perhaps that is a simplification, but I think there might be something there.

GS: If you have two groups of people like unionists and republicans and you ask them to sort the conflict out themselves they cannot, but when you have a third party like the British producing documents etc. the point of focus becomes less each other and more the third party. What would you say about that other dimension?

JC: The third party brings with it a difficulty for both. The unionists had to accept that that third party had no selfish strategic or economic interest, but that it does have a principled interest in the rights of a majority in a democracy, which is also a responsibility for the whole of society. On the other side, you have something which is quite different, which was a power-owning autocracy. So are they going to be a bit indulgent? Are they going to make some concessions? It is a very different perspective.

GS: The question of stereotypes, particularly in a conflict process, seems central to understanding if the divisions served by those stereotypes are to be addressed. Many people involved in the talks I have spoken to said that republicans were better on ambiguity than unionists, who preferred a more literal approach. In your experience, is there credibility in this stereotyped view?

JC: There is clearly a huge cultural difference between the Ulster/Protestant tradition with regard to the expression of identity compared with the Catholic/nationalist, even republican, emphasis. But, on the point of difference, there is as much gap between the nationalist North and South as there is between the two sides in Northern Ireland itself. In the South, the divisions are civil, but also more inherited. There was an almost moral ethical snobbery among unionists that they were the 'good people' and that those outside the tribe were the corrupted ones, and that snobbery was profoundly resented from the South.

GS: When you met republican leaders how did you view their approach?

JC: I cannot remember exactly when it was, but it was very early and when Adams and McGuinness were meeting ministers. The meeting might even have been in Canada. It was then that the question of decommissioning arms came up and, as I mentioned, Adams put his elbows on the table and put his head in his hands before acknowledging the difficulty. What I saw then was the emergent or butterfly chrysalis politician. He was not trying to pressure the situation by adopting a stance, but rather indicating that this was a really difficult problem and that we had to crack it together somehow. That was a big moment, and it was a real sign of change.

GS: Did they use the British to help them clarify their own position?

JC: Yes. But they were very much helped by John Hume, who mentored and interpreted for them in a number of ways.

GS: Did you also attempt to use John Hume, but more as a conduit for communicating to republicans?

JC: I think the only answer to that is, yes, because Hume was himself very much an innovator and a former of concepts. The referendum would not have come into being without John Hume – although it was not only his property. But the concept that nationalism was about people rather than territory, which was sent to the Provisionals and the Dublin Government, was very strong. Hume was very important, and I don't think his contribution has been fully realised.

GS: Can you describe the relationship between officials, politicians and the policy-making network? How did that work?

JC: It did not work in separated or horizontal layers, but through a lot of relationships, some of which crossed the official politician boundary such as North–South. A memory comes to mind of a meeting in Dublin when it became apparent that we had been talking to the Provos much to the horror of the Irish. We got into a pretty heated discussion, and it was heated on a political level with Albert Reynolds and John Major and the noise was getting louder and louder at the table. I simply put in a two-liner to John Major on paper suggesting that he take Albert into another room and keep everybody else out, which he did and it worked. The Albert Reynolds–John Major relationship was fundamentally more positive and constructive than the collective relationship in that meeting between the two sides, but perhaps this also indicates that international negotiation of this kind requires a degree of invention as well as planning.

GS: How do you determine how long a piece of text should be and if it is going to keep everyone involved in the process?

JC: I think it depends what stage you are at. Once you are in multiparty talks by agreement, inevitably between those preferably at the table at any rate, you can afford to do more in terms of both the rigour and the length of the text because you have more opportunity to explain what is going on, what the intended effect is and gauge whether the participants could buy into it or not. When you were dealing with officials, particularly between Dublin and London/Belfast, it was easier to pursue developments in the same way. There were obviously different styles, but there was much less need to worry about stamina or comprehension.

GS: How important was ambiguity during those early stages?

JC: Very much, and it was deliberate. The Iraq issue is terribly interesting on this too with the passage of the UN Security Council resolution 1441, because it was quite clear that there was absolutely no agreement between the Russians, the Chinese, the French and the Germans, on one side, and the Americans and perhaps one or two others, on the other. So to develop a consensual context, they agreed to draft and craft ambiguous text where afterwards each could claim they meant this and that. It doesn't solve the problem, but this was vital for Northern Ireland too. There was a competitive element about who would be the first to provide the most direction and influence in textual terms, and the British could draft and amend at great speed because they had more skilled people doing so, but, nevertheless, ambiguity was vitally important.

GS: Were you drafting tactically or strategically, for the short haul, the long haul or both?

JC: The proper British answer would be that we were drafting for strategic purposes, but actually not really. Although sometimes you need to drive through if you can, if you have enough words and strength, it can still be the case that the other side is too ambiguous or flaky. When that happens, it is better to back off because you do not want to invent florid text to cover the gap, so sometimes by pausing or waiting others then feel more inclined to move.

GS: Were there occasions when you drafted text without being clear about how it would shape events?

JC: Yes, we did that at Corfu at a European summit where right in the middle of things I invented a couple of what came to be known as the 'Corfu questions'. The main one asked would the Irish give up the constitutional claim if the British and the unionists agreed to the double referendum. That was a test to see whether they were for it or not because we sensed at that moment that they might just move. If it had been a year or two earlier we would not have done that, but would have waited and just carried the dialogue forward.

GS: How did the things that you could not write down differ from those that you could write down?

JC: You get into that kind of relationship when you are having a textual tussle on some genuine political question. Then you have a background where you are asking can I trust what the other guy is saying? That is, does he mean it? Taking into account that he will not be able to tell you everything you want to know, one still has to try to reach a judgement about whether what he is saying is credible. And, if you tell him something that you state he is not to pass around on paper, will he honour it? Those are the kind of issues that arise and that influence the context within which text is produced.

GS: So offering information to someone that you ask him not to share with others has a tactical function?

JC: It is a little gift, a little present, a sweetener, but when you get to know somebody properly in a working relationship you both need to know what you are doing. You can pass on advice or make suggestions without handing out paper, but you cannot go on doing it as a style of individual communication unless there is trust.

GS: Does trust make it harder for progress to be upset?

JC: I think that is more a question of moral character. If you have a properly trusting relationship with a counter-party, you should be able to respond or pass on bad news or a bad reaction more than the rest. But this comes down more to the nature of human interactions at an individual level rather than a measure of the situation or context itself.

GS: Did Sinn Féin oscillate between being certain and then being uncertain, with the latter more a reflection of strategic intent?

JC: Absolutely. In trying to characterise Sinn Féin, whatever its wholesale leadership, it is clear that it is a set of things, some of which are unwavering and principled and some which at any given moment remain in evolution. There were all sorts of sources to help form an impression or understanding of what was going on and why at that moment. That Adams and McGuinness have been able to exercise control over such a long period, with rising generations of Sinn Féin leadership, tells one immediately how good they are at managing both principle and pragmatism.

GS: Can you boil the peace process down to what you saw as a number of turning points or do you envisage the process as essentially a process of continuity?

JC: I would say it was a process of continuity with bumps in the road. Clearly, there is a continuum and there was great promise available in the early 1970s, which we all know was lost, and then there was a big bump in the road in the mid- to late 1970s. I think one of the unacknowledged, or not sufficiently acknowledged, things is that great shift in the mid-1970s on the British side to criminalise terrorism and give the police, rather than the military, primacy in dealing with the conflict as essentially a criminal matter – although this involved military support too and enabled the unionists to view terrorists as bad people doing the wrong things. That was profoundly resented by Sinn Féin, but that resentment could not be shared by the Irish governments, of whatever colour, so in that sense they were in the same position as we were. But did it have a catalytic effect in arousing in the minds of the republican movement a wish to confront, contradict or at any rate move out of the position where they could be accused of being pure criminals to something more principled? That was part of the engineering. So you had this quite large effect produced by indirect switches. When *The Observer* newspaper picked up on our back-channel talks, one of the dimensions of that was the effect this had on the Sinn Féin leadership for having talked with us. They would acknowledge that they were in indirect contact with the Irish Government and that was reasonably acceptable, but talking to the Brits, now how did they manage that? It was a question that certainly exercised us.

GS: Are surprises by and large a bad thing in a process like this?

JC: There is the old cliché about it being better with no surprises. You need to be able to acknowledge and stare in the face a change that has occurred, even if it is an unwelcome one or guides you off the line you were on, and you've got to be able to accept the possibility and then see if you can exploit it.

GS: Do you think creativity was required in dealing with this process? I am particularly thinking about dealing with the decommissioning issue.

JC: I think the first thing is to acknowledge the existence of the issue and its importance, not least on either side, of course, and then start to think about how you can address it and get round it, knowing that there is this complete block on the Provisional side about giving up arms to the enemy. So you create an alternative process, and that was where the decommissioning body and John de Chastelain came in. However, what was also important here was to get republicans to acknowledge the existence of this as a problem and engage with what to do about it, rather than claim it did not exist. Once that acknowledgement is there one can make progress.

GS: As a good negotiator, then, one needs to move across both hard and more malleable positions, but primarily because of the need to make the areas acknowledgeable as things that need to be addressed?

JC: A discussion we would have is do we build in a hard-line text to circulate to others with negotiating fat that we can give away, or do we give a softer text that they are more likely to accept, at least in principle, and then harden it up a little bit where it matters to us with red lines? You can do both at different points of time or in different contexts, but you have to judge it right and it is often a temperamental phenomenon, a utilitarian calculus.

GS: How did the Oxford or Cambridge system of education shape your thinking as a civil servant? I ask this because many civil servants appear to have been educated that way.

JC: Well, it depends what people read and with whom. I was reading English at exactly the time C. S. Lewis arrived and showed us a completely different approach, a much more sympathetic understanding and emotionally intelligent approach to reading literature compared with Leavis, who narrowly focused laser-like on text and what it meant. Lewis, on the other hand, was more interested in context and understanding the wider circumstances that may have shaped approach to text.

GS: So context was more important?

JC: Yes. It is hugely important to not really think and argue, but feel your way into understanding people's mindsets and hopes and expectations and fears, etc. There was a fine moment when we had just got the so-called 'constitutional parties' together in the talks around 1991 and we had to carve up some very expensive tableware at short notice to get the right shape so that nobody had to sit next to who they could not sit next to. But at the opening meeting John Alderdice said I think we should go round the table and just explain what our sense of identity is, and I have never forgotten it. Hume was a nationalist, Catholic and Irishman, but James Molyneaux choked and could not get anything out because it was too difficult. When we got to Ian Paisley he just said 'I am an Ulsterman, I am an Irishman and I am a British man', so multiple identities were evident then and this indicates the importance of understanding context and how one might work inside that context. A topic of constant interest retrospectively, as well as at the time, was that we appeared to be dealing with groups that had quite strict ethical limits and boundaries, but what was less clear was where those boundaries lay and where they came from.

GS: How important is the transition from minister to minister, government to government?

JC: When it was clear that New Labour was going to come in and Tony Blair had given the nod to Mo Mowlam to handle the Northern Ireland portfolio, I did not really know her at all, but decided to try to engineer a process whereby this might happen. My aim was to get to know her on a personal level, because she was not a disciplined, institutionalised processor, but more of a 'you–me' kind of person. So I invited her to dinner in London and gradually sought to win her confidence. I tried to take that thread through to after the election when she took up office in London at the Northern Ireland Office. One of the very first things that happened when she got to the office was that her private secretary told her that chancellor Gordon Brown was on the phone and wanted to have a word, so he was put through. The chancellor told Mo how delighted he was to see her in this extremely difficult post and said that if she needed any help from him she only had to ask. I thought this was good news and said to Mo we had better get a bid in quick, whereupon she told me that I did not understand a thing about what was going on inside New Labour, which was divided on a partisan rift, and that she belonged on Tony's side, but Gordon wanted to have her with him. I came to realise very quickly that any formal handover of policy issues and briefings would be dwarfed, at least in their own minds, for a bit. Nonetheless, we did do that and the second element of this transition was also just before the election, when I got Tony Blair to agree to an evening meeting with Quentin Thomas, Jonathan Powell, Mo and me in a club in London over dinner. I wanted to try to persuade them that Northern Ireland was a consensus issue, where there was both public interest benefit from pursuing a coherent line of policy and a set of relationships with Northern Ireland, and that it was better to have a success rather than a failure in political advantage terms. I remember a slight trope that I invented too, where I said that Number 10 and the Northern Ireland Office can play different roles, but they had to stay close to each other. I did not realise at the time, but it presaged an unhappy rift whereby Number 10 took over and Mo was there to guard or manage the green interest, but she had been very ill and none of us knew this. Tony knew, but I do not think anyone else did, and there was frankly a draining away of confidence in her and a shift in emphasis by Number 10 about the lead role.

GS: Is it advantageous to have a minister in place for a long period of time so that he or she can acquire deep knowledge and understanding of nuance, or is the 'long stay' disadvantageous?

JC: I think the only answer I can give is that it depends entirely on circumstances. If a senior minister has lost the confidence of his or her prime minister, then it is better to cut it off because there is no point in going on. On the other hand, in terms of the field of interest, the policy field, the arena, there is great advantage, short of the point where one or other of the main participants loses trust or confidence, or politically, cannot go on accepting the authority or influence of the British minister.

GS: Can having a clear picture of where you want to get to in talks and negotiations be disadvantageous?

JC: To use a military example, no plan survives first contact with the enemy, so you have to have a whole fan of possibilities and you have to be flexible, but at the same time you have to know what you are doing and why, in the highest strategic sense. Strategy is often about layers with the grand strategy more about what are we on this earth to do and what we want to get. Then at various intermediate levels one works towards that by being flexible and adjusting to shifting realities, means, resources and personalities.

GS: Is there a danger that people confuse tactics with strategy?

JC: That is the basic distinction in Army tutorials and I think a lot of low-level strategy is really tactics, but you can have tactical issues with very high-level strategic implications. In terms of the politics of the British Government, it matters to the extent that there are two sides to Parliament, leaving aside coalitions, which understand that, in the case of Northern Ireland, there is a common strategic objective, which there was certainly from the late 1980s on, and the tactics used to pursue it, along with what compromises and sacrifices might be deemed necessary. But I think there is a terrible risk in the modern age that, because the media track and record every phrase, for a minister in charge, or for advisers, there is the problem of being tied to every last syllable uttered. And this is a real problem because life isn't like that and one should not be hamstrung in that way.

GS: If one looks at the Anglo-Irish Agreement, the preamble is about historical continuity in the sense that the consent principle and the harmonisation or consultative roles are stressed. Given how much trouble this created for Faulkner at Sunningdale was this sorted out any further by the Agreement?

JC: It was two steps forward and one step back, because Margaret Thatcher felt that Garret FitzGerald had given her an undertaking that he was then neither in office nor in a position to fulfil, and that was the step back. But, in fact, the interaction between the two government machines was forward further than that. I do remember Irish secretary of government Dermot Nally being given a dinner in London with Robert Armstrong to do the honours, but he could not because of some crisis so I had to do it, and it became clear both in pre-dinner conversation and in words uttered around the table that we were in Kipling's terms 'in the jungle but of one tribe'. That is, we did not have the same positions on policy or national interest, but we did it the same way and trusted each other to do it the same way and that was hugely important, even if it had to be learned and re-learned.

GS: Can someone with a profound historical understanding get bogged down with that knowledge and not make decisions because of it?

JC: I think provided that there is enough collective grasp within the system, and challenge too for that matter, you can probably prevent that happening. There should not be a monopoly of wisdom or knowledge at the top of the system, and there should be room to create an atmosphere where it is possible to challenge. The risk otherwise is that you get to a conventional, almost status quo, position on your policy and objectives and stick there in the face of changing realities.

GS: If you get a catastrophic event, even in what you think is a reasonably coherent process, what does it do to the process?

JC: In the context of Northern Ireland, I think enormous credit to the British Government when the PIRA fired a mortar into the back garden of Number 10 and yet the process continued almost unswervingly. That is tremendous resilience, not a failure to respond. What it did lead to was Quentin Thomas and I drawing up the terms of a potential engagement with Sinn Féin/PIRA where everything was dependent moment by moment, meeting by meeting, on events on the ground. So the Canary Wharf bomb was an event on the ground, but we did not halt the process or change direction. You say that has cost you another six months or whatever.

GS: So control of a process such as the one we are talking about is very much about control of time?

JC: Time and the political cost of time passing. I think that by the mid-1990s Sinn Féin was finding increasing pressure coming from the nationalist community because they were the victims, they were the casualties and they did not have so much time to hang about. I also think there were forces at work within Sinn Féin/PIRA which meant that even Adams, McGuinness and Kelly and others would find it quite difficult just to wait another ten years.

GS: But bringing people into a process requires some fluidity. How good were Sinn Féin at using that fluidity?

JC: They had their own internal consultative processes, which we only knew a certain amount about, but they were very thorough and they were carefully maintained. It was a constant question, of course, and still is, of how Sinn Féin can continue to maintain authority, apart from the dissident fringes, and one way is the Ard Fheis, but they are also very sophisticated as a political culture. I do not say that the unionist community is not, but it does work at a different tempo.

GS: The republican narrative is constructed in terms of national unity, but if you look at the unionist narrative it is localised, regionalised. Does Northern Ireland need a messier, more ragged association with the Union to reflect a more fluid 'post-conflict' world?

JC: Bertie Ahern had just become taoiseach, or was just about to become taoiseach, and he gave me lunch and he said how he looked forward to the day when Ireland might be able to rejoin the Commonwealth, which does not imply the sovereignty of the British monarchy at all any more. There are lots of republics and people come in from outside, like Mozambique, and Ahern was saying how the Irish could do that. But what a sign of change that is. The other thing worth pointing out is the value of creating talking shops like the Council of the Islands. You might ask if these talking shops do anything or question what their relevance is, because people just talk and they are not too systematised and they do not have power and authority. But, in my view, you need as many of those as you can.

GS: Do you think there is a danger that the peace process might run out of process?

JC: A kind of 'carriage turns into a pumpkin at midnight' analogy? Well, I have a different concern, which is what happens when these extraordinary long-lived generations of Irish politicians all around the peace process eventually give way? Are there successors who can manage a power-sharing Executive and, if so, who are they? But, equally, is there any powerful driving force, and dissidents do not really come into this, of different perceived community interests, which might shatter the framework that was provided by the Belfast Agreement. That, it seems to me, is the most vital question now.

5 Resolving intercommunal conflict: some enabling factors

Sir Quentin Thomas

This chapter draws on ten years' experience (1988–98) working in Northern Ireland in pursuit of a political settlement, and considers this as one example of an intercommunal conflict or a dispute involving minorities within states. Are there in such cases identifiable preconditions, or predisposing factors, to the achievement of a settlement? Before addressing this issue substantively, there are one or two preliminary points to be made. First, my own position. I was the associate political director in the Northern Ireland Office (NIO) from 1988 to 1991, and thereafter political director until 1998. As such, I was responsible, with colleagues, including those in other departments (in particular in the Cabinet Office and the Foreign and Commonwealth Office (FCO)), and under the direction of two successive permanent secretaries (Sir John Chilcot, until 1997, and Sir Joseph Pilling, each of whom had previously supervised me in stints as political director) for advising ministers on political development, the scope for achieving a peaceful settlement and, in respect of Northern Ireland, for Anglo-Irish relations. I was extremely fortunate in the support, encouragement and guidance I received from John and Joe. In Whitehall, a key variable is whether, when you are in a hole, your superiors join in burying you or jump in, grab a spade and help to dig you out. John and Joe are both of the latter camp. Equally they, and indeed other close colleagues, were adept at spotting holes, however camouflaged, and avoiding them. More generally, my colleagues in the NIO over ten years were characterised by ability, commitment and collective purpose. I was very fortunate to work closely with David Cooke, David Hill and Chris Maccabe (who have chapters in this volume) and with Jonathan Stephens, but there are many others.

Secondly, this chapter is written from the perspective of a (former) British official and reflects that perspective. In practice, we worked closely with Irish officials, particularly those of the Anglo-Irish Division of the Department of Foreign Affairs whose perspective was inevitably and helpfully very different, at least in the early stages. The engagement with Irish officials, at times somewhat adversarial but increasingly in partnership, was both a challenge and a pleasure. For much of this time the head of the Anglo-Irish Division was Sean O'hUiginn, who, with great ability and charm, never failed to make us work hard for an agreement or to honour it once made.

Thirdly, it was the Northern Ireland parties who in the end drove this process and they who represented the people of Northern Ireland who took the strain of the conflict. It was a privilege serving as political director, most obviously at a time when round-table talks were under way, to work closely with politicians dealing with politics at its most raw yet potentially most creative.

Fourthly, officials in the NIO, because of its size and the nature of the work, see a great deal of ministers at close quarters and when dealing with intractable issues and challenging, and sometimes depressing, events. The scepticism of the age, agreeable though it is, means that the ability, commitment and courage of our leaders can be under-appreciated. For me, it was a privilege and pleasure to serve with Peter Brooke, who was instrumental in launching the process; Patrick Mayhew, who carried it forward for five long years; and Mo Mowlam, who skilfully steered it in the last year of my own involvement.

Fifthly, attempting, as this chapter does, to identify enabling features of a settlement might imply a judgement that a secure and enduring settlement has been achieved in Northern Ireland. It must be hoped that it has. But, as in the cliché about the possible success of the French Revolution, it is too early to tell. In any event, to draw on another cliché, achieving a settlement is not an event, but a process. Certainly, experience in Northern Ireland is consistent with this: the different building blocks to what may prove to be a durable set of arrangements have been put in place over at least two decades and, by some definitions, longer still. For example, even in the ten years with which this chapter is concerned some of the key developments were:

- establishing the basis for round-table talks held in 1991 and 1992;
- the Downing Street Declaration (DSD) (December 1993);
- the publication, by the British and Irish governments, of Frameworks for the Future, outlining a possible settlement (February 1995);
- the Report of the International Body on Decommissioning (the *Mitchell Report*, January 1996); and
- the Good Friday Agreement (GFA, 1998).

But there were, of course, earlier important elements, including the Sunningdale Agreement (SA) and the Anglo-Irish Agreement (AIA) (1985). And, while the GFA was a significant milestone, particularly when endorsed by referendum in the North and the South, it left, as other chapters in this volume bring out, much unfinished business.

Sixthly, one issue, considered below and elsewhere in this volume (e.g., David Cooke in Chapter 7), is the possible tension between the formal architecture of the successive rounds of talks in this period (1991–8) and the length of time over which a phased settlement must stretch. This meant that some of the subsequent important and difficult negotiations were governed by less formal mechanisms and, to some extent at least, bilateral exchanges displaced the multilateral model governing the process before the GFA.

Finally, while each conflict must be considered in its own terms, with its particular history and context, it is natural to attempt to make comparisons between them and draw out general lessons. This chapter covers, in the main, one phase of the pursuit of a settlement in respect to Northern Ireland. But it attempts also, by way of illustration, briefly to compare and contrast this with the prospects for a successful process in respect of the Israeli–Palestinian conflict.

Some features of intercommunal conflict

At heart such conflicts involve one or more groups within a state, actually or potentially, withholding consent to their inclusion in it, at least on the terms currently available. Many, perhaps most, contemporary armed conflicts involve, wholly or in substantial part, disputes of this kind, rather than war between sovereign states. Nonetheless, what one sovereign state perceives as an internal matter may be characterised differently by others. It may, indeed, lead to international conflict involving diplomatic action, sanctions or resort to arms. In practice, the two or more parties to intercommunal disputes within states may enjoy something close to parity (arguably, this was true of at least some of the parties to the various disputes at the time of the break-up of the former republic of Yugoslavia). But the more typical case involves one or more minorities within one sovereign state (like the Basques in Spain) or within several (like the Kurds, who have the misfortune to be minorities within Syria, Iraq, Turkey and Iran). It is also common that groups may simultaneously constitute minorities and majorities. The unionist community is a majority in Northern Ireland, but a minority on the island of Ireland and also, importantly, within the United Kingdom, as, of course are the nationalists. (A word of qualification is needed about the assertion that the unionist community constitutes a minority within the United Kingdom. It may be that a majority of the people of the United Kingdom support the maintenance of the Union between Great Britain and Northern Ireland, at least while that is supported by a majority of the people of Northern Ireland. That is uncertain, especially at a time when other aspects of the Union are in question. But even if that is so, it does not mean that there is an instinctive identification with the unionist community, with its distinct history, culture and preoccupations.) Biafra was founded to provide a political entity where the Ibo minority in Nigeria could form a majority, but within Biafra there were other minority groups. One result of this is that several, or all, of the parties to such disputes may seek to claim the privileges of victimhood, with its potential hardships, paranoias and morbid satisfactions (as well as other more positive features of distinct culture, history and tradition).

Despite this, there are typically incumbents, whose objective is to secure assent to the status quo, and challengers, who seek to depart from it. In many cases the incumbents exercise the constitutional power; they represent authority, while the challengers are dissidents, rebels, secessionists or insurgents. In Northern Ireland, the unionists, though not sovereign, comprised the authorities, at least until the imposition of direct rule. Thereafter, both sides within Northern Ireland were to some extent dispossessed. But, of course, the parties to the conflict included also two sovereign governments, in London and Dublin.

These conflicts typically

- involve differences, or perceived differences, in a mix of ethnic, racial, linguistic, religious or cultural characteristics;
- are of very long standing and are capable of persistence, despite sometimes lengthy periods of relative quiescence, are complex and difficult;
- involve contrasting versions of reality, and in particular contested historical narratives;
- involve moreover, often as a result of these varying historical accounts, different views of the legitimacy of the relevant sovereign state or states, and, therefore, differing views of what constitutes criminal behaviour and of the processes by which it is so defined;
- involve a profound sense of injustice, common to all parties (though obviously on different grounds), and carefully preserved records of past grievances and triumphs, real or symbolic, often accompanied by formal rituals of remembrance and celebration;
- provide at least some players with an incentive to perpetuate the conflict, for example, to sustain the player's political standing within his or her community;
- involve, almost always, conflicting territorial claims;
- are regarded by the parties to the dispute as exceptional, despite many features common to other disputes.

If these disputes typically involve incumbents, who may themselves constitute the relevant authorities, and challengers, it is worth considering the position of each of these separately. Incidentally, the characterisation of a party as an incumbent or challenger may itself be problematic. In respect of Northern Ireland, the unionists have arguably enjoyed some of the benefits of incumbency even after the imposition of direct rule, but probably few see it that way. Similarly, the Israelis have been conscious of, and anxious to emphasise, their victim status even long after many would consider that they have essentially won. But it is not suggested that the analysis here, and the division between incumbents and challengers, maps neatly on to the position in Northern Ireland. It does not (another point is the position of the Irish Government, which does not match neatly with either category). Nonetheless, the analysis may provide some suggestive and illuminating pointers.

The incumbents

The objective of the incumbents is to maintain the status quo and to avoid dissent. Where there is dissent, it must be neutralised, whether by repression, concession or some mixture of the two. Ideally, quiescence is turned to acquiescence. Where incumbents control the state, they have a range of tools at their disposal, including:
- suppression or control through policing, the armed forces and the intelligence agencies;
- adjusting the criminal law to criminalise and marginalise dissent;
- remedying grievances in the social, economic or cultural field to remove stimuli to dissent;
- making political concessions, such as granting or enhancing local autonomy (an important dimension is the extent to which territory is shared or partitioned);
- operating diplomatically to win international support for their view of the conflict and for their actions to bring it to an end.

Overall, the incumbents' objective is to make their victory secure by persuading the challengers, and their potential supporters internationally, that their cause is lost. In short, to deny the challengers belief in their eventual success.

The challengers

The objective of the challengers, naturally enough, is the opposite: to make clear that the strength of dissent is such that, as the cliché has it, the status quo is not an option. In a functioning democracy, this may be achieved peacefully by use of the electoral process. But, even in a democratic system, there is a risk that dissent manifested within the rules of the system will be misinterpreted as acquiescence to that system. Much depends on the size of the challenging minority, its character and its cohesiveness, which may in turn be a function, at least in part, of its geographical concentration. Where there is no democracy, and no effective means of registering dissent peacefully, dissent may be manifested in civil disobedience, crime (at least as defined by the incumbents) and violence, including terrorism. While media coverage of the conflict is significant for both sides, it is particularly important for the challengers. While all parties would prefer favourable coverage, even critical coverage, for example, following terrorist atrocities, has value to the challengers in demonstrating that the status quo is not stable. The challengers who resort to terrorism may, however, pay a significant price in terms of lost legitimacy, and establishing or maintaining legitimacy is an important objective of both sides. Securing coverage, domestically and internationally, is likely to be an important intermediate objective for the challengers. Among the objectives of the challengers are:

- maintaining the vigour and cohesion of their dissent;
- to this end, sustaining their grievances. If grievances are remedied, this must be ignored, downplayed or claimed as evidence of momentum towards eventual victory;
- creating new grievances, for example, by provoking the winners into obviously unjust and unjustifiable repressive action, thereby undercutting their own claims to legitimacy;
- creating disruption by any means available so as to undermine the status quo.

Differences between incumbents and challengers

At the risk of oversimplification, it may be worth bringing out some differences between incumbents and challengers. Incumbents, particularly those subject to the constraints of democracy or international opinion, need to demonstrate reasonableness, responsibility and lawfulness, or to show that any failures in this respect are the fault of the challengers' extremism. Challengers need not do so, or not all the time. Accordingly, unless suppression can be wholly successful (e.g., by extermination), which is difficult to ensure, the actions of the incumbents' police and security forces need to be restrained within some defensible set of rules and procedures (where, as is often the case, it is not, it may be serving the challengers' interests more than their own). The challengers, whose case is that their interests cannot be accommodated within the available rules, are much less restrained, at least in many circumstances. Incumbents may be happy to escape media coverage, but challengers typically seek publicity, even bad publicity, and while incumbents look for a comfortable life, reinforcing their victory, challengers thrive on discomfort both for their own community and for the opposition.

Preconditions to a settlement

Against this background, is it possible to identify some enabling conditions that are required for the achievement of a settlement of a dispute of this kind? Six such preconditions, or, at least, circumstances favourable to a settlement, may be considered.

First, continuation of the conflict imposes costs on all the main parties such as to constitute a significant incentive to find a settlement to bring it to an end.

Typically, the challengers in a conflict have an incentive to seek a settlement to improve their position. For example, where they are under occupation, or find themselves as citizens or at least occupants of a state whose legitimacy they do not accept, they seek remedies. In some cases, the incumbents have less incentive to seek a settlement, or at least one that involves new terms in which their privileged status as incumbents may be lost. But the conflict is likely to impose at least some costs: in maintaining order, repressing dissent and in resisting challenges to the legitimacy of the status quo, domestically and internationally. An important objective of the challengers is to sustain and increase the costs imposed by the conflict on the incumbents. Terrorism is one tool deployed for this purpose.

Secondly, none of the significant players believes that their best chance of securing their objectives lies in continuing the conflict.

Obviously, if a significant player believes, per contra, that his or her interests are best served by continuing the conflict, that is what he or she is likely to do, thereby posing an obvious threat to the prospects of securing or sustaining a settlement (for tactical reasons, a player may enter a settlement process, but not in good faith). If such a player, though significant (by definition), is isolated, it may be that the other players can successfully marginalise him or her. That is, transform that player from significant to insignificant by drawing his or her supporters behind the settlement process.

An important part of the preparation for a successful peace process will be to seek to undermine such beliefs. The challengers will seek to disabuse the incumbents of any idea that they can be reconciled to the status quo, while the incumbents will seek to deny the challengers the belief that they can succeed through continuing the conflict. As in all battles, and as in war, a crucial objective is to deny opponents belief in victory.

It is worth mentioning expressly one aspect of this. Unless outright victory is available, to one side or the other, the achievement of a lasting settlement is likely to require engagement in a process, and specifically dialogue between the 'incumbents' and the 'challengers'. But it does not follow that engaging in such dialogue is always and everywhere the right course of action, or that all the parties have an equal interest in doing so. Care is needed about the process itself and the terms on which it is established. For example, from the perspective of the incumbents, entering into dialogue at the wrong time or on the wrong terms may encourage the challengers' belief that victory is possible (perhaps with 'one last heave'). Similarly, from the challengers' perspective, entry into dialogue may give the impression, misleading or otherwise, that their will to maintain the conflict has been exhausted.

Thirdly, the grievances, or penalties, that underpin the conflict must be capable of remedy, at least to an acceptable level, in a peace process without so conflicting with other players' interests as to sustain the conflict or to create a new one.

This is something difficult to judge in advance, particularly as the parties are unlikely to disclose in advance (even if they know) the compromises they might be brought to accept. At the same time, if some sketch plan of a final settlement, however provisional, is available to the parties it may be highly conducive to initiating the settlement process – provided, of course, that it does meet the stipulated condition.

Fourthly, there must be some expectation by each party to the conflict that the other party or parties will, as part of the process, accept of themselves the prospective deal, or can be brought to do so. For example, by external pressure or by shifts in the views of their own supporters.

This can be another real difficulty. For one thing, each party is likely to maintain its bargaining position by stating its demands in maximalist terms. In the process leading up to the GFA in Northern Ireland, all the parties tended to withhold compromise on the ground that tough and experienced negotiators, as they believed themselves to be, would await the endgame. The process would, in their favoured phrase, 'go down to the wire'. In the end, senator Mitchell, who was chairing the talks, provided the wire by emphasising that the process really would end, as the legislation stipulated, by Easter 1998. This determination to await the wire had the unfortunate result that there was very little time to address and resolve a number of difficult substantive issues.

Another difficulty is that typically in such conflicts leaders, wisely and necessarily, devote much attention to their own supporters, to ensure their continued cohesion, for example. They cannot afford to be seen to be too preoccupied with the need, real though it may be, to give their adversaries in the conflict reassurance that they will be dealing in good faith and seeking the compromises on which a deal will depend (one factor exacerbating this is that, as the process approaches a settlement, the greatest tensions may occur within the respective communities. In the Northern Ireland case, for example, between Dr Paisley's Democratic Unionist Party (DUP) and Mr Trimble's Ulster Unionist Party (UUP), or within the republican movement with potential splintering away of the ultras). However, in Northern Ireland it was striking that many of those involved in the parties, despite (or because of) the length and bitterness of the conflict, were able to take a broad and imaginative view of the issues and of the interests of the community as a whole. In the case of John Hume and David Trimble, this was recognised by the award of the Nobel Peace Prize. But each of the parties included leaders who could look beyond their narrow interests.

Fifthly, there must be a process, involving all the main players, and enjoying their confidence, to manage the negotiation of a settlement and its implementation.

Precisely because conflicts of this kind are long-standing, complex and difficult, they are unlikely to be resolved speedily or at a single sitting. A process is required and, if it is to have a successful outcome, the main participants must have confidence in it. This means, almost inevitably, that much time and trouble have to be taken over procedural issues: rights of attendance, agendas, shape of table, location of talks, mechanisms for registering agreement and schemes for implementation.

Sixthly, the main external stakeholders, or interested parties, should be ready to support a settlement or could be brought to do so.

It seems clear that, in many cases, the active support and encouragement of outside supporters or sponsors of the internal parties to a conflict can be crucial in bringing about, and carrying forward, a settlement process; and in ensuring its implementation. The opposite is also true. In many cases, the external support or sponsorship of one or more parties to conflicts of this kind is significant and, indeed, in some cases some, or all, of the parties may not be able to continue in any active way without this. Similarly, external support may lead players to believe that their objectives may be best secured through continuation of the conflict (see second precondition above).

Northern Ireland: were these preconditions met?

It is worth considering briefly how far these conditions were satisfied in the case of Northern Ireland. It is probably not necessary to labour the first point: namely, that continuation of the conflict imposed considerable costs on all the parties. Both sides of the community in Northern Ireland suffered directly, and in a variety of ways. Those engaged in terrorism on both sides suffered hardship, danger, and the risk of capture and imprisonment. The British Government had to carry additional costs, a commitment of scarce military (and intelligence) personnel, civil disorder in Northern Ireland and a terrorist challenge there, in the rest of the United Kingdom and, indeed at times, abroad. There was also a diplomatic penalty. The Irish Republic and its government had incentives to settle the issue. Apart from various costs, including diplomatic costs, and its vulnerability to terrorism, the issue, striking as it did at the heart of its national ideology, constituted an obstacle to the widespread wish to normalise relations with the United Kingdom and to move on. Moreover, the republican movement, with its claim to be the true embodiment of that national ideology, and its rejection of the terms on which the state was founded, posed a direct subversive challenge to it and its institutions of a kind quite different from, and more serious than, that posed to the United Kingdom.

The second point, though it was far from obvious at the time, and remains in dispute, was that perhaps none of the main players believed that their objectives would be achieved by continuing the conflict (that does not mean that some parties, including the Provisional IRA (PIRA), had abandoned the view that violence, and the threat of violence, remained important to enhance their bargaining position). There may have been a time when the authorities, the British Government or before it the Stormont administration, had believed that the conflict could be resolved by military or policing means alone. If so, that time had passed. The British Government, like that in Dublin, sought a political settlement to bring matters to an end. The unionists and the constitutional nationalists were both ready, as events proved, to make compromises (of the kind in some cases rejected a few years earlier) to end the conflict. Loyalist terrorism was lethally dangerous, though it was largely reactive, specifically to republican terrorism (though not all the associated criminality was or is). Potentially it was (and conceivably is) reactive in addition to any perception of British betrayal.

The key question was whether the republican terrorists, and in particular the PIRA, continued to believe that their campaign could succeed. It was the singular success of the security forces and the intelligence community, coupled with the robust position taken by the main political parties in the United Kingdom, to deny the republicans belief in their prospective victory. There were, of course, other factors, including John Hume's patient efforts to challenge republican ideology on its own terms, getting Adams, initially, to see that the real obstacle was not the British Government, which no longer had a selfish strategic or economic interest in retaining Northern Ireland in the United Kingdom, but the million odd fellow Irishmen who did not want to join a united Ireland.

Thirdly, was there a deal available that was acceptable to all parties? With hindsight it seems that there was: more or less and keeping our fingers crossed. Those of us working on the process believed this in advance, partly as a matter of professional optimism and partly out of conviction stemming from analysis of the parties' positions, a conviction strengthened as our limited experience of round-table talks grew. But there were, of course, many sceptics, and the press regularly pronounced the process 'dead in the water'.

If the third condition was whether there was, as a matter of fact, a deal available, the fourth, closely linked, condition was whether the expectations of the parties of each other were consistent with this. It is on these two points that the British Government alone and the two governments (British and Irish) together, increasingly acting as partners, played an active part. Efforts were made, in round-table talks and separately, to identify and, equally important, to promulgate sketch plans of a possible settlement. If the apparent common ground, or zones of convergence, carried conviction, this could provide reassurance to potential participants to join the process, and an incentive to do so to influence the precise outcome. It would also condition expectations and remove the scope for surprise, although, since the process was inherently one of bargaining, it could not preclude rhetorical and histrionic expostulations at various points in the process.

This may be illustrated by reference to the constitutional position of Northern Ireland: what was its position now and how should its future be determined?

The British Government's position was that Northern Ireland was, *de facto* and *de jure*, an integral part of the United Kingdom, but that it could in future become part of a united Ireland if, but only if, that was the wish of a majority of its people. This was termed the 'consent principle'. The Irish position was set out in its constitution, Articles 2 and 3 of which asserted a claim to the island as a whole, and the Irish Supreme Court deemed this to amount to a 'constitutional imperative' on the government to pursue a united Ireland.

The two governments' first attempt to set out a formal position on this designed to help a settlement was in the AIA in 1985. It was a failure. Article 3 stated that: 'The two governments (a) affirm that any change in the status of Northern Ireland would only come about with the consent of a majority of the people of Northern Ireland', but this was instantly correctly decoded by the unionists as a statement of political reality, rather than as a declaration of a principle. They were right about this. It had been drafted that way precisely to avoid the need to amend the Irish Constitution. But that is what needed to be amended if the unionists were to be brought on board.

The next attempt was in the DSD (or Joint Declaration) of 15 December 1993. This stated, in the mouth of the taoiseach:

For this reason, it would be wrong to attempt to impose a united Ireland, in the absence of the freely given consent of a majority of the people of Northern Ireland. He accepts, on behalf of the Irish Government, that the democratic right of self-determination by the people of Ireland as a whole must be achieved and exercised with and subject to the agreement and consent of a majority of the people of Northern Ireland and must, consistent with justice and equity, respect the democratic dignity and the civil rights and religious liberties of both communities, including ...

Similarly, on the British side: 'The Prime Minister, on behalf of the British Government, reaffirms that they will uphold the democratic wish of a greater number of the people of Northern Ireland on the issue of whether they prefer to support the Union or a sovereign united Ireland.'

In February 1995, the two governments set out, in Frameworks for the Future, a sketch plan of what a comprehensive settlement might look like; the part dealing with the internal administration of Northern Ireland being the work of the British Government alone. This joint document included a more forward account of the constitutional position, such as in Part Two, paragraph 21, which stated:

As part of an agreement confirming the foregoing understanding between the two Governments on constitutional issues, the Irish Government will introduce and support proposals for change in the Irish Constitution to implement the commitments in the Joint Declaration [the DSD]. These changes in the Irish Constitution will fully reflect the principle of consent in Northern Ireland and demonstrably be such that no territorial claim of right to jurisdiction over Northern Ireland contrary to the will of a majority of its people is asserted, while maintaining the existing birthright of everyone born in either jurisdiction in Ireland to be part, as of right, of the Irish nation. They will enable a new Agreement to be ratified which will include, as part of a new and equitable dispensation for Northern Ireland, embodying the principles and commitments in the Joint Declaration and this Framework Document, recognition by both Governments of the legitimacy of whatever choice is freely exercised by a majority of the people of Northern Ireland with regard to its constitutional status, whether they prefer to continue to support the Union or a sovereign united Ireland.

In effect this settled the issue. While it had been a key issue in the 1991 round of talks, and had dominated those in 1992, particularly those held in Dublin, it was scarcely mentioned in the 1996–8 talks, which culminated in the GFA. That Agreement, of course, included provisions concerning the constitutional issue, including a proposed amendment to the Irish Constitution, consistent with the 1995 Framework Document.

Paragraph 1 (section iii) of the GFA states that the participants endorse the commitments made by the two governments that in a new agreement they will:

acknowledge that while a substantial section of the people in Northern Ireland share the legitimate wish of a majority of the people of the island of Ireland for a united Ireland, the present wish of a majority of the people of Northern Ireland, freely exercised and legitimate, is to maintain the union and, accordingly, that Northern Ireland's status as part of the United Kingdom reflects and relies upon that wish; and that it would be wrong to make any change in the status of Northern Ireland save with the consent of a majority of its people.

In effect, this recognises the legitimacy of partition. This set of provisions, though now endorsed by the people of Ireland, North and South, through referenda, provides both opportunity and potential difficulty. This is because it leaves the position of Northern Ireland as contingent, depending as it does in particular on the views of a majority of the people of Northern Ireland, which may change.

As to the fifth precondition, the need for a process, this, and the attendant procedural issues, were a major preoccupation at each step in the period (1989–98) under consideration. The round-table talks convened by Peter Brooke in 1991, after months of haggling mostly about procedural issues, were themselves dominated by procedural questions. However, this bore fruit in the second round, in 1992, when Patrick Mayhew was Northern Ireland secretary, as many of the procedures agreed, such as having an independent chair for North–South issues, were acted on. Similarly, when, following an election to select the participants, the 1996–8 talks were launched under senator Mitchell's chairmanship, the first lengthy sessions were devoted to agreeing rules of procedure. The process indeed came to have something of an existence and personality of its own. The communities in Britain and in Ireland began to invest hopes and expectations in it. There were periods when little happened in the process;

and hopes mainly depended on the reluctance of any player to accept the blame for having brought it to an end. A little more is said about this process later.

As to the sixth precondition and the readiness of external sponsors to support a settlement, it was striking that those concerned in the EU, the US and in other Anglophone countries with a significant Irish, and British, diaspora were actively interested in and supportive of the pursuit of a settlement on the right terms. This was reflected in the composition of the International Independent Commission on Decommissioning (IICD), under senator Mitchell, and the independent chairs of the 1996–8 talks: comprising distinguished representatives from the US, Canada and Finland.

Preconditions and other conflicts

Perhaps it is worth considering briefly how far the preconditions suggested above apply to other conflicts, and, more specifically, in the case of the Israeli–Palestinian dispute. First, it seems clear that the continuation of the conflict imposes very considerable costs on the Palestinians. It also imposes costs on the Israelis, though it is arguable that they are tolerable, given the rewards of victory, particularly since the construction of the security barrier has reduced suicide attacks markedly. The incentives to seek a settlement are arguably uneven or asymmetric.

Secondly, there are major players on both sides who probably judge that their best hope of securing their objectives lies in continuing the conflict. And it is not clear that an outsider would be justified in telling them that they are wrong. The considerable gains made by the zionists, and subsequently by the Israeli state, depend in substantial part on the deployment of military force, including in the early days in the form of terrorism. Similarly, some Palestinians, including most obviously Hamas and Islamic Jihad, clearly believe that they can secure acceptable terms only by continuing the conflict.

Thirdly, there must be serious doubts whether a generally acceptable settlement is available in present circumstances. There was probably some chance of this some time after 1967 when Israel's military success led to the adjustment of Palestinian expectations to the point where they might have accepted the return of the Occupied Territories, including East Jerusalem, even though these constitute only a fraction of historic Palestine. But the facts on the ground deliberately created by the Israelis, in the form of settlements (under governments of all shades), have probably succeeded in making an agreement on these lines impossible. Even if one were to posit an Israeli Government ready to hand over the Occupied Territories, how could it bring this about in the face of predictable resistance from some 400,000 of its citizens now occupying those settlements?

Fourthly, there are important players on both sides who have no expectation that the other side will agree to a settlement on terms they would find acceptable. Again, one has to say these pessimistic expectations seem fully justified.

Fifthly, for some years there has not been a process with any credibility or in which the key players have confidence. And sixthly, it seems clear that at least some of the external sponsors of the conflict, such as Iran, remain ready to encourage their clients to continue the struggle. Indeed, it is significant that none of the proposed mechanisms for advancing a settlement includes all the external sponsors.

The importance of process

As mentioned above, one feature of the efforts to secure a settlement in Northern Ireland in the period 1990–8 was the emphasis on a clearly defined process. When Peter Brooke was appointed secretary of state for Northern Ireland in 1989 he made it clear that he would devote considerable effort to the pursuit of a political settlement. It became apparent that a process would be required not merely as an enabling factor, as it is termed above, but as an essential prerequisite if the other potential participants were to join in. This partly reflected experience of earlier attempts at political progress, and the perception that a process established on the wrong footing could be worse than none at all. Accordingly, considerable reassurance was needed about the format, the agenda or scope of the exercise, the involvement of others and on what terms. The unionists also had a particular difficulty, namely, a refusal to enter a process while the AIA and the institutions established under it, in particular the Intergovernmental Conference and the Maryfield Secretariat, remained fully operational, while the British and Irish governments were anxious not to compromise the Agreement, something to which other parties would in any case have objected. It became apparent that a minimum requirement would be a text establishing some basic ground rules for the process and its procedures. This led to a succession of exchanges between the two governments and the parties to develop a text that would meet with general acceptance. This might be termed, accurately if pompously, an iterative process of successive approximation, with text that was in dispute or at least not yet accepted in square brackets. Although the outcome took the form of a statement by Peter Brooke to the House of Commons on 26 March 1991, the text was in effect one agreed among the potential participants in the talks convened soon afterwards (the text of the statement is given in the Appendix below).

This experience led to what became the dominant mode of this phase of the process (i.e., 1990–8, and possibly beyond). A text would be tabled and negotiations would be framed around attempts to refine it to the point where it could command general assent. In some cases, the initial draft might be tabled

Resolving intercommunal conflict

by one government or party or, later on, by an independent chair. In other cases, the draft might itself be an attempted composite, drawing on papers tabled by each of the other participants. For example, early on in the Strand 1 talks in 1991 (and those talks did not progress beyond Strand 1, dealing with relationships within Northern Ireland) each party tabled a draft agenda, naturally reflecting what issues they saw as important, but also the order in which they should be approached. This was followed by an attempted composite tabled by the British Government acting as secretariat and that text became a basis for negotiation.

The technique of 'single text negotiation', perhaps well known to some participants, thus came to be devised, or reinvented organically, collectively in the process itself. It proved to be extremely valuable and, as a generalisation, it might be said that where there was no text in play, lengthy oral exchanges would have little discernible outcome. In contrast, where there was a text there would almost always be an agreed product, though it might take much time and labour to achieve. Moreover, the agreed text resulting from such a collective negotiation always commanded respect subsequently in the process, even if its provisions were not always precisely adhered to.

Among the points made in the statement were:
- following extensive discussions with the main constitutional parties in Northern Ireland and with the Irish Government a formal basis for political talks existed;
- the two governments would be prepared to consider a new and more broadly based agreement (by implication in place of the 1985 AIA) if it could be arrived at through direct discussion and negotiation between all the parties concerned;
- to allow for an opportunity for such dialogue there would be a gap in meetings of the Anglo-Irish Conference, and during that period the Maryfield Secretariat would not accordingly be required to service conference meetings;
- the talks would take place in three strands reflecting the three key relationships; arrangements would be needed for liaison between the strands;
- all the parties would participate actively and directly in the North–South discussions, the unionists regarding themselves as members of the UK team;
- all accepted that all three strands should be launched within weeks of each other;
- there would be an open agenda in that any party could raise any issue it considered relevant; and
- 'It is accepted by all the parties that nothing will be finally agreed in any strand until everything is agreed in the talks as a whole and that confidentially will be maintained thereunto. However, in the final analysis the outcome will need to be acceptable to the people.'

Some features of these arrangements proved to be durable or provided the basis for a more developed position later on, such as the idea of an open agenda and the hint of the need to test any outcome in a referendum. Others, such as the wish of the unionist parties to regard themselves as part of the UK delegation, reflected a more temporary preoccupation. The requirement for a gap in Conference meetings was important in this round of talks and in the subsequent 1992 round. Indeed, the talks were ended by meetings of the Conference. But it did not figure much thereafter. The agreement for confidentiality was honoured more in the breach than in the observance. The rule that nothing would be finally agreed until everything was agreed implied, but did not state, that unanimity would be required. Since no final agreement was reached in the talks conducted under these rules the matter was not put to the test. In any event, an important feature of the rules of procedure drawn up for and during the 1996–8 talks held under the independent chairmanship of senator Mitchell and his colleagues made it clear that 'sufficient consensus' (as defined) was required, not unanimity.

The threat of violence and its leverage

One difficult, if unavoidable, issue concerned the implied threat of violence. The hope was that the achievement of a settlement would bring violence to an end, but how should this be achieved? An apparent aim of the AIA, perhaps most explicitly stated by the then taoiseach Dr Garret FitzGerald, was that it would marginalise Sinn Féin and demonstrate the progress that could be achieved by constitutional nationalists relying solely on peaceful methods. At some point, perhaps in the early 1990s, each of the two governments, initially separately, apparently came to the same view, which was that Sinn Féin would not be marginalised and that the better and more effective approach was to attempt to recruit them to an inclusive process, but on the basis that violence or its threat would be renounced. Underpinning this was the view that the democratic process was robust enough to accommodate a very wide range of political beliefs and objectives, provided they were advanced only by democratic and peaceful means. Accordingly, the formal position adopted by the two governments, and expressed most fully in the *Mitchell Principles*, was that a necessary precondition to joining, or remaining within, the formal talks process was a commitment to democratic and peaceful means.

Against that background, it was unsurprising, and perhaps inevitable, that the other participants would, in the process, seek reassurance from those with apparent connections to and/or influence over those with some paramilitary capability that this would be or had been brought to an end. The issue of 'decommissioning' of paramilitary weapons, and the matching demands for 'demilitarisation' from the security forces, came to dominate the 1996–8 talks, and thereafter. Indeed, the issue came close to providing a logjam. All sides were in difficulty. The existence of paramilitary capability meant that the participants had asymmetric influence: literally, an inequality of arms. Despite the formal requirement that violence, or the threat of violence, should have been renounced, the reality was of a process of transition, the completion of which would depend, to some extent at least, on the political outcome of the process. There was, in short, a tension between a 'static' analysis, whereby renunciation of force (and, by extension, weapons) was a requirement for entry into the process, and a 'dynamic' analysis, whereby a process of transition was involved which other participants could obstruct or encourage. And while all participants would be 'in transition' to some extent as they prepared to accommodate to the putative settlement, that process of transition was arguably more difficult, conspicuous and more necessary in the case of those parties that had, or had previously, 'paramilitary credibility'. But if, as seemed to be the case, the achievement of a political outcome depended on the perceived and authenticated abandonment of violence or its implied threat, then the risk was that the focus on this issue, which, to some extent, led to extensive bilateral exchanges in which the parties lacking paramilitary credentials played little part, gave disproportionate leverage to those whose commitment to constitutional and democratic procedures was less well established or accepted.

There is no easy answer to the difficulties of principle and practice this issue poses. It could be argued that it was better managed in a process, such as the talks chaired by senator Mitchell and his colleagues (1996–8), which culminated in the GFA, because it was independently managed, there were clear and accepted rules of procedure (including the requirement for sufficient consensus, which needed majority support from representatives of both sides of the community), and a transparent multilateral engagement. This meant that those who lacked 'paramilitary credibility' were nonetheless fully involved in the process. At the same time, it must be acknowledged that this process did not succeed in resolving the 'decommissioning' issue, and perhaps could not have done so. It is arguable, as other contributions to this volume bring out, that less formal exchanges, many on a bilateral basis, were needed for this.

Perhaps I could offer a tentative conclusion. Some of the necessary preconditions to a settlement can be identified with some confidence in advance. Much may need to be done before those conditions can be met. For example, it may take a lengthy campaign of counter-insurgency, or police action, before the challengers can be persuaded that they have no chance of victory by military means. Or it may take a prolonged campaign of terrorism and/or civil disobedience before the incumbents and those in authority accept that some new arrangements have to be made to reconcile the dissidents. But, unless the ground is prepared in this way, the quick fix of round-table talks is unlikely to succeed, even assuming the relevant people will attend at all, and may well make matters worse or, at least, prolong the conflict, for example, by exacerbating grievances or providing renewed hope to one side or the other that 'victory' is after all at hand.

Appendix

26 March 1991

NORTHERN IRELAND (Political Talks)

Mr Speaker: Before the Secretary of State starts, may I ask honourable Members who are not remaining for this important statement to leave quietly and without conversation?

3.30 pm

The Secretary of State for Northern Ireland (Mr Peter Brooke): With permission, Mr Speaker, I will make a statement about political development in Northern Ireland.

I am pleased to be able to inform the House that, following the extensive discussions with the main constitutional parties in Northern Ireland – the Alliance Party of Northern Ireland, the Social Democratic and Labour Party, the Ulster Democratic Unionist Party and the Ulster Unionist Party – and with the Irish Government, a basis for formal political talks now exists. I frankly acknowledge to the House that this would not have been possible without the good will and determination of the Northern Ireland parties and the helpful and constructive approach taken by the Irish Government. The stated positions of all these parties are well known. Her Majesty's Government reaffirms their position that Northern Ireland's present status as a part of the United Kingdom will not change without the consent of a majority of its people.

The endeavour on which we have all agreed to embark is an ambitious one. We are setting out to achieve a new beginning for relationships within Northern Ireland, within the island of Ireland and between the peoples of these islands. While a successful outcome cannot be guaranteed in advance, I am confident that all the potential participants are committed to a forward-looking and constructive approach. For their part, the two signatories of the Anglo-Irish Agreement – the British and Irish Governments – have made it clear that they would be prepared to consider a new and more broadly based agreement or structure if such an agreement can be arrived at through direct discussion and negotiation between all the parties concerned.

To allow an opportunity for such a wider political dialogue, the two Governments have agreed not to hold a meeting of the Anglo-Irish Conference between two pre-specified dates. All the parties concerned will make use of this interval for intensive discussions to seek the new and more broadly based agreement which I have just described.

As the conference will not be meeting between the specified dates the Secretariat at Maryfield will accordingly not be required for that period to discharge its normal role of servicing conference meetings provided for in Article 3 of the Agreement.

It is accepted that discussions must focus on three main relationships: those within Northern Ireland, including the relationship between any new institutions there and the Westminster Parliament; among the people of the island of Ireland; and between the two Governments. It is common ground between all the parties that hope of achieving a new and more broadly based agreement rests on finding a way to give adequate expression to the totality of the relationships I have mentioned.

Talks will accordingly take place in three strands corresponding respectively to the three relationships. Some arrangements will be needed for liaison between the different strands of these complex discussions. The Unionist parties have made it clear that they wish their participation in those talks to be formally associated with my presence and that they will regard themselves as members of the United Kingdom team. It is accepted by all those involved that, to make full use of the interval between meetings of the conference to achieve an overall agreement satisfactory to all, it will be necessary to have launched all three sets of discussions within weeks of each other.

A first step towards getting related discussions under way in all three strands will be the opening, as soon as possible, of substantive talks between the parties in Northern Ireland under my chairmanship. These will commence with a round of bilateral meetings before moving on, as soon as possible, into plenary sessions. It has been agreed by all the participants that before long, when, after consultation, I judge that an appropriate point has been reached, I will propose formally that the other two strands should be launched. My judgement as to timing will be governed by the fact that all involved have agreed that the three sets of discussions will be under way within weeks of each other.

The internal talks, like the talks in the other strands, will follow a demanding and intensive schedule. In order to ensure a full airing of the issues, it will be open to each of the parties to raise any aspect of these relationships, including constitutional issues, or any other matter which it considers relevant. All concerned have assured me that they will participate in good faith and will make every effort to achieve progress.

It is accepted by all the parties that nothing will be finally agreed in any strand until everything is agreed in the talks as a whole and that confidentiality will be maintained thereunto. However, in the final analysis, the outcome will need to be acceptable to the people.

6 Tactics, strategy and space

Chris Maccabe

In this chapter I will examine some of the practical steps that were taken to promote and consolidate the British and Irish governments' shared objective of inclusiveness in the Northern Ireland political/peace process. I will do so from the perspective of someone who was personally involved in many of the more obscure aspects of the search to find a viable accommodation. At the beginning of that phase, 1990–2, persuading the 'constitutional' parties to engage with each other and the two governments was paramount. That persuasion included dialogue between ministers, officials and members of those parties, particularly the unionist parties, ranging from grass-roots supporters, party officers and district councillors to MPs and other senior figures. It also involved dialogue with non-political 'opinion formers', such as church, business and trades union leaders, and community activists. There was no general understanding that ultimately a comprehensive, durable settlement would be achieved only with the participation of the political representatives of militant republicanism – (principally Sinn Féin) – and militant loyalism – principally the Progressive Unionist Party (PUP) and the Ulster Democratic Party (UDP) – but as events unfolded that would change. I will look at how the consequences of the changed circumstances were addressed so that following paramilitary ceasefires those groups were able to join the process as equal partners, before considering how dialogue with associates of the residual (and small but dangerous) republican and loyalist paramilitary groups that had not been present at the talks was established and maintained after the Belfast Agreement in 1998 and consequent devolution. And how the representatives of the PUP and the UDP, who had garnered little electoral advantage in the resultant elections, were encouraged to develop mechanisms and strategies that would allow them to put their creativity and energy at the disposal of their communities.

Growing up in Northern Ireland during the late 1950s and early 1960s, I was vaguely aware that local politics had a nasty side. But to a liberal Protestant, middle-class, urban family like mine, the 1956–62 border campaign of the Irish Republican Army (IRA) – Operation Harvest – had seemed remote and ineffectual, while the antics of a few headstrong unionists, such as the emerging Revd Ian Paisley and his enthusiastic supporters, were nothing more than a mild distraction. Later, in the autumn of 1964, when as a schoolboy I witnessed what came to be known as the Divis Street Riots – three days of running battles between West Belfast Catholics and members of the Royal Ulster Constabulary (RUC) following the forcible removal by the RUC of an Irish tricolour from the premises of an independent republican candidate during a Westminster general election campaign – I began to reflect on some of the rudiments underpinning my cultural birthright. The police, fearing a breach of the peace, had acted after Ian Paisley had threatened to remove the flag himself. That reflection was given renewed impetus two years later, the fiftieth anniversary of the Easter Rising, when a sinister loyalist terrorist group – the Ulster Volunteer Force (UVF) – appeared on the scene with a spate of sectarian attacks, including three murders.

Despite my revulsion at that lethal behaviour by some of my co-religionists, it was another two years before I was able to do much about it. By then I was a student at Queen's University in Belfast, and the civil rights campaign that had begun in Northern Ireland in August 1967 was gaining momentum. I was in general agreement with the campaign's objectives, and following the authorities' controversial, and ultimately violent, response to a civil rights march in Londonderry on 5 October 1968, I joined hundreds of Catholic students, and a substantial number of Protestant students, on two similar marches from the university campus to Belfast city centre in the days that followed. Both were blocked by the police. After that, as the situation deteriorated and the number of violent incidents increased, my appetite for street politics rapidly waned. But now my conviction, as Bob Dylan would have it, that in Northern Ireland, as in the United States, it was a case of 'the times they are a-changin' and that, somehow, I should be a part of that change.

In December 1973, after a spell as a researcher in the Northern Ireland Cabinet Office and its 'temporary' replacement, the Northern Ireland Office (NIO), I was delighted to learn I was to be assistant private secretary to the first chief minister of Northern Ireland, Brian Faulkner, leader of the Ulster Unionist Party (UUP). In my previous post I had been involved in aspects of the process that led to the Sunningdale Agreement earlier that month and Faulkner's appointment shortly afterwards as head of Northern Ireland's first power-sharing administration, one with a substantial Irish dimension. He would be working in harness with his old adversary, Gerry Fitt, leader of the Social Democratic and Labour Party (SDLP), who became deputy chief minister. Although the administration and associated assembly were short-lived, foundering in circumstances that are beyond the scope of this chapter, their very existence, and the cross-party goodwill I saw at first hand, showed me how a Northern Ireland at peace with itself, and equally important, at peace and in harmony with its southern neighbour, could move beyond the bounds of the sectarianism and bigotry that had blighted its first half century.

Fast forward almost two decades to December 1991. It was my fourth year as the director of regimes in the Northern Ireland Prison Service, with a remit that included the introduction of innovative policies for the treatment of prisoners and their families, life sentence reviews, and medical and chaplaincy services. The prison population was more than 3,000, spread across five establishments, and the majority of prisoners had been convicted of terrorist offences. The republican hunger strike of 1981, when ten prisoners died, still cast a long shadow over the prison system and there was a determination that it must never be repeated. I was encouraged to develop schemes to let long-serving prisoners go home for Christmas and other family occasions, enhanced family visiting facilities, in-cell televisions and telephone access. In fulfilling my remit, I had the direction and support of the imaginative controller of prisons John Steele, and above him secretary of state Peter Brooke and his ministerial team. If an issue was particularly sensitive, prime minister Margaret Thatcher's personal approval would be sought.

While the bureaucratic aspects of those reforms were being sorted out, I made it my business to canvass the views of the paramilitary prisoners, taking regular trips 'down the blocks' to chat with individuals and their 'commanders' over a cup of tea or coffee. On the outside, I met prisoners' families, including the parents, spouses and sisters of some life-sentence prisoners, and kept in touch with other interests such as the churches (particularly the Quakers who have played a significant humanitarian role in Irish affairs for more than 150 years, and the Methodists), the Northern Ireland Association for the Care and Resettlement of Offenders, and the International Committee of the Red Cross.

Although I was used to fairly regular career moves, the pre-Christmas 1991 phone call from the NIO's personnel director came as a bit of a surprise. It had just been announced that John Steele would be moving on early in the New Year, and I had assumed that I would remain in the Prison Service well beyond the appointment of his successor to provide some continuity. But it was not to be. I was to return to the NIO as head of the Political Affairs Division in Belfast. The Political Affairs Division, or PAB as it was more affectionately known (Political Affairs Belfast), had its roots in the turbulent summer of 1969 when the British Army was deployed on the streets of Northern Ireland 'in aid of the civil power' for the first time in more than thirty years. In August of that year, the government sent a senior member of the Diplomatic Service to Belfast to provide a hands-on resource. The primary job of the UK Representative, the diplomat's official title, was to establish good working relationships with key figures throughout Northern Ireland, especially those from a Catholic background, sharing ideas and information and reporting what he heard to London. When direct rule was introduced in March 1972, the UK Representative and his team were subsumed into the newly created NIO, reporting to the first secretary of state for Northern Ireland William Whitelaw.

Tactics, strategy and space

I was very pleased with my new appointment in 1991. I would be arriving at an auspicious time: the secretary of state had just outlined a fresh set of proposals hoping that they would breathe life back into the political negotiations – talks about talks – that had been suspended since July. Having been around the NIO since its inception, I was familiar with the scope of PAB's responsibilities and its role in keeping ministers in touch with the political temperature. I was sure the political and other contacts I had made during the previous twenty years would be invaluable. Although the head of PAB had not been a diplomat for some time, and both my immediate predecessors had been locals, I was the first person from a Protestant/unionist background in the post. I was also pleased that my deputies would be two of the department's finest, Ken Lindsay and Peter May. Ken, who had worked with me before in several sensitive areas, was a wise and shrewd Belfast man with extensive links in the community. Peter was an English high-flier with an impressive intellect.

In the week before taking up my new duties, I divided my time between handing over to my successor in the Prison Service and finding out as much as I could about the current political situation. As I drove off from Prison Service headquarters for the last time on Friday 17 January 1992, I was in high spirits. It wasn't that I had not enjoyed the last three years, for I certainly had, but I was relishing the prospect of getting close to the political action again. The car radio was on and I was not unduly concerned when a news flash interrupted the programme: 'We're receiving reports of an explosion in the Teebane area of County Tyrone. Further information will follow as soon as we have it.' During the Troubles such dramatic interruptions were commonplace and did not always turn out badly. Unfortunately, when I got home I discovered that the bulletin was one of the exceptions. A huge bomb had exploded by the roadside as a van carrying construction workers home from an Army base was passing. Eight men, all Protestants, had been killed and several others had been seriously injured. It was a tragic reminder of the lethal nature of Irish politics and the overwhelming need for closure.

When I arrived in my new office in Stormont House on Monday morning the atmosphere was understandably gloomy. But as the day progressed I began to focus on the job ahead. My predecessor, Danny McNeill, was a mine of information and, like Ken and Peter, had drawn up a list of people to whom I should present my credentials, as it were. Later I had meetings with my line manager, Quentin Thomas, and David Fell, the head of the Northern Ireland Civil Service and an old friend. The next day it was the secretary of state and Brian Mawhinney, minister of state in charge of political development. In every case, I was left in no doubt about the relevance of my job: I must get out there, work my contacts, providing them with explanations and reassurance where I could, then analysing what I had learned and reporting back. Although people associated with the political parties would be my main interest,

I should cast my net much wider, drawing in 'influencers' of all kinds, including some academics. Generally, I would be free to use my discretion when discussing what the government might or might not have in mind, but on some occasions I would be given precise instructions about what I should say and to whom. It was clear that if things were ever to move forward the political classes, especially the unionist political classes, would need a lot of encouragement, support and, sometimes, a little cajoling. And while I was precluded from dealing with members of proscribed organisations as such – which in 1992 included not only the Provisional IRA (PIRA) and other republican and loyalist paramilitary groups, but the PIRA's political wing, Sinn Féin – I was encouraged to cultivate 'associates' of those groups whenever the opportunity presented itself. In that context I realised 'associate' was a pretty flexible term.

That was the background against which I began to settle into my task. A week after my arrival the secretary of state said that it was not the right time to launch fresh substantive talks, and a few days later he added a unionist-friendly rider that in the absence of general agreement, following an impending Westminster general election, he could not rule out a bilateral deal with unionists. The response of PAB's contacts to that démarche was fairly predictable, with unionists broadly happy and nationalists, as represented mainly by the SDLP, clearly not. However, in Irish politics things rarely stand still for long, and, equally rarely, are all that they seem. So a combination of discreet dialogue with representatives of the four main parties engaged in the process and happenstance that saw taoiseach Charles Haughey replaced by the ostensibly more unionist-friendly Albert Reynolds allowed the secretary of state to announce that a talks plenary session would be held in Parliament Buildings on 9 March. PAB was very active in the run-up to that event, shuttling round our party contacts explaining how the session would be handled and what the government's goals were. On the day things went well enough, with the parties agreeing to reconvene after the general election that was expected to be called within forty-eight hours.

The election delivered a new secretary of state, Sir Patrick Mayhew, while an existing minister, Jeremy Hanley, took over Brian Mawhinney's political development portfolio. It had been decided that the talks would be conducted in three strands – the first dealing with the internal governance of Northern Ireland, the second with relationships between North and South, and the third with East/West relationships – with the Irish Government participating in Strands 2 and 3. Unionists were very nervous about the arrangement and a lot of ministerial effort was put into reassuring key members of the UUP, especially its leader, James Molyneaux. The charm offensive was conducted in several ways. For example, there was talk of a Northern Ireland Select Committee, which unionists wanted, and when a confidential paper by Sir Patrick on

North–South cooperation was leaked to the press and condemned by Molyneaux it was quickly withdrawn.

On 29 April the talks recommenced and continued in various formats: formal plenary, bilateral or multilateral between individual parties and one or both governments, and between the parties themselves. While the plenary sessions were invariably in Belfast some of the other meetings were in London, especially if the Irish Government was involved. As a member of the government's team, I was involved in all the internal strategy meetings where talks policy was refined, and was able to feed in tactical advice. That intimacy with the process also let me and my PAB colleagues transmit carefully calibrated information to our contacts, testing reactions and, hopefully, giving them some tasty food for thought. As time passed, I was able to build up close relationships with many of those people, though I never forgot that first and foremost I had a job to do. I was surprised how quickly I was able to perfect a system of almost total recall that allowed me to prepare a detailed note of a conversation, complete with an atmospheric commentary. It never occurred to me that any of those notes would see the light of day, at least during my lifetime. But I was wrong about that, as I would discover many years later when a copy of one – recounting a very frank conversation with the SDLP MP Eddie McGrady – found its way into the press by an unusual route. Fortunately, there was no lasting damage.

When the talks adjourned for the summer at the end of July that scene-setting activity continued in anticipation of their resumption. When they did resume, on 2 September, in Strand 2 format, the Democratic Unionist Party (DUP), led by Ian Paisley, withdrew, complaining that repeal of Articles 2 and 3 of the Irish Constitution wasn't top of the agenda. Those Articles asserted the Irish state's jurisdiction over the whole island of Ireland. The DUP's withdrawal was followed by a series of leaks to local newspapers about position papers prepared by the governments. Now I have always made a case-by-case classification of such leaks, on the basis of whether, in my opinion and in the overall scheme of things, they are likely to help or a hinder a particular situation. If it falls into the former category, which almost always has some degree of official sanction, I classify it as a 'good' leak. If into the latter category, a 'bad' leak. Like almost all the leaks that occurred during the talks, I placed those ones firmly in the former category.

With the DUP temporarily out of the picture, the way was clear for the UUP to make an historic visit to Dublin for a two-day Strand 2 session. That took place from 21 to 23 September in Dublin Castle, the seat of British power in Ireland for more than a hundred years before partition. The Irish Government had made lavish arrangements for the visit, including a coach that hurtled the British participants to and from our hotel each day amid a flurry of police outriders and wailing sirens. Each delegation had been allocated a suite of rooms in the castle, fitted out with the usual office equipment and garnished with a generous supply of refreshments. With a touch of Irish schadenfreude one of the rooms allocated to our delegation had a not altogether discreet plaque on the wall declaring that: 'In this room James Connolly signatory to the proclamation of the Irish Republic lay a wounded prisoner prior to his execution by the British military forces at Kilmainham Jail and his interment at Arbour Hill, 12th May 1916.' Seen in perspective the Dublin trip was successful, but the reality was that it was more significant for its symbolism than its substance, and although the talks continued on our return to Belfast, soon with restored DUP participation, it was clear that their days were numbered. On 10 November they stopped: the proximate cause was the resumption of work at the 'hated' Anglo-Irish Secretariat on the outskirts of Belfast, which had been suspended at unionists' request.

The year 1993 began as 1992 had ended, with UVF and Ulster Defence Association (UDA) attacks in Northern Ireland, PIRA attacks in parts of England – including a bomb in the north-west town of Warrington that killed two young boys – and more 'conditioning' by both governments. For example, tánaiste Dick Spring promised changes to the Irish Constitution if the circumstances were right, and the secretary of state said the government was 'neutral' on the question of Northern Ireland's position within the United Kingdom. In 1993, Northern Ireland had twenty-six district councils. A few were evenly balanced in terms of political complexion, but most were in the grip of a unionist majority, with UUP councillors outnumbering DUP councillors almost two to one. In some councils there was a chronic lack of cooperation and bitter debates, and in others palpable unionist distrust of the government stretching back beyond the 'perfidy' of the 1985 Anglo-Irish Agreement to the suspension of the Northern Ireland parliament in 1972. Paradoxically, unionist suspicion about the government's *real* intentions for Northern Ireland was not matched by the SDLP, whose members tended to take a 'what-you-see-is-what-you-get' approach. However, privately many members of all three parties held the view that Westminster had no particular attachment to their part of the United Kingdom and would love to get out if a safe and honourable way out could be found.

Power-sharing (or responsibility-sharing as unionists preferred to call it) was a central plank in the architecture for restoring devolution, and was already being operated voluntarily at a local level by several councils. To promote that practical example of what could be achieved if the necessary will existed, the secretary of state decided to launch a series of visits to council areas. It was hoped that he could undertake them at the rate of roughly one a month, but that transpired to be overly optimistic due to the other demands on Sir Patrick's time. The visits would have a common structure, starting with a meeting with the council in the council chamber, a call at a facility such as a school, hospital, factory or farm, and lunch with a selection of local people including the mayor or council chair, the relevant MP, shopkeepers, churchmen and women, a vet, solicitor or GP, and someone involved in community development. But the list was not exclusive. For security reasons the lunch invitations would be issued in my name, and it never failed to surprise me that the acceptance rate was almost always 100 per cent. In those days an invitation from the NIO was still prestigious. After lunch, Sir Patrick would engage with 'ordinary' people during a walkabout in the town centre.

We wanted to highlight the councils where responsibility-sharing was working well, so Dungannon seemed a good place to start. The UUP was the majority party with eight seats out of twenty-two; the SDLP came next with five; while the DUP, Sinn Féin and independents made up the balance. Towering over the council, at least figuratively, was the UUP MP for Fermanagh and South Tyrone, Ken Maginnis, who was firmly ensconced on the progressive wing of the party, and had proved that he had the courage of his convictions in the face of numerous PIRA threats and actual attacks. With Ken Maginnis' help and the organising skills of the town clerk, William Beattie, we drew up a programme that met our requirements and I put it to the secretary of state. He liked what was proposed, adding that as befitted a former attorney general he was a stickler for detail and wanted a brief that covered every issue that might possibly be raised with him.

In those days any contact between ministers and Sinn Féin was strictly off limits. Dungannon Council had three Sinn Féin councillors, but we were assured that none of them would be in the council offices during the visit and, as there was no question of inviting them to any of the other events, PAB's 'handshake prevention strategy' did not need to be put into operation. That strategy involved positioning an official close to any Sinn Féin representative who may have turned up unannounced. Then, in the event of an unacceptable hand being proffered to an unsuspecting secretary of state, the official would step forward, smile and shake the offending hand vigorously. An hour into the discussion in the council chamber I was congratulating myself on how well everything was going, when a councillor from an agricultural background asked the secretary of state what he intended to do about the growing number of dead cows being dumped at the roadside by irresponsible farmers wanting to avoid the cost of proper disposal. I knew the Department of Agriculture's section of the briefing material had not mentioned that abstruse subject and wondered how on earth Sir Patrick would field the question. But I need not have worried. He took it in his stride: 'Come from a farming area myself. Awful problem there too, and no easy answer. I'll make urgent enquiries and let you know exactly what I find out.' The councillor beamed his satisfaction and we moved on. It was a timely reminder of the pithy observation by the former US House chairman, Tip O'Neill, that all politics is local.

Three similar visits took place during the next six months. They attracted a lot of media attention and were a valuable way of getting the government's key messages across – especially the importance of cross-community cooperation. About the same time I was told to try to elicit an invitation for the secretary of state to address a meeting of a UUP constituency association, another confidence-building measure directed specifically at that party. Once again, Ken Maginnis' help was invaluable in producing the desired result. A vigorous DUP protest outside the venue in Co. Fermanagh only helped to make the event a success.

The appetite of PAB's contacts for information and a chance to share their thoughts seemed to increase in direct proportion to any increase in public activity on the political front. When those conversations involved senior members of the parties they tended to produce a range of opinions about where the process may or may not be going, speculation about the position of our interlocutors' political opponents, and gossip about the machinations and abilities, or lack thereof, of their colleagues. I recall spending several entertaining Friday afternoons in UUP headquarters after the party's weekly officers' meeting, listening to my hosts' colourful descriptions of how they planned to put the world to rights!

Such conversations, regardless of an individual's party, were invariably interesting, often illuminating, sometimes perplexing and, especially to a non-politician like me, instructive about the essentially solitary nature of political life. On the other hand, a small number of our contacts wanted to impart information about the thinking within the parties and groups that we were prohibited from engaging with directly, principally Sinn Féin, the PUP and UDP. It is fair to say that some of those contacts had an inflated sense of their own importance, but others had valuable insights and were willing to share them. Initially my greatest interest was the PIRA. I had inherited a sparse, and highly classified, file from my predecessor that included details of several people who had been in touch with him during the previous couple of years. None had any obvious republican connections. I was told to pick up those threads and in doing so soon decided that only three were really serious players. One was a former nationalist politician and the others were clergymen, one Protestant, one Catholic, who worked together very effectively. I gradually realised that their analyses, based on dialogue with their republican contacts, were almost the same: basically they were convinced that the PIRA was looking for a way to end the 'war'.

Contrary to my usual function as a two-way channel, during those delicate conversations I was under strict instructions to offer no opinions about the value or feasibility of any suggestions that were put to me. At that stage I was unaware of the 'link' that had been opened between the government and the PIRA, though I did know something of the other lines of communication with republican and loyalist groups that had existed at intervals throughout the

Troubles. One afternoon I met the two clergymen, who had asked to see me urgently. They told me they had been summoned to a meeting in London where 'an Englishman in a white trench coat' had told them courteously but firmly to back off. What should they do? I was puzzled by that turn of events and decided I must try to find out what was going on. Quentin Thomas was on leave, so I arranged to meet John Chilcot, the NIO's permanent under secretary. When I recounted my tale John grinned and told me:

The man in the trench coat was me. I'm afraid I can't tell you much but you do need to know that there's a credible process of engagement involved. It's being driven from London and it's starting to produce results. Your contacts have been useful in providing some corroboration for what we're hearing, but we're moving into very sensitive phase where the risk of sending mixed messages is too high to let you continue. However, I'll ensure you're told as much as you can be.

In the nature of such things I was soon able to fill in most gaps in my understanding of 'Chiffon', the name allocated to the covert activity, and as it picked up speed the pace of visible activity also quickened. Selective leaks ensured that certain pertinent information, such as the 'secret' dialogue between John Hume, leader of the SDLP, and Gerry Adams, the president of Sinn Féin, percolated into the public consciousness. The Queen visited Northern Ireland for the first time in sixteen years, delighting unionists, and the Irish president, Mary Robinson, shook Adams' hand in public a week later on a visit to Belfast. As the summer turned to autumn, speculation increased when what purported to be extracts from documents suggesting that government representatives and Sinn Féin were indeed in touch appeared in the press. The government's response to the speculation was blunt: there cannot be talk or negotiations with people who use violence or the threat of violence to advance their political ends. Period.

On 3 September, at a conference in England, an Irish journalist told me he had it on good authority that the PIRA was about to declare a one-week suspension of operations to coincide with a visit by an Irish-American fact-finding group to Ireland led by a former US congressman, Bruce Morrison, who had been taking a close interest in developments and who believed, like us, that the inclusion of Sinn Féin in all-party negotiations was an essential prerequisite for a successful outcome. I scurried off to put that serendipity – which chimed with other information we had received – into the system, commenting that the influence of Morrison and his colleagues should not be underestimated. The PIRA's suspension was duly declared the next day. Following several newspaper articles appeared claiming that the Hume–Adams dialogue, described by the two protagonists as being 'aimed at the creation of a peace process', had produced a request that the government should declare that it had no long-term interest in Northern Ireland. And with perfect timing, reflecting a call by

Martin McGuinness, nine days earlier, the secretary of state identified the right of self-determination of people living in Northern Ireland, as an important factor in any settlement. But, just as I was beginning to feel a real sense of momentum, my optimism was blown apart by the Shankill bomb and the Greysteele massacre. Those two terrorist attacks, the first by the PIRA in a loyalist heartland that killed ten people, including the bomber; the second, a shooting by the Ulster Freedom Fighters, a UDA affiliate, in a bar in Co. Londonderry in which eight Catholics died, seemed certain to bring everything to a halt. However, they had exactly the opposite effect, even though more press speculation about secret dialogue provoked vigorous denials by the secretary of state and the prime minister, with John Major declaring famously (or, depending on your point of view, infamously) that sitting down and talking to Gerry Adams and the PIRA would turn his stomach.

When news of the secret exchanges finally broke on Sunday 28 November, I was one of the small group of officials who accompanied the secretary of state to a hastily arranged press conference in Stormont Castle. There Sir Patrick outlined its origin and purpose to some of the most irritated journalists I have ever seen. The journalists' wrath was directed at all of us. They alleged that we had lied when we had denied on and off the record that any such thing was happening. As more details of the exchanges emerged and were routinely disputed by both sides, the violence continued with the PIRA murdering two members of the RUC, and the UDA murdering two Catholic civilians. However, so did the intricate choreography, greatly assisted by the publication by the two governments on 15 December of the Downing Street Declaration (DSD), a tour de force that received a cautious welcome across all sections of political and public opinion throughout Ireland.

As 1994 opened the sense of momentum increased again. The Irish Government lifted its broadcasting ban on Sinn Féin; John Major, whose personal and political courage and commitment to the peace process have not, I believe, been given all the credit they deserve, exchanged letters with Gerry Adams about the DSD; and Adams was given a visa allowing him to visit the US. On the flipside, there were PIRA mortar attacks at Heathrow Airport and multiple killings in Northern Ireland. While the exchanges with the PIRA were definitely *the* story, they were not the *whole* story. I was in touch with several people, including a Presbyterian minister, the Revd Roy Magee, who had excellent loyalist contacts, mainly in the UDP/UDA. Since 1991, the UVF and UDA had been constituent parts of an umbrella group – the Combined Loyalist Military Command (CLMC) – that also included members of the PUP and UDP. The CLMC had engineered a ten-week loyalist ceasefire in the early summer of that year. The archbishop of Armagh, Robin Eames, was also engaged and we were aware that the Irish Government was being briefed on loyalist thinking by intermediaries. The sum of our understanding was that the CLMC was anxious for dialogue with British Government representatives, primarily about the import of the DSD and the government's long-term intentions for Northern Ireland. Undoubtedly, some sort of direct engagement was desirable, but how could it happen given the prohibition on ministers and officials so engaging? We knew loyalists felt that they were defending themselves and their community against the threat of republican attacks and nationalist hegemony, and were deeply suspicious that peace was simply a way-point on Sinn Féin's road map to a united Ireland. So reassurance would be a central component of any dialogue.

On Wednesday 31 August, the PIRA announced that as of midnight there would be a complete cessation of military operations, a definition that caused the government some early difficulty due to the absence of any reference to permanence. The wide variety of reactions, which overall were positive, included renewed calls for us to grasp the nettle and meet the loyalists. By coincidence yet another significant unionist confidence-building event took place that week: the first visit by a secretary of state to a meeting of the Orange Order. After a lot of groundwork Sir Patrick met members of the order in their hall in Comber, Co. Down, where he was given a warm welcome. His core messages, which included the opinion that there was no reason why any cross-border bodies could not have some executive functions, were received with resignation rather than with untrammelled assent.

Days after the PIRA's announcement, the CLMC stated that it was engaging in a 'serious, in-depth analysis' of the announcement's implications, and that if it received satisfaction on six points of concern it was 'ready to make a meaningful contribution to peace'. We had seen a copy of the CLMC's statement before it was released and were being pressed to provide some answers. Hugh Smyth was a significant character in the story of loyalist politics. At the beginning of the Troubles he was a spokesman for the UVF, and was elected to the Northern Ireland Assembly as in independent unionist in 1973. Despite his close association with a terrorist group he was regarded as a moderating influence and that allowed him to build a successful political career. He was the first leader of the PUP. By September 1994, he had been a member of Belfast City Council for more than twenty years and had been elected deputy lord mayor in 1993 (when he was also awarded an OBE); and lord mayor in May 1994. I had known him since the early 1970s and respected his judgement. I thought talking to him about the current situation would not be a problem.

In contrast to Hugh Smyth, Gary McMichael was a relative newcomer to the political front bench. His father, John, had been a senior member of the UDA, and one of its sharpest thinkers, who was murdered by the PIRA in 1987. In September 1994, McMichael, still in his early twenties, was prominent in the UDP and had credibility with the UDA. Given his pedigree, he was the natural successor to Ray Smallwoods, the party's leading political strategist who had also been killed by the PIRA two months earlier. However, and helpfully for the work in hand, McMichael, like Smyth, was regarded as a 'civilian', a term used by some loyalist paramilitaries to describe associates with no record of active service. It was apparent to me that those men could provide a way out of our dilemma. After consideration of the proposition by the secretary of state, and with the approval of the prime minister, I was dispatched to Belfast City Hall to sound out Smyth on the feasibility of my meeting him in a personal capacity, not as lord mayor, and McMichael together. We thought a joint meeting was essential to prevent any negativity and point-scoring between the two groups. Smyth's response was encouraging and Roy Magee's assessment of McMichael's position was equally good.

In finalising the arrangements for the meeting I was at pains to emphasise the need for discretion. There was considerable media interest in what we might be up to and the last thing we needed was a press posse on our heels. Fortunately, a discreet venue was available: Quaker House near Queen's University. The facility was headed up by Alan and Janet Quilley, English Friends who had done extensive work with both loyalist groups and their republican counterparts and who were highly regarded. The meeting was fixed for Saturday 10 September. Responses to the CLMC's six points, which I could deliver orally, were prepared and cleared with the secretary of state and the prime minister.

I arrived at Quaker House in good time accompanied by Peter May, and was welcomed by the Quilleys. The upstairs room at the front of the Victorian terrace where the meeting was to take place overlooked a quiet, tree-lined avenue. As I gazed out of the window in apprehensive anticipation I was surprised, to put it mildly, to see the lord mayor's limousine, with its distinctive number plate, draw up outside. Surely lace curtains would start to twitch, urgent phone calls would be made and the media would be upon us? Gary McMichael arrived moments later in a relatively nondescript vehicle. After some preliminary small talk I opened the business by suggesting we should take the CLMC's six points as our agenda. Both men agreed, Smyth adding that they regretted we had confined the meeting to the two of them. He hoped it would be the first in a series and that other PUP and UDP members would be there in future. I was non-committal, pointing out that the joint meeting was in itself unprecedented and a sign of the importance the government put on both parties' involvement in the process. Smyth said that was all very well, but it was preposterous that members of the PUP could speak to representatives of the Irish Government whenever they liked, while their own government's door was firmly shut. I said ministers understood the need for parity of treatment between themselves and Sinn Féin. A loyalist ceasefire would get everything moving. Smyth, agreeing, said the prime minister should visit Belfast as soon as possible to assess the situation for himself.

Turning to the CLMC's six points, I said we shared the CLMC's concern about the absence of 'permanence' in the PIRA's statement, but cautioned that we should not get too hung up on words. Actions, or more accurately the absence of actions, were much more important. I said I could give explicit assurances on behalf of the government that no secret deals had been done with Sinn Féin and that Northern Ireland's status within the United Kingdom was guaranteed for as long as a majority of its citizens wished it. Anything else would be at odds with the government's primary objective of securing widespread agreement. I went on to address the CLMC's concern about the forthcoming *Joint Framework Documents*, likely to appear early in the new year. There was nothing to fear. The documents would be a distillation of all the information gleaned during the talks process, and in a sense would be an extension of the issues discussed in the DSD. They would probably reflect the governments' ideas about the kind of settlement that might command support, but the Irish document would not include material on the possible shape of the internal governance of Northern Ireland. That was a matter solely for the British Government and, ultimately, the people of Northern Ireland and their elected representatives. They seemed to take heart from what they heard, stressing that when the documents emerged they must be given to all the parties at the same time, not just the main ones. I said we would make sure they were not overlooked.

Finally, Gary McMichael emphasised the importance of doing nothing to create the illusion of a PIRA victory. The CLMC realised the PIRA's ceasefire would have consequences, some of which might not actually *be* concessions, but which would be *seen* as concessions by the man in the street. That needed to be recognised. Similarly, any financial peace dividend should be distributed equitably. I said post-ceasefire loyalists would be as free as Sinn Féin to take the credit for any good things that might happen, even though they could well have happened anyway. That was the stuff of politics. The government would act on the merits of a case, not on the basis of who demanded what. Fortunately, Hugh Smyth's high-profile arrival and departure drew no unwelcome attention to our liaison and during the weekend we heard the meeting had been useful. Unfortunately, our satisfaction about that suffered a violent reality check on Monday when the UVF left a bomb on a Belfast to Dublin train. It partially exploded, injuring two people.

The secretary of state had decided that while no further formal meetings could be held in advance of a ceasefire, informal dialogue should be intensified to reinforce the central messages. We knew the prime minister would be visiting Northern Ireland later in the week, and thought his visit would give him an opportunity to do just that. I was instructed to invite Hugh Smyth to a private meeting with John Major in Stormont House on Friday, 16 September. At the meeting, which was also attended by the secretary of state and me, John Major confirmed everything I had told Smyth and McMichael at Quaker House. He explained that if he was satisfied that the PIRA had given up violence for good, exploratory dialogue between Sinn Féin and officials could begin within three months. A similar three-month test would be applied to the PUP and UDP in the event of a loyalist ceasefire. Smyth said it would be helpful, in the context of the internal debate about a ceasefire, if we could repeat the messages I had conveyed on 10 September to a slightly wider loyalist audience. I understood that to mean a slightly wider loyalist paramilitary audience. John Major said we would do what we could. So clarification and reassurance by both governments continued apace. Like us, the Irish Government was involved in various configurations; in the case of the PUP/UVF at a high political level and with the UDP/UDA through intermediaries. By the end of September we were pretty sure a loyalist ceasefire was coming, and that optimism increased when a request was received for a group of loyalist leaders to go into the Maze Prison for a discussion with loyalist prisoners. Apparently the initiative was a success for shortly afterwards we heard that everything was in place for a decisive move.

Although I had some idea of what a ceasefire statement might look like, when it appeared on Thursday 13 October – delivered by Gusty Spence, one of the founders of the UVF, on behalf of the CLMC during an emotional press conference – I had a lump in my throat as I watched the live television feed in my office. In contrast to the announcement of the PIRA's cessation in a clinical press release, the CLMC's statement oozed sincerity and, crucially, included an expression of 'abject and true remorse' for victims of loyalist violence, albeit that 'victims' was qualified by the inclusion of the prefix 'innocent'. It was undoubtedly a significant moment, although subsequent events would show that the prime minister's description of 'another important piece of the jigsaw falling into place' was nearer the mark than the taoiseach's assertion that it 'effectively signifies the end of twenty-five years of violence, and the closure of a tragic chapter'.

On Friday 21 October, the prime minister came back to Belfast and had another private meeting with Hugh Smyth before addressing a business lunch in the Europa Hotel. Once again the secretary of state and I were present. John Major thanked Smyth for all he had done to help bring about the ceasefire. He said the route to democratic politics was open to anyone who renounced violence, and that he was anxious to ensure that loyalist representatives would be able to express their views in a meaningful way. He explained that during his lunchtime address he would disclose that he had made a 'working assumption' that the PIRA's cessation was permanent and, therefore, that exploratory dialogue between officials and Sinn Féin could begin before the end of the year, effectively before Christmas. He hoped a similar timescale would apply to the PUP and UDP.

The predominant view of unionists regarding the US was that there was a heavy bias in favour of Irish nationalism. However, president Bill Clinton's arrival in the White House in 1993 seemed to signal a shift of emphasis and a wish to become engaged on a more even-handed basis. The consulate general in Belfast was one of the first established after the foundation of the

US and has been in continuous operation for more than 200 years. Consuls general from the US are familiar figures on the local landscape and were significant contributors to the political/peace process as it developed. Val Martinez, a genial young man from Indiana, was the consul general in 1994. Arrangements had been made by influential Americans for a loyalist delegation, including Gary McMichael and David Ervine, who had emerged as a PUP spokesman with impressive political nous, to address the National Committee on Foreign Policy in Washington in the event of a ceasefire. Immediately after the CLMC's statement on 13 October the wheels were set in motion, but there was a hitch: certain US agencies were refusing to sanction visas for some of the delegates on account of their terrorist backgrounds. Ervine, for example, had been given an eleven-year prison sentence for possession of a bomb. However, the State Department had an eye on the bigger picture and was anxious to facilitate the visit as a confidence-building measure. Martinez was given the job of making the case for the defence. With my help he prepared a paper that described the current role of the questionable applicants, emphasising their commitment to a peaceful and democratic future, and the benefits that would flow from their being able to appear at such an influential forum. Their confidence would be boosted and, more important, their standing within their respective organisations was bound to increase. I knew ours was only one of several efforts to produce the same result – but I was sure our assessment, coming straight from the coalface, would carry some weight. A week later the delegation was in Washington.

As exploratory dialogue with Sinn Féin was set to begin in December, three months after the PIRA's declaration, then, if parity was to be maintained, exploratory dialogue with the loyalists should not begin until around the middle of January. However, there were advantages in starting both sets of dialogue at roughly the same time: any positive interaction between the two streams would be assisted, and the loyalists would see that we were taking them seriously. Moreover, Sinn Féin should not mind as it saw itself, and was seen by just about everyone else, as the main attraction. Happily, the prime minister's statement of 21 October about his working assumption on permanence provided the answer. If 21 October was taken as the starting point for Sinn Féin's clock the party would be at the table in about eight weeks, and starting the loyalists' clock on 13 October would produce a similar result. So, on 14 November at the lord mayor of London's banquet in the Guildhall, John Major was able to reveal that exploratory dialogue with the political associates of the UVF and UDA would also begin before Christmas:

Tonight, I can tell you that we have decided (as in the case of Sinn Féin) to hold exploratory talks with loyalist political representatives. I hope that these talks too will open before the end of December. The purpose in both cases is the same: to draw them into democratic politics and out of violence.

There was a chilling, if inadvertent, resonance about the choice of the Guildhall to deliver the news. The previous year the PIRA had detonated a huge bomb close by, devastating part of the City of London, killing one man and injuring fifty others. But the prime minister's statement was well received and prompted the understandable response, 'What next?' Strictly speaking there was still an embargo on direct engagement with close associates of the UVF and UDA, but it was only reasonable to give them some idea of what they could expect of exploratory dialogue so they could make adequate preparations. John Major's promise to Hugh Smyth that we would do what we could to reinforce our messages provided a way out of the conundrum and, again using the good offices of the Quaker Quilleys, another meeting was arranged for 1 December. On that occasion I was accompanied by my PAB colleague, Peter Smyth. The PUP's representatives were Billy Hutchinson, who had served fifteen years of a life sentence for murdering two Catholics in 1974, and whom I'd known since my time as director of regimes, and David Ervine. The UDP was represented by Gary McMichael and Joe English, putative commander of the UDA's East Antrim 'Brigade'.

I began by explaining that the meeting was a follow-up to my earlier one with Hugh Smyth and McMichael, in fulfilment of Smyth's request to the prime minister at their meeting in October. I said letters would very shortly be issuing to Smyth and McMichael inviting their parties to participate in exploratory dialogue. While I could note their responses to that news, I could not negotiate on any of the details. I went on to say that we thought it would be in everyone's interest if the dialogue was conducted with a joint PUP/UDP team. To proceed otherwise would create severe practical difficulties, and with Sinn Féin bound to be the principal focus of national and international interest, the image of a united loyalist delegation would be a powerful antidote to any perception of loyalists as bit players. Ervine and McMichael accepted the logic of that, but could not give an unqualified commitment. However, they said they were glad their government was taking them seriously for once. They and their colleagues had brokered the ceasefire and had not asked for anything in return. Now it was time for some government generosity, some 'baby steps' (an expression that would soon become David Ervine's catchphrase). For example, something that would show loyalist prisoners the peace process was not just for the benefit of republicans would send the right signal. More telephones in Belfast Prison and a significant extension of the Christmas home leave scheme would be a start. Hutchinson stressed the need for an enhanced social agenda, and for further confirmation that any peace dividend would be distributed fairly.

Regarding the modalities of exploratory dialogue, they were pleased with our assurances that the government team would not be prescriptive, and that their views on how business should be transacted would be taken into account.

The desirability of having a strong local element on the government team, with an innate understanding of the issues and compatibility with the 'Ulster psyche', was pressed on us with enthusiasm. They accepted the inevitability of exploratory dialogue with Sinn Féin starting first, but did not want to be in a position where they were always lagging behind. I was able to tell them that a statement by the secretary of state about the start of exploratory dialogue with Sinn Féin was imminent, and that a statement about loyalist exploratory dialogue would not be far off. (In the House of Commons that afternoon Sir Patrick Mayhew identified Friday 9 December, as the start date for XD – our shorthand for the dialogue with Sinn Féin – and a week later the prime minister specified Thursday 15 December for the start of LXD – dialogue with the PUP and UDP.) Finally, while they accepted that like our prior conversations, LXD would be covered by a veil of confidentiality, they shared our view that publishing an agreed communiqué on the opening day would give them the chance to send a positive signal to their supporters about their aims and objectives.

Everything was now in place for the parallel streams of exploratory dialogue to begin. A lot had already been done on the practicalities, and the arguments for and against possible venues had been considered by ministers. Eventually Parliament Buildings was chosen. Even though the premises were undergoing substantial refurbishment adequate accommodation was available for our purposes. We judged that while Sinn Féin might have some reservations about the historic resonance of a site at the heart of an administration that it and its PIRA associates had violently opposed, those reservations would be more than offset by the symbolism of its delegates entering as equals of the old enemy. The loyalists would, of course, have no such reservations, quite the opposite, but across the unionist family feelings would be mixed. Some people would be affronted – bloody footprints on the hallowed floors kind of thing – while others would derive wry satisfaction from the thought of 'the Provos' filing meekly into 'Stormont' at the behest of 'the Brits'.

Once the venue had been settled, the question of security came into play. Obviously the physical aspects inside and outside Parliament Buildings could be handled discreetly, but the thorny question of body searches was different. In 1994 frisking was a fact of life in Northern Ireland, but what would it say about trust if it were to be carried out on our guests? Fortunately, the answer was fairly self-evident: regardless of their pasts there was nothing to suggest that any of them would be joining exploratory dialogue with anything but pacific intentions, and, after confirming that no one on either of the government teams had any objection, the secretary of state approved a policy of no searching. I was a member of the LXD team, led by my colleague Stephen Leach, which began work on 15 December. On 13 December, I had a conversation with the prime minister about its likely course when he attended a conference in Belfast. To provide a direct link between the two streams I was also on the XD team led by Quentin Thomas, which, as agreed, met Sinn Féin, led by Martin McGuinness, for the first time on Friday 9 December.

There was no doubt XD was the big story, and the media thronged around Parliament Buildings on the opening day. But I was pleased to see almost as much interest when I arrived for LXD on 15 December. It is not necessary to include details of the proceedings of either set of dialogues here, and in any case my primary focus was the loyalists. Nevertheless, it is possible to make a general comparison of the two sets of dialogues, identifying some similarities and some differences. Sinn Féin had the advantage of being a single party with an eighty-year history of political activity, and was tightly coordinated in respect of just about everything. Its delegation's approach was predominantly strategic, but they were always on the lookout for tactical advantage. In contrast, the loyalists were a loose coalition of two relatively immature parties. They had an essentially anecdotal approach that depended a lot on the individual experiences of those who happened to be at the table, and had a tendency to analyse information to the point of destruction. Meeting the loyalists was a bit like meeting a set of community groups with political aspirations, whereas the Sinn Féin team often reminded me of veteran diplomats engaged in international diplomacy. They had a single personality and there was no point in looking for splits or personal opinions for if there were any they were securely locked away. Furthermore, Sinn Féin had a wealth of able people in its ranks, whilst the loyalists lacked strength in depth and had only a handful of seasoned political thinkers. For the government, the dialogue was ultimately about moving away from the ceasefires and building from there, to the point when ministers would be able to take control.

During the Christmas holidays fate took a hand in our carefully laid plans when an accidental fire caused serious damage to Parliament Buildings. Fortunately, the rooms we were using were not directly affected and it was possible to avoid the technical and psychological upheaval relocation would have entailed. Nevertheless, when we came back to the premises early in the new year there was a smell of smoke and the main corridor walls had a fine coating of soot. The place was a bit like a bomb site, an irony that was not lost on me. When the governments published the Frameworks Document on 22 February 1995, two sections caused an immediate wobble among moderate unionists and loyalists alike. The first was paragraph 47 of the British document, *A Framework for Accountable Government in Northern Ireland*:

> In the event that devolved institutions in Northern Ireland ceased to operate, and direct rule from Westminster was reintroduced, the British Government agree that other arrangements would be made to . . . promote cooperation at all levels between the people North and South, representing both traditions in Ireland . . .

The loyalists were worried that the commitment would allow Sinn Féin's strategists, if they so chose, to make any devolved institutions unworkable, creating a situation where much greater Irish involvement in the affairs of Northern Ireland was inevitable. The second concern was the concept of 'harmonisation' in the context of a new North–South body, which the other document, drafted jointly by both governments and titled *A New Framework for Agreement*, introduced: 'Again, by way of illustration, the governments would make proposals at the harmonising level for a broader range of functions'.

Although the loyalists were alarmed they agreed to reflect on what the sections really meant. We were able to help them with that and in due course their reflection allowed them to put the documents into perspective, identifying some positive points as well as some negative ones. Consequently. LXD proceeded fairly smoothly and sufficient progress was made to allow the NIO's political development minister Michael Ancram to take the chair on 22 March. That effectively brought LXD to an end and elevated the dialogue to a new level. Michael Ancram joined XD on 10 May.

The first engagement between a secretary of state and Gerry Adams, in his capacity as president of Sinn Féin, took place in Washington on 24 May, at an Irish investment conference hosted by president Bill Clinton. The event was memorably defined for me by an element of farce. Due to a mix-up with my reservation when I checked into the conference hotel, as a consolation the duty manager allocated me one of the finest suites available. Somewhat abashed by my good fortune, I immediately put my palatial accommodation at the disposal of the British delegation, and most of our internal discussions were held there. To dampen expectations it was decided that the meeting with Adams should be billed as just one of several with the party leaders who were in Washington. It was also decided that my suite should be the venue for those meetings due to its remote location within the hotel complex. That location would not be disclosed in advance to any of the party leaders, who would be escorted to the suite by me or one of my colleagues. Sir Patrick arrived incognito via the hotel kitchens and a service lift.

The meeting with Gerry Adams was scheduled as an early evening finale. Everything went according to plan until we were about to fetch John Hume for the SDLP's meeting. Someone said there was a lot of noise outside my front door, and when I looked through the spy-hole in the door I saw that the lobby was full of people, many of them journalists from home. We had been rumbled. A phone call swiftly produced an alternative venue, but it was in another part of the huge hotel so a hasty and rather undignified retreat was required. Despite the upheaval the meetings with Hume and Adams went off as well as we could have expected, and, of course, our friends in the press got a good story. When we returned to Belfast the kind of activity that had preceded XD and LXD resumed, with frequent meetings between the secretary of state or

Michael Ancram and the parties. My PAB team and I intensified our conversations with our contacts, who now included without restriction the associates of the UVF and UDA. Regrettably, I had few dealings with members of Sinn Féin who preferred to talk to ministers or London-based officials.

On 28 November, the governments issued a joint communiqué announcing the launch of a 'twin-track' process that envisaged parallel progress on the decommissioning of terrorist weapons and intensive all-party preparatory talks, with a start date before the end of February 1996 for the latter. Spirits were further lifted by an historic pre-Christmas visit to Northern Ireland by president Clinton when he met representatives of all the parties and made a number of public appearances. I introduced a DUP delegation to him at a reception in Queen's University. The delegation was led by Peter Robinson, the party's deputy leader, as Ian Paisley had insisted on a private meeting. Around the same time I got word that Peter Robinson would like to see me. That was unusual as, although we were on reasonably cordial terms, our relationship lacked the intensity of some of my other professional relationships, and I usually had to do the asking. We met for lunch and the conversation soon turned to the prospect of all-party talks. After rehearsing all the reasons why the DUP would not engage with 'unreconstructed terrorists', Robinson flew an unexpected kite: 'Look at it this way Chris, we're democrats and as democrats we're responsible to our electorate. Now if that electorate were to mandate us to sit down with Sinn Féin, or anyone else for that matter, we couldn't ignore their wishes. We would have to comply.' I was astonished. What Peter Robinson was offering was a route to inclusive negotiations, perfect in its simplicity. Reporting the conversation to the secretary of state I did not hide my enthusiasm for the idea, or my admiration for the DUP's pragmatism and, especially, Robinson's ingenuity and vision.

During the next few months the idea – which was initially rejected by the Irish Government and the SDLP, as well as Sinn Féin – was developed and refined. It was eventually agreed that the enabling legislation should provide for the ten parties with the most votes to be given seats on a 110-member forum that would deliberate on a variety of issues pertaining to Northern Ireland. But, essentially, the election would provide a body of people from whom party negotiators could be drawn. We calculated that setting the bar at ten parties would guarantee the inclusion of the PUP and UDP. In the undergrowth, however, all was not well. We were receiving reports that the PIRA was unhappy about the delay in starting the talks, but nothing specific. On Friday 9 February 1996, with a callous disregard for the spirit of the process, the PIRA gave vent to its unhappiness by detonating a huge bomb in the London docklands, killing two men and causing £100 million of damage. There was widespread condemnation of the attack, which came as a great disappointment to us all, including our loyalist contacts who spared no effort in trying to prevent any response in kind by their associates in the UVF and UDA. Thanks to that effort, and the persuasiveness and analytical skill of people like Father Alex Reid, Father Gerry Reynolds, the Revd Ken Newell and Chris Hudson, an Irish trade union official who for some years had been doing sterling work with the PUP/UVF behind the scenes, restraint prevailed, although the CLMC tempered that restraint by threatening to retaliate against any further PIRA action. Had the PIRA chosen to detonate the bomb in central Belfast rather than London things would have been very different.

The plans for the preparatory talks envisioned in the joint communiqué were swiftly revised to exclude Sinn Féin until the PIRA reinstated its ceasefire. That fact was communicated to the party when Quentin Thomas and I met Martin McGuinness, Gerry Kelly and Siobhan O'Hanlon on 26 February. Our note-taker on that occasion was Tony Beeton who, sadly, died in the Paddington rail crash on his way to work not long afterwards. Martin McGuinness said that Sinn Féin was still committed to peace, and thought the best way of achieving it would be to announce the start of 'peace negotiations', without conditions. He did not think our notion of an election was helpful and saw it as simply another time-wasting diversion. The proposed forum would be a 'bear pit'. Quentin's response was emphatic: as far as Sinn Féin's future involvement in any talks was concerned everything depended on events on the ground, and inconvertible evidence of a renewed commitment to peace.

The preparatory talks began on 4 March and were boycotted by the UUP, DUP and PUP, and, of course, Sinn Féin were not welcome. PAB was instructed to go round the dissenting parties testing out ideas and reporting back. We paid particular attention to the loyalists, especially those in the UDP who, although they were not involved in the boycott, were less self-assured than their PUP counterparts. The intelligence we gleaned supplemented what our senior colleagues and ministers were hearing, and alongside regular conversations with the Irish Government, helped us to build up a picture of how the early stages of the talks proper should be handled.

The forum/entry to negotiations election was held on Thursday 30 May. The UUP came first with 24.2 per cent of the vote, followed by the SDLP with 21.4 per cent, the DUP with 18.8 per cent, Sinn Féin with 15.5 per cent and the Alliance Party with 6.5 per cent. The remaining five places were filled by parties that got more than 4 per cent individually and included, as we had intended, the PUP and UDP. The others in that category were the UK Unionist Party, led by former UUP member Robert McCartney, the Northern Ireland Labour Party (NILP) and the Northern Ireland Women's Coalition, established earlier in the year with the help of people like the secretary of state's wife, Jean Mayhew. On Monday, 10 June, the delegates trooped into Castle Buildings to begin the negotiations that would soon settle into what the chairman, Senator George Mitchell, called 'a grim routine'.

Between his more formulaic duties, the secretary of state's visits to district councils continued to allow him to test public opinion for himself. Some of the most revealing moments occurred during his walkabouts in town centres. Tall and imposing, Sir Patrick cut an impressive figure as he chatted to shoppers and stallholders, elderly gentlemen taking the afternoon air and young mothers pushing prams. Some of the towns were in areas where support for Sinn Féin was strong. In other areas the DUP had a significant presence. He might therefore have expected to be given a rough ride on some occasions. However, it never happened – if you disregard a sad drunk who staggered across our path one day muttering oaths and was swiftly redirected by the local police sergeant. Good old-fashioned courtesy was the norm.

When the prime minister called a general election for 1 May 1997 the overall result was a foregone conclusion. Therefore, when my office door flew open on Monday 5 May and the new secretary of state for Northern Ireland burst in I was not in the least surprised, even when she sat down behind my desk and began to sketch a pretty flower on my blotter. Mo Mowlam had been shadow secretary of state for three years and I knew her well. For some months, with Sir Patrick Mayhew's authority, my colleagues and I had been briefing her and her affable deputy, Paul Murphy, about our responsibilities. New Labour's hands on the levers of power may have brought renewed impetus to the process. But, like those before them, prime minister Tony Blair and secretary of state Mo Mowlam knew real business would be done only when all the parties were at the table. Hopes were high that the emphatic shift in power at Westminster would be acknowledged by a swift restoration of the PIRA's ceasefire, but the PIRA had other ideas.

On 16 June I was passing the secretary of state's private office, on my way to a meeting in a conference room three floors above, when her private secretary called me over. He had just heard from RUC headquarters that two constables had been murdered in Lurgan, Co. Armagh, shot from behind at close range. The PIRA was thought to be responsible. If that was right, the officers would be the first it had killed since the end of its ceasefire. Would I please tell the secretary of state. When I went into the conference room and broke the news Mo Mowlam cancelled the meeting. As we hurried downstairs to get more details she was visibly shaken. 'How the hell could they do that?' she asked. 'Don't they know I'm doing my best for everyone here?' My reply was blunt: 'Mo, you may be the most honourable and understanding person on earth, but you're still the *British* secretary of state. In the eyes of some people you, and everything you represent, will always be a legitimate target.'

Senator Mitchell's grim routine continued until the PIRA restored its ceasefire 20 July. On 26 August, the two governments agreed to establish an Independent International Commission on Decommissioning (IICD) (of terrorist weapons), and three weeks later Sinn Féin's delegation took their seats at the table, accompanied by a great deal of unionist huffing and puffing. Later it was suspended again, briefly, on account of the PIRA's involvement in two more murders. To my dismay, the UDP was also subject to a temporary suspension due to similar infractions by the UDA, whose prisoners threatened to withdraw their support for the process and were dissuaded from such a course of action when the secretary of state paid them a visit in the Maze Prison. But despite all the setbacks and false dawns significant progress *was* made, albeit at the eleventh hour, and on 10 April 1998 – Good Friday – the deal was done and the Belfast Agreement (BA) was delivered. Among its most important provisions were a 108-member assembly and an accelerated release scheme for paramilitary prisoners. A few weeks later, when the Agreement received overwhelming endorsement in simultaneous referenda in both parts of Ireland, that should have been that. However, there was still work to be done.

The Irish National Liberation Army (INLA) was another terrorist group with a deadly capability. It had carried out some of the most ruthless and audacious attacks of the Troubles, including the assassination of Airey Neave, a Conservative MP and close friend of Margaret Thatcher, in the precincts of the House of Commons in 1979; the bombing of the Droppin Well bar in Co. Londonderry that killed eleven off-duty soldiers and six civilians in 1982; and the murder of Billy Wright, leader of the Loyalist Volunteer Force (LVF), in the Maze Prison in 1997. In the wake of the BA it was putting out feelers about a possible ceasefire and in due course, with the help of trusted intermediaries, I arranged to meet representatives of the Irish Republican Socialist Party (IRSP), INLA's political alter ego. The meeting took place early in August, at premises in Belfast owned by another church-related group. I was accompanied by a colleague, Robert Crawford. We did not know exactly who would be there until three men came into the room. To my surprise one was a man who had taken part in a recent fact-finding seminar that I had arranged for a group of well-connected republican women. Later I discovered he was more IRSP than INLA. When the other two introduced themselves I knew they were the genuine article.

I began by explaining the ground rules. They were familiar. Acknowledging the significance of the meeting, the secretary of state had authorised us to participate on the strict understanding that we were not there to negotiate. Although the government wanted the political process to be as inclusive as possible, there was no question of formal dialogue with the IRSP before an INLA ceasefire and a public declaration that the organisation was committed to an exclusively peaceful and democratic future. I added that in my opinion there would never be a better time for it to do that. After answering several questions about the implications of the BA for the political landscape, I outlined the potential consequences for INLA prisoners of a credible INLA ceasefire and the appointment of someone to liaise with the IICD on the organisation's behalf. I did not agree to a further meeting – everything depended on events – but said that I could see no objection in principle. I was able to promise to recommend to the secretary of state that a forthcoming visit by the IRSP to the Maze Prison should be enlarged to include all seven members of the party's Ard Comhairle (ruling council), and that they should be allowed to meet the twenty or so INLA prisoners.

Summarising the discussion in my preliminary report to the secretary of state, I described the delegation as 'intelligent, charming and witty'. It is instructive to compare that assessment with the assessment of one of my NIO predecessors who had a secret meeting with two PIRA leaders, one Gerry Adams, in 1972, a year when 470 people died violently in Northern Ireland and there were more than 12,000 terrorist incidents:

Their appearance and manner were respectable and respectful... Their behaviour and attitude appeared to bear no relation to the indiscriminate campaigns of bombing and shooting in which they have both been prominent leaders.

It says a lot about the inherent qualities of Irish republicans that we could both be impressed by people who were capable of such dreadful things. Like the INLA, the loyalist LVF was a small and extremely volatile terrorist group. It had emerged as a separate entity in 1996, when Billy Wright had acrimoniously split from the UVF, and established itself in the Portadown area of Co. Armagh. On 15 May 1998, five months after Wright's death, the organisation declared a ceasefire 'to create the proper climate in people's minds, so when they do go to vote [in the Belfast Agreement referendum] they will make the proper decision for Ulster and that is to vote no'. It was seen as a hollow gesture.

For some time I had been having occasional conversations with a former loyalist life-sentence prisoner turned minister of religion and sometime politician, Pastor Kenny McClinton, who had been close to Billy Wright and acted as a spokesman for LVF prisoners. By a strange coincidence, McClinton's brother had been the singer in a 1960s pop group of which I had been a teenage member. During those conversations, I would press for an LVF ceasefire and emphasise the benefits that could follow a start to decommissioning. I was aware that members of the UUP were engaged in a similar persuasion offensive. Three days after I met the IRSP delegation, I had another meeting with McClinton when we went over the same ground. On that occasion I had an inkling that something was afoot.

But, before my colleagues and I had an opportunity to assess fully the import of either meeting, on Saturday 15 August a Real IRA (RIRA) bomb devastated the centre of Omagh in Co. Tyrone, killing twenty-nine people. The shock and distress the attack caused was evidently shared by the leaderships of the IRSP and INLA, for, on 17 August, the day its delegation visited the Maze Prison, the IRSP issued a statement calling on the INLA to reach a decision quickly on a ceasefire declaration. The INLA responded on 22 August, declaring that 'We have accepted the advice and analysis of the Irish Republican Socialist Party that the conditions for armed struggle do not exist... The Irish National Liberation Army is now on ceasefire.' The LVF took longer to act, but on 13 November it announced that it would decommission some of its weapons if the PIRA matched the gesture in the ratio of ten to one. The PIRA did not take the bait, but the government responded immediately, accepting that the organisation's 15 May ceasefire was genuine, and that its prisoners were thus eligible for early release. The decommissioning event, in which Pastor McClinton played a part, happened on 18 December and included a theatrical flourish when a variety of small arms were cut up in front of the chairman of the IICD, General John de Chastelain, and several journalists. Although it was the first decommissioning by any Irish terrorist group, and despite its intrinsic value, it was largely discounted as another exercise in self-promotion.

With Sinn Féin now in the political mainstream, and all the paramilitary groups (with the exception of republican 'dissidents' like the RIRA) on *de facto* ceasefires, care was necessary to ensure that the two main loyalist groups, which had political pretensions but little electoral support, did not become inflamed again. Thanks to some modest electoral success by the PUP, the political maturity of David Ervine and Billy Hutchinson, and the steadying hands of people like Gusty Spence and Billy Mitchell, the UVF was reasonably content. However, when the UDP failed to secure any seats in the 1998 Assembly election the UDA began to show signs of restiveness. Moreover, neither the UVF nor the UDA had decommissioned any weapons. The UDA's disenchantment and internal power struggles led to the eventual demise of the UDP and the CLMC, the latter succeeded by a Loyalist Commission set up with the help of the leader of the UUP, David Trimble, and archbishop Eames. The Commission's immediate concern was a bloody feud that broke out between the UVF and UDA, and it was soon struggling to find an alternative to violent loyalist sectarianism associated with the Holy Cross School in North Belfast. In due course, the UDP was succeeded by the self-consciously apolitical Ulster Political Research Group (UPRG).

Although I had gained another promotion, in due course becoming the NIO's political director in Belfast (a post that was coupled with appointment as the British joint secretary of the British–Irish Intergovernmental Conference, the successor to the unionists' anathema, the Anglo-Irish Intergovernmental Conference), I remained as the NIO's point-man with members of all the loyalist groupings, alongside my shrewd and resourceful deputy and head of PAB, Mary Madden. I also lobbied for funds for various loyalist projects in the US, on my own and once in support of secretary of state John Reid, and at home. Throughout that period, which lasted almost seven years, the prime minister and his chief of staff, Jonathan Powell, were kept in the picture. At critical stages Jonathan's intervention was decisive.

The Irish Government's outreach to the PUP/UVF remained coordinated by Chris Hudson, while its engagement with the UPRG and its affiliate the UDA was conducted at arm's length by Martin McAleese, the husband of the Irish president. From time to time he and I would compare notes. In the same way that the quiescence of the main loyalist groups could not be taken for granted, the attitudes of the INLA and the LVF still needed to be monitored. With that in mind, I continued to meet members of the IRSP and LVF associates on an occasional basis, advising them, among other things, about how best to approach officialdom on various matters that concerned them.

The slow pace of decommissioning, interparty rivalry and wrangling between the main political blocs continued to hamper full implementation of the BA, and it was not until Tuesday 8 May 2007 that almost all the outstanding pieces fell into place. On that day the two old antagonists, Ian Paisley and Martin McGuinness, stood side by side as first minister and deputy first minister of Northern Ireland, flanked by Tony Blair and taoiseach Bertie Ahern. As I watched the drama unfold in the Great Hall of Parliament Buildings my emotions were decidedly mixed. Unquestionably, it was a day for celebration. But for me, and I suspect some others present, it was celebration tinged with sadness. Whatever way you looked at it, the historic compromise we were witnessing bore a striking similarity to the courageous deal my old boss, Brian Faulkner, had cut with his political opponents at Sunningdale almost thirty-five years before.

If only, I thought, if only . . .

7   The Joint Declaration and memory

David Cooke

This chapter is about trying to prompt myself to remember the Joint Declaration (JD) of spring 2003. I put it that way for several reasons. I am not a historian or a political scientist, but rather someone who ceased to be a British civil servant in autumn 2004, and who played a minor supporting role in the Northern Ireland peace process between 1990 and 1993 and then between 2002 and 2004. It is surprisingly difficult to remember work you did a decade or more ago. So this chapter is at least partly an account of my struggle to remember, prompted by books, but unprompted by any revisiting of the unpublished government records of the time. Secondly, for reasons which I hope to shed some light on, I think the JD initiative is a somewhat neglected phase of the peace process. It was nothing less than an attempt to secure 'acts of completion', to conclude a settlement on some of the most difficult issues left over from the Good Friday Agreement (GFA) of 1998. Though there are signs, even in 2014, that there is still unfinished business.

When I was studying history at university (a past I share with many Irish and British talks participants) there was a vogue for a 'high politics' view of history, epitomised by historians such as Maurice Cowling and John Vincent, which held that activity within the political elites was what counted, and it was, and should be regarded by historians as being, untainted by social, economic or cultural developments. Such a philosophy sometimes seems to be at work in writing about the peace process. You even sometimes thought you could detect it among talks participants. And this chapter may not be immune from such a temptation.

And yet the 'high politics' approach does not seem adequate to the history of the peace process. The build-up in Northern Ireland after 1922 of disadvantage and discrimination, and the resulting changes in mentalities, not to mention restriction of political opportunities, must be central to the analysis. And I do not mean these points to be confined to just one side of the divided community. But a historical understanding of the peace process needs a wider context still. Wherever you go in Northern Ireland, and in the Republic of Ireland too, you sense a different attitude to history from that on what one quickly learns not to call 'the Mainland'. The past feels a more important reference point, for good and for ill. Historians are pundits in the way they are usually not in, say, England or France. Personal, phenomenological time, the most important time for most of us, is subordinated to a time of legendary events and identity affirmation.

Soon after starting work on this chapter I watched *Nostalgia for the Light*, Patricio Guzmán's brilliant documentary on the admittedly very different issue of 'the Disappeared' of the Pinochet regime in Chile. By focusing on the Atacama Desert, the place on Earth with the least humidity, the film establishes strange connections between remembering the dead and astronomy. Prisoners in desert camps studied the stars until their guards thought they were using them to plan escape routes. Women searching the desert for the bodies of loved ones found fragments of calcium that the astronomers surmised to have come from the origins of the universe as well as from the dispersed bones of human bodies. Astronomers and archaeologists in the film lament that there is less ignorance and oblivion about their disciplines than there is about Chile's recent past. The cosmos becomes a vast metaphor for the sorrows of near contemporary history. The subject of the legacy of the past is scarcely less vast, charged and fluid in Northern Ireland. I will not be able to live up to that thought in the chapter that follows, but I will at least try to keep it in mind.

This chapter is in three parts. The first gives the context for the JD, and the intensive negotiations for which it was just one possible organising device. This section comes mostly from books. The second is more personal, and is about trying to remember what role I played in drafting the JD. The third is an attempt, again personal, to explain what I think was going on. I have added an outline chronology, but I have retained no official papers from my time in the Northern Ireland Office (NIO), and I have consulted none in the process of trying to prompt my memory.

Background

The JD is associated with a particular phase of the Northern Ireland peace process between 'Stormontgate' (the police raid on the Sinn Féin offices in Parliament Buildings) and the suspension of devolved government in Northern Ireland in October 2002, and the Assembly elections of 26 November 2003, following on from the fiasco of the failed choreography at Hillsborough Castle on 21 October 2003. It was a period of intensive negotiations in a variety of formats, including meetings between David Trimble and Gerry Adams and their respective teams at a frequency not seen before. It was punctuated by great set pieces, such as the visit of president Bush and his team to Hillsborough on 7 and 8 April 2003, but it was a phase that, although it appeared to end in failure, also prepared the winding paths for the final climb to the summit. As with all phases in the Northern Ireland peace process, the period that I am considering here (October 2002–October 2003) can easily assume a baffling complexity. But the bare outline can be simply stated.

After the 1998 GFA, the devolved government that was established with David Trimble (Ulster Unionist Party (UUP)) as first minister and Seamus Mallon (Social Democratic and Labour Party (SDLP)) as deputy first minister functioned precariously. David Trimble faced both anti-Agreement and sceptical opinion in his own party, and the Democratic Unionist Party (DUP) opposed and wished to amend the Agreement, though it took up ministerial office. Between 1998 and 2002, the proportion of Protestants who believed that the GFA had benefited equally both unionists and nationalists had fallen from 41 per cent to 19 per cent.

Acts of Provisional IRA (PIRA) decommissioning in October 2001 and April 2002 were hard to secure, while continuing paramilitary activity culminated in 'Stormontgate' in October 2002, when the police mounted an operation in Parliament Buildings after it emerged that Sinn Féin had a source within the NIO who supplied much political information as well as some that, the police indicated, could be used for targeting. The Assembly was suspended on 14 October 2002, unionists having indicated that they would withdraw from government. The alternative of excluding Sinn Féin from the Executive had been considered, but the SDLP did not support it. Prime minister Tony Blair made his Belfast Harbour Commissioner's speech on 17 October, saying that a 'fork in the road' had been reached, and calling for 'acts of completion'. Then Paul Murphy replaced John Reid as Northern Ireland secretary on 24 October.

The period between October 2002 and April 2003 saw negotiations involving the British and Irish governments and the Northern Ireland parties on the acts of completion agenda. On 3–4 March the prime minister and taoiseach held two days of talks at Hillsborough with the pro-Agreement parties, and the prime minister announced the postponement of Assembly elections until 29 May. On 7–8 April, president Bush visited Hillsborough for an Iraq War summit with Tony Blair, and the two governments held further talks there with the parties. This resulted in the publication on 1 May of a JD, which aimed to constitute a comprehensive set of proposals for dealing with the outstanding issues.

The prime minister posed three key questions to the PIRA on 23 April, seeking to remove ambiguity about decommissioning, the ending of paramilitary activity and the ending of the conflict. This was followed by the announcement on 1 May that the Assembly elections would be further postponed, with the aim of creating more space for the negotiations to be concluded, but in the knowledge that Parliament would review matters if an election date had not been announced by 15 November.

On 21 October, with some misgivings, the prime minister and the taoiseach returned to Hillsborough for a day of timed announcements centring on a new and major act of decommissioning by the PIRA. The act took place, but the chairman of the Independent International Commission on Decommissioning (IICD) overseeing decommissioning, General John de Chastelain, was not in a position to give sufficient detail to enable David Trimble to go into elections on a basis of re-entering the devolved administration. Subsequent weekend salvage negotiations at Hillsborough on 25–26 October made a serious attempt to resurrect the deal, but eventually failed. My chronology sets out what was on offer on 26 October, and suggests if that had been available when General de Chastelain gave his press conference, the choreography of 21 October might well have been successful. The Assembly elections proceeded in November 2003, and the DUP and Sinn Féin emerged as the largest parties from their respective sides of the community. The JD phase of the peace process was over, and a new phase had begun.

The politics of the JD phase were complex, and filled with drama. The British and Irish governments, under Tony Blair and Bertie Ahern, worked well together, and relationships between the teams reflected the trust and candour between the principals. But the UUP was preoccupied by challenges to the authority of David Trimble's leadership by Jeffrey Donaldson and his anti-Agreement supporters. Sinn Féin was critical of the British Government for what it saw as an unnecessary suspension of the Assembly, and a breach of private negotiations in mid-April and public allegations that a British agent, 'Stakeknife', had operated for some years within the PIRA, were unsettling the Provisional movement. The SDLP faced an electoral threat from Sinn Féin and felt marginalised, particularly by the British Government. The DUP was seeking to make gains at the expense of the UUP, and had an agenda, whose scope was as yet unclear, for renegotiating the Agreement. Of the smaller Assembly parties, Robert McCartney's near one-man band the UK Unionist Party (UKUP) remained a thorn in the flesh, capable of unsettling the pro-Agreement parties. Led by David Ford, the Alliance Party (AP) continued to appeal to moderate opinion on both sides of the community, but could be more challenging than that might suggest. The Northern Ireland Women's Coalition, led by Monica McWilliams, again had cross-community appeal, but faced a more uncertain future than the AP. The United Unionist Assembly Party was perhaps the least conspicuous of the smaller parties. And Cedric Wilson's Northern Ireland Unionist Party was a breakaway group for the UKUP. The Progressive Unionist Party had links with the Ulster Volunteer Force (UVF), and its leader, the late David Ervine, known in republican circles as 'Dictionary Dave', was a thoughtful, if demanding, participant in the talks.

Of the paramilitary groups in Northern Ireland at the time of the publication of the JD, the PIRA, the Irish National Liberation Army (INLA) and the UVF were regarded as being on ceasefire. The Real IRA, the Continuity IRA, the Ulster Defence Association (UDA) and the Loyalist Volunteer Force were not, although the UDA had announced a twelve-month cessation of activities. Concern about the criminality organised by most of these organisations was growing, alongside the more politically well-established concerns about paramilitary activity, such as punishment beatings, and capability. As well as this parades and marches remained a volatile issue, as they were to continue to be even after 2007, although the 2003 marching season was unusually calm, partly as a result of intensive cooperation and preparation between the UUP and Sinn Féin. There was also cooperation on the matter between Sinn Féin and the British Government, which helped.

The 2001 census recorded 53 per cent of the population as Protestant and 44 per cent as Catholic. Northern Ireland during this period had a higher proportion of children than any other part of the UK and a smaller proportion of the elderly than anywhere except London. Unemployment among both Catholics and Protestants had fallen sharply between 1991 and 2001, but was significantly higher among the former than the latter, and Northern Ireland had a higher incidence of low-income families in 2003 than anywhere else in the UK. Further, educational achievement outstripped other parts of the UK, but the population was among the least healthy. Cities such as Belfast had a more vibrant feel in 2003 than they had a decade before and inward investment had made great strides, but multiple indicators showed that disadvantage was a serious problem in parts of both sides of the community. Yet, compared with other areas of conflict in the world, Northern Ireland was unusually prosperous. It has been remarked that there have not been many other trouble spots where Marks & Spencer stayed open throughout.

Between the late 1960s and 2002, over 3,500 people were killed in the conflict in Northern Ireland. Over 40,000 people were injured, although the real figure was higher since not all injuries were recorded. The overall death rate from the Troubles of 2.25 per 1,000 population was on a par with the Middle East or South Africa, but much lower than Salvador or Cambodia. My former senior colleague Sir Kenneth Bloomfield, reporting in May 1998 on his work on behalf of victims, said that the letters he had read and the stories he had heard would be burned in his memory forever. Over 40 per cent of deaths resulting from political violence happened in Belfast, although its population was only about a fifth of that in Northern Ireland. Of these deaths, over 60 per cent were in the north and west of the city.

The British Government had the twin objectives of bringing about the ending of politically motivated violence and establishing durable and stable institutions of government involving both sides of the community. We regarded ourselves, with the Irish Government, as facilitators, though facilitators with some powerful levers under our control. We would sometimes say that we would support any outcome if it had the potential to secure convergence and agreement. That may be too simple a way of putting it, but it remains true that we were not normally to be found advocating doctrinaire positions. But neither were we innocent of error or misjudgement. So-called 'securocrats' formed part of our circle of colleagues, but, in my own experience, they were people of decency and integrity.

Northern Ireland continued, at this time, to be a more important issue in US politics than most British observers appreciated. President Bush was perhaps less personally involved than president Clinton, and also less inclined to second-guess the British Government, but his adviser, ambassador Richard Haass, was a frequent visitor who had top-level contacts with the parties. Political figures in Washington, such as senators Ted Kennedy and Christopher Dodd, and congressmen Pete King, Richie Neill and James Walsh, took a keen interest, and were briefed by visiting teams from Dublin and London. I was personally involved in briefing senators Kennedy and Hillary Clinton during the period under discussion. Northern Ireland affairs were also followed closely by a number of EU countries, and by Australia, New Zealand, Canada and countries in the Far East. A number of distinguished international figures played significant facilitating and monitoring roles at or around this time, but none of the talks participants would have regarded it as appropriate to try to hand the issues over for international resolution. This was the background against which we sought to advance the peace process during the period October 2002–October 2003.

If you know where to look in the JD some ten issues stand out as the leading elements of the negotiations. The first is decommissioning of paramilitary weapons. This had emerged in late 1993 and early 1994 as a vital requirement and, sometimes, as a precondition and stumbling block. Partly because decommissioning does not tell the whole story, and partly to widen the focus beyond the stumbling block, decommissioning was joined by the two further issues of ending paramilitary activity and establishing definitely that the conflict was over. I explain this more fully later. The fourth element is 'normalisation', a term of art for scaling back security arrangements in line with changes in the threat. The synonym 'demilitarisation' has a more republican sound. Then come three issues often taken together: fifth, concluding the implementation of the Patten recommendations on policing; sixth, Sinn Féin joining the Policing Board and related institutions; and, seventh, an outstanding matter left over from Strand 1 of the GFA of 1998, the devolution of justice and policing (which was only finally resolved in 2010). The eighth point is the vexed and sensitive question of how to deal with the 'On the Runs' (OTRs). To explain an issue that may be unfamiliar: the equally sensitive issue of prisoner releases, a focal point at the time of the Agreement in 1998, left over the unfinished business of what to do about those who were at large but wanted by the police. It resulted in a policy for judicially administered resolution of suitable cases and, ultimately, in highly controversial legislation which Parliament found objectionable.

The last two points again went together. The ninth element was the proposal for an Independent Monitoring Commission (IMC), which was originally envisaged as focusing on paramilitary activity, but subsequently acquired a wider remit. And, the tenth was sanctions for any breaches of the settlement. These ten points cover most of what was needed to finish the implementation in full of the Agreement, the 'acts of completion' of which Tony Blair spoke in the Belfast Harbour speech.

I have provocatively left out some further points to which great importance was attached, and which, as I remember very clearly, were the subject of many hours of negotiation. They included restorative justice, the protection of human rights, and, above all, specific reforms of great importance to the different identities within Northern Ireland, for instance, relating to emblems and symbols, and to the Irish language and Ulster Scots. I do not mean to belittle these significant and often emotive issues. I relegate them only because of a sense that they were capable of falling into place if the ten issues listed above were resolved, but not vice versa. Two more absolutely crucial variables, although neither of them could quite be described as acts of completion, were the date of the next Assembly elections, and the goal shared by all parties of getting the devolved institutions up and running again (restoration).

During the phase I am writing about, some great issues of the peace process were *not* on the table. These included the dual consent principle at the heart of the constitutional accommodation confirmed by the Agreement. Joint authority was no longer an issue, though it had been at the time of the Anglo-Irish Agreement (AIA) of 1985. In addition, the arrangements under the Agreement for the Northern Ireland institutions, for the North–South machinery, and for the east–west institutions, were not in play. They were known to be firmly on the reform agenda of the DUP, but at this stage they were not participants. However, it was known that a review of the working of the Agreement was due in December 2003.

Memory

I was associate political director in the NIO from 2002 to 2004, working with John Reid and then Paul Murphy as secretary of state, with Jane Kennedy and Des Browne, and then John Spellar, as security minister and political development minister, respectively, with Jonathan Phillips as political director, and with my old Oxford friend Jonathan Powell, the prime minister's chief of staff, who was the leader of our little team which hurtled around between Belfast, London and Dublin like a squash ball bouncing off hard walls and floor. There was also the formidable figure of permanent secretary Joe Pilling to brace and cajole us when we needed it. I had previously worked in the NIO as a head of division from 1990 to late 1993, and had had a hand in the drafting of the Downing Street Declaration (DSD) of November 1993 and the messages exchanged between the PIRA and the British Government. As always with a British civil servant, I was operating under political direction, and my senior colleague at the time, Quentin Thomas, supervised, guided and encouraged me. (Quentin, in turn, reported to the then permanent secretary John Chilcot, who was a key player more generally in efforts to nudge republicans onto an exclusively peaceful political path.) I was fearful that my second stint would not live up to the excitement and satisfaction of the first. But it did! (I should add a comment about drafting the messages to the PIRA in 1993. The aim was to send text that was frank and honest, but also constructive and encouraging where that was possible. I was closely supervised by Quentin Thomas. When one is playing the lead adviser role under prime ministerial and ministerial direction, as he was then, it is sensible if possible to find someone else to wield the pen. So mine was an inky fingered scribe role, but nevertheless one of the most absorbing tasks I have ever had in the Civil Service. We were convinced that the initial message from the PIRA that 'The conflict is over but we need your advice on how to bring it to a close' was genuine, though subsequently real doubt has been cast on that. The lesson I learned above all others from that work is that channels of communication of this sort have their own dynamics and there may be more distortion than one thinks.)

When you have been away from Northern Ireland for years, with your attention focused on other things, it never leaves you, but settles into a series of panels or vignettes. So, before I clicked print and renewed my acquaintance with the JD, all I could remember were things like these. Negotiating with the Sinn Féin team for fourteen hours in Windsor House in the centre of Belfast, watching Gerry Adams and Martin McGuinness take it in turns to stretch their legs and stand contemplatively at the back of the room observing their colleagues metaphorically torturing us as they worked through the apparently infinitely detailed Sinn Féin briefing documents. Dr Paisley bursting into a backroom group of British officials in Parliament Buildings, commanding magnificently 'Let me smell your breath!', and then roaring with huge laughter. US secret service divers in the lake at Hillsborough. Standing next to Condoleezza Rice and Colin Powell when George Bush gave his press conference there. Sitting with Mark Durkan and his SDLP colleagues in a waiting room at 10 Downing Street and then being mistaken by Tony Blair for an SDLP councillor. David Trimble giving me a very painful lesson on the UUP sensitivities over the treatment of North–South matters at Sunningdale and in the 1995 leaked *Frameworks Document*. The frequency of Gerry Adams' genial exhortations to British officials that we should 'get real' and 'cop on' (we must have been more sceptical than is sometimes claimed). Grabbing a sneaky Mars Bar for lunch in Castle Buildings, which Tony Blair has said was one of his least favourite places. And so on.

Jonathan Phillips and I, as political director and associate director, worked for much of the time as a double act, sometimes splitting on who went where when there were simultaneous meetings in, say, Belfast and Dublin, and often dividing topics between us. In the language of the time, Jonathan was a director general and I was a director. We got on extremely well, often finishing a hard day by having dinner together at Stormont House, sometimes just the two of us, and sometimes in the company of members of the ministerial team, other than the secretary of state. The secretary of state, or SOSNI as he was sometimes known, would more usually be based at Hillsborough, to which he would sometimes invite us to taste the latest consignment of the Chateauneuf du Pape, a controversial appellation for the peace process which used to amuse Paul Murphy, who was often cheerily greeted by Dr Paisley as 'The Apostle Paul', and who is a papal knight in real life.

There was never any doubt that Jonathan was the senior partner, and his contribution to the peace process, both during the JD phase and then in its final stages, was truly heroic. Jonathan has a prodigious command of, and appetite for, detail, but he combined this with a constant grasp of the big picture, great resilience, and a high degree of resourcefulness in dealing with the innumerable twists and turns of the process. He would sometimes describe himself as a control freak, but what this really meant was that I was lazier than him! Jonathan is one of the least lazy people I have ever met. From time to time, a convivial dinner à deux would be interrupted by a telephone call from Jonathan Powell requiring a new document to be produced before we went to bed.

A key player at all times was my fellow director Chris Maccabe. In formal terms, Chris' responsibilities included overseeing the Political Affairs Branch, which he had himself previously led, our main source of information about the machinery and agendas of the Northern Ireland political parties; running the British side of the Secretariat which supported the East–West institutions; and coordinating the NIO's outreach to the loyalists. Informally, Chris, who had become a friend during my earlier period in the NIO, was an unrivalled source of insights and advice. He was ideally placed to say, when necessary, 'look, you just have not got the nuances right here'.

Most work in the Civil Service is done at the level of the division, but the division that supported us on political development, led by Alan Whyshall, was sometimes having to play catch-up because of the sheer pace of events. Alan, a brilliantly gifted man, bore this with amazing equanimity, but made a vital contribution. His team produced huge volumes of policy papers, briefs for meetings, draft speeches and more at great speed. Alan himself was an excellent judge of both the politics and the substance of the process, and combined this with a deep knowledge of the constitutional documents and legislation. His team was split between London and Belfast, with Alan, like Jonathan and I, shuttling between the two on a draining but unpredictable schedule. One of the team's responsibilities was one of those nightmare subjects, the logistics of talks meetings held on NIO territory. This could range in scope from tracking down the next stately house for hothouse negotiations through to ensuring that the right combination of orange and green vegetables was available at mealtimes.

Neither we nor indeed Jonathan Powell and our political masters could have functioned without our subject experts. These were colleagues in other parts of the NIO, and in parts of the Northern Ireland Civil Service as well, who knew all about, for instance, policing, or parades, or human rights or tackling disadvantage. Some of these were important players in the talks in their own right. Most senior of these was David Watkins, who was the main point of contact with the chief constable and the Army. This meant that David was the lead NIO official on the vital subject of security normalisation. Again, David was a friend from my earlier period and, like Chris Maccabe, a vital source of less formal advice and guidance. He also uncomplainingly allowed Jonathan and me to hijack his Belfast office and his PA from time to time. David was well supported by Nick Perry, who later took over from him. Stephen Leach and Paul Priestly were the kings of criminal justice policy, and Robin Masefield of Patten implementation on policing arrangements and reform, a subject so intricate in places that he could, without exaggeration, be described as the world's leading expert on it.

I must acknowledge many other vital colleagues, whether in ministerial private offices, at Hillsborough and Stormont House, or in other parts of the NIO. Some of these, for instance, Robert Hannigan, who held the key post coordinating the NIO's dealings with the media, went on to become leading players in the later stages of the peace process. But I will end this incomplete account by hailing a very special breed, the PAs who organised and looked after us. My own PA, Julie Harwood, was a star, who could type vital documents direct from dictation by someone, that is, me, babbling over her shoulder without the slightest sign of stress. She often did similar work for Jonathan. She also had a brilliant Belfast turn of phrase. On one occasion I was trying to hunt Jonathan down in the London office, and asked Julie if she had seen him. Her reply was 'Sure, he's away down to the Video Conference Room like a whippet, so he is!'

All of this activity proceeded under the watchful and undeceived eye of Sir Joseph Pilling. Joe had been a superb political director in a previous phase, and the temptation for him, as permanent secretary, to reprise that role now must have been considerable. But he self-denyingly gave Jonathan and me space, while supplying the extra angles and perspective that we might not have had ourselves. Every week Joe pulled together everyone in the organisation who had a role of any sort in the peace process and we met, usually in the video conference room, to ensure that all were briefed and up to speed. Given the difficulties of keeping everyone in the loop, this was a vital function. Above all, Joe was the prime mover of the NIO team, and this chapter mentions just one among countless crucial interventions that he made. If it does not sound too ungrateful to colleagues in the Foreign and Commonwealth Office, the Cabinet Office and elsewhere, we were tremendously fortunate during this period in having such a short communication line to the prime minister's chief of staff, Jonathan Powell. In other periods of the peace process there could be tension between the NIO and the watchers in other parts of Whitehall. Jonathan's role meant that there was no such problem during the period covered in this chapter.

When I first discussed this chapter with Graham Spencer, he expressed fascination about how British officials went about their various tasks, and what conditioned us to behave and perform as we did. It would take a book to answer him. But I told Graham that I thought some early Civil Service experiences were formative. This included discovering that you could not reproduce your university weekly essays, but instead had to ask, for each document you wrote, whose name it was going to be in, what it was seeking to achieve and what nuancing was required, as well as advising ministers on legislation and the intense drafting under pressure that went with that, and hanging around for long hours in the disorientating settings of Westminster and ministerial meetings, in which so much could go wrong, from nose-bleeds to heart attacks. I think, too, that for many of us, though not all, there was the realisation that we were not cut out to be politicians, while we nevertheless experienced a growing fascination with the political decision-making process.

What has all this got to do with the JD? Well, I may be hallucinating this, but I nevertheless firmly believe that, after receiving my marching orders from Joe Pilling and Jonathan Phillips, I dictated it one grey afternoon late in 2002 in an office overlooking the Thames, on Millbank. What I dictated certainly was not the complex and rather baroque text called the JD that came out of my printer when seeking to refresh my memory for this chapter (how different it was I cannot know for sure without seeing my draft, which is not available to me). But it certainly expanded a great deal, divided itself up several times, and became more intricate with the language of many different hands. By early 2003, following several joint drafting sessions near Dublin, it had become well and truly a joint British–Irish production, in a sort of reverse of the process that took place with the DSD of 1993. Probably no one could establish now how many authors this palimpsest could claim in its final form, and still less who wrote what.

Why did we produce it in that initial version? I have a blurry memory of Joe Pilling, at some time in late 2002, coming into Jonathan Phillips' room, where the two of us were closeted, and telling us that if we did not offer Number 10 a possible strategy within twenty-four hours then they would probably turn elsewhere for advice. That concentrated the mind. There was a market for something like this, and an urgent one. 'Stormontgate' was a big trauma, which had made another suspension inevitable. The necessary trust had drained from the Agreement institutions in those circumstances and the SDLP did not think it was right to ask them to support the only alternative, of excluding Sinn Féin. But, on the bicycle theory, so vividly set out by Jonathan Powell in *Great Hatred, Little Room* (2008), we had to find a way to keep the process going. More, we had to gather the threads together again so that the politicians could re-engage. We did not seriously doubt that, from their various perspectives, they would want to. But a new version of the bike had to be found. To torture the metaphor, a vehicle needed to be found that could carry the freight of the necessary acts of completion. And the urgency, indeed, went deeper than merely keeping going and coming up with a new framing device. I mentioned above the extent to which unionist support for the GFA had leaked away since 1998. Political engagement in late 2002 felt disenchanted and centrifugal, and it was a pressing concern to try to reverse that.

There is a perhaps still more important consideration. In my previous spell in the NIO in the early 1990s, we had distinguished between political development and political movement. By the former we meant the three-stranded all-party talks. By the latter, we meant indirect and for some of the time secret contact with republicans with the aim of securing the ending of the conflict. In late 2002, the world had moved on, but we needed to address the totality of the outstanding acts of completion, including both those relating to substantive political issues, such as policing, and those relating to components of political movement, such as decommissioning and ending paramilitary activity and capability. By late October 2002, Jonathan Powell was putting strategic papers to Tony Blair on how this might be done. But he was in the market for a framing device. This was where the drafting from me, commissioned by Joe and Jonathan, came in.

I cannot reconstruct from my memory exactly what was done with my text. Joe Pilling and Jonathan Phillips will have looked at it, and then it will have gone to secretary of state Paul Murphy. It will then have been sent, with a covering letter from Paul Murphy, to 10 Downing Street, where the recipient will have been Jonathan Powell. Jonathan then embarked on what I believe was quite a sustained and intensive process, involving iterations with us, of knocking it into shape and establishing whether Tony Blair thought the proposed process, framing device and content were the right approach. It is also perhaps worth bringing out that this account of the drafting of the JD does not support Gerry Adams' claim that it was largely based on the fifty-seven-page Sinn Féin 'wish list' document, since we received this only in late December 2002 (a not entirely welcome Christmas present, though one that we took seriously and did a great deal of work on).

The draft JD was intended initially for discussion with the Irish Government and Sinn Féin. It may seem unfair that it was not produced for more even-handed and inclusive discussion. Perhaps that was wrong, but it reflects the reality that one of the purposes of the document was to incentivise and create pressure for movement by republicans on weapons and paramilitary activity. David Trimble was briefed on it and then shown it early in 2003. The other parties were first engaged on it in March. Drafts such as that early version of the JD do not come to you *ex nihilo*. I will have known from discussions with Jonathan Phillips in particular, but also Joe, what sort of approaches we collectively thought might be promising. I will have known well the minds of Paul Murphy and his ministerial colleagues, Des Browne and Jane Kennedy, and also Owen Smith, Paul's clever and congenial special adviser. As for Jonathan Powell, Northern Ireland was a subject I had been discussing with him ever since I stayed with him in Washington in the early 1990s, when he was still a diplomat. But when I explained this process to Graham Spencer, he made clear that he had found that my account did not even begin to explain how one would set about such a task. I think such an exercise of introspection would have been difficult in late 2002, and it has not become any easier with the distancing perspective of time. But I can offer these reflections.

The parallel with the DSD of November 1993 is one starting place. The comparison is highly imperfect. The DSD was much concerned with questions of legitimacy and consent, and with even more charged concepts such as what might be meant by 'an agreed Ireland' and what, if anything, the British Government was prepared to become a 'persuader' for. It did not start its life as a British document, and that shows, notwithstanding the highly significant changes that the British Government needed before it could become party to it. Nevertheless, the DSD was short enough to serve as a model. In both cases the link was there (although not overtly in the case of the DSD) between constitutional principles and 'movement', as tested by what happened 'on the ground', in the shape of 'cessation' in the case of the DSD and decommissioning and ending paramilitary activity in the case of the JD. At a much more personal level, my involvement in the former, however minimal, gave me the confidence to attempt the drafting of the latter. A big difference from the DSD was the attitude to be taken towards ambiguity. In the DSD, ambiguity, in places, was still the drafter's friend and the handmaid to the process. In the case of the JD, it was time to start pinning down ambiguity and setting out the tests against which acts of completion would be judged. But there were many other things about the requirements of the wording that as drafter you were aware of, and indeed would have internalised to a high degree. The language should not appear slanted, or unbalanced, or use known provocative phrases. Nevertheless, some phrases might be acceptable which yet displayed their provenance to those in the know. It is a good bet, for instance, that if in these documents you encounter words such as 'deficit' or 'transcend', then the phrases in which they appear originated in Dublin rather than in Belfast or London. Crucially, we knew the positions of the parties. Our Political Affairs Branch produced endless but essential reports on conversations with party members, and we were avid students of their speeches and publications. The difficult bit was not to apply the formula, but rather to spot the subtle shifts.

One had to have absorbed the theology and the detail of the three strands, whatever blind-spots that might risk. It was a seminal political construction, but was it blind to the Belfast–London axis? I ask that not to make an integrationist or related political point, but simply as a political analysis. In my own case, I had not been on the scene at the time of the heroic achievement of the Agreement in 1998, but I had been present at the Brooke and Mayhew talks at the beginning of the 1990s, and could even remember the contributions of the DUP, absent in 2003. Those talks established much of the theology of the post-AIA stages of the peace process. I think that there had, in the draft JD, to be material, even sections, at a level that rose above the detail, even detail so important that it would require primary legislation. There had to be an admixture not of windy rhetoric, but of principle. And there had to be some examples of the language of acknowledgement and accommodation. Nevertheless, there were differences of taste and nuance between British and Irish officials about this, and I will return to them.

The key heads of negotiation, my ten points, together with the others I also mentioned above, had to be identifiable; identifiable, but not bald or unbalanced. There was no point in including irrelevant or inherently intractable issues. Questions to do, for instance, with overarching approaches to the legacy of the past were not ready and might bog things down, though individual aspects of such questions did need to be resolved, and left their mark on the JD. Finally, although the language must not be confusing, it was more important that it should promote convergence than that it should be elegant. Nevertheless, it should be clear. You knew that if the draft JD did its work, it would attract many subtle minds and pens, and would become greatly more encrusted than when it started out. So it should not start off too knotty. At a more personal level, I knew that Jonathan Powell would not accept language that he considered to be 'heavy-handed'. He had disliked that ever since he was an undergraduate.

In case it is of any interest to political scientists, I can report that at the time of putting together the first draft of the JD some of us had indeed read some of the work on consociation theory. I found it reassuring to know that more abstract thinking about the political institutions for divided societies such as Northern Ireland was not wildly out of line with the task in hand. But the point should not be pushed too far. The task in hand in late 2002 did not centre on questions of self-determination, consent, joint authority (which was off the agenda in a way that would not have been true of earlier periods in the peace process) or the design of power-sharing institutions in Strands 1 and 2. At its heart were more substantive policy questions about guns, bread and butter. In any case, we were not political scientists.

One of the odder and less satisfactory features of the British Government's performance during the peace process has followed from discontinuities of personnel. Changes in the ministerial team at the NIO are a matter of public record. For instance, in the summer of 2003, John Spellar replaced Des Browne as political development minister: both Des and John put a great deal of thought and effort into the discussions with the parties, and particularly into trying to make a potentially divisive process seem more inclusive. Less familiar are the changes in the teams of officials. A typical NIO posting used to be three years. Some officials changed jobs within the NIO, but others, like me, were secondees from other departments such as the Home Office, Ministry of Defence and Foreign and Commonwealth Office, and might do just one or two postings in the NIO. This pattern is in contrast to the generally much greater continuity of experience in the talks teams of the Northern Ireland parties. But when you are *in situ* in roles such as mine, associate political director in 2003, you can and do make efforts to smooth out these discontinuities. You have access to the official files, though there are only so many of them you can keep at the front of your mind at any one time. You can talk to your predecessors, who may be people you know quite well. And the NIO used to equip us with invaluable collections of what were known at the time as 'Sacred Texts', or more formally, to take one example, as 'Key papers in the talks process, 1991 to 1997'. Some colleagues, such as David Hill and Alan Whysall, achieved an extraordinary mastery of these documents, on which others of us were necessarily very dependent. In the NIO in late 2002 we felt a degree of discontinuity from the talks at Weston Park in July 2001. Jonathan Powell was there, but Jonathan Phillips and I were not. Jonathan Phillips' predecessor was Bill Jeffrey, a friend and senior colleague of mine from the Home Office, while my predecessor was first Jonathan Stephens, who had worked for me in the early 1990s, and then William Fittall, who was Patrick Mayhew's principal private secretary at the time.

I am pretty sure that when I was attempting the first draft of the JD on that grey afternoon in late 2002, I had close to hand the text of the letter that John Reid and Brian Cowen had sent to the party leaders on 1 August 2001, three weeks after Weston Park, setting out the elements of a package to help to deliver the full and early implementation of the GFA. I have a sense that, while I was familiar with the contents of this document, I did not feel I knew it from the inside. Partly for that reason, and partly because we needed a fresh start with the JD, I tried not to take too much account of the Weston Park package in my drafting. I have the Weston Park document in front of me as I write and it makes a curious contrast with the JD as it was published on

1 May 2003. The two documents are less than two years apart, which makes them close enough in time to have considerable continuity of purpose. And yet both the presentation and the agendas are subtly different. The August 2001 document is far less encrusted than its May 2003 counterpart, and it has the elegance of a style of drafting that has been much less picked over. On the other hand, the agenda, at least on the face of it, seems less ambitious. The expressed aim is not acts of completion, but merely to 'help to deliver the full and early implementation' of the Agreement. The same holds true when you look at the substance. Perhaps this is just a matter of presentation, but the Reid–Cowen letter says the package covers 'all four outstanding issues – policing, normalisation, the stability of the institutions and decommissioning'. Only four? Nothing about ending paramilitary activity or ending the conflict? Nothing about monitoring or sanctions?

On the matter of the OTRs, which are alluded to in the post-Weston Park document, my recollection is that Jonathan and I inherited a well-developed draft scheme from Bill and William. So this very difficult and sensitive issue was less of a late developer than monitoring and sanctions, which assumed a higher profile with such major breaches as 'Stormontgate' (and before it Castlereagh and Columbia). Of course, all such generalisations as this invite a back and back genealogical quest. The OTRs were an extension of the prisoners issue, a prominent Sinn Féin demand in 1998. And the GFA had almost foundered in the endgame over exclusion, which was an important subset of the sanctions issue. Anyhow, such issues morph over time, and by 2003 sanctions had a new context, established by the idea of an IMC, versions of which both the UUP and the AP had been considering the previous year.

However, some issues seem to have loomed larger at Weston Park than they did during the JD phase. A good example concerns the sensitive cases from the past, some relating to serious allegations of collusion by the security forces, which are covered in paragraph 18 of the August 2001 proposals by the two governments. By the time of the JD phase, the Canadian judge Peter Cory was at work reviewing the cases. A combination of this review and the significant changes made to the government's *Implementation Plan* for the *Patten Review* enabled the SDLP, but not Sinn Féin, to join the Policing Board in November 2001. This, I should acknowledge, was one very significant outcome of Weston Park. But, for me, perhaps the most striking specific difference between the Weston Park documents and the JD is the absence from the former of material about ending paramilitary activity and acknowledging that the conflict is over, two of the key counters in the JD that I identified earlier. I may be wrong about this, but I suspect that these two ideas, although implicit earlier, did not really start to be worked up until the meetings at Clonard Monastery in west Belfast from July 2002 onwards between Jonathan Powell and Bill Jeffrey from the British Government and Gerry Adams and Martin McGuinness of Sinn Féin.

An early version of what became paragraph 13 of the JD, dealing with these matters, is to be found in Tony Blair's Belfast Harbour speech of October 2002. As far as I can remember, Jonathan Phillips and I inherited comparable forms of words from Bill Jeffrey and William Fittall when we took over from them in the late summer of that year. Jonathan Powell has said, looking back, that the dynamics were not right for a deal at Weston Park, and that a lot of joint work was done on specific papers by the British and Irish governments for which there was no sufficient quid pro quo from republicans. That, it seems to me, must have been a crucial difference between the two phases.

And what about the experience of re-reading the JD? British officials are not big on discourse theory, but it is a fair bet that a number of us knew and approved of G. M. Young's dictum that in studying history one should continue reading until one can hear the voices speaking. And in reading published sources in preparation for writing this chapter, I found that this was what happened to me. Once again, I could understand, and even speak, the languages of the JD. In the process of doing this, I found that the voices did come back. I could hear Mark Durkan telling Tony Blair in October 2003 that the British Government's approach was one of 'moral setaside'. He did not explain what he meant and he did not have to. Martin McGuinness is the most courteous of men, but defends himself eloquently when under attack: on one occasion when we were pressing him and Gerry Adams on paramilitary activity, he said that 'Hugh Orde [the chief constable] sneezes every time a mouse farts.' David Trimble used to refer to the greener parts of the JD as 'guff'. This may sound disrespectful, but in a private context was far more constructive than that: he was saying that he was prepared not to quibble, and to deal with any hit he might take. I can hear Ian Paisley describing the nearly deal of 21 October as 'a dunghill of deceit'. This must have been a public observation, but it was exactly what one would have expected Dr Paisley to say about the outcome of a process to which he was not party, and we were to rediscover in the months after November 2003 that he could be much more engaging in private discussions. Every peace process needs its healers, and Paul Murphy was perhaps the greatest of these during this phase. After the agony of 21 October, he had kind words for all parties, and I can hear him saying, of David Trimble: 'Well, David and I will just go and have some Fronsac at the Oxford and Cambridge.'

When I re-read the JD now I cannot say for sure where a particular phrase comes from, but I can find points of interest in every paragraph. I will not subject readers to that, but will attempt a broader-brush analysis. It is clear to me that parts, but not all, of the set of documents were subjected to a considerable 'greening' process, coming primarily from the Irish Government, and to a lesser extent from Sinn Féin. Two components in which I recognise my original drafting almost unamended are the papers on 'Devolution of Policing and Justice' and on the 'OTRs'. This tells me that these documents were not explored in much depth, which, after a certain point, were parked or banked. By contrast, the opening paragraphs of the JD have evidently been much worked over. They are far more repetitious than a British official would draft. It is instructive, for instance, to count the number of appearances of words such as 'trust', 'confidence', 'definitive', 'historic' and so on. I stand to be disproved, but I believe that phrases such as 'dwelling forever on the undoubted wrongs and associated hatred of the past' would have come from an Irish pen. The word 'confidence' is a classic indicator. In the first paragraph of the *Agreement on Monitoring and Compliance*, a contentious document much disliked by Sinn Féin and worked over by Irish colleagues, 'confidence' occurs three times in the first three sentences. Semantically, it is an even-handed term. But it has its roots in the 'confidence issues' which used to have their own item on every meeting of the Anglo-Irish Intergovernmental Conference, and which to unionists represented Irish Government 'interference' in Northern Ireland.

My recollection is that the British Government's approach, a little like David Trimble's in this respect, was to accept a certain amount of green-tinged language of acknowledgement and recognition in return for solidity on substantive points that we knew would be essential to one or more parties. It has to be kept in mind that it was common practice among both British and Irish officials to accept a first draft from the other team and then amend it to deal with problematic material. We were always clear that our test was to hunt out material that would be unacceptable to any party, and we did not regard ourselves as interpreters of unionism to our Irish colleagues, who in any case had their own meetings with the UUP, just as we did with the SDLP and Sinn Féin. One consequence of this acquiescence is that in the published texts it takes twelve paragraphs until one comes to the most famous paragraph in the entire collection, paragraph 13, which sets out in detail the types of paramilitary activity that must end. I am sure that Irish colleagues saw it as an advantage, and politic, not to belabour republicans with this language right at the very start of the document. For us, I think, the important point was not its placing, but that it should be comprehensive and clear. Here one might reasonably be asked why there was so much focus on forms of words about paramilitary activity both in the JD and in statements in April, May and October by the PIRA, and by Gerry Adams glossing the PIRA words. Why did all this matter, given that a monitoring regime was being set up anyway? Well, even the monitoring regime needed a benchmark, and that is what paragraph 13 provides. Moreover, Sinn Féin never accepted the monitoring proposals, as Gerry Adams' statement on 21 October made clear, even if it could be construed as tacit acquiescence. Actions may often speak louder than words, but in this case words were needed too, not least as republican recognition that unionists had requirements too. Some of the formulations used by Gerry Adams on 21 October had been agreed in advance with David Trimble.

A good example of British insistence on a key point of both substance and rhetoric is to be found in the conditionality of the language about security normalisation. Both in paragraphs 18 and 19 and in the Annex that dealt with this, there is massive use of the conditional 'would' to underline that normalisation would take place only in the context of acts of completion. Although as a generalisation it is broadly true that Irish colleagues were keener on expansive rhetoric than we were, there is a rhetorical aspect to our insistence on the repetition of 'would': we could, of course, have said instead that we 'will' do what is set out if the conditions are met. The trigger for normalisation shows signs of having been a battleground. The phrase 'In the context of the definitive transition to exclusively peaceful and democratic means' leaves the start point of security normalisation open to interpretation, and yet an endpoint of April 2005 is set. In paragraph 5 of the Annex, the start point is glossed as 'On the basis of the historic leap forward by the [P]IRA we would undertake a normalisation programme over the period between now and April 2005.' This is all a bit messy, but our bottom line was protected because it would be for us to judge both whether the clock had started and whether any subsequent changes in the threat assessment required modification of the normalisation programme. In the event, both governments judged (the Irish Government also having a significant interest through the security cooperation programme) that a PIRA statement later in May was insufficient to trigger the full security normalisation programme, although some interim measures were taken in line with the threat assessment.

An example of a test of British provenance is that for devolution of justice and policing. Indeed, this could not have been an Irish Government test because of the doctrine that the Irish Government should not play a role in Strand 1 matters. But the British test is revealing: devolution on a basis that 'is robust and workable and broadly supported by the parties'. There is a hint here of the British Government having a position beyond a purely facilitating one: the idea is that policing and justice are government functions of fundamental importance, and the British Government has an obligation to be satisfied that they are devolved in a way which is not merely agreed, but robust and workable. In paragraphs 13–21 of the Annex, which look to me to be much as I drafted them, there is a classic instance of the British Government in facilitating mode, putting forward a range of possible institutional models for the parties to consider and narrow down. That is a very Whitehall approach.

Leaving aside the key issue of devolution of policing and justice, paragraphs 20–24 of the JD, on policing and justice, will be impenetrable to most readers. This is the effect of the intense political interest since the Agreement in these two vital functions of state. Police reform issues could now be viewed in four categories: the proposals in the original *Implementation Plan* for Patten; the revisions to that plan agreed at Weston Park; further measures by now included in the policing legislation of 2003 but conditional, for their statutory commencement orders, on acts of completion; and yet further measures, going beyond Patten, being sought by Sinn Féin, such as total ending of the use of plastic baton rounds.

It is worth noticing some more specific points, some small and some more important. In paragraph 25, the two governments 'rededicate' themselves to human rights and equal opportunity. I am not sure whether the word came from a British or Irish pen, but it is a quintessential John Reid word, which he often used in press conferences in Dublin. Paragraph 24, on criminal justice, has a New Labour flavour, including the keyword 'modernisation'. And something interesting happens in paragraph 27, where the British Government undertakes to 'encourage the devolved administration, when restored, to prioritise and take forward a review of policy on good community relations'. This is a clear breach of devolution: it is unimaginable, for instance, that the British Government would have said such a thing in the Scotland White Paper of 1997: devolution means devolution. I suspect that in this case the British Government was responding to a proposal urged by the Irish Government or Sinn Féin, and judged that the contribution of the initiative to acts of completion was more important than the purity of devolution doctrine. An interesting British Government act of completion, in addition to those on security and the OTRs, is in paragraph 9, which states that in the context of acts of completion the British Government would repeal the power in the Northern Ireland Act 2000 to suspend the Northern Ireland institutions. In one sense this could be read as a rebuke to the Mandelson and Reid suspensions. More constructively, it was an expression of faith that in a context of genuine acts of completion such suspensions would no longer be needed. But a political realist might note that if in the future suspension should nevertheless be needed to safeguard the Agreement's institutions, this could still be achieved by emergency primary legislation at Westminster.

The text also sheds light on a tricky question of interest to both participants and analysts: was the JD intended to form the basis of a single text negotiation? The GFA might be viewed as a relatively clear example of a single text negotiation document. Although in reality it was a complex collection of texts and side letters, and was not endorsed in the same manner by every party, it was designed to pull all the issues together for agreement by all the participating parties. The JD is not quite like that, as can be clearly seen from paragraph 36, in which the two governments in effect commend the JD's contents to the parties without seeking their endorsement (similarly, in his subsequent Statement to the House of Commons on the Joint Declaration, the secretary of state said that the pro-Agreement parties approved of the JD, but made clear that its proposals were those of the two governments). It thus falls somewhere between the 1998 Agreement and the 1985 AIA, which was much closer to being an imposed blueprint. One could write a great deal about the typology of texts of this sort. In a sense, the JD is *sui generis*. It is much richer in policy content than the DSD of 1993, though it shares that document's aim of securing transition to exclusively peaceful political means. The JD reflects the especially high degree of solidarity between the Tony Blair and Bertie Ahern administrations, but it nevertheless tries harder to bind in the parties than, say, the DSD or the 1985 Agreement. But perhaps its most important function of all is to set out the benchmarks and tests for all-round acts of completion. This makes it both an interesting text and an unusual one in relation to what went before.

Conclusions

What was the point of this year in the peace process, from October 2002 to October 2003? Gerry Adams has said that the negotiations were even more intensive, and tougher, than those leading up to the GFA of 1998. I am not in a position to second-guess that. But, certainly, during the year there were hundreds of meetings, phone calls and documents. No single person was involved in them all. But Tony Blair, Paul Murphy, Bertie Ahern, Brian Cowen, David Trimble, Gerry Adams and Martin McGuinness all, from their different perspectives, were involved in a high percentage of the action, and leading advisers such as Jonathan Powell, Jonathan Phillips, Michael Collins from the taoiseach's office, Tim Dalton, head of the Irish Justice Ministry, David Campbell (David Trimble's chief of staff) and two or three people from the Sinn Féin team could make a similar claim.

At the heart of this intensive effort was a quest to hold Assembly elections and restore the Northern Ireland Executive in return for verifiable and completed decommissioning, the ending of paramilitary activity and the ending of the conflict itself. In order to clear space for this central deal, the other outstanding issues, such as normalisation, the OTRs, Sinn Féin joining the policing board and the devolution of justice and the police, had to have agreed implementation plans and agreed sequencing. Depending on where we were at a given time, one or more of the parties could, and often did, seek to narrow the agenda or, by contrast, to broaden it and reintroduce banked elements. It is important to understand that there was no absolute, non-relative yardstick for judging how much was enough on a given issue. This could change, especially if, for instance, one or more of the sides judged that its supporters were getting the sense that a rival was getting the better of them. For an adviser and minor participant such as me, it was a bit like swimming. You had to be in the water to get the feel for the judgements and improvisations which your part demanded.

If you take the ten key issues that I singled out in the first part of this chapter, some were more fixed, or less variable, than others. With restoration of the

Executive, the election date and Sinn Féin joining the Policing Board, there was not really any policy content to negotiate: the questions were essentially ones of conditionality and sequencing. The others did raise outstanding policy issues. Sometimes these could feel like a John Coltrane saxophone solo, in which the issue was held up to the light of the negotiations and twisted first this way and then that, so that different angles and aspects were exposed to view. Take decommissioning. It was reluctantly accepted during this period that filming and photos were not on. 'No Spielbergs', as both Brian Cowen and Martin McGuinness used to say. Witnessing by respected clerics did feature in the discussions, but was not in the final package. That left questions of timetabling and transparency. Some claim that these variables were never truly tied down, but it was even more complicated than that. What, for instance, was required for transparency? Would an inventory of decommissioned weapons be necessary, would headings and examples suffice, or would simple rhetoric to the effect that the weapons decommissioned could cause mayhem and mass destruction have any value? The answer varied according to political circumstances.

In an attempt to give some sort of shape to the intricate chronology of events, I can make out a number of broad phases. Between October and Christmas 2002, the British side was seeking a framework for corralling the necessary acts of completion, eventually coming up with the draft JD. Tony Blair gave a revealing interview to Frank Millar at Downing Street on 9 November, in which he repeatedly stressed paramilitary activity as the reason why the British Government could not yet deliver its own acts of completion, why David Trimble had had no option but to leave the Executive, and why unionist opinion was not coming back behind the GFA. In January and February, the two governments refined the approach, and the Irish pushed us to a more forward position on security normalisation, which was then cleared, with some difficulty, with the army and the police. These discussions were also vital in achieving joint ownership by the two governments of the text of the JD.

The intensive negotiations of March and early April had the effect of pulling out the highly sensitive issues of OTRs and sanctions, and parking them by balancing them off against each other. This is why they take the form of separate documents within the JD package. Mid-April focused on decommissioning, paramilitary activity and the ending of the conflict, which were the subject of Tony Blair's three questions to the PIRA. This was seen as a serious breach of protocol by Sinn Féin and the Provisionals, but may have been a factor in securing the further movement that was necessary to the UUP in particular. The next discernible phase ended in the publication of the JD on 1 May: this was risky, because the package could have been seen as unbalanced, and it was challenged, for instance, by Trimble's opponents within the UUP. The advantages of publishing the JD were that it set a benchmark

The Joint Declaration and memory 169

for PIRA acts of completion, to which they could have regard without having to endorse in language that would be unacceptable to them. It bracketed out and parked issues such as the OTRs and sanctions, and to a lesser extent normalisation, devolution of justice and policing and Sinn Féin joining the Policing Board, albeit not definitively in any case, and gave visibility to all parties and to the public of the shape of the package of required acts of completion.

July was a quiet marching season, partly the result of intensive cooperation between the UUP and Sinn Féin, which helped with the mood for the autumn push. Back in London, I took a couple of calls from Gerry Kelly from Sinn Féin on the subject, and I know that he played an important calming role. September saw acute focus on the question of the election date: this was one of the rare issues on which the two governments did not see eye to eye. The interlinked policing issues also loomed large at this time, although much of the focus was on sequencing rather than substance. Finally, there was the narrowing down to the agreed sequence for 21 October (originally planned for the day before), the statement by Gerry Adams including some of David Trimble's language which most found positive, the foundering of the choreography because the IICD representatives were not in a position to give a sufficiently transparent account of PIRA decommissioning, and the tantalisingly close-run failure to revive the deal on the weekend of 24–25 October. Could this have culminated in success rather than failure? I do not see why not. The weekend salvage operation, by which time the moment had perhaps passed, demonstrated that the necessary ingredients for success could have come together on the day of 21 October.

What lessons did we learn? This is more difficult to answer than it seems. I was, as I now see, shielded from recriminations, but others, such as Jonathan Powell, were not, and showed their class in absorbing them without transferring their pain or becoming discouraged. The obvious points were almost too obvious to be worth calling lessons: that there was a collective failure to pin down the fine detail on the transparency and timetabling for decommissioning; that more grip could have been exerted; that what happened to John de Chastelain should not be allowed to happen again; that things might still have been different if his press conference could somehow have been more upbeat; and so on. But once the salvage operation of the following weekend had failed we were into the run-up to elections, and then a completely new phase of the peace process, centring on proximity talks involving Sinn Féin and the DUP, so not all of the lessons would have been relevant anyway.

I say there was a collective failure to pin down decommissioning. The irony is that we now know that it was a substantial act (even though that in 2005 was more substantial still). It did not help that there were at least six key players, namely, the British and Irish governments, the UUP, Sinn Féin, the IIDC and the PIRA, and more specifically their representatives. I know myself of at least a dozen concerted efforts to settle how the act could be described, and there must have been more. We know, for instance, that there was a serious focus on this issue in the direct discussions between the UUP and Sinn Féin. It is very difficult, and perhaps fruitless at this stage, to assess how far the failure came about through a negotiating miscalculation rather than a breakdown of the criss-crossing communications. The intensely frustrating thing is that the substance of a sufficient solution was potentially there, as the subsequent salvage discussions demonstrated.

What would have happened if the deal had come off? My time as a student studying history came too early for the vogue for counter-factual history, though one of my professors, H. R. Trevor-Roper, would probably have enjoyed it. I find the speculation almost impossible to carry through, not least because it is so hard to estimate what the outcome of the Assembly elections might have been in different circumstances. I think one can be confident that certain outstanding issues would still have given much trouble, not least because relatively little substantive progress was made on them during the year I have been writing about, and because it was more expedient to park them. Devolution of justice and policing would come top of the difficult list. What would the DUP have done? Another impossible question. On a naively optimistic interpretation, they would probably have participated again in the Strand 1 institutions, and that might have had the effect, given a fair wind, of drawing out that their agenda for amending the Agreement did not inherently include show-stoppers. But the key development of the personal bond that grew up between Tony Blair and Ian Paisley would have been deferred. More generally, the DUP would have been far more reluctant negotiators than they became after the November 2003 elections. Perhaps, in the end, it would have been a slower route to the summit if the 21 October sequencing had come off. But that was certainly not the calculation we made at the time. The central push for a deal was between the UUP and Sinn Féin, especially in September and October, and it was that to which we were committed.

In an important pamphlet *Misunderstanding Ulster* (2007), David Trimble, now Lord Trimble, gives a penetrating analysis of the continuity of the peace process from the Brooke–Mayhew talks of the early 1990s onwards, cautions against oversimplified application of the Northern Ireland model to conflict resolution in Spain, the Middle East, Sri Lanka and elsewhere, and criticises the British Government for departing from the policies through which the GFA was reached in its attempts to move the process on after 1998. Seamus Mallon has taken the last point further, arguing that the two governments betrayed the moderate centre in Northern Ireland politics. Others, too, have argued that during the four main episodes between 1972 and 1992 in which the British Government had contact with the PIRA, this contact had some damaging consequences in terms of undermining moderate nationalism.

David Trimble is right that any prescription of unfettered negotiations with terrorists as a key ingredient of world conflict resolution is imprecise in a way that is likely to mislead those trying to secure exclusively peaceful politics. The exchange of messages in 1993 was very clear about the conditions that had to be satisfied before the British Government could engage with republicans, or before they could participate in all-party talks, although at that stage they did not expressly include decommissioning (it is true that members of the link did on a couple of occasions take more forward positions, but these were not authorised). Our discussions with Sinn Féin in 2002–3 were not unfettered, or open-ended, and involved clear insistence on the required endpoint and the necessary acts of completion. One of the main purposes of the JD was to set this out. The language in paragraph 13 of the JD, for instance, on the requirements for ending paramilitary activity, is a case in point. Parts of it go back at least as far as the *Mitchell Principles* of 1995. We strengthened it from its October 2002 version in Tony Blair's 'act of completion' speech, and it stood from May to October 2003 as a clear, public benchmark. We knew that the PIRA were not going to re-use this language. Apart from the certainty that they were not going to abase themselves in this way, repeating the language would have looked like an admission of guilt. Nevertheless, the requirement was clear on the public record. Similarly, on ending the conflict, neither we nor David Trimble insisted on the humiliating term 'disbandment', but the requirement was again clear. Tony Blair caused a fair amount of angst by putting his three questions publicly to the PIRA in April 2003, but he was driving out the ambiguity in the way he said was needed in the 'acts of completion' speech.

Imprecise versions of the 'dialogue with terrorists' argument might lead one to expect that in 2002 and 2003 we were talking to the representatives of dissident republicans. To the best of my knowledge, we were not! They did not have a realistic or constructive enough political agenda, and such dialogue would have rendered our discussions with Sinn Féin impossible. Tony Blair did on several occasions propose to Gerry Adams that he should directly meet the PIRA, but these suggestions were played into the long grass. There is good reason to believe that Adams and McGuinness did not have things all their own way with the PIRA over this period, whether with volunteers or with the leadership on the PIRA Army Council. The published literature refers to occasions on which they were rebuffed, as well as to their commanding mastery of republican aspirations. It seems likely to me that the leadership called for from Gerry Adams and Martin McGuinness was a formidable task requiring vision and skill of a very high order. That said, it seems plausible that Adams and McGuinness were assisted in being able, as so often in diplomacy, to play both ends against the middle to some extent. That is another reason why requirements and benchmarks were needed, even if, as I have argued above, the values of these variables could shift according to the requirements of the context.

What about Lord Trimble's argument that the British Government departed from its pre-Agreement approach, succumbed to another inch-by-inch negotiation, and abandoned the moderate centre among the Northern Ireland parties? This has some force, but here, it seems to me, the position is quite complicated. So, did we betray the moderate centre by eventually not seeking further postponement of the elections? I do not think so. There were two deferments, both at significant political cost, in order to create the space for the deal to be done. Logically, there would have to be elections at some point. Seamus Mallon's argument is weakened by the fact that the SDLP were consistently in favour of early elections. David Trimble signed up to a planned sequence that included as an element the announcement of the election, and it was an essential trigger for restoration of the Executive, a *sine qua non* of the deal. There is more scope for legitimate disagreement about the precise way in which the election card was played during the course of the September discussions in particular, but that would take me to a level of detail that I cannot now assess without being able to see the official papers.

In a recent, illuminating conversation which I greatly appreciated, Mark Durkan told me that in his judgement it would have been much better if the whole of this phase of the peace process had been conducted as a fully inclusive, and where possible multilateral, sequence of negotiations, focusing on a timetabled set of acts of completion. I find this approach intellectually coherent and ethically appealing. My only reservation, and it is a major one, is whether this could have worked in practice. Mark Durkan's arguments are detailed, and I cannot do justice to them here. He has strong views on a number of the more specific points I cover in this analysis. On the point about practicability, he would probably say that if particular parties were uncooperative, the two governments should have maintained firm positions until those parties returned to the fold. I can only reply that the approach actually taken was messier, both practically and morally, but achieved better results and fewer compromises in the long run than other possible courses of action. I would not expect Mark to agree with that!

On the argument that elements in the British and Irish governments were advocating a switch to a 'deal of the extremes', that is, between Sinn Féin and the DUP, some distinctions are needed. Chris Maccabe and his team were indeed keeping in touch with the DUP and analysing the leadership challenges within the UUP, but they would not have been doing their jobs if they had not done so. But that does not mean that in, say, September 2003, the DUP would have been the British Government's preferred interlocutors. At that time no one in the British team was in any doubt about the seminal importance of the intensive direct dialogue between the UUP and Sinn Féin. In a real sense, it was their deal that we were working on.

But that does not exhaust the debate. Could and should we have avoided further inch-by-inch negotiation with Sinn Féin? And could we have played a tougher hand? My answer to the second question is: probably yes. As to the first, I am not so sure. Not all the unfinished acts of completion fell to the republicans. It is true that Sinn Féin were masters of trying to squeeze out every last drop, and that this was a recurring tactic, though one we were well aware of. But we did at least have a good idea of where the lines were for the other parties, checked back with them as often as we could, and made it a key test not to concede anything that was either unlikely to command agreement as part of an overall package or was not in the public interest. Yes, of course, as a matter of procedural fairness, it would have been better if Sinn Féin had been compelled to negotiate every line of their fifty-seven-page document with all the other parties. It would certainly have saved us the odd fourteen-hour meeting! But as a matter of practical politics, that was not going to happen.

David Trimble argues that we abandoned the 1998 principle of sufficient consensus. I am not sure that we did. Some form of the principle was at least indirectly in play in the construction of the JD. One could argue that it was only an attenuated version of it. My own feeling is that we were simply trying to address the political realities of the circumstances in 2002–3. One could also argue that after November 2003 sufficient consensus could be delivered by the DUP and Sinn Féin rather than the UUP and the SDLP, but that is an anachronistic point for the period covered in this chapter.

Some recent accounts of the period from November 2003 to 8 May 2007 have sought to argue that the British Government could have played a tougher hand, and that events such as the Northern Bank robbery, the murder of Robert McCartney and the reactions to these, were more important in bringing about the completion of decommissioning and the formal end to the PIRA campaign. I am not in a position to comment from first-hand knowledge, which in my case ended in September 2004. But I am suspicious of the first part of the argument, and do not think that the second part is applicable to the period covered here. External events leading up to 'Stormontgate' had indeed played their part in shaping the position of republicans, but I think it is misleading to divorce this from the substantive content of the intensive political dialogue over the period. The parties were rational negotiators, if sometimes unpredictable ones. And it bears repeating that much of the direct negotiation was between the UUP and Sinn Féin. Leaving aside the certainty that these arguments could be pursued with further distinctions and further detail, my conclusion remains that this was an intensive and vital period of the peace process. In his autobiography,

A Journey (2010), Tony Blair called it an 'intermission', but that perhaps reflects his frustration that 21 October 2003 did not come off. As I have argued above, I believe it could have. At the time, David Trimble referred to the need for both sticks and carrots. In this, as in much else, he was right.

Towards the second day of the salvage negotiations at the end (that is, on 26 October), the brilliantly professional staff at Hillsborough Castle said they were bringing us hot pies and curries. David Trimble said he preferred to eat his dinner at home. Jonathan Powell wryly remarked that so did he, when he had the chance. But for me it was a privilege to be a participant in these talks, and also in the early stages of the subsequent phase marked by the return of the DUP. If I am a little more sceptical than some about the applications of 'lessons' from Northern Ireland to other parts of the world, this is neither to deny that there are such lessons, nor to downplay the magnitude of what was being attempted. When I first started visiting Northern Ireland in 1990 we were in the middle of one of those terrible phases of tit-for-tat killings, the despair was palpable, it was received wisdom and almost orthodoxy that the issues were insoluble, and that local people were incentivised to ensure that the problems were not solved. That view has always struck me as insulting. The people I worked with showed courage and vision. David Trimble had perfected techniques for ensuring that a cut-off point was reached in fraught negotiations (spurning the pies and curry was a minor example), but it should never be forgotten that he sacrificed his illustrious leadership career for the peace process. It is both exciting and moving to prompt one's memory of this period in Northern Ireland. If someone could make a film about it as thought-provoking as Guzmán's *Nostalgia for the Light* I should be very happy!

Appendix: brief chronology

2001

9–14 July: Weston Park talks.
11 September: 9/11 attacks in the US.

2002

17 March: Castlereagh break-in.
August: Three republicans arrested in Colombia.
4 October: Police raid Sinn Féin offices in Stormont.
14 October: Suspension.
17 October: Tony Blair's 'acts of completion' speech to the Belfast Harbour Commissioners.

26 October: Gerry Adams' Monaghan speech.
December: British first draft of the JD.
19 December: David Trimble temporarily walks out of talks.
24 December: Sinn Féin send fifty-seven-page document to the British Government.

2003

28–29 January: British and Irish teams meeting at Farmleigh, outside Dublin.
12 February: The two governments meet the parties at Hillsborough.
18 February: British and Irish officials meet Sinn Féin for fourteen hours at Windsor House.
3–4 March: Multiparty talks at Hillsborough. Assembly elections postponed from 1 May to 29 May.
14 March: St Patrick's Day. Meetings in the US.
7–8 April: President Bush at Hillsborough. The two prime ministers decide to hold back publication of the JD.
23 April: Tony Blair puts his three questions to the PIRA.
1 May: Publication of the JD. Second postponement of Assembly elections.
June–September: Challenges to David Trimble within the UUP.
July: A quiet marching season, partly resulting from intensive UUP–Sinn Féin liaison.
September: First private handshake between David Trimble and Gerry Adams.
4 October: The prime ministers meet at an EU summit. They send a joint letter to the PIRA seeking an end to paramilitary activity and private instructions to volunteers.
19 October: Tony Blair's heart flutter.
21 October: Choreographed announcements. Assembly elections to be on 26 November. Statement by Gerry Adams. Press conference by General John de Chastelain. He states that he is not in a position to describe the major act of decommissioning by the PIRA that he has witnessed. David Trimble puts the sequence on hold.
25–26 October: Unsuccessful salvage negotiations at Hillsborough. The final republican offer is a twenty-four-month period for decommissioning, a percentage for the arms decommissioned thus far, plus an annex listing the types of weapons. But by mid-afternoon, David Trimble's supporters are drawing in their horns.

References

The JD can be found at: http://cain.ulst.ac.uk/events/peace/docs/bijoint010503.pdf.
Blair, T. (2010). *A Journey*. London: Hutchinson.
Powell, J. (2008). *Great Hatred, Little Room*. London: Bodley Head.
Trimble, D. (2007). *Misunderstanding Ulster*, available at: www.davidtrimble.org/publications_misunderstanding.pdf.

8 Movement and transition in 1997: Major to Blair

Sir John Holmes

My aim in this chapter is to describe the transition between John Major and Tony Blair in the area of Northern Ireland policy, from the perspective of someone who lived through it at close quarters. What stayed the same, and what was different? Why was Blair able to take what Major had started through to a successful conclusion? Did they have different views, or was it just their political circumstances that were different? These are questions that I will consider and elaborate on, but, before I do so, it is important to provide some background context to political conditions at the early stages of the peace process and the influences on the process.

The Downing Street context

I took over from Rod Lyne as John Major's overseas adviser at the beginning of 1996. The role was wide-ranging, covering all international and defence affairs, including overseas aid, and was all-consuming. There was little substantive policy support for the role in 10 Downing Street at that stage, although the administrative back-up was formidable. While there was advice to be had in some areas from the Cabinet Office Overseas and Defence Secretariat, I had only one Foreign Office assistant of my own to help me cover everything going on in the world. Even that was a relative novelty – my predecessors until Rod Lyne had had no such help, reflecting the then prevailing wisdom that Number 10 advisers should essentially be intelligent links between the prime minister and his ministries rather than independent sources of advice and policy expertise. All this may seem rather quaint in the age of a National Security Council, and it no longer quite represented the reality even then (think of Charles Powell's role with Mrs Thatcher). But the sensible idea behind it was to stop overweening and overambitious prime ministerial advisers second-guessing line departments and ministers or, even worse, developing rival policies, as was seen to be the damaging case in Washington, with the national security advisor constantly at the elbow of the president, backed by the resources of their National Security Council, and vying counter-productively with the State Department and the Pentagon for influence.

Like my predecessors, in addition to foreign affairs, I had to devote large amounts of effort to Northern Ireland, and to the continuing search for a lasting peace settlement. Over the next three and a quarter years, until I left Tony Blair's office in March 1999, I often spent up to a third of my time on Northern Ireland, and occasionally even more when the pressures were particularly great. This was not because international affairs were lacking in interest, controversy or activity – for example, 1998, the year of the Good Friday Agreement (GFA), also saw the UK presidencies of both the G8 and the EU, in both of which I was centrally involved – but was simply a reflection of the crucial, life-and-death demands of the Northern Ireland issues, and the huge personal role played in them by both prime ministers. It was, of course, rather ironic that the prime minister's overseas adviser should deal with Northern Ireland when it was certainly not an overseas territory, but that was how it had been for a number of years, no doubt because of the importance of the issue for relations with the Irish Republic and, to a lesser extent, the US.

One particular feature of the role that I inherited was its importance for the unionists. Their suspicion of the Northern Ireland Office (NIO) and its supposed hidden 'green' agenda of handing them over to the South knew almost no bounds, even when a secretary of state such as Patrick Mayhew could hardly be seen as any kind of Provisional IRA (PIRA) sympathiser. Number 10 was viewed, rightly or wrongly, as more understanding of, and sympathetic to, unionist fears and aspirations. This meant that unionists were always particularly liable to phone or come into Number 10, and to use the overseas adviser as the first port of call, in the absence of instant access to the prime minister, to complain about NIO duplicity or incompetence, and press their case. It was not that others did not do the same, from the Social Democratic and Labour Party (SDLP) through Sinn Féin, to the loyalists, but in my experience Number 10 and the prime minister's overseas adviser had to be ready to lend a particularly sympathetic ear to unionist concerns and demands in order to keep them onside and engaged in the peace process, wherever it stood at the time.

Another particularly important part of the role was to be the link with the taoiseach's office in Dublin. There were, of course, multiple other contacts with the Irish, from the NIO and elsewhere. But it was important that there was this channel too, so that the Irish had a fuller idea than they might necessarily get from the NIO of where British (and unionist) concerns and bottom lines really lay. This channel proved vital at many stages. This was therefore the kind of role I played for both prime ministers, including in the transition between the two in May 1997, after Tony Blair's landslide victory in the general election of that year. It was relatively unusual for the same official to stay on in the same role for any length of time when prime ministers changed, particularly when the incoming prime minister came from a different party. But it was by no means unprecedented, given the unpoliticised British Civil Service tradition. People often ask me about the difference between the two prime ministers for whom I worked. My habitual reply is that the crucial difference was not so much in their policies, views and attitudes, though these were not of course identical; or even in their personalities, though these were certainly very different; but in the political circumstances in which they were operating. I hope to show that this was largely true in the Northern Ireland context too, but that there were also some significant differences of attitude and approach from Blair that were appropriate to the moment, and that helped to make rapid progress possible.

John Major

In my time with John Major, in 1996–7, he was coming to the end of eighteen years of Conservative Government, with all that implied for the exhaustion of energy and ideas of the party, if not of the prime minister himself. He lacked a secure parliamentary majority, was fighting an endless battle against opponents in his own party, particularly the Eurosceptics, and increasingly lacked authority and power through no fault of his own. It was a minor miracle, for which he is still given insufficient credit, that he was able to keep going and achieve so much in such unpromising conditions. Nevertheless, it was almost universally assumed that he was bound to lose the 1997 election, with all that implied for how much effective business could be done in key areas when everyone was waiting to deal with his successor.

This was certainly a factor in Northern Ireland too. The different parties and their leaders could have been forgiven for being increasingly inclined to hang back to see what would happen with a new Labour Government, especially in the last few months of the Major administration, rather than take risks with the outgoing Conservative one. We did indeed see this reluctance to commit beginning to be visible, but it did not take hold seriously until a surprisingly late stage before the election. The political situation was also particularly complicated because the unionists could in many cases be the swing votes for the government in the House of Commons, which gave them at least a theoretical stranglehold on policy in areas of particular interest to them.

It has often been alleged that the unionists were, as a consequence, somehow given a veto on Major's Northern Ireland policy, and that this explains the lack of movement and consequent nationalist and republican frustration in the last period of the Major administration. This is in my view, and in the light of my experience, a serious misreading of the situation. In particular, it completely misjudges the degree to which Major, whose commitment to making progress towards lasting peace in Northern Ireland should never be underestimated, despite the risks for him, was determined precisely to avoid becoming the hostage of the unionists. If he had indeed been obliged, or been content, to be in that position, he could have had a much easier life. He could certainly have effectively given up the struggle to move forward much sooner than he did. But he was never willing to do that except right at the end, as we shall see. He continued to look for objective ways forward and for credible compromises as long as he could. Many of the things he did in his later years in office certainly annoyed the unionists more than the nationalists, for example, the negotiation of the so-called Frameworks Document with the Irish Government in 1995, whose supposed 'green' tinge (more in language than substance) infuriated even moderates like the then Ulster Unionist Party (UUP) leader, James Molyneaux.

Having said all this, there is no doubt that Major did at times have to be even more than usually aware of the neuralgic points for unionist opinion, and to take care to avoid antagonising them and their Conservative Party supporters and sympathisers too far or unnecessarily. Unofficial intermediaries like Robert Cranborne and Brian Mawhinney, then chairman of the Conservative Party, were constantly working to keep the relationship on the rails. They had a good deal of success, and the show was indeed kept on the road. But there were nevertheless still political limits to the new steps that could be taken during that period, not just because the unionists would have objected, but also because it would have been impossible to create enough support in the Conservative Party itself, or more widely in the press and public opinion, for moves too far out of respective comfort zones at a time when there was no general inclination to trust the republicans. For example, Major would in principle, for all his strong language of condemnation at times, have liked to take the dramatic step later taken by Blair of meeting the Sinn Féin leaders himself. But this was politically out of the question in the particular circumstances of the time, with PIRA violence never far away.

My own time with Major started in the most inauspicious way possible on the Northern Ireland front when on 9 February 1996 the PIRA broke their 1994 ceasefire, one hour after stating publicly that it was at an end, by exploding a bomb in the City of London, killing two innocent civilians in the process. There had been rumblings about this possibility for months before it happened, because of a strong republican view that what they saw as a firm promise to hold all-party talks including them had not been met. But it was still a shock when it actually occurred – perhaps even to some of the Sinn Féin leadership, at least in its timing. It obviously posed an immediate challenge to the strategy of trying to engage Sinn Féin in the political process, and created a great opportunity for those opposed to this strategy from the beginning, mainly on the unionist and Conservative side, to say 'We told you so'.

The immediate precursor to the bomb had been the early January 1996 report of US senator George Mitchell and his colleagues from an international panel that had been asked to look at the thorny question of the decommissioning of illegal weapons by the paramilitary organisations. This report proposed that the idea of prior decommissioning, that is, at least some decommissioning *before* talks including Sinn Féin and the loyalist parties linked to their paramilitaries could start, should be given up as, however desirable in principle, it was not going to happen in practice; and that the concept of parallel decommissioning, that is, at least some decommissioning *during* the negotiations, should be substituted. Prior decommissioning had long been dear to the unionists, for obvious reasons of democratic legitimacy, to avoid the appearance or reality of negotiating under the duress of a threatened return to violence, and to try to ensure that all concerned were genuinely committed to exclusively peaceful means to achieving their political goals. It had been picked up explicitly by Patrick Mayhew on behalf of the Major Government in a speech in Washington in March 1995 in a not unreasonable form (which the unionists thought at the time did not go anything like far enough). One of the so-called 'Washington Three' conditions stipulated some decommissioning as a condition that those representing the paramilitaries should fulfil in order to join the negotiations quickly thereafter. Unfortunately, however reasonable in theory, in reality even this became an obstacle to moving forward both because it represented, in the eyes of republicans in particular, a departure from the claimed tradition of 'putting the pike in the thatch' rather than taking steps that could be interpreted as implying defeat or surrender, and because there were men in the PIRA, and among the loyalists too, who were simply not yet ready to abandon all thoughts of a return to violence and who, therefore, had to be brought slowly and with great difficulty to accept exclusively peaceful and political methods of promoting their cause.

Decommissioning was to become one of the greatest bugbears of the negotiations before, during and long after the GFA. Its difficulty is illustrated by the facts that there was no actual decommissioning until 2001, and that the process was not declared completed until 2005 (and even then, despite international verification, was not accepted as a full reality by some on the unionist side). This shows both its central importance as a tangible symbol of the end of the war, and its ability to get in the way of progress. One counter-argument to the demand for decommissioning, beyond the psychological concern raised by the Irish and Sinn Féin themselves about the need to avoid appearing to humiliate the paramilitaries, was that the PIRA or their successors would always be able to get hold of more weapons if they decided to go back to violence, so that whether they had got rid of their existing stock, while obviously of practical as well as symbolic value, was not the be-all and end-all for the future that the unionists made it out to be. However, the real point was that in a context where neither side trusted each other at all, the possession of weapons by one of them was always bound to be a major factor.

It is an interesting question whether the decommissioning obstacle could have been avoided, or at least reduced, if the 'Washington Three' conditions had never been enunciated in the way that they were by secretary of state Patrick Mayhew. There is no doubt that they did constitute a hook on which the Major Government impaled itself, and that getting off this hook became a serious problem in the future for British Government policy. My own view, coming in after it had happened, was that this was indeed a regrettable, if understandable, move, in that it reduced our room for manoeuvre when it was in any case often rather too narrow. On the other hand, the possession of illegal weapons was always (rightly) bound to be a problem, and the unionists were always bound to be insistent on some proof of the abandonment of violence, as they showed consistently over time after the GFA. There was absolutely no point in convening talks attended by Sinn Féin but not by the unionists. In substance, therefore, the decommissioning impasse was no doubt unavoidable at some stage, but it would have been better to tackle it when the political process had gone further. 'Washington Three' was an unhelpful hostage to fortune at the time, and putting it up front and centre led to real concerns on the nationalist and republican side about British good faith.

In any case, John Major's reaction to the decommissioning recommendations in the *Mitchell Report* of January 1996 was politically astute, but in this case a good deal more welcome to the unionists than to the nationalists. He implicitly accepted the proposal on parallel decommissioning, but avoided saying so in so many words. He focused instead on endorsing six fundamental principles that Mitchell had put forward as requiring acceptance by all parties wanting to join the talks before they could actually do so. What became universally known thereafter as the *Mitchell Principles* consisted of total and absolute commitment to:

1. democratic and exclusively peaceful means of resolving political issues;
2. the total disarmament of all paramilitary organisations;
3. agreeing that such disarmament must be verifiable to the satisfaction of an independent commission;
4. renouncing for themselves, and opposing any effort by others, to use force, or threaten to use force, to influence the course or the outcome of all-party negotiations;
5. agreeing to abide by the terms of any agreement reached in all-party negotiations and to resort to democratic and exclusively peaceful methods in trying to alter any aspect of that outcome with which they may disagree;
6. urge that 'punishment' killings and beatings stop and to take effective steps to prevent such actions.

As well as playing up the importance of these commitments, Major also seized on a brief reference in the *Report* to the possibility of elections as a legitimising element for democratic parties. He put forward a specific proposal for the election of a new body in Northern Ireland whose main aim would be to produce party delegations for the talks. This was initially angrily dismissed by the nationalist side, and by the Irish Government, as at best another delaying tactic and at worst a dangerous sop to the unionists, who had long wanted such an election. They argued that it threatened a return to the bad old days of rule from Stormont, and that, in then tánaiste Dick Spring's graphic phrase, the proposal was 'adding petrol to the flames of republican frustration'.

In fact, Major was playing a clever game which could command support at Westminster and among the unionists, while keeping the door open for all-party talks including Sinn Féin. The election idea was no doubt not crucial to the future of the process, but it did put a democratic gloss on what was being offered and provided a possible way forward. Nevertheless, it was a hard sell to the nationalists and republicans. In the short term, it redoubled their accusations that the British were doing everything possible to avoid the all-party talks, which they believed had been promised two years earlier – a promise that had played an important part in bringing the PIRA leadership to agree to the ceasefire.

Given that the PIRA broke the ceasefire a few weeks after the publication of the *Mitchell Report*, and John Major's response to it, there were, and no doubt still are, accusations that this electoral proposal by Major had been the straw that broke the camel's back, finally exhausting PIRA patience. But it is not at all clear that this represents the truth; the PIRA decision to break the ceasefire almost certainly predated the publication of the *Mitchell Report* in January – the preparations for the London bomb certainly did. Major's own response to the end of the PIRA ceasefire when it came showed once again both the strength of his determination to continue with the peace process if at all possible, and the limited room for political manoeuvre he had at his disposal. He could have used the fresh violence as an excuse for ending efforts to move forward with Sinn Féin, given the breach of faith it represented for most outside the republican community, and the extent of his personal anger over another deadly bomb on the British mainland. But he was still not willing to give up. In addition to condemning strongly the terrorist attack, therefore, he reiterated the vital nature of the *Mitchell Principles* and the need for any party entering talks to accept them fully, and also repeated his proposal for elections in Northern Ireland to allow parties to demonstrate their democratic mandate. He also made clear, in a way which Blair was to echo just over a year later, that the talks would go ahead with or without Sinn Féin, and that the ministerial contacts that had been started with them would end until the ceasefire was restored. But he also spelled out that Sinn Féin still had the opportunity to join the talks if they so chose, by reinstating the ceasefire and accepting the six *Mitchell Principles* (which, of course, included a commitment in principle to full decommissioning).

This was reinforced at an Anglo-Irish summit in London a few weeks later, when the Irish finally bought into the idea of the election in return for the setting of a firm date of 10 June 1996 for the start of the all-party talks. The nationalists and the Irish continued to think that the British could have set this date earlier and thus avoided the breakdown of the ceasefire. But, to repeat, this ignores the simple fact that meaningful talks involving Sinn Féin without some major gesture from them, such as some actual decommissioning or a clear statement that the violence was over for good, could not have happened at that stage anyway because the unionists would have refused to sit down with them. The key point for me is that, under great pressure from difficult events and toxic domestic politics, Major had nevertheless found a way to keep the Northern Ireland show on the road.

The elections were duly held on 30 May, and Sinn Féin, having decided not to boycott them, did surprisingly well, recording some 15 per cent of the vote – causing much debate at the time about whether this should be interpreted as a vote for continuing violence or for them to continue their efforts to join the normal political process. The latter was more plausible. In any case, Sinn Féin used their success to step up their demand to be allowed into the talks on the basis of this fresh democratic mandate. But since the PIRA had not declared a fresh ceasefire, and they had not accepted the *Mitchell Principles* in any meaningful way, there was no way that this demand could be met. The talks were therefore launched without them on 10 June, though in practice they never got beyond essentially procedural issues, including the vexed question of wider participation in them. The Sinn Féin case was further undermined when a huge bomb was detonated in Manchester city centre on 15 June, the day of the Trooping of the Colour in London, causing widespread destruction and injury. The following weeks also saw a deterioration of the situation on the ground, with further PIRA attacks and worse than usual trouble over the marching season, particularly at the flashpoint of Drumcree.

This was hardly conducive either to progress in the talks, which in any case had hardly got off first base, or to the chances of Sinn Féin getting into those talks. Again, John Major could have been excused if he had given up so close to the general election that he looked so much like losing, and in such unpromising circumstances. Intensive private discussions nevertheless got under way again in the autumn, mainly between the two governments. Once again, they were apparently at the initiative of John Hume, working with Adams, and they took a familiar form, with a familiar goal: to find a form of words for a public statement by the British Government that would reflect British long-standing positions, but somehow also contain enough comfort for nationalist and republican views, this time including the point that talks would not be allowed to drag on indefinitely, to help convince the PIRA to declare a new ceasefire.

One aim was to set out the process by which Sinn Féin could be allowed into the talks, once the government was convinced that any ceasefire was genuine and intended to be lasting, and to provide assurances that this process would not be too long drawn-out. The draft statement did this. However, Major was not willing to set a specific timeframe in advance, given his suspicions about the nature of the previous PIRA ceasefire. This was a serious stumbling block for the nationalists and Irish, who wanted no period, or at worst only a short defined one, to test the PIRA ceasefire.

As always, these were difficult negotiations, with many voices involved and constant demands upon the British side to go the extra mile to make progress possible. There was also another familiar problem: the unionists were not involved in these talks, but they were inevitably aware that something was going on, and were highly suspicious that something was being cooked up behind their backs which they were going to hate when it came out. Major nevertheless took this process as far as he believed he possibly could. But there came a moment in late November when the demands to go further from the Irish and nationalist side were continuing, when the fact of the discussions had become public (apparently leaked by Sinn Féin), and when unionist and Conservative Party suspicions were reaching a crescendo. Major decided that the process could go on no longer. He therefore decided to bring the negotiations to a halt, and to set out publicly what had been happening, including the latest version of the statement on which we had been working.

This provoked a furious reaction in Dublin, who had received very little notice of this move, and among the nationalists and republicans. My own relations with the taoiseach's office, normally very good, broke down for a period under the strain amid accusations of bad faith. The unionists, while happy that the private negotiations had ended, were also dismayed by how far the prime minister seemed to have been prepared to go to bring in Sinn Féin. The net result was that, although there were some further discussions and thrashings around, and the multiparty talks continued to discuss procedural issues before they were suspended in March 1997 until after the elections, this British statement effectively brought a halt to serious efforts to make progress with Sinn Féin before the British elections five months later.

Major's attempt to bridge the differences and to take risks for peace had therefore finally hit the buffers. But it is still instructive to look at what was behind, and in, that November statement, beyond the usual verbiage that had to go into any statement on Northern Ireland. Notwithstanding denials, the British Government had in fact once again been negotiating with Sinn Féin at one remove in an attempt to bring them into the talks, and had signalled clearly that a renewed ceasefire would be enough to trigger further contacts and discussions with the aim of letting Sinn Féin into the talks relatively quickly, despite the violence still going on at the time. All this was happening in the worst possible political context. It is worth comparing this with what happened later after the election, described below, when Blair was faced with the same conundrum of how to bring in Sinn Féin, and how quickly, in completely transformed political circumstances.

One of the constant questions behind all this activity was how far progress could be made without Sinn Féin (and the loyalists) at the talks. The focus on Sinn Féin was irritating at times to all the other parties, nationalist as well as unionist, who could point to their far greater share of the popular vote and therefore their much greater ability to represent important parts of the population. There was always the risk that the chase after Sinn Féin would send the message that violence worked. But the overall view was nevertheless that talks without Sinn Féin would in the end be Hamlet without the prince of Denmark – while there were many things that could be agreed without them, and it would certainly have been possible to set up a new political order in Northern Ireland without Sinn Féin, the prospect of an incomplete, non-inclusive agreement was in the end unattractive not only because it would contain the seeds of further violence, but because a significant strand of opinion would have been left out. Genuinely inclusive talks, to use the jargon expression of the time, had to include the republicans too.

The private Irish view at the time, attributed to a senior official, Sean O'Huiggin, namely, that talks without Sinn Féin were 'not worth a penny candle', might therefore have been exaggerated therefore, but it did represent the underlying reality. Hence the continuing attempts to bring them in, and the lack of ultimate credibility of regular British statements that they would be happy to press on without Sinn Féin if the latter insisted on excluding themselves. It was not that these statements were not sincere – the multiparty talks did after all get under way without them in June 1996 – but somehow everyone knew that if Sinn Féin could not be enticed into the process, if not at the beginning, then at least later, the chances of success and of successful implementation would be much reduced. The Irish and the SDLP in particular, despite their own many frustrations with Sinn Féin, were in the end unlikely to have negotiated very seriously without them.

The ultimate basis of the argument for bringing them in had to be that while republican violence, however unacceptable in itself, might have helped to create a situation where Sinn Féin's views could not be ignored, and in which they should be brought into the talks if they wanted to be there, nevertheless it was Sinn Féin's political activity and its ability to represent an important strand of opinion that were the crucial game-changers. The continuation of PIRA violence once the principle of allowing Sinn Féin into the talks had been agreed was therefore not only unacceptable, but also obviously ineffective and futile. If the PIRA thought they could still bomb their way to the table, it had to be clear that in fact the only obstacle to the republicans being there was precisely the continuation of their violence.

The transition

This was the situation inherited by Tony Blair in May 1997. He did not necessarily know a huge amount about Northern Ireland in advance, but he had prepared for this moment in several important ways. He had moved the Labour Party away from the position it had been drifting into, of being somehow neutral between supporters of the Union and partisans of unification, and even becoming 'persuaders for unification'. Kevin McNamara's replacement by Mo Mowlam was one obvious signal of this, even though Mo was never a great fan of the unionists, or they of her. Blair had also made a point of praising Major's efforts to bring about peace in Northern Ireland, and of supporting them, even at difficult moments – the so-called 'bipartisan approach'. He had visited Northern Ireland and reassured the unionists of his own attachment to the Union; he had also been to Dublin and made connections not only with then taoiseach John Bruton, but also his likely successor, Bertie Ahern, with whom he got on extremely well (a relationship that was to prove absolutely crucial later). His chief of staff, Jonathan Powell, had also made a lot of contacts and immersed himself in the detail, and was to play a central role in everything that followed. The broader background was that Blair, like Major before him, was determined to make a huge personal effort to bring about peace in Northern Ireland, even though he, like Major, had been warned by old timers in his party that such efforts always ended in tears, and in any case did little to impress mainland British voters. Both men regarded it as wholly unacceptable and an affront to British democracy that violence should continue in any part of the United Kingdom without every effort being made to bring it to an end. Both were also rightly convinced that in the end London and Dublin had to work closely together if a lasting settlement was to come about.

Blair had huge confidence both in the power of reason and in his own ability to persuade people to do what he wanted, and to negotiate successfully even in the most unpromising circumstances, through personal charm and engagement. He had developed a technique of appearing to tell people privately that he agreed with them, while saying something on the same lines privately to people on the other side of the argument. This was not without risks, and he sailed close to the wind at times in Northern Ireland, but in general it served him extremely well. Whether Blair would have made the attempt at Northern Ireland peace as he did if he had really known at the beginning just how much personal time and effort would be involved, not to mention the deep frustration and near heartbreak at times, must be a matter of speculation. But I am confident that he *would* still have made the same choice. Certainly, peace in Northern Ireland was an enormous achievement, even if still incomplete today, and a very important part of his legacy – sadly, and wrongly, for some people it is virtually the only credit they are prepared to give him. At the same time, importantly, Blair has always been careful to say that much of the credit belongs to John Major, and that it was Major who had done so many of the hard yards, not least through ground-breaking initiatives such as the Downing Street Declaration (DSD), to create the opportunity which Blair himself now had. This was not just words. He knew it was true, and fully appreciated the role Major had played over the seven years of his prime ministership.

Major was well aware at the end of his time that only a new British administration, with new vigour and authority, and a new five-year mandate, would be able to take the peace process forward successfully. Blair was even more strongly conscious of the fact that, in this area above all others, the enthusiasm and authority that his massive electoral win gave him had to be used quickly, or the chance would pass and the process would fall back into the usual quagmires. His advantages were indeed multiple. His own party was unlikely to cause him any trouble on this issue; the opposition in London was condemned to years of introspection and weakness, but he could still call on them with conviction for a continuation of the bipartisan approach he had himself stuck to in opposition; public and press opinion was ready to give him the benefit of the doubt on almost any issue for the immediate future; there was a friendly government in Dublin; he had excellent relations with president Clinton in Washington, which he could use to wean the US administration away from too much unthinking support for Sinn Féin and towards a more balanced attitude to the unionists; the unionist community, admittedly still suspicious of where a Labour Government might go on the issue, was partly reassured by prior contacts and was in any case in no position to resist too far a British prime minister with such a big majority who was likely to be there for at least two terms; and the nationalist/republican community was ready to do business with someone they hoped would be more instinctively sympathetic to some of their concerns, as well as being reluctant to fall out with someone likely to be in power for a long time who could so obviously make the political weather. That was the good news. The bad news was that there was still no PIRA ceasefire and republican violence had continued even through the electoral period. Moreover, the unionists remained highly sceptical of the possibility of ever doing peaceful business with the republicans, with both sides likely to be inflamed even further by the forthcoming marching season.

Tony Blair

Form the beginning, Blair knew that his best chance of making progress was to move quickly to create a new sense of momentum, and to give the naysayers no chance to start to dominate the narrative once again. Clearly, he had to meet the main parties quickly, but, as always in Northern Ireland, he also had to put out some words on what he thought and what he wanted as prime minister, to frame the future discussion in the right way, and to prevent others from claiming on his behalf that they knew what his real views were. The top priority, therefore, was to make an early speech, and to make it in Northern Ireland, in order to carry the arguments to the place where they most needed to be heard. It was decided to use the opportunity of the Royal Agricultural Society of Belfast's annual show to do this, two weeks after the election, on 16 May – this was very much traditional unionist country, and therefore a chance to take the argument to the unionists directly.

There were two basic objectives for the speech, and they were not easy to reconcile: to set out the conditions under which Sinn Féin could come back into the talks fold; and to reassure the unionists that Blair as prime minister valued the Union and was not about to give it away. The first was urgent, but the second was more important because it was always the unionists who could effectively veto progress whenever they wanted – if their goodwill were lost, it might prove impossible to recover. I had already been working on such a speech before the election, based on my perceptions of what needed to be said to both sides, and I was reassured when Blair and his team accepted my draft as the basis for what the speech would become.

The first objective was met by a passage in the speech which made clear that Sinn Féin would be welcome in the talks, but that the talks would not wait for them. In a metaphor that quickly became tired, and indeed irritating, Blair said that 'the settlement train was leaving', and if Sinn Féin were not on it, it would leave anyway. To board the train, the essential requirement was a renewed PIRA ceasefire, as well as commitment to the *Mitchell Principles.* This was accompanied by a lengthy denunciation of the futility of continued violence. The message was spelt out: the PIRA and Sinn Féin had to choose between negotiations and violence. If they chose the former, the response from his government would be rapid and forthcoming. If they chose violence, the full force of the security forces would be brought to bear. In order that there should be no misunderstanding about the government's message, Blair made clear that contacts at official level with Sinn Féin, which had been effectively cut off after the breakdown of the ceasefire, could resume.

The second aim was covered by an explicit reaffirmation of the government's commitment to the Union, and his own in particular. He said that he valued the Union, which would continue as long as a majority of Northern Ireland's inhabitants continued to want this. A political settlement was not a slippery slope to a united Ireland, and his government would not be persuaders for unity. He added, in a striking phrase, that he did not expect to see Northern Ireland as anything but part of the UK for the lifetime of anyone in the room, even the youngest. These were not just empty words. I can testify from my own private discussions with Blair that he had absolutely no wish or intention to reduce the size of the UK, and what this meant for the country's role and influence in the world – for example, he hated having to go to Hong Kong a few weeks later to witness the Chinese takeover, and often joked, with a serious undertone, about how to make the United Kingdom bigger and more populous, and therefore more powerful in the world.

Overall, the speech was a balanced success in the toxic, zero-sum-game world of Northern Irish politics, where what one side liked was by definition almost certain to be viewed with the utmost suspicion by the other side. Sinn Féin hated the words about the Union (and the Irish were hardly thrilled either), but for the most part, and after an initial burst of criticism, kept their unhappiness about it to themselves, especially when reassured by the Irish, briefed by us, that it was after all no more than a restatement of recent British policy about the principle of consent. The unionists were grudgingly pleased by the reassurances about the importance of the Union. They were not at all happy about the apparent speed with which Sinn Féin would be let into the talks if the PIRA did declare a ceasefire. But their reactions were not show-stoppers – it was difficult for them to appear not actually to want a renewed PIRA ceasefire, even though many unionists secretly found the situation politically easier when they could rail about republican violence without having to confront the problem of what they would do if it actually did stop for good.

One of the issues of the speech was, of course, what to say about the problem of the decommissioning of illegal weapons. Blair, with my full encouragement, was in no hurry to impale himself on the hook of decommissioning as a precondition for progress, as Major had felt obliged to do. At the same time, he could hardly argue for less than what Mitchell had proposed, that is, some decommissioning in parallel with the talks. He, therefore, confined himself to endorsing that concept, since he was well aware of how difficult decommissioning of any kind was likely to prove in practice. The unionists were, of course, alert to every nuance in what was a critical area for them, and redoubled their efforts to make sure that there could be no backsliding on what they regarded, in many ways quite justifiably, as a crucial principle. The issue was once again set to cause endless trouble.

How different in substance was the approach that Blair set out in this speech from that pursued by Major before him? The emphasis on the importance and likely longevity of the Union was striking, and intended to be so, but it did not represent any change of policy. It was there in part because, as a Labour leader keen to make progress with the cooperation of all sides, he had to provide reassurances in this area, given the party's perceived 'green' bias over many years. His predecessor, as the leader of the Conservative and Unionist Party, did not face the same need – the reassurances of impartiality were more necessary for the other side. On Sinn Féin, the fundamentals were the same: insistence on a ceasefire and acceptance of the *Mitchell Principles*. What was also apparent, however, reading between the lines, was a greater willingness to move quickly and to be less demanding on the *quality* of a ceasefire than the previous government had been. One of the reasons why Major had been so wary of PIRA/Sinn Féin good faith after the 1994 ceasefire had been the knowledge, from intelligence and other sources, that the PIRA had continued to recruit, procure weapons, plan attacks and targeting, as well as continuing the so-called punishment beatings and killings that were such a frequent and horrific feature of Northern Ireland life at the time. Blair was certainly concerned by the likelihood of a repeat of this pattern, but he was readier to take the basic fact of a ceasefire for what it was, and to understand that some in the republican movement were not likely to give up lightly the possibility of going back to violence, at least not until they had seen the shape of a future settlement. He also had more faith in his own ability to draw the republicans into the political process, and to make it as difficult as possible for them ever to go back.

This was in some ways the most difficult area. We often discussed among ourselves how far Adams and McGuinness were really committed to peace and democratic methods. It was hard to have any certainty about exactly where they stood, quite where they fitted into the PIRA hierarchy and precisely how much support they had among the decision-makers of the republican movement. Intelligence helped a bit, but could never be definitive. Like others, we often joked about the Sinn Féin leaders going back home to talk to the mirror when they referred, usually very indirectly, to having to take some bit of necessary movement in their position back to the PIRA. However, we also knew it was a lot more complicated and subtle than that. We did believe that they were often out on a limb, compared with important parts of the PIRA leadership, and were indeed at times risking their own lives as they tried to move their hard men along the path towards declaring the conflict definitively at an end and towards some actual decommissioning of their weapons. We were also aware that this could sometimes, perhaps even often, be a negotiating tactic on their part. We could watch for ourselves how they played on the susceptibilities of the Irish Government, and John Hume, by suggesting that renewed violence was imminent if we did not soften our position on this or that issue, in order to get them to put pressure on us to change. This sometimes led the Irish and John Hume to tie themselves in knots. They were constantly telling us, on the one hand, that the republicans were serious about peace, really had given up their old ways, and would surely make the definitive move if we just made this or that concession, before then coming back to us days or even hours later in a panic to say that the ceasefire was in imminent jeopardy, having clearly been on the end of some pretty direct threats of renewed violence.

Our conclusion on balance was that leaders like Adams and McGuinness *were* now serious about peace, whatever their past involvement in violence and continuing membership of the PIRA. They seemed genuine when they talked about their desire for their children not to have to live under the threat of death and destruction as they had done. This was not to say that we were certain that they would never go back to violence if their aims had been completely thwarted in the political process. But we did think that they had genuinely concluded that there could be no military solution, and that they wanted to make progress politically if it was at all possible. In any case, the point was that Blair was probably more prepared to go the extra mile in taking what they said at face value than Major had been, and was, of course, better placed to do so both because of his own overall political position of virtually being able to walk on water at the beginning of his first mandate, and because, unlike Major, he did not have a substantial part of his own party, and indeed his own Cabinet, predisposed to take the unionist side and regard the republicans as unreconstructed terrorists who could never be trusted. Let me be quite clear about this: Blair was not at all naive about Sinn Féin or the PIRA. He knew the risks and uncertainties as well as anyone. My view is that he was simply more prepared intellectually and better equipped politically to test to destruction the possibility that they could be brought to embrace real peace. For my part, I encouraged him to take that attitude, having seen the downsides of too much potentially self-fulfilling suspicion under his predecessor.

This confidence in what might be possible was justified by what happened next. While there was no immediate response on the ceasefire front – indeed, two Royal Ulster Constabulary officers were killed by the PIRA a month later, which made both Blair and taoiseach Bruton very angry – the mood music gradually began to be increasingly encouraging. A month after his speech, on 25 June, Blair spelled out not only that he needed, and was expecting, the ceasefire to be renewed within five weeks, in good time before the talks resumed in September, but also that he would accept just six weeks of peace thereafter as enough to justify Sinn Féin being allowed to enter the talks, with no mention of decommissioning as a precondition. This was a gamble, and a very short period to allow the nature of the ceasefire to be verified, but Blair was clear that momentum was everything, and that the opportunity to move things forward rapidly was too good to be missed.

The ceasefire was renewed on 19 July, and Sinn Féin thus crossed the main obstacle to their participation in the talks as from 29 August. On 9 September, they accepted the *Mitchell Principles* and, though the effect was spoilt by a PIRA statement shortly afterwards making clear that this was not them speaking, it was decided not to allow this to derail progress. The talks duly restarted on 9 September, with Sinn Féin. Unfortunately, it was without any of the unionist parties, who boycotted the event in protest at the speed with which

Sinn Féin had been admitted. Nevertheless, the UUP relented five days later and joined the talks themselves. The gamble had therefore paid off, and the political pressures engendered by a new, powerful prime minister had worked their magic. It was true that the other main unionist party, the Democratic Unionist Party (DUP) of Ian Paisley, were not at the talks, but that had always been likely to prove a bridge too far, given their implacable hostility to Sinn Féin at the time. They were kept informed of the progress of the talks, and the prime minister's door remained open to them. They did not, in the end, come on board until well after the GFA, when the lure of office eventually proved too much for their leaders to resist, particularly as they had by then become the largest unionist party – Trimble and the UUP had sadly paid the price for their political boldness in making peace. To see at a later stage Peter Robinson, who took over as leader of the DUP, and Martin McGuinness governing together from 2008, however uncomfortably at times, seemed to me to be another clear vindication of the strategy started by Major and taken forward by Blair.

The resumption of the talks, and the inclusion of Sinn Féin, was of course more like the beginning than the end of the problems. The talks finally entered their substantive phase in October, but progress was glacial, despite George Mitchell's best efforts as the chair of the talks. Even participation remained an issue, as occasional violent incidents on one side or the other called into question the good faith of the parties linked to the paramilitary groups. The loyalist Ulster Democratic Party were banned for a period in January 1998, and Sinn Féin were excluded for seventeen days in February because of PIRA involvement in two killings. These decisions were heavily contested from both sides, with protests from those excluded over the evidence behind the decisions, and from the mainstream parties at the short, even token, extent of the exclusions.

The agenda for the talks was essentially the same as it had been for some years, based on the three-stranded approach, the notion that nothing was agreed until everything was agreed (enabling trade-offs between the strands), and the outlines set out first in the DSD, and then in more detail in the Frameworks Document (despite the latter's rejection by the unionists). Blair did not introduce new elements to this agenda, but as events were to prove, he was probably able to be more flexible about the exact content of the final agreement in non-crucial areas than Major might have been, for example, on policing and prisoners, and no doubt a little more inclined to be flexible overall. His attitude tended to be that, as long as vital UK interests and principles were protected, and the overall balance between the communities preserved, he could go along with more or less whatever the parties themselves could agree between them.

His other ability was to see the importance of symbolism in changing mindsets. One good example was the decision to set up a further judicial enquiry into the events of Bloody Sunday, given the evidently unsatisfactory nature of the original *Widgery Report*, widely seen by the Catholic community in Northern

Ireland and by the Irish as a whitewash. I had recommended this to Blair on its own merits, having looked again at the *Widgery Report* myself and what had emerged since. But it was still a brave prime ministerial decision to endorse such a conclusion, given the unhappiness it was bound to cause among so many of the British military establishment, as well as among the unionist community. Although we had no idea at the time that the enquiry would take so long and cost so much, its eventual conclusions and the British Government's acceptance of them under prime minister Cameron justified the investment. I also believe the decision played an important part in creating the context in which the GFA could succeed – in some ways it was the psychological equivalent for the nationalists of the reassurances about the Union offered to the Protestant community.

Most of the talks agenda was contentious in one way or another, and for one party or another, but in some key areas the basic deal could be discerned: a fair deal on power-sharing (which the UUP and SDLP agreed with remarkable speed at the very end of the process, once other elements of the deal were in place); Irish repeal of their constitutional claim on Northern Ireland; and acceptance by all concerned of the principle of no change in the status of Northern Ireland without the explicit consent of the majority of the people there. In other areas, the way forward remained very hard to trace – above all, perhaps, decommissioning, and the arrangements for North–South cooperation in practical areas which would give the South a say in Northern Ireland affairs (and, of course, vice versa, though this point was usually ignored). Both these were to give huge trouble. Both nearly derailed the GFA, and disagreement on both delayed setting up proper government structures for years, above all on the decommissioning dilemma. These were not the only problems. Changes to Northern Ireland's policing and the early release of paramilitary prisoners were hugely difficult for the unionist community to accept, and policing was later to cause huge problems about implementing the GFA. But they were in the end swallowed and put into practice more easily than decommissioning and the North–South cooperation bodies.

The latter was a good example of where the Blair/British position was essentially to accept whatever the two parties who were most exercised about the North–South arrangements, that is, the Irish and the unionists, were able to agree between them. We had to be the mediators, because the emotion on both sides was such that they could not negotiate anything directly. For the Irish, the North–South cooperation arrangements were the one tangible advance to come out of the talks in exchange for giving up their constitutional claim. They were also important for Sinn Féin as a sign that not everything in the way the province was governed would remain the same after any agreement. For the unionists, while purely practical cooperation in non-core areas could be contemplated, anything more than that was seen to be smacking of joint sovereignty and the beginning of the slippery slope to unification.

In such circumstances, the British Government could easily misjudge where the acceptable limits for either side lay. On the eve of the final Belfast negotiations in April 1997, after a frustrated George Mitchell had set an Easter deadline for the conclusion of the talks, the whole process hung in the balance after papers that Irish and British officials had prepared on the North–South bodies were given to the parties. The unionists threw an immediate, major and largely understandable fit at the length and sensitivity of the list of areas proposed for North–South cooperation. The NIO had assured us in Downing Street that the list would be broadly acceptable to the unionists, at least as the basis for negotiations, but they had in fact completely misunderstood, or decided to ignore, obvious unionist red lines – John Taylor famously said that he would not touch talks on such a basis 'with a forty-foot pole'.

The deadlock was broken and the talks put back on track only when the Irish, in the shape of taoiseach Bertie Ahern, reluctantly agreed to revisit the list. His willingness to do so, having been pressed to move by Blair, despite having just lost his mother, was hugely important in convincing the unionists of Irish good faith and allowing the rest of the negotiations to proceed. The list eventually agreed for GFA purposes, not without further last-minute alarms, was just about acceptable to both sides at the time, but their interpretations of what it implied were still very different. This led to a further negotiating crisis in late 1998, which was overcome only by huge involvement once again by Blair and Ahern in a cliff-hanger late December summit, when the final list of so-called implementation bodies and areas for joint cooperation was agreed.

Decommissioning came even closer to derailing the GFA talks at the very last minute during the Belfast talks, when the unionists understood that the text was not going to contain the unequivocal commitment to some early decommissioning as a condition for joining the future devolved government that they had long sought, and which they thought they had been promised by the British Government and by Tony Blair in particular. In vain did we explain that this had proved completely un-negotiable with the parties representing the paramilitaries – loyalist as well as republican – and argue that the unionists should not lose sight of the big prize in the negotiations, namely, universal acceptance of the fundamental principle of consent. Combined with language on policing and prisoners, which was also deeply unsettling for the unionists, the lack of certainty on decommissioning was very nearly enough for David Trimble to lose control of his own delegation and to refuse to endorse the painfully negotiated final text.

Changing his and their minds took concerted appeals from president Clinton and Blair, as well as a hastily cobbled together letter from the latter that promised that the British Government would support changing the provisions within the Agreement to allow for the exclusion of Sinn Féin from government in Northern Ireland if they had not started to deliver on decommissioning after six months. While hardly a watertight promise, this was just enough for those members of the UUP who wanted to do a deal, and we scraped through. This sort of last-minute manoeuvre was hardly ideal and, of course, contained the seeds of future trouble, but in our view it was still definitely worth it. The GFA changed everything, and made a return to the previous violence in Northern Ireland more or less unimaginable. Once the parties had signed up, it was very hard indeed to imagine going back to the previous stalemate. It was a huge achievement for Blair, with immense help from Ahern, to get the parties to go so far. His persuasive abilities and charm, combined with mastery of detail when he needed it, and massive personal commitment to a positive outcome, were in many ways the foundations on which the whole edifice was built. However, these strengths also had corresponding potential weaknesses: as I have already mentioned, Blair was a master at making all his interlocutors think that he really supported them and their views, through private warmth and assurances of understanding, and at saying things to different interlocutors that, while not necessarily contradictory, would not always have been easy to reconcile with each other if stated in public and compared with each other. Of course, this is in many ways a standard negotiating technique, but he took it to a new level, not least in Northern Ireland. In the case of decommissioning, he was no doubt assuring the unionists that he understood and supported their insistence on some actual decommissioning, while telling the republicans that, while he certainly wanted decommissioning, and it would definitely have to happen in the end, he also understood the practical difficulties they might have in actually getting this through their hard men. Some of these ambiguities were bound to come home to roost.

Let me be clear here. I am not criticising Blair's approach. Such constructive ambiguities were crucial to making progress in the particular circumstances of Northern Ireland. I was at times as guilty as anyone else of a degree of equivocation. But we had to be aware, as we were, that the real issues they concealed could not all be dodged indefinitely. In the case of decommissioning, I suspect Blair never really believed, at least in the early stages, that it needed to have the importance given to it by the unionists, since he could see that if politics got the upper hand, then the weapons themselves would eventually become irrelevant – which was my own position, too. In those early days he often asked me what the solution to the decommissioning conundrum actually was. I always had to confess that I did not have a magic solution. We would just have to go on plugging away at both sides – trying to persuade the unionists that its speed did not matter quite as much as they thought; and the republicans that their good faith and commitment to democracy and peaceful means would always be suspect as long as they did not actually not only make clear that they had given up violence once and for all, but also demonstrate that they had done so by putting at least some of their weapons 'beyond use', as the jargon had it. I always knew this was going to be difficult, but, if I am honest, I little suspected when I left Downing Street in February 1999 that the issue would continue to derail attempts to establish stable devolved government in Northern Ireland for another six years.

One other significant change in approach between Major and Blair came in the attitude to contacts with Sinn Féin. We have already seen that, in his first speech at the Royal Agricultural Society in Belfast, Blair had authorised the resumption of official-level contacts with Sinn Féin, even before there had been evidence of any PIRA intention to renew the ceasefire. Once the ceasefire was again in place, ministerial-level contacts with Sinn Féin could also resume quickly – and, indeed, quickly become routine. But there was one card still to play, namely, direct contact between Sinn Féin and the prime minister himself. Blair was keen to be able to get a direct feel for himself of what sort of people Adams and McGuinness were. Once the talks were under way, with Sinn Féin inside, this became politically doable, though not without risk.

It was decided it would be slightly easier to manage in Belfast than in London. A meeting was duly arranged in mid-October. It was not a very substantial encounter, lasting only about twenty minutes, and it was awkward for all concerned. But the importance of what it symbolised and the new opportunities it opened up were huge. There had been a lot of agonising in advance about whether the prime minister should shake hands with men who had until recently been regarded as terrorists, and were still so regarded by many people. In the end he did, which had to be the right thing to do if any kind of working relationship were to be struck up – but it was done in private so that there was no picture. The press coverage, in Northern Ireland, the rest of the United Kingdom and round the world, was massive and mostly favourable, except of course from the unionists and their supporters. A giant taboo was thus broken and another psychological hurdle to a lasting settlement crossed. Direct communication between the main protagonists had to be worthwhile in reducing misunderstandings and increasing the chances of a lasting settlement.

There was one more piece of drama to come, when the meeting was repeated in Downing Street a couple of months later in December 1997 with, if anything, even greater media coverage and even sharper symbolism as the Sinn Féin delegation went into the building that their PIRA colleagues had mortared only a few short years before, and that they saw as the source of so many decisions taken against the interests of the Irish people, not least when Michael Collins had entered its doors to negotiate Irish partition in 1921. Again, the substance was slight and the atmosphere was tricky, but the important point was that the two sides were beginning to talk directly, and could continue to do so. Once that meeting was over, it was surprising, and a useful lesson, how quickly meetings between the prime minister and Sinn Féin leaders became a routine and normal part of the landscape. The same thing happened a year later when

David Trimble decided to have a bilateral meeting with Sinn Féin in an effort to break the deadlock in setting up the Northern Irish devolved government – the unionists had had no direct dealings with Sinn Féin all through the talks, although they had, of course, to cross each other in the corridors and the washrooms. The first Trimble–Adams encounter was a major media story and a psycho-drama within the unionist community, with many accusations of sellout and treachery. The second was still a story, but much less so. Thereafter such encounters rapidly became a natural part of the political life of the province. Stranger things were to come, of course, when the DUP finally decided to get in on the act of governing, and Ian Paisley and Martin McGuinness sat at the same table for a jokey teatime encounter. But that was much later.

No account of the time I spent with Blair would be complete without a reference to the campaign to win the referendum on the GFA in Northern Ireland in May 1998. There was little doubt that the overall vote would be won, given overwhelming Catholic support for it, but it was vital to be able to say that it had attracted majority Protestant/unionist support, too. This was far from assured, given implacable DUP opposition and divisions within the UUP – Trimble had won a series of internal votes backing his stance, but there was still a significant unreconciled minority. The underlying problem was that many unionists were convinced in their heart of hearts that the GFA represented a defeat for them and their ideas, incorporating too many concessions to the men of violence, without certainty about decommissioning, and could even be the beginning of the slippery slope leading to the united Ireland they had always feared. Part of the reason for this was that Sinn Féin had cleverly portrayed the outcome as a victory for them, even though they had little substantive reason to do so. This was enough in the all-pervasive zero-sum game of Northern Irish politics to convince the unionists that they had somehow been conned. They could not see what we in London profoundly believed to be the case: that acceptance of the principle of consent by all the other parties gave them the key point they had always craved, that is, no change in the status of Northern Ireland without the consent of the majority there (leaving aside the longer-term fear that the Catholic population would one day be a majority because of a higher birth rate).

This feeling of having somehow been outmanoeuvred, reinforced by the unpalatable but necessary moves on prisoners and policing, meant that the unionist leaders, even those who had signed up to the GFA willingly at the time, tended to sound unconvinced and defensive themselves when talking about it. This was hardly the way to win over the many doubters.

Blair quickly realised not only that he would have to throw himself into the campaign personally, but that he would have to produce some hard-sounding assurances to convince the unionists that they were not being sold out. The result was his famous five handwritten pledges that featured on many posters

in Northern Ireland. They had to be brief, striking and attractive, which indeed they were:
(1) no change to the status of Northern Ireland without the express consent of the people;
(2) the power to take decisions to be returned from London to Northern Ireland, with accountable North–South cooperation;
(3) fairness and equality for all;
(4) those who use or threaten violence to be excluded from the government of Northern Ireland; and
(5) prisoners to be kept in prison unless violence is given up for good.

It was, of course, not enough for these pledges to be catchy. They also had to be compatible with the GFA itself. My role within Downing Street was to certify the latter point, particularly for the fourth and fifth pledges. To be frank, both were on the edge of truth in literal terms, even after a lot of drafting modifications, but they were accurate in spirit and certainly not contrary to the provisions of the Agreement. I agreed to them going ahead on that basis, but not without some misgivings. I do not know how big a part the pledges themselves played in the eventual result – there were many other factors, including an important visit by John Major to support the 'yes' vote. But I am sure that without Blair's full engagement, persuasive powers, political skills and readiness to make such promises, the referendum might well not have attracted the majority vote in the unionist community, which it just about did. This political triumph, for that is what it was, was of course followed by the bleakest day possible when twenty-nine people were killed by a Real IRA bomb in Omagh on 15 August 1998, the worst single incident of the whole Troubles. Blair was able to find the right words and emotions to deal with this tragedy, including, as Major had so often shown before him, the determination not to be deflected from the search for lasting peace by such mindless attacks. It was, of course, helpful that, in this case, Sinn Féin were ready to condemn the violence together with the other parties.

Conclusion

I hope that my impressions and judgements about the similarities and differences between Major and Blair, and how this affected the dynamics of the peace process in Northern Ireland, have emerged reasonably clearly from this brief run-through of some of the main issues. To sum up, I am convinced that they deserve equal credit for the Good Friday breakthrough, and not just because I worked for both of them. Both insisted on devoting huge time and effort to Northern Ireland when many tried to dissuade them. Both were never prepared to take no for an answer, and were ready to go the extra mile. Major had a much more difficult political context to deal with, and yet still laid so much of the essential groundwork that would enable later success. He was more cautious about Sinn Féin and the PIRA, and their good faith, at a time when this was arguably more necessary; more likely to insist on upfront proof in the form of decommissioning; and less inclined to be flexible about key problems and principles. There were advantages as well as downsides to this, not least in keeping the unionists onside at a very difficult time.

Blair had a much easier political context, and used brilliantly the chance to create rapid momentum in order to get everyone over the many obstacles in the way of an agreement. He was more confident of his own powers of persuasion, more inclined to be flexible about issues as long as the main principles were respected, more likely to wing it in discussions in order to keep the process moving, and more inclined (as well as more politically able) to take risks. Those were exactly the qualities needed in the circumstances of the post-election opportunity. If many others too played a crucial role in the final success, John Major and Tony Blair were a complementary double prime ministerial act over Northern Ireland for which we should all, and most of all the people of Northern Ireland, be grateful.

9 The challenge of symmetry in dialogue: an interview with Sir Joseph Pilling

Interview

GS: Can you give me an overview of what your job was and what it involved you doing?

JP: From 1997 to 2005 I was the permanent secretary, and I used to describe myself then as the person who tried to make sure that the Department of the Northern Ireland Office (NIO) was fit for purpose to serve the secretary of state and the other ministers. I had a responsibility for the broad direction of policy and for involving myself in any matters that were going wrong, and from time to time in public affairs things do go wrong. That cannot be avoided. At such times I tried to support colleagues who were taking the lead in different policy areas, which involved having a pretty good idea of what they were up to.

GS: Was the role of the NIO to totally complement British Government policy or was it autonomous in what it was doing?

JP: The formulation of policy and tactics comes about through a dialogue between government departments responsible for different areas and the government who have been elected to run the country and the detailed manifesto that they wish to implement. In the case of Northern Ireland, it is quite hard to find a period between 1972 and the present day when any British Government has had a policy significantly different from any other British Government. That is to say, the objective was always to try to stop the killing and hand responsibility for running Northern Ireland over to local politicians and, from a pretty early stage in that forty-year period, it was clear to all British governments that that had to mean handing power over to people from both communities and not just to people from one community. So power-sharing, in a phrase, was the policy on the political front and on the security front it was peace. The policy really never needed to be debated much. The question was always how to try to achieve those two key aims.

GS: Can you recollect when you first heard the term 'peace process'?

JP: It post-dated the 1985 Anglo-Irish Agreement. The NIO had begun to think that there might be a step-by-step process that could eventually lead to the achievement of the policies that I have just described as having been around and having been pursued since the early 1970s. So, the talks that I took part in during 1990–1, when Peter Brooke was the secretary of state, were certainly not seen as an isolated venture. They fitted a sort of scheme at that stage where we did not have a ceasefire. We certainly had some aspiration for achieving a ceasefire and seeing former terrorists come in and take part in the process. But I do not recall that we used the term 'peace process' for it as early as that.

GS: What was the view in 1991 about Sinn Féin being outside the talks?

JP: We had a different level of consciousness from our day-to-day, week-to-week engagement with the political parties who were in the process and, alongside that, trying to get others involved.

GS: At that time in 1991, did you foresee Sinn Féin committing to a ceasefire and coming into the talks process or did you see them becoming even more peripheral as the talks progressed?

JP: We did not have a detailed road map in our heads as to what would happen after a ceasefire. At that stage we were seeking to convince Sinn Féin that there were possibilities for them with a ceasefire, that the British Government was not irrevocably committed to keeping Northern Ireland within the United Kingdom if a majority of people in Northern Ireland wanted to leave the United Kingdom and form part of the Republic of Ireland. And I would not underestimate the significance of this. We continued, not just through a political process, but through other work being done in the NIO and in the security and intelligence community to try to convince republicans not that they would lose the military campaign that they were engaged in, but that it was not a campaign that they had any particular prospect of winning. In other words, the military conflict as they saw it, and the terrorism as we tended to see it, was a stalemate and would never be better than a stalemate for either party. Some put the emphasis entirely on political negotiations and talks, and the NIO tried to underscore a big picture which saw how those efforts could work together and help the other. It was very important that the work of the security forces was undertaken in a way that did not undermine the political or 'peace' process. For me, it is rather questionable that we would ever have got as far as we did in political talks if Sinn Féin had believed that the Provisional IRA (PIRA) were likely to achieve their goals by shooting and bombing, and get the Brits to leave and achieve a united Ireland that way.

GS: If you call it a political process, it really becomes a matter of political positions, but if you call it 'peace process', then the notion of politics appears to be subsumed into a moral frame of reference do you not think?

JP: Peace was something that might have been achieved as a result of the ceasefire full-stop, but we were interested in more than that. We were interested in political development. We were interested in returning the government of Northern Ireland to the people who lived there, who had strong affiliations there and who had an electorate that supported them there, rather than Northern Ireland being governed by politicians who had no votes at all from within Northern Ireland, and whether they were Labour Party ministers or Conservative Party ministers I think that is properly described as a political process. This was important in its own right, but also as a way of underpinning a lasting peace.

GS: Was the political approach framed by a moral dimension?

JP: I would be more conscious of moral conflicts than I would about a moral imperative, that is to say, weighing up what the right thing to do was in a situation where nothing you could do was free of some sort of moral downside. One of the most obvious moral dilemmas was the release from prison of a lot of people who committed very serious offences, but who were going to be released two years after the Agreement. Where was the morality there? Well, the morality there was that there was a goal available where the problem of the prisoners could be dealt with, which was not only worthwhile, but would save human lives. Does one want to keep on with massive gaol deliveries on the basis that people can commit murder and get out after a couple of years regularly? No, one does not want to do that. Could it be justified in quite exceptional circumstances morally? I believe yes it could and I think it was rightly done.

GS: Was there a moral tangle round that?

JP: People who are in senior posts in government or in political parties are not unsophisticated, and they are well used to weighing up conflicting circumstances and deciding where the morality is, so I do not think anybody that I knew spent a lot of time agonising over whether it was right or not. A critical judgement that needed to be made was the length of time, that is, one year, eighteen months, two years or three years. Where do you draw the line in order that it did not undermine the referendum that was to follow? An awful lot of unionists who very much wanted to see people serve long terms of imprisonment for murder were going to be needed to vote for the overall package. The judgement was two years, and since they did vote for it that must have been a reasonably good judgement. Would they have voted for it if it had been six months? Probably not.

GS: Can you paint a picture of the extent to which the process was conversational and informal in relation to the heated, pressurised and formal aspects of talks and negotiations?

JP: Going back to 1990–1, I can remember both formal and informal talks in that period, in Dublin and in Belfast, and I remember rather more tedium than excitement and shouting. I am sure that there were moments when people lost their temper, but it was not a regular experience. Informal and formal conversations could be equally heated and pressurised.

GS: Can you say something about creativity within this process, because although clearly the success of the peace process came down to getting parties to sign up to an agreement this says little about reflexivity and imagination within those constraints?

JP: One of the things that are pretty difficult is to give up a technique that has proved successful and move on to some other approach. But one of the more creative ideas that came up after 1997, and I cannot recall it ever being used between 1972 and 1997 in Northern Ireland, was the notion of a residential occasion where people were taken to a country setting that was relatively isolated from the press and other people, and put in a situation where it was quite difficult not to talk to each other in the corridor, or not have a cup of coffee together, or a glass of something together or even eat together. The absence of other commitments in those times helped the process forward more quickly. I have a hunch that this eventually became rather counter-productive, or certainly a bit worn out as a technique, but it was very successful when it was first introduced and this made it quite hard to give up. Possibly the Brits stuck with it longer than was sensible though.

GS: Why did it begin to not work, what went wrong?

JP: People became rather frightened. Possibly this was because they developed defences against making any concessions to such an extent that it might have been better not to have tried that technique, but something less ambitious and a bit more time-consuming, a bit more prolonged, as a way of getting them to think about a possible need for some small adjustments in their position, so they could meet other people making similar adjustments in their position.

GS: Can you say something about the relationship between detail and context, since without the context you do not get people involved to begin with and only from that context can one build towards detail?

JP: What I felt about the process was that there was nothing on which ambiguity could safely remain to the bitter end. There came a moment when clarity was needed on pretty well everything, but to have attempted to obtain clarity on everything at the beginning would have been a bit too much. So one of the slogans that led to the April 1998 Agreement was 'nothing is agreed until everything is agreed', but one of the underlying big issues, policing, was simply put into a siding to be dealt with later, and if the everything that had to be decided or nothing was decided had included the name of the police force in Northern Ireland and the badge that that police force would use, along with what sort of uniform they would wear, etc., it might not have been possible to get the Belfast Agreement as early as April 1998.

GS: On the question of ambiguity, do you think that Sinn Féin were slightly more comfortable with ambiguity because they just saw everything as a stepping stone to the next stage, whereas the unionists were more literal people, more interested in the exactness of meaning, and so ambiguity was a bit more difficult for them?

JP: That was a view that most people in the NIO took. There was a big cultural difference between the community that most of the unionist leaders came from and the community that most of the nationalist and republican leaders came from. It is probably broadly true that the unionists were more suspicious about things not being nailed down in some detail than the nationalists and the republicans, and it is interesting that the votes for the Good Friday Agreement (GFA) were rather more on the green side than on the orange side. It was a process that you could almost see torturing David Trimble because he won narrow vote after narrow vote among his own supporters, and we had all seen his supporters as the best hope for the process as opposed to the Democratic Unionist Party (DUP), who have become pillars of the process more recently. At that stage they were standing outside the process and criticising it, and that illustrated, on the unionist side, ambiguity in a rather different sense, which was the ambiguity that many in the unionist community felt about the process, whereas I do not think there was ever quite the same sense on the green side about people being in two minds about the process.

GS: Does negotiating hard boil down to saying no to a lot of things?

JP: It means producing a whole series of things on which one is seeking satisfaction and then gradually over time agreeing a form of words that seems to be acceptable to both sides on those issues, and then everybody on the other side feeling that the process is there more or less. And then another shopping list of issues appears that had not actually been mentioned before. You may feel that that shopping list was probably in their minds from the beginning, and that it was produced at a point in time when they felt that they had the best chance of getting some progress on those topics, because if they had brought it in at the beginning they might have been given short shrift and people might have despaired and walked out. But having got to the point where they thought they had got the deal that then created a big incentive to see if their demands could be met on this fresh shopping list. That is what hard negotiation in this situation seemed to mean. There were many items sought by parties to the process that could not be accepted.

GS: What would have happened if the governments had said 'no', we have already dealt with your initial shopping list which was the most important stuff, we are not actually going to get sucked into these other issues?

JP: One lesson is that negotiating with an organisation that has a terrorist arm is rather more difficult that negotiating with an organisation that does not. So, for example, I have never negotiated with anybody who has not told me that they personally are the most reasonable person that I could ever hope to meet, but unfortunately you know they are only there with the consent of some truly unforgiving people and if they were to accept what I was asking them to accept, it would not be them I would see at the next meeting but somebody else because they would be got rid of. But if the people that are being referred to in a negotiation by the other side's leaders are actually gunmen, who on the whole are not taking part in the political process, it is much more difficult to get a sense of where they are actually at. But, as I have said, every party experienced a failure to get all they wanted.

GS: And of great advantage presumably to have these people that are hidden in the background who could potentially cause damage?

JP: Yes, and it is a benefit that the unionists did not have.

GS: When the PIRA ceasefire broke down with Canary Wharf did you think that the process would end with that action?

JP: It is easy in a negotiation to become over-respectful of the other side and to attribute to them almost magical qualities that they do not possess, and I always reminded myself that the republican movement was as capable of making mistakes as the British Government were and I knew the British Government's capacity for making mistakes, because I was one of the people making the mistakes. Of the incidents that occurred during the process, the Northern Bank theft of 2004 would be quite a good example. Anybody looking for a smooth, successful process might have taken the trouble to stop that from happening, because it was certainly a bit of a nuisance, putting it mildly. But the fundamental analysis was that it was in their interests to take part in this process, and in the end to cut a deal. One point I could make, which I might have made earlier and which I did not quite get in, is that for me one of the difficulties about the negotiating process was that the Irish Government had a natural and entirely understandable affinity with the nationalists and the republicans and a perfectly good and improving relationship with the unionists, but it was a different relationship they had compared to their relationship with those who wanted a united Ireland. But the British Government, who might have achieved symmetry by having a different and rather closer relationship with the unionists than they had with the nationalists and the republicans, in fact had no such different relationship. The process depended on the British Government being neutral, but not on the Irish Government being neutral. So the unionists always were, and still are, at a disadvantage in having no sovereign government particularly committed to their cause. That made for an imbalance in the negotiation that was a real difficulty in the way of making progress. I was always conscious of it and its impact, but could see no way round it.

GS: Looking back would you say that quite often in these talks and negotiations too much was said and the more you talk the more you potentially open up to your opponents, opportunities or weaknesses? Is there, to try to put it more clearly, a problem in trying to gauge whether you are not saying enough or saying too much?

JP: That question seems to be founded on an assumption that the more talking you do, the more likely you are to provoke issues, and draw attention to issues that might better not be drawn attention to. I am not sure that assumption is correct. I have known people who are very terse but capable of raising a lot of issues in a very few words, and other people who can speak for hours at once without apparently saying anything at all! So I do not think that there is a clear correlation between the amount of talking that is done and the extent to which you jeopardise the process by bringing things in almost by accident that you did not intend to talk about.

GS: But was it better to get to a number of points quickly rather than allow people to talk for hours or days without it going anywhere?

JP: Every conversation takes place between a minimum of two people, otherwise you are in danger of being committed for talking to yourself if there's nobody else present, and often there is more than one other party present and an effective form of dialogue depends not just on the intonation of the person who is doing the talking at any one moment, but also the people that are doing the listening. I once worked for somebody who, however difficult the situation was that we were dealing with, liked to begin every meeting with five to ten minutes of, as it were, inconsequential chitchat, and I eventually came to realise that this was not time-wasting, it was a psychologically necessary sign on his part that we were not rattled, we were not in despair, we were going to cope, we were not panicked into talking desperately about what on earth we did next.

We could afford to, as it were, waste a bit of time in civilised inconsequential discourse and then turn to whatever it was that we had come to sort out, and the worse things got the more he was committed to that particular technique. It was a psychological need that he was meeting, and it had some benefit as well for others once they understood what was going on. It drove you absolutely bananas until you thought it through and understood it. So I do not think there are absolute rules about this. I have known very effective people who speak very tersely and when you meet them for the first time you do not realise that this is their style, and it can be rather off-putting and you feel it is a rather cold process, but I do not think that I saw too much of that sort of approach in Ireland, North or South.

GS: Were people good at listening and, indeed, did they listen so much they started hearing things other than what were said? A kind of paranoid listening?

JP: How can one generalise about the whole lot of people, some of whom were unfortunate enough to be listening to me? I would not have been necessarily thinking about what sort of listening they were doing whilst I was talking. I do think, however, that we would not have got anywhere in the process if a certain measure of listening on all sides had not been what I call good quality, empathetic listening, where you are really understanding where other people are coming from, and what matters to them and what matters to them not quite so much. To talk about a technique I have used in negotiations that I have led, but not in Northern Ireland, I have had people on my team who have been told by me that it is their job only to listen to the other side and not under any circumstances to speak, so they never needed to be thinking while somebody else was talking about what they were going to say next when it was their turn, because it was never going to be their turn. And then when the talks ended the first thing I would do, would be to turn to them and say what did you hear?

GS: In the early stages, in talks, Sinn Féin would often have a person sit at the back and say nothing, which could be taken as intimidation by the people talking. But in not having to function under the pressure of involvement, those people could listen to the nuances. Do you think enough attention was given to such observation, noting body language, subtle shifts and inconsistencies and underlying intentions?

JP: Some of the teams that were deployed on some of the bilateral talks were very small. There might have been only two or three people in the room on each side, and they might all have been expecting to speak at various points. In representing 'management' in dealing with trade union negotiations, I would often, as said, set somebody the task of not actually listening, but watching the body language on the other side of the table, because one would be interested in splits between people on the other side. Where did they sit in relation to each other? How much did they look at each other? You would sometimes get someone turning revealingly half their back to their own side looking away from the people they were supposed to be joined with in the negotiation and, because in those circumstances I was doing a lot of the talking from my side, I had to ask other people to watch specially for that and then talk about it afterwards, as well as listen to what was said.

GS: Do you think that at the start of the peace process there was any clear idea or plan on where the end of the process would be?

JP: We always suspected that policing and justice would be the most difficult thing to devolve, and that it would probably come at the end of the process. We probably did have ambitions in 1998 that there would be less agreements than resulted and the agreements would at least be closer together than from 1998 to 2010. I do not think that we were planning on that timescale. It is not the end of the process in the sense that you close the book and take no further notice of, or interest in, this subject again for the rest of recorded time. I became pretty concerned, before I retired, that London and Dublin should not fall into the trap of thinking that they could take their eye completely away from Northern Ireland. If you look at the arrangements between 1922 and 1972 for the UK Government, what Northern Ireland sometimes called the 'imperial government', they were not a very good model, and part of the reason for the conflict is that after 1922 London did its absolute best to wipe its hands of Northern Ireland and leave it to the lawfully appointed government of Northern Ireland. There is obviously a delicate balance to be struck between taking a continuing interest, knowing what is going on, showing respect for the fact that powers have been dissolved and are being exercised by local politicians without trying to interfere in those areas, so you have to strike a balance. But, I do not think that London was very well informed for most of the period between 1922 and 1972.

GS: If one looks at the development of the policies that shaped the peace process, in what sense was there an historical continuity with Sunningdale and the Anglo-Irish Agreement?

JP: In one sense there was no policy to be discussed in Northern Ireland after 1972. The government was trying to get out of it again and, from a very early stage, London wanted to see the return of devolution, but did not see how stable devolution could be achieved without a sharing of power between the two major communities. The majority and the minority community in Northern Ireland and everything that went on after 1972 was about trying to find a way to deliver what had been defined as the objective in policy terms, almost as soon as Stormont had been suspended. I am not sure that in 1974 if you had said to the people in Sunningdale that if they were to hang around a bit longer they might be able to get Sinn Féin into this process they would have thought that was a promising outcome. You would have needed to have been a very considerable visionary in 1974 to see that that could happen in the lifetime of quite a lot of people who were then participants in the process.

GS: Was the sense that the situation was stalemated and that politics was necessary widespread?

JP: The people I talked to were of that mind. There would have been occasional individuals in the Army, less the police, who thought that we needed to be tougher and we would win and that the problem would be sorted. This is in the nature of the duties and conditioning that a soldier goes through, which is about winning campaigns rather than losing them. But at senior levels, if you are talking about the British Establishment then you are really talking about the people at the top of the structures. I do not personally recall anybody who was not pretty realistic about the difficulty of 'winning a war'. On the other hand, I do think that people believed they could contain the problem in a fashion that would be ultimately frustrating for the other side, who were trying to win a war and who would see that it was not going to be very easy to win.

GS: The idea of the stalemate is interesting because one could ask why that was not obvious years before and at what point did people come to see that it could only ever be a process of containment rather than an outright win or lose situation?

JP: I cannot paint an honest and fair picture that everybody on the British side of this process moved at exactly the same speed in their perception of the situation and in exactly the same way, and it would be ridiculous to pretend that people were not conditioned by what they were paid to do. If you were a diplomat, for instance, or a civil servant involved in Northern Ireland, you might rather more quickly reach the view that no stable satisfactory arrangements for life in Northern Ireland could be achieved by military defeat of the PIRA. But if you were a lieutenant colonel in the British Army, who had been trained at Sandhurst and who had been brought up to think about military campaigns, you would be likely to see it very differently. It would be silly to say that there were never tensions, there must have been. I do not remember great examples of it, but there certainly would have been different perspectives and people moving at different speeds, and it is not the case that the heroes of this story are the soft-handed diplomats and home civil servants and the villains are the Army and the police, because if the Army and the police had not actually done their stuff in the way that they did, and one should include the intelligence services as well, there would not have been a deliverable deal on offer from anybody.

GS: In the republican tradition there is the myth of the 'glorious defeat' that underscored the impulse of armed struggle. But political transformation has, on the face of it, meant settling for not getting the British out of Ireland. There must have been considerable persuasion and coercion to carry the PIRA to this changed position. It must also have aided the Sinn Féin leadership very much to have Adams photographed with Hume and Reynolds in Dublin early in the peace process, as well as getting access to visas for trips to the United States where Adams could internationalise republicanism and lend it more respectability in the process.

JP: Yes, but some people believe that you negotiate by asking for what you want to get and others believe you best negotiate by asking for much more than you expect to get. As I said, if they convinced people that they were very tough negotiators and had achieved the best deal, then they achieved no more than the truth. I do not think they could have been better negotiators and they no doubt convinced their base that there were things they had to ask for but also jettison, because that secured in the end a better bottom line than if they had not asked for those things in the first place. I also think that you should not underestimate the fact that however objectionable some thought the unionists and Alliance Party were, they had, and have, the great merit of being from the island of Ireland, the whole of which is a single entity in republican thinking. Having them involved in the governance of the six counties in the northeast corner of the island, is, in principle, a very different matter than having a London secretary of state involved, and the police service is an Irish police service if you believe in a united Ireland. It is not the same as the Gardai, but it is on the island and it consists largely of Irish men and women, and so it could be seen as a sort of staging post to the ultimate goal and it is better than direct rule. You also have the merit of the participation of several important republicans in the governmental process, which is more than some mild consolation. It is certainly a step forward.

GS: Is a good negotiator always a tough negotiator?

JP: No, but it is one way of doing it and I do believe that anyone I know would have struggled to do better than Sinn Féin's negotiators did in this process. There may have been other ways of skinning the cat, and they may have been more congenial to the people they were dealing with, but I do not think they went back to their base and said what they were doing step-by-step once every two years. This was pretty well a daily process with some people whom we did not see and to whom they were talking most of the time. They would have been seen as tough negotiators on that basis.

GS: Were the unionists tough negotiators?

JP: I thought David Trimble was a tough negotiator. What always struck me about David Trimble was that he was not bolstered by someone who had a better or a bigger vision than him, or saw the long distance scene better than him. In my view, he was not bolstered and supported by people who had a better eye for the detail than him. He always seemed to me to be the best man on vision and the detail, and that is a rather demanding combination of roles if you are a very key player in a multiparty negotiation of this sort.

GS: In Alastair Campbell's book *The Irish Diaries* (2013), he says that Sinn Féin were like a solid football defence, moving forward and back together in a line, whereas the Ulster Unionists would often argue in front of each other in the room. Was that your perception?

JP: It is not always wise to disagree publicly, and parties make a big effort, particularly approaching elections, to present as united a front as they can. But one knows that there is a ferment of disagreement going on behind the scenes and people are often prepared to brief off-the-record against their colleagues in London-based political parties. Sinn Féin never felt to me like a political party of that sort at that time. They presented a much more disciplined face to outsiders, and it was very difficult to tell outside what the pressures were inside and who was arguing against whom. It was also, therefore, very difficult to know whether or not to believe the leaders of Sinn Féin when they said they wished they could help, but actually the pressures on them were such that they could not because the 'boys will not stand it'.

GS: So you could not see a weakness?

JP: At a time when these meetings were going on, I occasionally went out and visited a local authority where I would talk to the councillors from different political parties. It was a way of keeping in touch and keeping myself informed, sensing what the mood was in Northern Ireland a bit closer to the grass-roots than in Stormont. It was very common to find other people in political parties who would tell you what a dead loss their party leader was. It was very difficult to find anybody in Sinn Féin who would tell you anything other than what you were hearing from the top of the organisation, and there were other features that made them more characteristic of a religious movement than a political party. For instance, look at income. I do not know the detail of what they did with their salaries once Stormont was up and running, but I remember being told that they handed over their income to the party and the party gave them back what they needed. So, if they had large families they got rather more money and if they had smaller families they got rather less money. That does have some of the feeling of a religious organisation about it. You could not see the Labour Party, even with its commitment to socialism, asking its MPs to hand over income to the party and getting a smaller sum back.

GS: Principles or pragmatism?

JP: What one hoped is that the leaders, the people, as it were, at the very top for a long period saw that the process had a real potential benefit to their community, and that without the process there was no hope for the benefit. For example, we are talking about a deal that would remove offensive parts of the Irish Constitution that would commit the Irish Government and Sinn Féin to a united Ireland only on the basis of a majority vote in Northern Ireland, that would require the consent of the Northern Ireland people as a precondition to a united Ireland, that would bring an end to violence and provide positions in government in Northern Ireland for Northern Ireland politicians, including unionists who would have expected on the basis of their strength in the electorate to have the top job. There were a number of historically important things on the table for unionists. I felt that David Trimble's greatest contribution was that he never wavered in the clarity of his vision that this deal offered things to his community that were vitally important and that they were not going to get by walking away from the process. Now, you could say that that is the rational case for pragmatism over principle. Although it is said that the unionists attach greater weight to truth, to the word and to principle that might make their attachment to gains not as strong as the green side's attachment, they did see that they had an awful lot to lose by walking away from the process. In the end, it was that that just about carried them across the line.

GS: On pragmatism and principle, to what extent does pragmatism work before it begins to make principle look ridiculous?

JP: Well I think it depends on what the principle is. If you have a principle about not putting arms beyond use, or not handing over weapons to the authorities, and it goes deep into your psyche as an organisation, it may be a principle that means a great deal inside your own movement, but it is probably quite a difficult principle to get other people to understand. But if you have a principle that decisions should in the end be taken democratically with an electorate that are properly informed about what the choices and what the options are, a lot of people would subscribe to that sort of principle and it would have greater resonance with participants in a process whatever side they came from. Principles can also come into conflict. It is not just pragmatism that is the problem with principles or the absence of pragmatism as a result of adherence to principles. It is also the case that if you have a principle that you do not hand over your weapons and the other side has a principle that society should be conducted in a peaceful way without murders and bombings, then there is a sort of conflict of principle that has to be solved in a pragmatic way, arguably with some ground being given on both sides in relation to the principles at stake. Decommissioning may be an example of neither side sticking absolutely to the principles that were in conflict with each other, so it had to be accepted as having gone far enough by governments and unionists, and Sinn Féin possibly felt that they had had to give ground on an important principle for them, but the ground they gave did not carry them all the way to what unionists would have wanted.

GS: If you are assuming Sinn Féin's commitment to exclusively peaceful means you might argue that not using the weapons for five or ten years shows that there is no real intent to use them. Yet punishment beatings carried on and were not viewed as a violation of the exclusively peaceful commitment. Why do you think that was?

JP: I do not think punishment beatings, which by definition were in nationalist or green republican communities, ever seemed so politically significant as the habit of killing people outside those communities. Did that mean we did not care about people who were shot in the back of the legs? I hope it did not mean that. But what I gradually realised was that, just as in England, you can find people who are suffering from crime waves in their community (who by definition tend to be living in poor communities where crime waves seem worst) who are often remarkably hawkish in their view about how criminals should be treated, and remain remarkably unattached to things like fair trials and laws of evidence and all the things that I have spent a lot of my working life fussing over. It seemed to me that in both communities in Northern Ireland speedy punishment of anti-social behaviour was not unpopular among victims of crime, and that the efforts of the police and the courts were seen as pretty ineffective by comparison, as well as amazingly time-consuming and not very successful in their impact on would-be criminals. All that needed to be taken into account when assessing punishment beatings as opposed to shooting policemen, or bombing police stations and killing people in other communities. An ability to conduct a terrorist campaign does depend on a little bit more than just weaponry and, although weaponry is quite important, you need a structure and you need people to be, as it were, battle-hardened in the way the PIRA was and performed from the early 1970s until the mid-1990s.

GS: How important were key principles like consent, mutual respect and equality in galvanising the different sides to the prospect of a settlement?

JP: Probably both sides had a tendency not to do too well on those features of the Agreement that were less appealing to them. As equality in Northern Ireland tended to be a code word for evening up the discriminated-against Catholics from the deprived position that they had been in, that shift was generally seen as detrimental to the established majority. Equality was a word that was powerfully attractive to the green side and one hoped the orange side did not really dwell on. One would not have said to them look how important it is that we have got this reference here to equality. You would not go out of your way to highlight it in discussion with them, but the more sophisticated would have understood that there was no way that you could get an agreement that would include a hymn of praise to the concept of inequality. It may have been painful, and they did not know where it was going to lead, but they knew that they had to put up with it in order to get some other things, and I have already listed some of the things that were attractive to them.

GS: Did republicans dislike the principle of consent because their past had relied on consent being somewhat ignored, at least politically?

JP: I always imagined that when political leaders of the minority community went round and sought to sell the deal to their own people, they did not say 'You will be very pleased to start down this road and see where it gets to.' I think they probably said that within a measurable number of years, one way or another, this would lead to a united Ireland and they did not dwell on the detail there when it came to it. They knew very well what the agreements said. Of course, one of the things that all political leaders can rely on is that only a relatively small number of people follow these things with immense care. They had very, very few voters who read whole documents. The Belfast/Good Friday Agreement was a much shorter document to read than the Treaty of Rome, but it was still not the sort of thing that most ordinary people in Northern Ireland would have had as bedside reading, so they relied on the sales pitch of the leaders of their communities to know what it was really all about. And, as I say, understandably they would put the emphasis on the things that were attractive and tend to ignore those things that were unattractive. It is not surprising.

GS: What are the differences between strategic, pragmatic or practical thinking?

JP: Once the policy became a power-sharing Stormont with Sinn Féin as part of that process, the tactics that one would engage in from day to day and week to week in pursuing that goal must always be conditioned by keeping sight of the ultimate ambition. To take a practical point, you would not want to push any party in the process to the point where they decided they were going to 'take their bat home', as the English might have put it, and leave the game completely. If you push them to that point, then the chances of getting to the ultimate policy aim, which the strategy was trying to achieve, would be quite seriously damaged. I suppose you hope that they might leave briefly and come back again, but one of the objectives was to keep everybody in the process.

GS: Does that mean you never really pushed Sinn Féin as far as you could have because you were worried they were going to go over the edge or walk away?

JP: It is another way of stating the judgement you have to make in any negotiation, which is whether you can believe them or not when they tell you what the breaking point is for them at any particular time. Sometimes you find out later that you got it right, and sometimes you find out later that you got it wrong. And at other times you never find out and are left wondering whether you got it right or wrong.

GS: Was there ever a view that we have drawn these guys a fair way into this process and they are not likely to run away now, because if they did they would be sending out a message to their own base that what they have staked their credibility on is now defunct? Realistically, how are they going to walk away given the seriousness of the implications for them?

JP: Well, of course, that is all part of the analysis that one makes; what are the pressures on them to stay in the process? There are pressures to keep them in the process, clearly, but there is a limit to how effective those pressures are if you require them to do things that are unsaleable to their own constituency. It is partly in relation to that kind of awkward but critical judgement that different layers of communication between the two sides come into their own, because, whether it is true or not in practice, most people might believe that in a one-to-one conversation there is a better chance of reaching a judgement about what the bottom line is than in a big meeting with note-takers and teams of negotiators on both sides making speeches at each other. Humanly speaking, we perhaps all believe that we have a much better chance of finding out what people really mean in that situation, where one might be better able to tell if one is dealing with someone who is being straight with you, or possibly more capable of deceit than you imagine. However, one must also be aware of the danger of deluding oneself into thinking that because there is a full, frank and private discussion going on one necessarily has a better sense of what is going on, because this was far from always the case.

GS: Would you say that conversation and negotiation shape text, or is it text that shapes conversation and negotiation?

JP: I would say that it is interchangeable. When you first draw up a text you are not thinking only of what you want to achieve yourself, but of the people who want to share with you in supporting this text. You are doing your best to judge where the bottom lines might be, and what points and forms of words and what presentation and substance might give you chance of getting the 'buy-in' that you are looking for. And what informs those judgements are all the conversations you have ever had and all the information you have available to you about the parties that will eventually join in the process. Having got the piece of paper in existence you then go into a 'document-specific' series of conversations that might lead to further refinement and change.

GS: How did text shape or inform the relationships between people?

JP: As I mentioned before, there comes a moment for textual barter and it is a very important part of the process, but if you come at it cold, I think you are less likely to make progress than if the ground is prepared and that preparation of ground happened in different ways at different times. It is difficult to provide a formula that says this is exactly how human relationships and personalities interacted with the need at some point to get down to talking about and settling an agreed text as to the way forward. It happened in different ways at different times.

GS: Does that mean that you prefer more text to play with?

JP: It just carries one back to finding the right moment. The right moment for sorting out policing was not in 1998 so the text was rather thin and rather brief, but there came a moment for Patten and the detailed *Patten Report* that did not in itself solve some of the issues. In order to solve the badge we had to have a Policing Board that at that time did not have Sinn Féin on it, but it did have the SDLP on and they had to cut a deal on the badge, which they managed to do. I remember the moment of euphoria when the Policing Board managed to sort out the badge. Now that was not text, that was a visual symbol, but it was the same as text. It was very specific, detailed and clear, had to be agreed by all parties, and could not be departed from once it had been agreed. But that came at the right moment.

GS: Were you ever taken by surprise by the level of attachment that any particular side gave to something that perhaps you did not think they would give such attachment to?

JP: No, I do not think I was ever taken by surprise. I had been at the Northern Ireland game since the 1960s on and off, so I do not think there was that much unpredictability as far as I could see. I was slightly surprised that what seemed to me to be major features of the April 1998 Agreement, which was essentially a change to the Irish Constitution and a general acceptance that there would be a united Ireland only on the consent of the majority of the people in Northern Ireland, did not seem to get the credit they deserved from the unionist community. That had been the policy of the British Government for many decades, but the point about that Agreement was that it was being signed up to by all the parties to it, including the Irish Government and Sinn Féin. I am sure that if you talk to a lot of people from the unionist community they would say that the history of Northern Ireland since 1998 has been a history of the erosion of their position, which completely fails to acknowledge the significance of those features of that Agreement. I do not believe for one second that the significance of that escaped David Trimble, in fact, I think he led his community into that Agreement precisely because he understood the deep significance for them.

GS: If one looks at the 1997–8 period one can see that choreography and symmetry were important, but how difficult was it to do that in a zero-sum climate?

JP: There have to be things on offer for both communities in order for the process to carry on. You cannot have a very prolonged period of one community feeling as though they are losing all down the line and not gaining anything or you would not get anywhere. Of course, there were some features of the arrangements that were perhaps significant for both communities. It would be easy to describe the whole process as a 'game' where one party could only gain at the expense of the other party, but the whole apparatus around Stormont means that, with devolution, there is a sort of financial infrastructure that was not there to the same extent before, and pretty well all the politicians in Northern Ireland must actually welcome that, whether they prefer to talk about it or not.

GS: One remembers when John de Chastelain was expected to sell the decommissioning argument and it went badly wrong, and Trimble just sort of pulled the plug on the choreography. What happens when the choreography goes wrong?

JP: What that puts me in mind of is what I am certain I have stolen from other people and have usually said about planning in government, whether for the Northern Ireland political/peace process or for any other form of business, which is that there is great advantage in undertaking really detailed planning, examining the 'what ifs', having contingencies in mind as to what you might do in certain circumstances that may or may not arise, and so on. It is vitally important that you do that planning and then when you are in it for real, it is vital that you throw the plans away and proceed, if you like, off the seat of your pants or instinctively. The reason I put it that way is that your instincts, the seat of your pants, will be better for having done the planning beforehand, but if you do the planning and then believe your own plans you will almost certainly get it wrong, because you will not have been listening and paying attention to what has actually gone on between the start of the process and the disaster that has now ensued, whatever it happens to be.

GS: One gets the impression that there was a lot of running around going on for a very small number of people, who would try to nudge and push things along in ways that seemed quite spontaneous, but do not actually fit this kind of formalised picture of people in the negotiation setting.

JP: My own belief is you make much more progress if you have a relationship with people in negotiation. It would appear that the talking that was done through the so-called 'link' between the British Government and the PIRA from the 1970s (and Brendan Duddy and Michael Oatley have talked quite openly about the nature of their friendship) would not have been sustained as long as it was, or have been useful as it was, without an acknowledgement of the importance of that dimension. And that is only a rather well-known, perhaps slightly surprising, example of the phenomenon that you are asking about. But, of course, you may find yourself in a situation with people who are not entirely congenial, but you still have to find a way of doing business with them, and you might not achieve a friendship that lasts beyond the need to meet each other in order that you can both do the jobs you happen to have at that time. But, in some circumstances, it will go beyond that and a relationship will develop that is sustained because you both enjoy the relationship.

GS: Did you get the sense that people actually found themselves warming to those who instinctively they were telling themselves they should loathe because of meeting on a regular basis?

JP: Rather conventional British civil servants and politicians would not expect to find in any way congenial people who had been committed to a campaign of violence over decades in pursuit of their political goals. That may be what you are alluding to. What I would say about that is when I was a very young man, and possibly a bit older than a very young man, I was quite happy to use the sort of nouns and adjectives that British statements tended to feature, such as 'despicable' and other psychopathic words, in relation to those who had planted bombs and shot other people. But, at some point, and quite a long time ago, it dawned on me that these people were pursuing what *they* saw as a principled course. I did not agree with them, but actually it was a terrible mistake if you believed your own propaganda that these people were little more than proponents of mindless violence or psychopaths. It simply led to a fundamental failure to understand their motivation and, as they would see it, their ideals. You could say that the sort of lives that these people led, running risks to their own safety, not having stable everyday family lives because they could not always sleep in the same place night after night, demonstrated a commitment to a cause and meant that they had to be taken very seriously. So I was not altogether surprised to find that some of them had attractive, almost charismatic, personalities, and others had rather unattractive and off-putting personalities, and in that respect they were extremely similar to British civil servants and British politicians, who also personified a wide array of character differences.

GS: To what extent did ego feature in this process? Was it at one level like a competition of intelligences or philosophising?

JP: You may have a very particular theory of exchanges in mind when asking that question. I do not know that I would describe it as ego-driven. Sure, ego has had a lot to do with this process, as it does to any human endeavour, but it is certainly the case that there have been moments in negotiations between the two governments when the two participants have got a lot of satisfaction from realising that they were dealing with an interlocutor worthy of every bit of skill that they could bring to bear, and the sort of tussles that that led to generated quite a lot of enthusiastic members of the audience on both sides. I have heard it said that for certain sorts of negotiation, you could have sold tickets because it was so sparky and so challenging, but I am not going to name the names. I do not think that there was any particular shouting in the exchanges I was involved in. There was more sharpness than shouting. It is a way of conducting a debate, and whether it goes somewhere depends on a lot of other things not just the quality of people's minds.

GS: Can you actually be persuasive without conceding or giving away, and how were concessions used?

JP: Obviously concessions were made all round fairly regularly or there would never have been any progress. It is not a mathematical thing. It is a matter of mood and emotion, and all sorts of things that are not really to do with the content or the substance of the negotiation can have a bearing on when you arrive at the moment that you actually get a deal. And you do not say, well you have to make 15.5 per cent concessions to this side and 15.5 per cent concessions to that, and then we will be there. It does not work like that. It might be easier if you could make that sort of calculation, but you cannot. Timing is quite important and tone is quite important, and sometimes it may be necessary to say I am afraid there is nothing else on this point that I can add and that if you will not take what I have just said now, then I am afraid that this process has come to an end. But you have to be very careful about saying anything like that, and, if you do, you have to be extremely careful to stick to it.

GS: Like decommissioning?

JP: I've heard it said on the part of Sinn Féin that they had a number of things promised to them that they never achieved. They may have come to regard or assume that a category of promise would be made that they had to discount and they could not calculate on that promise ever being honoured. It is one way of negotiating.

GS: What you say is very interesting in that you have demonstrated to your opponents that you have conceded on certain points, or that you have been willing to accept less than you would like. So, achieving and not achieving are an essential part of the process if it is to work.

JP: And sometimes perhaps being given a promise of something but not the substance, not having the promise delivered, had to be something that people had to settle for, and they may have preferred a promise to nothing at all or to a straight rejection. It was part of the courtesy of life. You know it is almost as if you said, you can have this chocolate that you like and then pick it up and eat it yourself, with a wink as it were! That is, you are making a promise, they know that you are not going to keep it, you know you are not going to keep it, and you know that they know that you are not going to keep it, and so on. It is easier to make the promise and keep the atmosphere sweet than it is to say, 'Look, let's get real here for pity's sake, there is no way I can do that and you must know that there is no way I can do that.' So instead of putting it as starkly as that and rather dampening the atmosphere, chilling the atmosphere, you promise something that you are not going to deliver.

GS: Did you find that in the communications process metaphors were an important part of shaping context, such as Blair's 'peace train' that was leaving?

JP: Well they always bring things home to people and some people have a gift for vivid forms of speech. Seamus Mallon very famously said that the process was 'Sunningdale for slow learners'. A very vivid phrase, and you could pick it to pieces and nit-pick about the details and some of the differences between Sunningdale and the GFA, but it was not altogether wrong. So metaphor can be good, and it is possibly closer to sound bites since we remember the things that stir our emotions rather than things that simply register at an intellectual level.

GS: From your experience can humour be used to shoot straight to the argument, or move things along or block things?

JP: I did sit through quite a few of the talks, the plenary talks that led eventually to the April 1998 Agreement chaired by George Mitchell. And there was an occasion, I think in Dublin, when we were planning to throw Sinn Féin out of the talks for a period. One group of loyalists had been suspended from participating for a week or ten days, and there had been a terrorist death on the republican side and something similar was going to be done with Sinn Féin because of that. They were filibustering to try to keep the talks going to avoid this happening while they sought an injunction from the Irish court. They were quite good humoured about it and asked for adjournments and so on, and there had been a number of deadlines that had passed and George Mitchell was clearly running out of patience because they were having trouble finding a judge. We came together again at something like seven in the evening, and they asked for another very short delay because they were almost sure that they were about to be able to speak to a judge in Dublin about this matter and seek an injunction. And George Mitchell, speaking as someone who had worked as a judge, said 'I have to tell you that it's one thing to get hold of a judge to speak to, but it's another to get him to agree to what you want him to agree to.' In the rather tense atmosphere that helped to change the mood a bit.

GS: Did people laugh at things you did not expect them to laugh at?

JP: Or possibly laugh more uproariously than you thought something was worth laughing at because of the release of tension and so on. There is nothing distinctive about these negotiations in that respect from other negotiations. When there is a release of tension you will often get an over-the-top reaction of humour or whatever.

GS: Looking back on that whole period of your involvement do you think that what came out of the process was as good as it could have been in terms of political outcome?

JP: At this moment we have the constitutional arrangements that we wanted, but there are a number of questions one can ask oneself, such as did it happen as quickly as it could have happened?, or could it have been handled in a different way and got a much earlier and identical result? Another question is could it have been handled in a way that would have bound in everyone on the republican side who had ever been inclined to violence so that there were no so-called 'dissident' groups continuing a campaign of violence? Could we have found a constitutional arrangement that would have allowed a more coherent plan for the government of Northern Ireland to be developed and implemented? If you take an issue like the future of grammar schools in Northern Ireland, which the parties seem to be incapable of resolving, you could ask if we could have developed a constitutional arrangement that would have made it easier to sort that problem out. Given that there are always people who have to present themselves to the electorate, and given that they are not of the same political parties, there are bound to be stresses and tensions and moments that they choose to point out the disagreements. I think the broad position is that we are as far forward as we ever dared to hope.

GS: How does text and context work to influence what you were doing?

JP: I do not think it is possible to argue in a situation like Northern Ireland that you need only look at the words on the page and that you do not need to think about how those words might be understood differently by different communities. For reasons that I never completely understood, the term Good Friday Agreement, which was, as it were, the popular title of something, an example of three words that might be described as text, was always perfectly acceptable to the minority Catholic/nationalist/republican community in Northern Ireland, but unacceptable to the majority Protestant/unionist/loyalist community. So it was called the GFA to some people in some company and the Belfast Agreement – its official title – to others in other company, and it seemed to me to be perfectly fitting to be aware of the context in which that text would be viewed by different people.

GS: Why was it not called the Belfast Agreement to begin with, which presumably would have catered for everybody all at once?

JP: Despite the formal title, 'Good Friday Agreement' was quickly adopted in popular speech, and we were slightly taken aback by the wish of the unionists not to call it the GFA. Their motivation may have been no more than the fact that they wished to be obstreperous and difficult over something that did not terribly matter either to them or to us. But the whole process of political negotiation makes you think about the context, and if you do not think about the context, then you will not make very much progress. On the other hand, a colleague of mine always used to describe it as a process of 'textual barter', and it was certainly the case that the words on the piece of paper were terribly important and were argued over. It was a focus, a method, as it were, by which we could secure agreement.

GS: On the process of re-drafting the text, how did the initial version differ from the final one?

JP: Anyone who earns their living in a government department knows that the person who puts the first words down on a piece of paper, the first draft of anything, is invariably the person who exercises the greatest influence over the text that eventually emerges. There may be changes made, but, unless you consciously tear up the original version and throw it in the bin, you are always somewhat confined by the way the person wrote it down the first time. Therefore, if you are in a negotiation, a multisided negotiation, you are very conscious of the advantage you have if you produce the first draft. One of the strengths a government department has to balance is the fact that in Northern Ireland neither the Irish Government nor the British Government had any votes really, but one of the sources of power and influence that we both had was people who could write the pieces of paper, and that is always the starting point and the major shaper of the eventual outcome. Certainly, there are changes, not always to clarify things, sometimes to obscure things, and sometimes it is part of human nature that changes are made, that you believe have absolutely no effect on meaning at all. But you find a way of making a change to please people who are unhappy about it and they may persuade themselves that they have secured a concession, and that may lead them to agree to something that they might not otherwise have agreed to.

GS: Typically, would the draftsman overwrite and cut it down, or would he write barely anything and build it up?

JP: I do not think write barely anything and build it up. The changes would be balanced between excision and addition, so there would be occasions when you would expand something, there would be occasions when you would abbreviate something, or just leave something out rather than abbreviate it, and agree not to address that particular aspect at this stage in that particular document. There are all sorts of things you have to do to try to get to an agreed text, and it is an illustration of where context is important, because if a person who has put all their money on the text believes that is all that is important, but is told that this version is superior to that version, and they look at them both and believe that they meant exactly the same thing and that there is no difference between them, you would have no way of explaining to someone who did not understand context that the difference between the two was that the second version had had changes made to it. That it reflected changes made to the first version and, whether or not those changes made any difference to the meaning, they made a difference to its acceptability to one of the parties, because that party believed that those changes had been made in response to their unhappiness and they felt reassured by that response.

GS: So, often the appearance of the changes made was important to pacify the resistance or unease?

JP: Yes, it gives people a sense that you are listening to them, that you are responding in some way to their concerns, and anyone who has any experience in this game knows that, with the best will in the world, you try to judge what the effect of a particular document is going to be when it is put into practice, in real life as it were. But you cannot always be sure what that is, and when you have seen it happen on a number of occasions, you cannot get too excited by exactly what the text says. People do get very excited about it and therefore one does take it seriously in making these changes.

GS: Was the peace process a textually driven process where you had to have this piece of paper that would bind people in?

JP: Timing is quite important in terms of when you introduce text. Where people disagree, in the end you have to work at it through text, but I would say that understanding the context allows you to get the timing of the introduction of text more right than wrong, so you have a chance of not having people walk out at the wrong moment.

GS: How important is it to look at spaces, gaps or perhaps things that are not said in order to try to find this thing called 'common ground'?

JP: I think I would prefer the term 'emotional intelligence' really. That you have to empathise with the people you are talking to and you have to draw them into talking in a relatively unguarded way. This is easier to achieve with some participants than others, and easier in some areas of life than in others, in terms of getting a sense of where they might be willing to compromise and where they are not willing to compromise. If you find an approach that both parties could agree on, you could say that that was a piece of creativity and, even though it does not match writing a piece of music or poem, it does involve some empathy and some imagination in the sense of putting yourself into the position of people who have a very different upbringing and very different values to yourself. It is true, though, that text possibly mattered somewhat more to one party than the other.

GS: Would you say that there was a 'Catholic' analysis underpinning republican and nationalist approaches to the peace process that involved seeing things more as part of a journey?

JP: I think for sure that people on the green side of the community who were the leaders and negotiators seemed to accept with greater comfort a feeling about something that had not been honoured. This was less the case on the unionist side. I always felt that if unionists caught you out in what they might have seen as a lie, they saw that as a pretty devastating blow to the process because it destroyed confidence on their part in a way that it did not quite destroy confidence on the part of the green side, who perhaps did not have such high expectations of the people they were talking to. I mean, they would not have taken the British Government as a model of perfect human behaviour.

GS: Why did the British agree to others like de Chastelain and Mitchell coming into the process?

JP: It was partly their neutrality and, in the case of Americans, it had the advantage of reassuring the governments that both had a potential to help with this process by speaking at various points to various people. One of the things that infuriated a lot of unionists is how little recognition was given to the vast number of Irish Americans who come from a unionist background and the number of US presidents who have had Ulster Protestant blood in their veins. Americans tend to be thought of as influenced by Irish-Catholic thinking, with little or no input from people with an Irish-Protestant origin.

GS: Did the thinking of 'the outsider' have any impact or bring about any change in how the British were thinking about this process?

JP: I do not really remember that happening. I am sure that on the technicalities of decommissioning John de Chastelain might have had more influence, and certainly with George Mitchell you had a very impressive senior figure who was taken seriously by everybody. But I doubt if anyone ever sat down at the beginning and said that it would be rather clever if we went into this with those who have big reputations and great standing, and who could not be identified as either sympathetic to unionists or nationalists and then draw them in. Having done it once as a tactical matter, then you almost retro-fitted a strategy to the tactics being developed and produced the rationalisation as something that was carefully thought through in the first place, when it was not.

GS: Did the one-to-one conversations play a particular role throughout that process?

JP: I have always found it to be so, not just in terms of the negotiations we are talking about here, but in that if you try to do it all across a table in a formal structure with everyone who has an interest in the room at one and the same time, you might, if it is not very important, get there in the end, but it will take an awful long time and, if it is important, you might never get there at all if that is all you are prepared to do. In my experience, you have to operate always both at the one-to-one level and at the more formal level.

GS: Do you think that when negotiations start, the participants know exactly what they want at the end of it?

JP: My experience has been that people do generally know what they want to achieve, and know what they would have to achieve to make an agreement worth having, that is, what their bottom line is. But it would be a very surprising world if, in the course of talking to other participants, you never learn anything that you did not know before and that might cause you to adjust, as it were, your aims and/or your bottom line in a negotiation.

GS: 'The bottom line' is an interesting expression and many people use it. Were there occasions when people negotiated to the minimum with the view that if they got anything else it would be a bonus?

JP: I do not think that you can make a rule about it, particularly if you are in a relationship that is ongoing. My experience here is that you knew what you thought was right for the public of Great Britain, and you knew what you thought your ministers regarded as absolutely imperative to go to Parliament, or go to the newspapers, and say what had been achieved. Whether you pitched miles above that or a bit above it slightly depended upon your reading of the other side and on your style. One thing you would avoid if you were negotiating year in year out with the same people was the use of overblown rhetoric that would later be shown to be garbage, because you had your own reputation to protect as a careful, thoughtful, straightforward person. In such a meeting you probably would not ever reveal your bottom line, but you might, particularly if an early deal was important for some extraneous reason, seek out the leader of the other side and say 'There's absolutely no point in persisting in asking for that because believe me I cannot give it to you and I will never be able to give you that. You know, I can go back to my side and plead all day, but I will be told not to be so stupid, so you had better get yourself used to the idea that you are not going to get that. But I might be able to help you with a bit over here, and if you want to ask for something there I might be disposed to give it to you.' So you can reach a point where you almost stage-manage the full negotiation by informal contact, but you really need to be able to trust the other person in order to be able to do that, and that, in my experience, depended on building relationships at a point where you were not at a crisis. You got through a crisis best if you had been talking to people when you did not absolutely have to talk to them. So you built a relationship, built an understanding, built a measure of trust that you could, as it were, call in, and so did the other side. You know, both sides are at this game, it is not a one-sided process.

GS: Sinn Féin documents in the early 1990s insisted on a date for British withdrawal. Does that strike you as strange, putting a minimum requirement and then ignoring it down the road?

JP: They had a number of quite distinctive marks to their negotiating style. One of them was certainly to make sure they did not knowingly under-bid, on the one hand, while another feature was that after an exhausting negotiation, when you thought you had finally got to a deal and you were congratulating yourself on it, they would come back and ask for just a little bit more. Sometimes what they were asking for seemed so insignificant when set against the irritation that they were causing by coming back and asking for it, that you wondered whether they had got the judgement right. But I suppose standing back and looking at that pattern over the years, they probably did make quite a lot of progress by being ready to come back, not at the eleventh hour, but at the thirteenth hour, and just ask for a little bit more.

GS: One can see that the momentum of the Blair Government was much more urgent, if you like, for various political reasons. The impression is that it was not such a formal or controlled process under Blair as it had been under Major, with Jonathan Powell and others conducting a multitude of one-to-one sessions. Would you say that it was a very controlled process under Blair?

JP: Reports have been written about differences in styles of governance, stretching across the whole front of domestic and international issues, the so-called 'sofa government' about which people have written and about which Tony Blair and those close to him have argued back that that is a misunderstanding of what was going on. Tony Blair is very good with words and he writes very well, but I do not think that he had a particular taste for lots and lots of written words. In my experience working within a government department with different secretaries of state, when the political leadership changes, the department has to adjust the way it works to fit in with that person's predilections. It is not party political in the sense that all Tories read everything and socialists do not, or the other way round.

GS: The need to listen and the spontaneity of conversation is clearly a skill in the negotiating process, but actually it seems to be an important part of peace-making that tends to get overlooked.

JP: My observation would be that some people are very secure and confident in conversation, whether one-to-one or in groups. Life has taught them that they are as fluent and as quick thinking and judicious as they need to be in order to be effective and safe in what they are doing. Others lack that confidence and do not really want to put themselves in a position where they might be taken advantage of by people who are more eloquent and more quick-witted than they are themselves. What I would say of Tony Blair is that I do not think that he had any doubt at all about his ability to hold his own in conversation with any modern leader in the world. He was from the top division on that particular quality.

GS: Blair was often seen as a charismatic person. Is charisma an important part of talk and negotiations, and is it a powerful motivating force?

JP: I might not use the term charisma, but a slightly more neutral term like personal presence, because to say somebody is charismatic is generally to describe them as a fairly attractive sort of figure. People did find Blair attractive when they met him and I think charismatic is a reasonable term to use of him, but it is not the only way you can make a powerful impact in a room. If you hardly ever speak in a negotiation, it can be utterly terrifying to the other side. If you only ever ask a question and never give any indication of what you are feeling yourself, there is quite a lot of research that shows that it drives people to distraction.

Reference

Campbell, A. (2013). *The Irish Diaries 1994–2003*. Dublin: Lilliput Press.

10 Why was the Good Friday Agreement so hard to implement?: lessons from 'Groundhog Day', 1998–2002

Sir Bill Jeffrey

When I was a young civil servant in the Home Office in the 1970s, I served as secretary to a committee chaired by Lord Franks, arguably the most distinguished British public servant of the postwar generation. When I came to draft the committee's report, his instructions were for me to write to be understood by an interested general reader, of reasonable intelligence, 'who was paying attention'. I am not sure how many general readers there will be for a book of reflections by former servants of the British Government in Northern Ireland, but I have tried to follow that prescription here.

This is not a memoir of my time in Northern Ireland. I do not believe that civil servants should write memoirs, and, even if I did, most of the decent anecdotes have already been told by Jonathan Powell and other chroniclers of the period. What it is, is an attempt, after a gap of more than ten years – most of it spent in other busy jobs in Whitehall – to order my own thoughts about what was actually going on in the turbulent period between the conclusion of the Belfast (or Good Friday) Agreement (which, to avoid needless controversy, will from here on be referred to as 'the Agreement') on 10 April 1998 and the collapse of the institutions, for the third time, on 14 October 2002. Although not a politician myself, my perspective on these events is political and practical rather than historical or theoretical. As a civil servant, I was always at the pragmatic end of the spectrum, interested principally in what works (and what does not) and how outcomes can be delivered in the real world. The approach I have adopted is to start with some basic facts about the Agreement, which I believe are essential to an understanding of what was going on, and then offer a highly compressed account of the main efforts to break the deadlock over decommissioning and devolution. By my reckoning, there were seven such attempts, or passages of events, in the period between Good Friday 1998 and the point when I departed the scene in October 2002. Gerry Adams memorably described these as 'Groundhog Day', because there was a certain repetitiveness about them, but there were also differences. I will then, as it were, hold that account up to the light, and attempt to answer why it took so long to implement an Agreement that was rightly applauded around the world as a major breakthrough and to consider whether anything could have been done differently, as well as what lessons might be learned from the experience that might help to resolve similar conflicts elsewhere in the world.

The Agreement was an attempt to be comprehensive, to resolve, to the extent possible, all the outstanding issues that had bedevilled earlier attempts to solve the Northern Ireland problem. It did not settle the constitutional position of Northern Ireland for all time, but it did provide, through the application of the consent principle, a mutually acceptable way of addressing it in future. The new institutional framework – the Northern Ireland Assembly and Executive, the North–South Ministerial Council, and the British Irish Council – was sketched out in enough detail in the body of the Agreement to make implementation relatively simple had there not been political obstacles in the way. In different degrees of detail, the Agreement addressed human rights safeguards and equality, economic, social and cultural issues, decommissioning, security, policing and justice, and the release of prisoners. In that sense, the aspiration to comprehensiveness was achieved. But, inevitably, not everything could be pinned down to the same degree. This was partly because the negotiations in the weeks and days before Good Friday were intensive and time-limited, and partly because the issues that were not pinned down were among the most difficult and intractable. Policing is a good example. The Agreement described in relatively uncontroversial terms the need for a new beginning for policing in Northern Ireland, and the characteristics of a police service that would be 'capable of attracting and sustaining support from the community as a whole'. But the detailed working through of these ideas was handed to an independent commission, whose report was not published until September 1999.

But the prime example of an issue that could not be pinned down in the Good Friday negotiations is the decommissioning of arms. The paramilitary organisations were not parties to the Agreement, although their political representatives were. The decommissioning section of the Agreement includes a commitment by all participants to the total disarmament of all paramilitary organisations, and confirmation of 'their intention ... to use any influence they may have to achieve the decommissioning of all paramilitary arms within two years [following the referenda on the Agreement] and in the context of the implementation of the overall settlement'. Decommissioning – and the fact that those who could deliver it (the paramilitaries themselves rather than their political representatives) were not committed by the Agreement to do so – was at the heart of the problems that unfolded over the succeeding years.

There were two other related provisions of the Agreement that should be added to the mix. The first was the early release scheme for prisoners. The

Agreement committed the British and Irish governments to 'put in place mechanisms ... for an accelerated programme for the release of prisoners'. Prisoners affiliated to organisations that were not maintaining a complete and unequivocal ceasefire were not to benefit. Release dates would be set taking account of the seriousness of the offences and the need to protect the community. The intention was that 'should the circumstances allow it, any qualifying prisoners who remained in custody two years after the commencement of the scheme would be released at that point'.

The second is the provision for removing a Northern Ireland minister from office for failure to meet his or her responsibilities, including those set out in the 'Pledge of Office'. This can be done on a cross-community vote only. Although the section goes on to declare that 'those who hold office should use only democratic, non-violent means, and those who do not should be excluded or removed from office', it clearly relates to ministers themselves rather than their paramilitary associates and makes no direct reference to decommissioning obligations. Concern on this point led David Trimble to seek and receive from Tony Blair at the end of the negotiations a letter reassuring him that 'if, during the first six months of the shadow Assembly or the Assembly itself [the provisions for exclusion from ministerial office had] been shown to be ineffective, [the British Government] would support changes to enable them to be made properly effective'.

These three sections of the Agreement – on decommissioning, prisoner releases and exclusion from Executive office – and the supposed connections between them, dominated the long-running argument about the establishment of the new institutions. For readers unfamiliar with the Agreement, the other salient fact is that, in order to function, the institutions require willing participants from both communities. In other words, if unionists are unwilling to accept ministerial office in the Northern Ireland Executive, the implementation of the whole institutional framework is stymied.

In Northern Ireland there is a caricature that unionists tend to be over-literal (as Tony Blair found to his cost with his hand-written pledges during the referendum campaign), whereas for nationalists the question is whether the language used is politically and culturally sympathetic, and the details matter less. In this case, the roles were almost reversed. Unionists argued that, unless and until the Provisional IRA (PIRA) decommissioned their arms, Sinn Féin should be excluded from ministerial office, and that, since both the decommissioning and prisoner release sections of the Agreement included an aspiration for completion within two years, the one should not proceed without the other. Sinn Féin took the literal view. They were not the PIRA. They were using such influence as they had. The prompt establishment of the prisoner release scheme was an obligation on the governments, and the establishment of the institutions was an obligation on all the parties to the Agreement.

These positions were entrenched by public statements on both sides. On 5 September 1998, as the end October date originally set for establishing the institutions approached, David Trimble said in terms that decommissioning was necessary before the Ulster Unionist Party (UUP) would enter an Executive with Sinn Féin. On the same day, Gerry Adams said that there was nothing in the Agreement that prevented the immediate establishment of an Executive including Sinn Féin. On 19 September, Gerry Kelly of Sinn Féin said that there was a 'looming crisis' if the unionists insisted that prior decommissioning was the bottom line before Sinn Féin were allowed to enter the Executive. They had 'unrealistic expectations'. On 23 September, Adams was more explicit. Decommissioning was not within Sinn Féin's gift. Trimble was trying to 'impose conditions' and renegotiate the Agreement. At the UUP annual conference a week before the end of October deadline, Trimble said that Sinn Féin members could not become part of the Executive before decommissioning. All of this was in the public domain, but in private the positions were the same.

The first major set-piece event to address the decommissioning impasse was at Hillsborough Castle from 29 March to 1 April 1999. The discussions centred on a text, which was largely the work of the two governments, and was refined through bilateral discussions between the prime minister and the taoiseach, on the one hand, and the main party leaders, on the other. The text attempted to deal with republican objections to decommissioning being made a precondition of the establishment of the institutions by saying that it was not a precondition but an obligation deriving from the parties' commitment in the Agreement, which should take place within the timescale envisaged by the Agreement, and by describing a sequence of events that would start with the nomination of those to take up office as ministers. But it also provided reassurance for unionists that, if they nominated ministers and decommissioning did not take place within a reasonable time (the statement eventually published assumed a month), there was a way out. The nominations would fall to be confirmed by the Assembly on a cross-community vote, in which the unionists could withhold their support.

One element of the Hillsborough proposal that did not feature in later attempts was the idea of a 'collective act of reconciliation', on a date to be proposed by the Independent International Commission on Decommissioning (IICD), but within a month of ministerial nominations. On that date, some arms would be put beyond use, there would be further British moves to reduce the military footprint, the institutions would be formally established, and there would be ceremonies of remembrance for all victims of violence. (The 'collective act of reconciliation' was, as I recall, an Irish suggestion. It would have provided cover for a move by the PIRA, with the putting of some arms beyond use being seen as a contribution to reconciliation. It was ingenious, but the likelihood that the 'victims of violence' would include members of the PIRA killed on operations raised issues of 'moral equivalence' and therefore apprehensions among unionists, and indeed to some extent within the British Government.)

Like others who were involved, by the end of 31 March I was optimistic that agreement could be reached on these lines, in which case the text would have been a joint statement by the governments and the parties. By the morning of 1 April, it was clear that this was not to be. Sinn Féin's position had hardened noticeably overnight. The prime ministers took the decision to publish the text as it stood, as work in progress – a draft declaration on which the parties' views were sought. By 3 April, Brian Keenan, a senior member of the PIRA Council, had made a speech in which he said that the PIRA would not be forced into a surrender in the form of decommissioning; and the following day Gerry Adams' reaction to the Hillsborough statement was that it 'may have merit, but may also be counter-productive if it amounts to an ultimatum to the armed groups'. This was soon followed by formal rejection of the Hillsborough declaration by Sinn Féin.

The second attempt to break the deadlock was at Downing Street a few weeks later. This involved a much less elaborate proposal, under which ministerial nominations would have been made the following week, with full devolution and the establishment of the institutions by the end of June, following a report by the IICD. This was Hillsborough shorn of the collective act of reconciliation (which unionists would be glad to be rid of, fearing that the proposed acts of remembrance would be an occasion for 'moral equivalence' between terrorist and other victims), but also of the assurance that a decision to nominate ministers would not be irrevocable. Although David Trimble appeared at the time to be willing to contemplate recommending it to his party, it was never likely to be acceptable to unionists (he soon reached that conclusion himself) and it was rejected by the UUP Assembly within a day or so. This prompted Tony Blair to set 30 June 1999 as an absolute deadline for establishing the institutions, and the third major push was therefore in the latter part of June, this time in Belfast.

The proposal that emerged from these talks, again in the form of a paper by the two governments (*The Way Forward*), bore some resemblance to the Hillsborough declaration. All parties would reaffirm the principles of an inclusive Executive, decommissioning of all paramilitary arms by May 2000, and that decommissioning should be carried out in a manner determined by the IICD. As at Hillsborough, there would be a sequence of events. Since the talks did not conclude until 2 July, the 30 June deadline was extended to 15 July. The nomination of ministers-designate would take place on that date, with devolution following on 18 July. But before then the IICD would confirm a start to the process of decommissioning, begin discussions with representatives of the paramilitary organisations, and specify that actual decommissioning was to commence within a set time.

There would be three progress reports from the IICD, running through to May 2000. The most significant difference from the Hillsborough package was that if commitments under the Agreement were not met, either on decommissioning or devolution, there would be a fail-safe mechanism. The two governments would automatically, and with immediate effect, suspend the operation of the institutions. The British Government introduced, and took through Parliament at great speed, legislation to create powers of suspension, which would assume greater significance early in 2000 after the *Mitchell Review*. In procedural/sequencing terms, these were the bare bones of the proposal, which had the support of the nationalist parties. It required the unionists to jump first, by enabling the Executive to be formed without decommissioning having occurred. But it gave them the assurance that, if expectations of PIRA decommissioning were disappointed, they would not be expected to continue to sit in an Executive with the political representatives of militant republicanism. How likely these expectations were to be fulfilled was the crucial question. Around that time, there was a view within both governments that, if the institutions could be established, the PIRA were ready to move on arms decommissioning – the so-called 'seismic shift'. Whether this was the case or not is beyond the knowledge of this writer, but the more the unionists probed the assertion that a significant shift in PIRA thinking had taken place, including with the Sinn Féin leadership, the less reassured they were.

The other difficulty for unionists was that the 'fail-safe' was one that brought the whole house down, rather than excluding from government those responsible (as they would have seen it) for failure. The combination of this feeling that all parties would be punished for the failure of one, together with the fact that they were not convinced that the 'seismic shift' was for real, led the UUP to reject the proposals on 9 July.

A recurrent issue over the previous twelve months had been whether to attempt to establish the Executive, even though the political prospects of doing so successfully were poor to non-existent, by moving the Assembly to run the 'd'Hondt' procedure for the nomination of ministers. (Under the d'Hondt procedure – named after its Belgian originator – seats in the Executive are allocated in proportion to the parties' numerical strength in the Assembly. The largest party has first choice of ministerial portfolio. Thereafter that party's assumed strength is reduced by a formula in which the numerator is the number of seats held and the denominator is one plus the number of ministerial posts held. Making that assumption, the next largest party has second choice, and so on. At a certain point, even reduced by the formula, the largest parties' assumed strengths are greater than those of the smallest, and they are therefore entitled to several ministerial posts.) Hitherto, with some wavering, the pragmatic view that there was no point in doing so unless unionists were willing to play their part, had prevailed within the British Government. But there was a strong view among the nationalist parties (and to some extent in Dublin) that there was an obligation on us to attempt to create the Executive, however poor the prospects (there was, of course, a political dimension to this, because formal unionist refusal to accept ministerial posts played into a narrative that they were reluctant to share power and were intent on blocking progress). Part of the understanding underpinning *The Way Forward* proposals was that, whatever the outcome, the d'Hondt procedure would be run on 15 July. As might have been expected, the UUP absented themselves. No unionists were nominated, and an Executive could not be formed. A frustrated Seamus Mallon, angry at what he saw as unionist attempts to extract concessions on the back of the decommissioning impasse, chose that moment to resign as deputy first minister-designate.

The fourth attempt to break the impasse was the *Mitchell Review*, which began on 4 September 1999. As chairman of the talks that led to the Agreement, senator George Mitchell had the depth of understanding, the authority and the skills to command the trust of the parties. His *Review* was different from its predecessors in several significant respects. First, the governments and the prime ministers consciously stood off from the process and did not participate in the discussions with the parties. My Irish opposite number, Dermot Gallagher, and I briefed the senator in New York before he embarked on the review, and were briefed by him, in confidence, as it progressed. Secondly, the discussions were more genuinely private, and unattended by media publicity, than could realistically be achieved when two prime ministers and a wide range of party representatives were involved. Mitchell brought the main parties together, memorably at Winfield House, the London residence of the US ambassador to the UK, rather than engaging in a series of bilateral meetings, and worked to build trust at a personal level.

At the heart of the *Mitchell Review* was the idea that, with sufficient trust on all sides, the institutions could be established without decommissioning having taken place, in the expectation that their establishment would before long create the conditions in which it would occur. In a pre-arranged sequence, senator Mitchell obtained from the IICD and published on 15 November an assessment of the current state of the decommissioning issue, which endorsed his view that successful establishment of the institutions would transform the situation, and called on the paramilitary organisations to appoint representatives to discuss modalities. This was followed two days later by a PIRA statement indicating that, following the establishment of the institutions, they would appoint an authorised representative, and by positive statements from the parties. There was, from the *Review*, a private understanding about the timescale on which it was expected that decommissioning would follow, and public statements (in slightly different terms in London and Dublin) by the two governments to the effect that if there was default on devolution or decommissioning, they would take the necessary steps to suspend the institutions.

The *Mitchell Review* was successful in the short term. David Trimble persuaded the Ulster Unionist Council (UUC) to 'jump first'. The institutions were established on 1 December. But, trust having 'crept in' (in words quoted by George Mitchell on the conclusion of his *Review*), it soon dissolved. Republican sources were reported within days to be playing down any expectation of early decommissioning. David Trimble committed to a further meeting of the UUC in February 2000, and made it known that he had lodged a post-dated resignation letter with the chairman of his party to be actioned in the event that there had been no decommissioning by that date. The PIRA's New Year statement described their contribution to the *Mitchell Review* purely in terms of the appointment of a representative, and criticised 'subsequent attempts by the UUP to set preconditions on further political progress' that were not part of the understanding. It soon became clear that there would be no early movement on substantive decommissioning on the timescale expected in the *Mitchell Review*.

The suspension of the Executive by Peter Mandelson on 11 February was, in this writer's view, no more than the necessary fulfilment of the undertakings given in November. It was the only occasion I can recall in almost five years when there was a real and deep difference of view between London and Dublin, which extended to Irish colleagues at official level whose judgement I respected then and still respect. Although the Irish Government had gone along with the concept of suspension in *The Way Forward* proposals and at the end of the *Mitchell Review*, and must have been aware of the timescale Mitchell had assumed, they reacted strongly against the suspension decision. The fact that Sinn Féin seized on the suspension as an example of spoiling by the colonial power, and demonised Peter Mandelson was no surprise, but the Irish reaction was harder to explain. Whether the *Mitchell Review* failed to deliver its intended outcome because David Trimble injected open conditionality into the UUP's acceptance of ministerial office or because the PIRA never intended to decommission arms at that stage is an even greater imponderable.

The fifth attempt was largely the product of bilateral negotiations between the two governments and Sinn Féin in April 2000. In Washington, during the St Patrick's Day celebrations in March, David Trimble had hinted that he would be willing to re-enter the Executive if the PIRA made a convincing statement to the effect that the war was over. The statement that the PIRA eventually made (on 6 May) did not include that phrase, but it did include an undertaking to open some arms dumps for inspection by international inspectors and to 'initiate a process that will completely and verifiably put [PIRA] arms beyond use'. There were some accompanying 'normalisation' measures to reduce the British military footprint. The inspection of arms dumps (by Maartti Ahtisaari, former president of Finland, and Cyril Ramaphosa, a senior figure in the African National Congress), with regular re-inspections to confirm that the arms remained secure, was the new element, which in one sense built confidence and indicated that the PIRA's weaponry was no longer sacrosanct. David Trimble recommended to his party that he re-enter the Executive. Devolution was restored on 30 May 2000.

The sixth major negotiation was at Weston Park, 9–14 July 2001, following David Trimble's resignation as first minister on 1 July. In the intervening thirteen months, there had been successful inspections of PIRA arms dumps by the international inspectors, but no substantive progress on decommissioning; the debate about the implementation of the *Patten Report* had intensified and polarised; and (in response to a motion at the UUC in October calling on him to leave the Executive if the PIRA failed to decommission) Trimble had proposed – and carried – a motion committing him to prevent Sinn Féin ministers from taking part in cross-border bodies until the PIRA had fully engaged with the IICD. In the run-up to the UK general election on 7 June, Trimble had also committed himself to resign on 1 July unless the PIRA had begun to decommission by then. He duly resigned, and – to create space for further negotiations – John Reid, by then Northern Ireland secretary, suspended the Executive for twenty-four hours. (Under the implementing legislation, this had the effect of preserving the status quo for six weeks, and was a device which was to be used again.)

Although security normalisation measures had featured in earlier negotiations, Weston Park was the first occasion on which discussions were on a much broader canvas. The talks themselves were inconclusive, but they generated a package that the two governments published as an *Implementation Plan* on 1 August, covering the whole range of issues – policing, decommissioning, normalisation, the stability of the institutions, and others that had not even featured in the Agreement, such as the investigation of controversial cases from the past, a review of the operation of the Parades Commission, and the treatment of people suspected of terrorist offences that predated the Agreement, the so-called 'On the Runs'. In contrast to previous attempts, decommissioning was not dealt with in detail in the document. It was described as 'indispensable' and something that 'must be resolved in a manner acceptable to and verified by [the IICD]'. In the weeks that followed, there were several false starts. The IICD reported on 6 August that they had received a proposal from the PIRA that they believed 'initiates a process that will put PIRA arms completely and verifiably beyond use'. The following day, the UUP rejected this and the Weston Park plan as falling short of what they needed, which was to see actual decommissioning. There was a further suspension of the Executive on 10 August to create more time, upon which the PIRA withdrew their proposals.

There were then two events, which in different ways affected the mood and dynamics of the process greatly. The less significant was the arrest of suspected PIRA members in Colombia on suspicion of providing support for the Colombian insurgent group FARC, which appeared to come as a surprise to Sinn Féin and put them on the back foot. The more significant was the Al Qaeda attacks in the US on 11 September, which was massively distracting for political leaders in the US and elsewhere, not least Tony Blair; but in the US the impact on attitudes towards the PIRA – and by extension Sinn Féin – was palpable. Support for the political process in Northern Ireland by the US had always been vital, from Bill Clinton's behind-the-scenes exhortations in the run-up to Good Friday, to the Bush administration's more conventional but no less supportive efforts, in particular through special envoy Richard Haass. But the combination of 9/11 and the Colombian escapade definitely hardened attitudes in Washington in a way that the Sinn Féin leadership cannot have failed to notice.

On 20 September, the PIRA re-engaged with the IICD 'with a view to accelerating progress', but the UUP were no more impressed than before. There was yet another suspension on 21 September, which had the effect of setting a new deadline of 3 November. The UUP tabled a motion in the Assembly to exclude Sinn Féin ministers from the Executive. If it failed, they would withdraw their ministers. It duly did fail, and unionist ministers resigned from the Executive on 18 October. After all that, Sinn Féin and the PIRA acted. On 22 October, Gerry Adams called on the PIRA to make a ground-breaking move on the arms issue. On 23 October, the International Commission reported the first act of PIRA decommissioning. This was enough for unionist ministers to resume their seats in the Executive, and by 6 November (after a hiccup because – interestingly for the purposes of this analysis – David Trimble did not at that stage command a majority of unionist votes in the Assembly for his re-election as first minister and was only elected at the second attempt after an Alliance member re-designated himself as a unionist) the show was back on the road. By the most tortuous route, the Weston Park *Implementation Plan* had arguably succeeded.

The seventh and final passage of events in the period I was involved occurred in the summer and autumn of 2002. There had been a second tranche of decommissioning in April 2002, which the International Commission described as 'substantial', though no details were given. The institutions were working with some notable successes, but a good deal of friction as well. But a series of events conspired to bring about a further collapse. At its root was the problem for which arms decommissioning had long been the proxy: the continuing activities of the PIRA. Throughout the period, there had been credible evidence that – while the ceasefire held in the sense that there were no paramilitary attacks on civilian and security force targets – punishment attacks on individuals, targeting activity and other illegal activity inconsistent with an organisation that was preparing itself for a peaceful future persisted. The arrests in Colombia in August 2001 had an unsettling effect, and during 2002 more information came into the public domain that kept the issue alive. A break-in at the Special Branch headquarters at Castlereagh on 17 March 2002, in which sensitive personal information about police officers and informers was stolen, was credibly attributed to mainstream republicans, as was a major bank robbery in Belfast. The last straw was the discovery in October of the so-called 'Stormont spy-ring', which led directly to the institutions being suspended again on 14 October. David Trimble made it clear that in these circumstances it was no longer sustainable to be in government with Sinn Féin. He would take his ministers out of the Executive unless the British Government proposed Sinn Féin's expulsion. Throughout that period, there were strenuous efforts made by both governments to save the situation, but no formal talks as such. On 30 October, the PIRA announced that it had ended its contacts with the IICD. On 17 October, Tony Blair made an important speech in which he pointed the way towards the next phase of the effort. The PIRA were, he said, at a 'fork in the road'. It was time for 'acts of completion'.

How then would I answer the question with which I began this chapter? Why, in October 2002, after almost five years and a rollercoaster of failed or only temporarily successful attempts to embed the Agreement by establishing the institutions, did we appear to be no further forward – indeed, as it seemed, actually further back, since few, if any, at that time were optimistic that the Democratic Unionist Party (DUP) would be willing to do the deal? The first point to make is the obvious one made at the beginning of this chapter. The Agreement was an admirable attempt at a comprehensive settlement of outstanding issues, but it was not and could not be completely comprehensive. Had there been a commitment to decommissioning of arms on a set timescale, of a kind that bound the paramilitaries, or had there been the kind of explicit linkage that David Trimble sought between PIRA decommissioning and Sinn Féin membership of the Executive, or decommissioning and the prisoner release scheme, things might have been different. But there was no such commitment or linkage (it is extremely doubtful, to put it no higher, whether one could have been negotiated in an Agreement that commanded the support of all parties) and, in its absence, the negotiation around the pace of PIRA disarmament and the basis on which others fulfilled their obligations under the Agreement was arguably bound to continue.

Two other bits of unfinished business are also relevant. The first is policing, which could not be addressed in detail within the compass of the original negotiation, and was remitted to Lord Patten's Independent Commission. On an optimistic view, that Commission would have reported at a point when the institutions were already well established. In fact, when Patten reported on

9 September 1999, there had already been three unsuccessful attempts to establish the institutions, and the fourth (the *Mitchell Review*) was about to begin. Policing was a touchstone issue for both nationalists and unionists, which aroused strong emotions. The fact that the *Patten Report* was being decided on, legislated for and implemented while the devolution/decommissioning wrangle continued probably made both negotiations harder. The symbolic loss, as it was seen, of the Royal Ulster Constabulary (RUC) (the *Report* recommended the adoption of a new name for the force, and badges or other symbols free from any association with the British or Irish states) added to unionists' sense that the Agreement was a one-way street, and explains, for example, David Trimble's insistence on formal legislation to preserve or incorporate the RUC within the new Police Service of Northern Ireland (PSNI) as part of the understanding when the institutions were restored the first time on 30 May 2000. The unresolved issues over policing also had an arguably malign impact on the later negotiations, including those at Weston Park in 2001, to the extent that both SDLP and UUP attitudes were coloured by a fear that, in our desire to bring about PIRA decommissioning, the British Government would make further unwelcome concessions to Sinn Féin on Patten implementation.

The other piece of unfinished business in the Agreement was security normalisation. The British Government committed itself to reduce the numbers and role of the armed forces in Northern Ireland to levels compatible with a normal peaceful society, and to the removal of security installations and emergency powers. There was a published strategy for normalisation (see the *Strategy for Normalisation of Security and Policing*, 1999), but inevitably the scale and precise timing of steps to reduce the military footprint were a matter for judgement in the light of the security threat at the time. The fact that there was no hard and fast programme led Sinn Féin to argue that the pace of 'demilitarisation' was too slow, and to press in negotiations for specific steps to be taken, including the closure of bases and the removal of military installations. This required careful handling, because, in the end, as we were all keenly aware, the first responsibility of government is the security of the people, and all normalisation decisions were taken on military and police advice. But, although less toxic than policing, the fact that these matters featured as they did in political negotiations fed the sense among the other parties that Sinn Féin were milking the process.

My second point is about opinion within the Protestant unionist population, political unionism and the UUP in particular. At the time of the referenda, exit polling in Northern Ireland suggested that, of those voting, 96 per cent of Catholics and 55 per cent of Protestants had voted 'yes'. It tends to be the case in Northern Ireland that anything welcomed overwhelmingly on one side of the community is viewed with suspicion on the other, and subsequent polling suggested that, if anything, the percentage in favour among Protestants reduced over the following few years. From the outset, although they subsequently took their seats in the Assembly and, indeed, ministerial posts in the Executive, the DUP was hostile to the Agreement, in whose negotiation they had played no part, and harried David Trimble at every turn.

Within the UUP, Jeffrey Donaldson's departure at the end of the talks weakened Trimble, and there was throughout a small but active minority of anti-Agreement Assembly members, with a majority of the party's Westminster MPs opposed. The UUC supported Trimble at each key stage, but by a diminishing margin over time, and with enough equivocation for him to feel – as after the *Mitchell Review* – that he had to bind himself in the future in order to carry the day, thus fuelling Sinn Féin accusations that he was setting 'preconditions' on their participation in the institutions. The way in which implementation of the Agreement was sequenced did not help. Of the significant benefits for unionists, acceptance of the consent principle and the associated constitutional changes were either too esoteric to be noticed or (somewhat unfairly in relation to the Irish changes) already factored in as long-standing policies of the two governments. The restoration of devolved government was (at least in unionist eyes) being put at risk by republican intransigence on arms decommissioning, and it was unfair that the best the governments could come up with (and even then controversially) was a fail-safe that had the effect of excluding everyone. The argument that should have carried weight – that it was an extraordinary achievement for unionism to have negotiated a settlement that saw Sinn Féin participating in devolved government in part of the United Kingdom, indeed, complaining at being excluded – somehow did not, despite great efforts by David Trimble and others. The fact that the release of paramilitary prisoners came early in the implementation of the Agreement also ate at unionist support. The governments have been criticised for pressing on with the release scheme in the absence of progress on other issues, and it is true that the two-year period for both the release scheme and decommissioning was suggestive of some kind of political connection. But, for better or for worse, there was no explicit connection, since the governments' commitment to release prisoners (subject to conditions) was a commitment to more than best endeavours, and it would have given a disastrous signal (as well as probably driving apart the two governments, on whose unity of purpose so much else depended) to have done otherwise. There is, however, no doubt that, essential as it was to reaching the Agreement, the release scheme offended unionist opinion deeply. What is known in the academic penal policy world as the 'just deserts' principle runs quite deep in the Protestant psyche. The suggestion I have heard from some overseas commentators, that the fact that the scheme included loyalist prisoners as well as republicans should have made the scheme easier for unionists to accept, completely misses the point, at least in relation to the middle ground unionists to whom the UUP looked for support.

Overall, the political context within unionism was therefore unpromising to say the least. David Trimble was at times over that period criticised, particularly in the US and by some commentators in Ireland, for not selling the Agreement more enthusiastically and with less reservation to the unionist community. Personally, I think this criticism was misconceived. For one thing (and as someone who grew up in the Church of Scotland I can make the point more easily than others) it underestimates the essentially sceptical cast of mind of the predominantly Presbyterian audience Trimble was addressing. But even allowing for that, the political constraints I have described would have made it difficult for him to adopt anything other than the crab-like approach he adopted, however infuriating it was at times. The fact that, in these conditions, he twice brought the UUP to 'jump first' into the Executive was, in context, a remarkable achievement.

On the republican side, the real political dynamics were inevitably less transparent. Gerry Adams and Martin McGuinness never wavered (even in the most private conversations) from the position that they were not the PIRA, and exploited the leverage that the decommissioning issue gave them with great skill. To the question of why did they not persuade the PIRA over that period to move faster, more decisively and more convincingly there are several possible answers. Some would say it was purely tactical, when as long as they were extracting concessions from the British Government, why should they stretch the patience of harder-line colleagues in order to enable the formation of local institutions for which they did not care much anyway? There is something in that view, but I do not buy it as a complete explanation of what was going on. Of course, there were tactics in it, on all sides, and one of the challenges for the government negotiator was to separate out the tactical from the substantive in dealings with people who were past masters at mixing the two. But there was substance as well. The Sinn Féin leadership knew that, as the Agreement was implemented, they would lose the support of some of the more hard-line elements, but they were sufficiently aware of and fearful of the historical precedents to be determined to avoid a major split in the Provisional movement. Although they came to accept that it was a proxy for a much more important issue – whether the PIRA was actually out of business or not – their initial instinct was to treat decommissioning as something got up by unionists and security-minded elements within the British state (whom they always regarded as the real enemy) to obstruct the process and/or to humiliate the PIRA. On that analysis, the real achievement was that the ceasefire held, and if the guns were silent, why fuss about decommissioning?

The Sinn Féin leadership was almost certainly more in charge of the whole agenda within the republican movement than they were prepared to admit, and there is room for doubt about how consistently they acted as persuaders. But, to my mind at least, there is no doubt that some persuasion was necessary, and the accounts of well-placed observers of how the Adams–McGuinness political project developed over the years (Moloney 2002) tend to bear this out. It is interesting that, in the extended interviews that form the basis of Frank Millar's excellent *David Trimble: The Price of Peace* (2004), admittedly in the context of a slightly later period than the one I am describing, Trimble takes essentially the same line and is quoted as saying:

> My own hunch . . . is that the political leadership within the republican movement were in fact actually committed to doing things in terms that would have satisfied our needs – particularly on the transparency of decommissioning – but the problem came from elsewhere . . . from people on the paramilitary side who didn't want to go ahead with the decommissioning with the implication that it's going to be completed and we're going to wind up the [P]IRA.

At times (notably at Hillsborough in March 1999), Adams and McGuinness appeared to get ahead of the hard-liners, and then decide, in effect, to rein themselves in.

The Sinn Féin leadership were also well aware of the divisions within unionism. Although they had grudging respect for David Trimble as, at that time, the best hope for the Agreement, their world view tended to be that intransigent unionism would always find an excuse for excluding them. Whether they consciously withheld the PIRA's best shot at persuading unionists and others that the war was really over until the DUP were fully engaged is something only they can say, but they were far too astute not to have noticed that the electoral balance was shifting the DUP's way, and they must have been aware of the risk that, just as the PIRA made their big move, the unionist public would shift their allegiance to the more intransigent party. From mid-2002 onwards, I suspect that that factor alone significantly reduced the chances of a breakthrough. None of this is to say that the movements actually made by the PIRA over that period – the facilitation of the Ramaphosa/Ahtisaari inspections, the putting of some arms beyond use – were not significant. They were, but they appeared to be so grudging and cloaked in mystery as to play into unionist suspicions that they were purely tactical and designed to extract concessions from the British Government.

The other factor affecting attitudes on all sides was the continuing level of paramilitary violence and public disorder. Reading the chronology of the period to help prepare this chapter, I was struck – probably more than I was at the time – by the steady drumbeat of attacks and killings, as well as incidents of serious disorder such as those around the annual stand-off over the Orange parade at Drumcree and the demonstrations at Holy Cross School in the Ardoyne (on 7 November 2001, in answer to a Parliamentary Question, the then Northern Ireland Office (NIO) security minister Jane Kennedy said that there had been 840 paramilitary attacks so far that year, with 620 by loyalists and 223 by republicans). The good news was that the main ceasefires held, and levels of violence were much reduced compared with the period before the Agreement – a point which supporters of the Agreement had to keep making – but the steady drip of evidence that normality had not yet been achieved aggravated both the public and the politicians who represented them and of whom compromises were being asked. The long-running dispute over Drumcree was particularly damaging, because it revived sectarian enmities, reinforced unionism/loyalism's sense of loss, and exemplified for both sides the intransigence that each suspected of the other.

Could things have been handled differently over this period? Undoubtedly they could, but whether it would have affected the outcome is open to question. I have dealt with several of the political 'if onlys' – 'if only David Trimble had been a more enthusiastic advocate of the Agreement within unionism', and 'if only the governments had used the prisoner release scheme as leverage to achieve decommissioning'. But there were others. One is 'if only decommissioning had not been elevated in significance to the point where it held up everything else'. It is, of course, true that the decommissioning of arms is, in itself, of no great substantive significance. They can always be replaced. What matters is the mindset and intentions of those who hold them. The PIRA ceasefire was increasingly persuasive over time, but in the period of which I am writing, unionists (and, to be fair, others) were by no means persuaded that the PIRA was out of business or definitely heading in that direction. Throughout the period, and particularly towards the end of it as things unravelled during 2002, there were too many signs that, while the ceasefires held, PIRA activity continued. In these circumstances, while my own view is that the attempt in the mid-1990s to make Sinn Féin participation dependent on decommissioning will be judged by history as having been a mistake, it was, I think, inevitable that, when it came to establishing real, continuing devolved government, with Sinn Féin holding ministerial office, decommissioning – or more accurately the issue for which it was a proxy – would be an obstacle.

Perhaps a more interesting 'if only' is 'if only it had been possible to get the Executive going without Sinn Féin, either on a power-sharing basis, but with a more conventional voluntary coalition, or by excluding Sinn Féin'. These are, of course, two different cases. The form to be taken by the Executive was the aspect of the Agreement that was left most to negotiation among the Northern Ireland parties, principally the UUP and the SDLP. The system adopted, in which ministers are appointed through the operation of the d'Hondt formula in proportion to their parties' holding of seats in the Assembly, had the effect that Sinn Féin were entitled to (at that time) two seats in the Executive. To that extent, the Agreement therefore created the dilemma. On the other hand, if the Agreement had allowed instead for a voluntary cross-community coalition – or even at that stage a compulsory coalition of the largest unionist and nationalist parties – Sinn Féin would not have had the stake in the institutions (and therefore the Agreement) that they had, or indeed the incentive to persuade the PIRA eventually to stand down. Frustrating – and ultimately almost destructive – as the devolution/decommissioning impasse was in the years after the Agreement, there is a strong argument that a settlement whose governance engaged Sinn Féin and recognised their democratic mandate with ministerial office, was in the longer term likely to be stronger than one that did not. Whether, during the turbulent period I am describing, it would have helped or hindered to exclude Sinn Féin from the Executive under the Agreement as it actually stood, or credibly threaten to do so, is a different question. It turned out to be a largely theoretical one, because under the Agreement such exclusion requires a cross-community vote, in which the SDLP would have had to vote for the exclusion or removal of Sinn Féin ministers from executive office.

As the party whose agenda was most reflected in the Agreement, and which, through the Hume–Adams dialogue, had contributed greatly to the PIRA's ceasefire and Sinn Féin's involvement in the process, the SDLP's position was pivotal. Their leadership was frustrated by what they saw as Sinn Féin's and the UUP's exploitation of the decommissioning issue for party advantage, and of the governments' readiness (again, as they saw it) to indulge them. This frustration was most evident in Seamus Mallon's resignation as deputy first minister-designate on 15 July 2000, and, to an extent, in the approach the SDLP subsequently took to the *Patten Report*. There were moments when it seemed possible that the SDLP might be willing to join a cross-community vote with unionists to exclude Sinn Féin. In a significant speech to his party's conference on 13 November 1998, Mallon captured well the fears of unionists and republicans. Unionists feared that 'Sinn Féin would pocket maximum sectoral advantage and then fail to honour their decommissioning obligations within the specified two-year period'. Sinn Féin feared that, whatever they did, 'unionists would up the ante by contriving new demands and conditions to exclude them from Executive office'. The SDLP guaranteed, Mallon said, 'to remove from office those who dishonoured their obligations'. This scrupulously even-handed guarantee, to the extent that it bore on Sinn Féin and decommissioning, appeared to relate to the two-year period that expired in May 2000 (then comfortably far into the future), but that deadline came and went with no sign that the SDLP were ready to take such action. It is a moot point whether, had they been willing to do so, it would have changed the dynamic in such a way as to make early decommissioning more or less likely. It would certainly have been hugely divisive within nationalism.

Later, as evidence mounted of continuing illegal activity by the PIRA, the issue became whether the UK Government would act to exclude Sinn Féin from government. That was, in effect, David Trimble's demand when news of 'Stormontgate' broke in October 2002, but it was not something that was provided for in the Agreement. For the British Government to have excluded Sinn Féin would have required primary legislation at Westminster to step outside the terms of the Agreement – feasible, but as a unilateral assertion of British authority so redolent of earlier times as to be even more provocative for nationalists of all hues (including the Irish Government) than suspension had been in May 2000.

One thing that might have been handled differently is relations with the DUP. Some of David Trimble's closest confidantes (and possibly Lord Trimble himself) suspect that the NIO's long-term plan was to rely on the DUP, and that they therefore regarded the UUP as expendable. That was most definitely not how it felt during the period I am describing. It may have been a failure of imagination, but the strong assumption at that time was that DUP opposition to the Agreement, although it clearly had a tactical dimension, was for real, and that, if they gained the political ascendancy and/or Trimble lost the argument within the UUP, all might well be lost. Whether it would have affected the outcome or not I rather doubt, but if anything opportunities may have been missed both to put the DUP on the spot for so blatantly having it both ways, and to understand better where their true position lay.

Whether the process of negotiations could have been handled differently is one for the process geeks. With the exception of the *Mitchell Review*, the basic technique in the set-piece negotiations was for the two prime ministers to lead talks with the parties, with occasional plenaries but a strong emphasis on bilaterals with the main players, which Tony Blair and Bertie Ahern conducted together. These were usually prefaced by private exploratory talks, involving British and Irish officials, with Tony Blair's chief of staff, Jonathan Powell, prominent on the British side. At some point, either at the beginning (as a product of the exploratory talks) or as the negotiations unfolded, the governments generally floated a text as a basis for discussion. There was invariably a deadline, real or invented. The weakness in the approach was that, because the initiative tended to lie in London and Dublin, the parties could simply wait for the governments to come up with proposals and be in reactive mode. This did not always happen, but it was a constant risk, and the concentration on bilaterals meant that the parties that were not centre stage could become frustrated and feel that their collective weight was being undervalued. On the other hand, the commitment, sense of urgency and common purpose of the prime minister and the taoiseach were a huge asset, without which progress simply could not have been made. The concentration on bilaterals with those from whom concessions were needed did not in itself build trust between the parties, but it was the product of the pragmatic, problem-solving approach that both men brought to the table. It was also no more than common sense. They were busy heads of government, and time was at a premium. The approach taken by the *Mitchell Review*, as described above, was different, more spacious, and intuitively more likely to build trust. It probably succeeded in doing so at the leadership level, but the time was not right, and even the redoubtable senator could not cure the legacy of mistrust in the wider communities that the leaders represented.

At a more technical level, it may be worth reflecting on the way in which the content and coverage of the negotiations developed over time. The central problem was that, to share Executive responsibility, the UUP needed either confidence in the peaceful intentions of the PIRA (of a kind that convincing arms decommissioning would have brought) or confidence that, if they moved first and were disappointed, they would not be expected to continue in government with Sinn Féin. Sinn Féin, on the other hand, needed to avoid any suggestion that decommissioning was a precondition to taking their place in the Executive as of right, or any sense of defeat for the PIRA. Both had sceptical constituencies to manage. The early attempts to resolve that dilemma involved explicit sequences of events. The Hillsborough declaration was built round the notion of the 'collective act of reconciliation', which would have provided cover for a move by the PIRA had they been willing to make it, but turned out to be more explicit than republicanism could bear about the expected move and the revocability of the unionists' decision to enter government with Sinn Féin if expectations were disappointed. The proposal that emerged from the Belfast talks in July 1999 again had a sequence that would have established the Executive on the basis of a Decommissioning Commission report that the process had started (but no actual 'product'), but, beyond offering progress reports through to May 2000, it was unspecific about timescales, and relied on the two governments to suspend the institutions if expectations on decommissioning were disappointed (which turned out to be insufficient assurance for unionists).

The three attempts that led, albeit only temporarily, to the establishment of the institutions were notably less explicit, at least in public, about sequences of events. The *Mitchell Review* relied on a private understanding – not, in the event, fulfilled – and the senator's own judgement that the conditions existed for devolution to go ahead. The PIRA statement in May 2000 permitting the inspection of arms dumps was the product of private discussions between the governments and Sinn Féin. The Weston Park published *Implementation Plan* was, as I have said, remarkably uncommunicative on decommissioning. To the extent that there was an unpublished understanding about a sequence of events, it was insufficient to dissuade the unionists from withdrawing from the Executive that autumn, upon which the PIRA made their ground-breaking move to put arms beyond use. The Weston Park *Implementation Plan* therefore (eventually) succeeded, probably because the other elements of it gave Sinn Féin benefits they did not want to lose, but the sequence of events that it had assumed did not. The later attempts were also characterised, as I have observed, by an expansion of the coverage of the negotiations, which moved from being not much more than single-issue talks addressing the decommissioning impasse (although even at Hillsborough security normalisation featured) to multi-issue talks, as at Weston Park in July 2001. Whether this broadening of the canvas helped or hindered the main effort is difficult to say. As a matter of general principle, it helps in political negotiations to have more than one issue on the table, because trade-offs become possible and there is more likelihood of win/win rather than win/lose. In this case, however, one also has to factor in the sense among the other parties that Sinn Féin was using the expanded agenda for its own purposes to up the price of decommissioning.

What conclusions can be drawn from all this and to what extent are they relevant to other conflicts elsewhere in the world? One thing that surprised me looking back on the chronology was that, in the four years between October 1998 (the earliest when the institutions could realistically have been established) and the collapse in October 2002, the institutions were operating for more than half the time. This was not a four-year stand-off. Risks were taken. Much ingenuity was shown by governments and Northern Ireland parties, but it always felt precarious. Some of the reasons for that were political, the divisions within unionism and the self-imposed absence of the DUP being the most obvious. But at root the problem was the absence of trust. The belief that unionists would always find excuses to exclude republicans from power, combined with historic mistrust of the British Government, made it less likely that the PIRA would wind down their activities as decisively as the new situation demanded. The bizarre sequence of events involving the PIRA in 2002 reinforced unionist suspicions that republicans were intent on having it both ways, and made the collapse in October 2002 all but inevitable. The other factor that tends to be overlooked, and that certainly applies in other deep-seated conflicts, is time. By October 2002, the PIRA ceasefire had been in place for over five years. But in the context of a thirty-year insurgency, in which few families on either side of the community had been untouched by tragedy, and of a much longer history, spanning centuries, of intractable division on the Irish question, that is perhaps not so very long. Although the formal PIRA ceasefire held, there were plenty of reminders over this period that paramilitarism, both republican and loyalist, had not gone away.

Local or regional conflicts, based on ethnic, religious or national identity, tend to have deep historical roots and create enduring grievances. It is, in my view, a mistake to read across directly from one to another. No two are the same. But among the lessons I would draw from the Northern Ireland experience are the following.

First, and most obviously, the need for patience, persistence and political commitment over a long period, of the kind provided by the two prime ministers and the Northern Ireland political leaders. Secondly, where an insurgent group is laying down its arms as part of a political settlement, the need to have in mind both the self-respect of those concerned and the reassurance of others that the laying down of arms is genuinely intended to create peace and is not just a tactical manoeuvre. In Northern Ireland decommissioning became, for a time, the measure against which that judgement about long-term peaceful intentions was made; it was not, however, best calculated to protect paramilitary self-respect. By 2001, it was clear that the real issue was continuing PIRA activity and the unacceptability of participants in government (even those with a democratic mandate) having such strong links with a still-active private army. Thirdly, it often takes the courage of the moderates to get a potentially successful peace process going, but the commitment of the extremes, sometimes under pressure from the moderates, is required to complete it. This is delicate territory in Northern Ireland, because the UUP and the SDLP felt, and still feel, that the governments courted the extremes in such a way as to expose the moderate parties electorally. But it is a phenomenon that can be observed elsewhere, and reflects the fact that the unreasonable are usually harder to get into the tent than the reasonable, and that in a mistrustful, divided society the safety play for the public is often to tack towards the extremes. Fourthly, at what I have described as the 'technical' level, this experience exposes the limitations of pre-plotted sequences of events, especially when made public in circumstances under which the requirements of the two sides are, strictly speaking, incompatible. In such circumstances, there is definitely room for what Jonathan Powell describes as 'creative ambiguity', provided that someone remembers what is actually supposed to happen and no one is left with a lasting feeling of having been misled. I do not, however, conclude from this that pre-plotted sequences are a bad idea. When well designed, they can build confidence and the measure of trust (not necessarily unqualified) on which progress depends. And, fifthly, progress should be made where it can be, but – despite some of what I have said here – the more comprehensive a peace settlement can be, the better. The Agreement was a remarkably comprehensive political settlement, albeit one that had, with slight variations, been on the table for many years. It did not, and could not, settle definitively the related questions of paramilitary activity and fully inclusive government, but the fact that Sinn Féin and the loyalist parties were bought into it was very significant, because it meant that the Agreement was the means of securing the peace, even if it took almost another ten years to bring it fully into effect. That, and the fact that it was as politically comprehensive as it could be at the time, helps to explain why the Agreement was a fixed point of common understanding, which survived for as long as it did only partially implemented, and did not go the way of its predecessors.

The other part of the explanation – and I am indebted to my old NIO boss Joe Pilling for this insight – may lie in the democratic pressure exerted by the people of Northern Ireland on their elected representatives. This was not wholly consistent, and there were times when the politicians may have felt constrained by the views of their constituents into a more intransigent position than they might otherwise have taken. But, as year succeeded year with the ceasefire intact, people became used to (relatively) threat-free Saturday nights out in Belfast (and their equivalent), and the politicians were accordingly less constrained, and, to the extent that they had not already, drew the conclusion that there was no going back. That process of accommodating to the peace – which it would be a mistake to call 'normalisation', because Northern Ireland is still, in many respects, an abnormal and divided society – was always bound to take years rather than months. Whether it needed to take as long as it did is a matter for others to judge. The important thing is that, in 2007, the point eventually came, and that the opportunity was seized.

Finally, some reflections on what it was like to be a senior civil servant in the NIO at that time. In one sense, the role was the same as in any other department of government. Ministers are in charge. They have the democratic mandate, and they take decisions for which they are democratically accountable. They are the figures in the limelight, criticised when things go badly and taking (and deserving) credit when they go well. The civil servants' role is to muster the best-informed, wisest advice they can, to set out the options and risks clearly, and often to express a view on the best way forward. They also do essential underpinning work on legislation, the preparation of public statements, etc. All of that was true in Northern Ireland, but there was one significant difference. In Whitehall, while good Civil Service advice must, in my view, be politically astute, the tradition of impartiality and readiness to serve the government of the day whatever its political complexion means that political advice as such is not, and cannot, be part of the deal. In Northern Ireland, at the time of which I am writing, the requirement to behave with propriety and without political favour was as strong as in any other part of government, but any difference between the Westminster parties (although there was some) was not at the heart of what we were doing. Understanding, and attempting to influence, complex political forces within Northern Ireland, in the service of a political settlement, was central to the whole effort. The three Northern Ireland secretaries for whom I worked (Mo Mowlam, Peter Mandelson and John Reid), though they were, to put it mildly, different personalities, all knew their own minds, and each made a very substantial contribution to the process; but each of them wanted and received political advice and support from their senior civil servants. Working relationships between ministers and officials were closer than I experienced anywhere else in government.

Personally, I found this invigorating, but it brought responsibilities. To be credible with Northern Ireland politicians, and indeed with Irish colleagues, it was essential for there to be no doubt that one knew the minister's (and on occasion the prime minister's) mind, and was not running any kind of agenda of one's own. This is evidently right in principle, but it was also good tactics, since Northern Irish politicians are not above directing the most ferocious public criticism at officials when their real target is ministers (to be fair, their real target *was* sometimes actually officials, and not having a personal agenda was not always an effective defence!). In such a charged atmosphere, it was more than usually important to be seen as a straight dealer, who would tell it as it was, and could be relied on to report back accurately. The other responsibility was to try to understand as well as possible what was going on, and interpret it for ministers. There were others tilling this field, of course, as is clear from Chris Maccabe's chapter, and we relied greatly on the insights of colleagues who had grown up in Northern Ireland. But as political director, I always felt that it was incumbent on me to get beyond the tactical (which tended to dominate) into an understanding of the real political and social dynamics. A problem for the negotiator in dealing with the parties to any dispute is how best to separate out the tactics from the substance, or at least how much weight to give to each. In Northern Ireland at that time, there was plenty of tactical exaggeration going on, but behind it lay deep substantive concerns, which needed to be understood and which it would have been unwise in the extreme to ignore.

A personal view is that this is particularly true of unionism. The view taken by many unionists that the NIO (and, indeed, the British Government generally) should have been more of an advocate of the unionist case, to match the instinctive nationalist sympathies of the Irish, is in my view unrealistic. The policy of the ministers whom I served was not the policy of the unionist parties. But I always felt that the NIO owed it to those who profess a British identity to have as good an understanding as possible of where they are coming from, and to reflect it in the analysis. As it happened, the Irish officials with whom I had the closest dealings had a better-developed instinct for unionist sensitivities than they were given credit for, but the point still seems a valid one.

References

Millar, F. (2004). *David Trimble: The Price of Peace*. Dublin: Liffey Press.
Moloney, E. (2002). *A Secret History of the IRA*. London: Penguin.
Northern Ireland Office (1999). *Strategy for Normalization of Security and Policing*. London: HMSO.
Ulster Marketing Surveys (1998). Northern Ireland Assembly Election Exit Poll, conducted for RTE, 25 June.

11 Text and context: an interview with William Fittall

Interview

GS: Can you explain the mechanics of drafting text?

WF: I think it depends a lot on the nature of the document that you are talking about. To go back to 1992, which was my first intensive involvement in Northern Ireland business, the name of the game was constitutional talks. That meant the political parties excluding Sinn Féin, because at that point the PIRA was still waging a campaign. There was a lot of formal text around the three strands involving the Ulster Unionist Party (UUP), the Democratic Unionist Party (DUP) and the Social Democratic and Labour Party (SDLP). We produced it within the Northern Ireland Office (NIO) both in preparation for and during those talks. They did not in the event get that far, but at the time they did break what appeared to be a number of logjams and achieved what were a number of 'firsts'. There had to be a substantial quantity of text, not least because in Strand 1 the aim was to try to secure agreement on what new devolved institutions of government would be. With those sort of exercises, when you were into constitutional matters and defining the powers of bodies, by definition the text had to be full, comprehensive and deal with all the issues, and it had to be pretty careful. If you come to a different phase, such as when I was involved from 2000 to 2002, the dynamic was different. The PIRA had gone to a ceasefire in 1994, come off in 1996 and then gone back on again after the 1997 election. You then had the 1998 Agreement and the subsequent successful cross-border referenda. So it was a very different phase. We were much more into crisis management, running repairs and rescue operations. Essentially, following the Agreement it took a long period before devolved government was established mainly because the Agreement had been so contentious within the unionist community, and from the outset David Trimble, who had done the deal, was under huge pressure. To many unionists it seemed that the republican movement had got onto the 'inside track' and had achieved a position of great influence, while still having a private army that might be reactivated as and when. And decommissioning had not happened. So, in August 2000, it was all about private negotiations over what might eventually emerge with quite spare public texts to try to help David Trimble stay in government. Therefore, you are talking about a different sort of texts and you cannot talk about text as if it is a singular, indivisible thing.

GS: So, by 2000 text was more about marginal gains rather than foundational positions and big leaps as established in the early period of the peace process?

WF: In 1992, the NIO was living off the intellectual capital of twenty years and more of analysis. That analysis had been fundamentally sound. After the Troubles started and the NIO was created, there was serious analysis and the Sunningdale Agreement of 1973–4 was based on essentially the same set of principles that led to the Belfast Agreement in 1998. The underlying analysis was that you had to have government arrangements that commanded cross-community consent, a North–South dimension with a productive relationship between Belfast and Dublin, and that all this needed to be set in a less tense relationship between the two islands. All this was there in the 1970s, and that was what subsequently prompted Seamus Mallon, in his rather vinegary phrase, to say that the Belfast Agreement was 'Sunningdale for slow learners'. In the early 1990s, there was an intellectual framework where the analysis had been done and people lived off that. Now that is not to say that others were not trying to do other things. There were still many on the unionist side who hoped that somehow or other they would get devolved government back in Northern Ireland without the sort of concessions to nationalists and republicans that were likely to be negotiated. The big issue that was unresolved and unresolvable in 1992–3 was the gap between the two concepts of what in the NIO we called 'political development' and 'political movement'. Political development was the notion that you worked with the constitutional parties, because you could not in a democracy have direct negotiations with people who were letting off bombs and not accepting the framework of the law. It was about trying to agree new institutions of government and new ways of working that came from building up the centre to marginalise the extremes. But there was also political movement, which was about seeing whether there were other ways of bringing influence to bear to persuade the PIRA to stop the violence for good. In other words, how did we get those who were breaking the law to stop doing so? And that was very current at the time because the Hume–Adams talks and the indirect 'link' that the government had with the PIRA were active. Within the NIO there were those who thought that the political development process would prevail, that Sinn Féin would be nervous of the bus leaving the station without them, and that the political process would encourage them to make the shift to a democratic approach. So there were those who believed that political development would produce peace. There were others who believed that you would not get a proper political deal until the violence had stopped and that political movement was the way to do it. The orthodox view in the NIO was that you simply could not know for sure which would prove best, so you had to pursue the two together in a twin-track strategy. This was entirely consistent and defensible. The messages that were sent to the PIRA via 'the link' were about making it clear that if the republican movement wanted to be part of politics, then the violence had to stop. As it happened, those who believed that you had to have political movement before political development proved to be right because the experience of the talks in 1992 was that the Irish Government and the SDLP under John Hume were not actually interested in doing a deal on texts or on governmental institutions in the absence of Sinn Féin coming into the process. All the work on text in 1992 was in a sense a useful limbering up for what happened subsequently. At the time the nationalists, understandably, were not prepared to make sacrifices because of all the memories from 1972, even though they were prepared for it to happen on the right terms in 1998. The process in 1992–3 was a slightly strange one because nationalist Ireland had its eyes on political movement, but the NIO did not know whether that approach would work. We had to have constitutional talks, and I do believe that the fact that the Irish Government and John Hume were prepared to sit down was a way on the nationalist side of putting pressure on Sinn Féin because it signalled to them that it was just possible that a deal might be done without them – as it had been at Sunningdale in 1974 – and that this time it might stick. The nationalists were, however, not very interested in serious engagement in the run-up to the 1992 election, because they thought that John Major would lose and Neil Kinnock would become prime minister and Kevin McNamara would become the Labour secretary of state, giving them more fertile partners for negotiation than John Major and Peter Brooke.

GS: But in what way did the text reflect the tension between political development and political movement?

WF: I do not think it cashed out in the text at all, because you were talking about two quite different strategies and you could run them together and see, in the light of events, which one would work. Republicans were not at the table because they were still fighting and that had a direct bearing on things. Obviously, once Sinn Féin became part of the negotiations, then that changed the dynamic on the nationalist side. In 1992, it was the SDLP and the Irish Government who were, as it were, 'carrying the banner', and once you had Sinn Féin involved you had three participants. At that point the significance of the SDLP became diminished and that has been the political reality since.

GS: In trying to make the argument for democratic politics while trying to draw extremists into that process, to what extent was language necessary for this?

WF: What was completely absent from all the items discussed in the political development constitutional talks in 1992 were prisoner releases and dealing with the past. Those issues did not feature at all. When I went back in 2000 many of the discussions of the issues, the deals and the texts were about the past and 'On the Runs' (OTRs), and these were the most acute problems because the pressure from Sinn Féin was to move beyond the early release scheme agreed in 1998 and get to something more radical. As far as texts and political movement were concerned, obviously there had been the public speeches made by Peter Brooke such as the 'no selfish strategic or economic interest' speech, and that was a way of publicly sending a message to the republican movement, which was supplemented by the fact that John Hume was talking to everybody. The first day I joined I was due to get the plane early in the morning to go to Northern Ireland and I was suddenly told we would start in London. The reason for this was because John Hume was going in to see John Major at Number 10 with Peter Brooke to say how he was getting on in his discussions with Gerry Adams. You also had the government using this indirect link to the PIRA through which messages were passed and that became very lively. The message that was received, which seemed to signal that the PIRA did want to stop, was carefully crafted. They had sent nine paragraphs, so we had to send nine paragraphs in response.

GS: Was that how it was conducted, in terms of a parallel between what came and what went?

WF: There was a view that what we had received was a long and careful and quite wordy piece, so it was thought to be a matter of psychology and signalling and that we were taking it seriously if we sent something of equivalent length. Peter Brooke was secretary of state until after the 1992 election, and Patrick Mayhew took over and this message came about early 1993. I can remember that there was a period of considerable reflection after this long message came in, and obviously the text that went back had to be approved by the Northern Ireland secretary and the prime minister. The stakes are pretty high when you are communicating, even indirectly, with a paramilitary organisation that is running a terrorist campaign and still killing people. I recall that the authorisation to send the message back, the nine-paragraph response to theirs, was actually given on the day before the Warrington bomb went off and killed the two boys. The prime minister had agreed it could go back and we were discussing on the Friday the arrangements for it, and the view was taken that having got the clearance we should get this back quickly because you never knew what might happen. So it was a sad irony given what happened the following day, though, taking the long view, it was right that the message went when it did.

GS: Do you recall in the 1991–2 period talk in the British Government about defeating the PIRA?

WF: This idea of 'defeating' the PIRA needs a bit of deconstruction. By the early 1980s, the PIRA had moved explicitly to the duel strategy of 'the Armalite and the ballot box', and there was no question of defeating the republican movement to the extent that it was pursuing a perfectly legitimate objective, if illegally, that Northern Ireland should be part of a united Ireland. That is a perfectly legitimate aspiration if you can persuade people of its merits. There was a view, over a long period, that helping the PIRA to see that they could not defeat the British Government was part of securing peace. They had to see, as they did indeed come to see, that they could not win. What worries me about the phrase 'defeating the PIRA' is that nobody sensible thought that Northern Ireland could be sorted by some sort of security victory over the PIRA. We did think that security successes against the PIRA were a necessary part of putting pressure on them, and we had to do it anyway because they were trying to kill people so we had to try to stop them from doing that by arresting those responsible. In that sense, the criminal justice approach was an integral part of the strategy, so gaining intelligence and disrupting operations and getting evidence and locking people up was all part of the strategy to help them to see that they were not going to win and that this was not the way to go. To go back to that period in the early 1990s, as mentioned, the two concepts of political movement and political development ran in parallel, where making political progress between the SDLP, the Ulster Unionist parties, the Alliance Party and the Irish Government might eventually help to weaken and marginalise the PIRA to the extent where republicans would enter the political process. It was an open question at that stage whether this would work, because the PIRA had been operating against the wishes of the SDLP and the Irish Government for the past twenty years. But there emerged a point in the early 1990s when the Irish Government were not willing to do a deal and make significant concessions alongside the SDLP with the unionists and the British Government, because they were mesmerised by the fact that they thought that Adams and McGuinness were moving towards a ceasefire and that this was such a big prize that everything had to become secondary to that. They certainly did not want to start making compromises until that part of the nationalist family in Northern Ireland was within the tent, as it were.

GS: Can you explain what you think were the potential or discernible differences in how the Irish interpreted text in comparison with the British?

WF: I think there are two separate issues here, and you have to be a bit careful over not confusing them. The first is that the Irish and British governments had a qualitatively different role from each other. The British Government had no selfish strategic economic interest. Its agenda was to try to secure agreement, and almost anything that anyone could agree was okay by the British Government. Of course, the Irish Government was in a different position. Going back to the early 1990s before the Good Friday Agreement (GFA), it had Articles 2 and 3 of its Constitution and the historical weight of that on it, so it was a player in a different way from the British Government. It also did not have the responsibility for Northern Ireland, and when you have responsibility there are certain constraints and burdens that you do not have without that responsibility. The other thing, of course, is that the Irish always saw themselves in some sense as a protector for one part of the community in Northern Ireland, namely, the nationalist community, so the first thing to say about the approaching of text, or negotiations or anything else, is that the Irish approached it through a very particular prism. However, although the SDLP mattered in the early 1990s it mattered rather less to the Irish Government by 2000 because Sinn Féin was in the ascendancy by then. The second point to bear in mind is that the Brits have a reputation in European discussions and elsewhere of being very literalist, where once they have signed up to something they will do it. I do not think it is true at all that the Irish signed up to things because they would interpret text fairly broadly and worry about it less. No, they were extremely attentive to texts, and bear in mind that, as representatives of the minority community in Northern Ireland, there was that edginess that comes with looking after the interests of the underdog, as well as the British–Irish relationship characterised as it is by a history of the powerful alongside those who feel oppressed, colonised and victimised. It is certainly not the case that the Irish were easier about texts or would regard them as merely a general statement. They were tough on them.

GS: Did they have a tendency to be more conversational in the process and put greater emphasis on the value of dialogue in comparison with the British?

WF: It is the case, having warned against cultural stereotyping, that the way that people relate to each other and do business in a small society, and this would be true of Dublin and Belfast, is different. There is a tendency in a small, intimate society for business to get done more informally and through relational situations. In a larger society and culture, particularly one that imbued the high Victorian spirit of the Northcote–Trevelyan Civil Service reforms, which were all about impartial analysis, coolness and civil servants being advisers to ministers, there is perhaps a more formal approach to business. One of the important functions of ministers is being able to bring legislation to Parliament, so the Civil Service has traditionally functioned to support ministers around legislative texts. Perhaps that does mean that the natural strengths and instincts and default mechanisms of British civil servants are a bit different from the way people do business in Belfast or Dublin, and in that respect both those places are different from London. In that sense, the differences are partly to do with scale and partly to do with culture.

GS: Does that impact on trust? If you are part of a bigger society that is built on a politics of analysis, measurement and risk assessment, etc., then surely the means of creating and building trust is different.

WF: We are talking about points along a spectrum here, and I do not think one should be too stark about it. Large numbers of people understood the importance of personal relationships and confidence-building; after all we have the diplomatic service which spends much of the time doing that. The civil servants who were intrinsically cooler may have been so because that is our Northcote–Trevelyan training. Also, think of people in the NIO who had not spent all their life living in Northern Ireland, but had spent a lot of time working in Whitehall and perhaps only went to Belfast for periods of time. People who work in government in London do not socialise greatly with people they work with in London. It is a cooler relationship among colleagues, which is different from people working in Dublin and Northern Ireland.

GS: When you talk about civil servants having this cool, analytical approach can you elaborate on how that comes into play in dialogue? Are you looking for what might go wrong rather than what might go right?

WF: I come back to the additional responsibility that falls to you if you are in power, and bear in mind that the British Government was in power for long stretches of direct rule. It was not just the sovereign power for Northern Ireland, but it was running the place because devolution had been suspended. So you have the responsibility, as Hugh Dalton famously put it, of being congenital 'snag hunters'. You are always thinking what might go wrong and what the practical consequences of that might be. About how we might legislate if such and such happens and about who is left carrying the can. You have to think that way to some extent, but the trick is not to become defensive and bureaucratic so that all imagination and opportunity goes. I think that all of us working on Northern Ireland issues over a long period knew that it was going to take some nerve, boldness, creativity and risk to deliver what was needed. After all, we were asking people who had fundamentally different constitutional objectives and who thoroughly disliked each other to do deals and to prepare to work together in a government. This involved a lot of risks and living with the consequences in respective communities of what might happen if those communities were not behind this shift, so we were very conscious of the consequences. You had to assess things carefully, and there was a dynamic in 2000–2 when, as has been documented by Jonathan Powell and others, there was perhaps a bit of a creative tension between Number 10 and the NIO, where

Number 10 thought that the NIO was a bit cautious and risk-averse, and the NIO thought that at times Number 10 cut rather quickly to the bottom line without always weighing the downsides as well as the upsides.

GS: If we fast-forward to 2001 when the Assembly collapsed, was text as influential as dialogue in getting the Assembly up and running again?

WF: Drawing too sharp a distinction between text and dialogue is artificial because all processes produce text by way of agreement, whether it is something quite complicated like the GFA or whether it is rather shorter agreements that occurred at stages in the process about who was going to do what next about this or that. Indeed, sometimes that included private agreements, and that is one of the bones of contention at the moment with the OTR issue. The government would privately promise Sinn Féin that it would do something or other in the context of Sinn Féin getting the PIRA to decommission weapons and so on that was about sustaining the Assembly and enabling David Trimble to stay in government, and the dialogue was about how we were going to write that down and what we were going to say publicly and privately.

GS: You mention private agreements. Do they cause you more pain in the long run or do you think they are justified?

WF: There are those who believe, though even they do not practise it, that almost the whole of human life should be conducted transparently and in full public gaze. Those who are most passionate for freedom of information and most suspicious of executive power think Parliament and Assembly proceedings are for everybody to witness and that is how you do all public business. Complete nonsense. Human life does not work like that. All institutions have to manage a boundary between what is public and what is private. Even institutions that are in the public sector and accountable to the public for a whole range of reasons have to be able to account business in private, because some of it is about commercially sensitive things and some of it is of a candid political kind and about people. You have to be able to talk about all that privately before you then decide what you are going to make public. That publicity is, or should be, on the basis of private assurances. Now we would never have got to the point of the PIRA ceasefire in 1994 if there had not been private, indirect exchanges with the PIRA. You would never have got the GFA in 1998 if there had not been all sorts of dialogue of an intensive kind in private, because people have to be able to think aloud, explore positions and see where compromises might be struck and this involves testing things out privately. You have to be able to do that. Of course, alternatively, if you attempt to keep private that which has been agreed, there is a risk that it will get up and bite you. What Ireland has in common with the Church of England is that neither keeps secrets for very long, so what is private will not stay that way for very long, with the risk that misrepresentation of what was private will be quite considerable. In a process that is about building up trust, situations that are private manifestly have a tendency for those who are not part of them to create distrust and mistrust, and so you have to be careful about that. Having said that, I think that it is perfectly legitimate to have private understandings on some matters as long as you are clear about how you handle them when they come into the public domain. And, because they will come into the public domain in some way, you had better draft communications at the outset with that in mind. What you have to avoid is perceived dishonesty or deception of people. Being economical with the truth is often seen as code for being misleading or being disingenuous, and those things are not right. Nevertheless, you do not give everyone the total story all the time because that is not how life is or how political relations work.

GS: When you write a piece of text is there a way of doing it where the text is both concealing and revealing? By that I mean does the text act as a seduction to draw people into a process without necessarily offering detail or substance? Is there text as 'bait'?

WF: It is difficult to generalise about that because you are talking about a very wide range of circumstances. A lot of the process of drawing people into serious discussion is done generally by more informal conversation. It is not text-based to start with, so by the time the constitutional talks started in 1992 all the preparatory work had been done by Peter Brooke to get the unionists to agree to engage with the SDLP and potentially with the Irish Government if we got into Strand 2. There had been many rounds of private meetings before my time that involved understandings shared with the SDLP and the Irish Government about the terms of trade for talks, and particularly in terms of Strands 1, 2 and 3. While the talks were going on the unionists had insisted that the operation of the Anglo-Irish Agreement (AIA) was suspended. It is usually the outcome of the initial discussion – talks about talks – that some texts emerge recording the basis on which the various parties are prepared to engage. But if you look at various stages of the process over a long time span, it becomes very difficult to generalise. It depends a little bit on what the rhythm is. Gerry Adams and Martin McGuinness used to refer to the rounds of discussions in 2000–2 as 'Groundhog Day', meaning that all these talks were doing was going round on the same old issues. They liked to imply that the British Government was not living up to its responsibilities and should sort them. However, if you are looking rigorously and academically at how things worked you have to break things down in order to see how varying forces came to shape power-sharing in Northern Ireland, a new North–South relationship and a new 'defused' British–Irish relationship. You also have to distinguish between three different sorts of exercise: intensive periods with a desired big deal at the end of them; periods that were fallow because nobody thought it was a good moment to talk; and periods of the kind we had at several times in 2000–2, when you were not expecting to produce some big defining document, but simply trying to do little deals to stop confidence and trust sliding backwards, and stop what had been created unravelling. That period 2000–2 included within it proximity talks at Downing Street, Chequers, Hillsborough and Weston Park, and longer periods of bilateral discussions in a sort of continuous drama with a changing list of characters. The problem at the time was dealing with David Trimble's threat of pulling out of the Assembly by such and such a day if there was no movement on PIRA decommissioning. So the questions that dominated then related to crisis management. What movement could be created by getting the PIRA to shift a bit? What price would Sinn Féin seek to extract for 'bringing their influence to bear'?

GS: What value does a public speech have?

WF: It has a number of potential advantages. It depends on the context. Obviously, it was used as a technique of speaking to people you could not speak to directly, and particularly in the early 1990s when some people were letting off bombs. Then the purpose was mostly about speaking to their community and trying to bring influence to bear on the leadership. There was also the Blair speech made soon after the 1997 election at the agricultural show in Northern Ireland, which was quite a warm unionist speech. There are two reasons for making speeches of that kind. One is to put things on the public record so the people can hear what is said, and the other is to try to reach over the heads of the politicians to do that. Now that is quite a dangerous game to play in a democracy because you want the politicians to support the process of change, but there is a sense too that at times you want the politicians to respond to what the people really think rather than rely on them to tell you what people think. The other thing, and it may seem paradoxical, is that on occasions you might want to almost paint yourself into a bit of a corner publicly. This is not something that politicians naturally want to do and good civil servants, generally speaking, advise ministers not to paint themselves into corners because life is intrinsically unpredictable so you always need room for manoeuvre. Having said that, although the government's part in negotiation was largely facilitative it still had to make clear where the boundaries were. So it was important to draw some lines that were both binding, but also defining what the name of the game was.

GS: When you send a public message it obviously becomes a declaration of intent, but how much consideration is given to problems of interpretation among divergent groups who receive such a message?

WF: From my experience in the NIO, people were always keenly aware that on every issue the see-saw was a rather rigid one, and that in all conflict situations something that appears to give something to one side is immediately perceived by the other for that reason alone as being difficult. Because of this we did not have rushes of blood to the head. There was a lot of careful musing about who should be given advanced notice of what was to come. And for some people it may be shocking that we were privately communicating indirectly at all with the PIRA before the ceasefire, so what you say has got to be something you stand by on the day it does go public and subsequently.

GS: Is a good speech within a context like Northern Ireland a mixture of the static along with the dynamic? That is, is it about reassurance through principles mixed with the uncertainty of change by pragmatic emphasis?

WF: I do not think I would go quite that far, but it is a normal technique in any dispute resolution process to try to start with the common ground and then to build it up from that around the things that are contested to see if you can either resolve them or manage them in some new way. I do not think that is just specific to Northern Ireland. It is common elsewhere too and it is quite a continental thing, much loved of European treaties with long preambles and established principles, which all sounds like good motherhood and apple pie stuff, and then you get to the difficult bit.

GS: To what extent does text function as a form of persuasion?

WF: Text was crucial to reaching agreement, but a lot of what was going on in the room where we were doing that at successive meetings was about building trust so that people had confidence that the text could be read straight, meaning you could read the words and not be fearful of hidden agendas, and that there was a willingness to proceed in the light of principles with proper independent review and scrutiny. The best negotiations are those where people do not end up looking back at the text much afterwards unless they have to turn it into legislation. What you are trying to do is to create the circumstances in which people can make things work. In general, we all have a preference as between rules and principles, but my own view is that, except when you are legislating, it is better to proceed by way of principles rather than rules. Nevertheless, you also have to have some text to hang on to as well because you cannot do it all by trust alone.

GS: Bertie Ahern has said he and Tony Blair wanted to make the talks as comprehensive as possible, and spent a lot of time doing that because they did not want a disenfranchised element to scupper the process, so inclusivity was the main emphasis. But how do principles enable a convergence of differences whilst maintaining an ethos of inclusivity? How is a broad terrain of contestations focused onto a narrower terrain while retaining an image of comprehensiveness?

WF: The core objective is to get to a position where people are prepared to live and work together within as normal a democratic framework as a deeply divided society will allow. Therefore, you are trying to gain acceptance of certain rules of the game, even if the most fundamental issue of all – which country to be part of – is not one on which people will agree. The secret is keeping people in the same church, so to speak, even though they have significant theological differences of opinion. The difficulties of this should not be underestimated in Northern Ireland, because you have a situation where people have historically contested what we might see as conventional democratic structures and rules. The rules have not been normal in Northern Ireland for all sorts of reasons, not least where one section of the community was prevented from exercising power, so it was not in any sense a normal situation. It is, and was, not a simple 'Let's have elections and who gets the most votes wins power' argument, because the historical majority did not command cross-community consent. So you had to create arrangements that could command confidence on both sides of the community. You had, to put it another way, to try to drain some of the poison out of the North–South relationship as Lemass and O'Neill tried to do tentatively in the 1960s before the Troubles. It was, and is, actually in the interests of unionists as well as nationalists for North–South relations to be better. It is a small island, and economically and socially it makes sense for this to happen, so we had to try to draw the sting from the British–Irish animosity. In recent years we have seen Martin McGuinness raising his glass to the queen at Windsor Castle, which is not something you would have bet your mortgage on ten years ago.

GS: Can you talk about constructive ambiguity and the shift to clarity after the GFA?

WF: It has a place, but only a limited place. My own view is that the circumstances in which you should go for constructive ambiguity are where the two sides almost collude in it. In other words, you, as the facilitator, have got a problem that both sides find very difficult. They will find it difficult with their own constituencies too if you resolve it completely or too quickly, but you find something that both can live with while being aware that it is a fudge. But you should not fudge where there are differences of view, since this will quickly come home to bite you. Sometimes constructive ambiguity is a way of enabling movement on a difficult issue and helping the two sides to defer a problem while you make progress on other things. So it is a sort of holding position. I think if you are trying to run a process you should not be trying to obfuscate for others, and it does not work anyway. Such negotiations take forever and people will pick everything apart. It is a device you would use only among consenting adults.

GS: When you were there in 2000 considerable change had taken place. What was most evident for you about that change from 1992?

WF: Well, the context was completely different. As I said, in 1992 the nationalists were interested in having political talks as a warm-up for what they thought would be big talks once the violence had stopped, but they did not want to do deals until then, not least because people were always frightened of being outflanked by more extreme elements. So once these more extreme elements were part of the discussion it was easier for talks to make real progress. That was an issue for the nationalists. What we have not talked about so far is that the unionists wanted some power back in Northern Ireland. They knew they would have to share it in some way, but they wanted a new Assembly. The thing that was high on their minds was that they were still smarting from what, for them, was the historic affront of the 1985 AIA. One of the complexities of the talks in 1992 was that the unionists decided to make it part of their position that they would not talk while the AIA was in force. Now, of course, this was where a bit of constructive ambiguity was essential, because the Agreement could not be abrogated since it was an international agreement. So, a means was devised whereby the operation of the Agreement was suspended, with the British and Irish governments taking the view that it was not working normally. This slightly elaborate fiction was created where, in order to have these talks, it was determined that the Agreement would in some way be put into suspended animation. However, by making a fuss over this the unionists gave the Irish Government an absolute veto over whether talks happened or not, because the British and Irish governments had to agree the length of the period of suspension. So, as soon as the Irish Government thought the negotiations were getting a bit difficult, they could say that they could not agree any extension of the suspension because it was a very important agreement and so they could draw negotiations to an end. There were a couple of dramatic moments I remember from the talks. We had got into Strand 2 discussions about North–South bodies in the summer of 1992, which, of course, the nationalists wanted lots of and the unionists were very wary about. We were coming up to a deadline, and we were pretty clear that the Irish Government and the SDLP had had enough of the talks. As I say, they had not expected to have to enter into them. But a period of violence had enabled John Major to get a commitment before the April 1992 election that talks would resume in earnest afterwards. Most people had expected a Kinnock victory, which, of course, did not happen, so the Irish and SDLP were pitchforked into talks they had never really wanted. There was then a dramatic moment in Dublin, about June or July that year, when the Irish view was that the talks had to stop and that the Agreement had to be re-established. We had been making a bit of progress on texts and issues, and in the end the Northern Ireland secretary said it would be ridiculous and quite irresponsible to suspend talks given that we were making progress. So, the British line was that we had to have longer at this, which would put pressure on the men of violence. It was agreed with the Irish that there would be another couple of months' suspension of the Agreement while we continued. The talks stopped in the September on the renewed date because, at root, the Irish and the nationalists did not want to get to the point of having to make very complex compromises when they had never planned to get into such talks in the first place, and were much more focused, quite reasonably, on trying to get the PIRA to stop the violence. But the other and earlier dramatic moment that is of interest, given what Dr Paisley did subsequently, was that because of all this complexity about suspending the Agreement there had been quite tight deadlines. We had had Strand 1 talks first, which the Irish were not part of because they were about internal government, so at that point the participants were just the British Government, the unionists, the SDLP and the Alliance Party. Of course, the SDLP then felt rather exposed because Sinn Féin and the Irish were not part of it, and they wanted to get through this into Strand 2 quickly so the two strands could run in parallel. However, the unionists insisted that we must get some kind of outline agreement or make some progress on the texts in Strand 1 first, and there was a very difficult day when we had made progress, but the question was would the unionists agree to move into Strand 2, which meant bringing the Irish Government into the talks? The UUP and James Molyneaux were prepared to do it, but it was a very difficult issue for the DUP, and there was a big row during which they kept having meetings. We resumed in the middle of the Friday evening when it was not quite clear whether Ian Paisley had got a mandate from his party or not. We were with all the parties around the table, with Patrick Mayhew in the chair, and it was John Chilcot who in the meeting drafted on the hoof a sort of half sentence or sentence and Paisley said 'Yes I can live with that', so we got into Strand 2.

GS: What was that sentence?

WF: It was something about the Strand 1 arrangements and Dr Paisley said he would go with it, but the DUP was very unhappy about it. Dr Paisley and his colleagues did take part in Strand 2 talks, which started at Lancaster House in London, and that was the first time that he had sat down with Irish Government ministers so it was, in its way, a breakthrough.

GS: In what way did the unionists interpret text which might be seen as different to how republicans interpreted text? Clearly, viewing the Agreement as copper-fastening the Union for unionists and as a stepping-stone to a united Ireland for republicans indicates two very different reference points. One might be seen as static and the other dynamic. How did such reference points shape reactions to text?

WF: I think you have to be careful to avoid generalising too much. Of course, there were different underlying aspirations and dynamics, but I do not think one side was any less receptive to text than the other. The hardest of the hard in negotiations were Sinn Féin, however. In 2000–2, with any text involving them, they were absolutely remorseless, as suggested by George Mitchell's phrase about them being 'chisellers'. But it is important to be clear that there was not that much of a gap where you could say one was pedantic and the other was not.

GS: What about the suggestion that whereas unionists 'read the lines', nationalists and republicans were particularly concerned with 'reading between the lines'?

WF: I am quite cautious about that, and I think there is an element of simplification and stereotyping there as well. Yes, temperamentally and culturally the Protestant Presbyterian tradition is very different from the Irish Catholic tradition with the resonance of imagery and all of that, but I think you have to be careful about drawing overly simple conclusions. I think the more significant point is that strategically the unionists are in a defensive position, indeed, you could say they have been since 1886. The Home Rule controversy was about staying in the United Kingdom, and ever since they have been trying to ensure that they have access to power and do not have their position eroded because they are a minority in Ireland. Even within Northern Ireland, they fear that with migration and differential birth rates they will get pressed back, so their position is a defensive one. With the nationalists, you have the sense of grievance at what happened at the beginning of the twentieth century, and then what happened after 1921 over the way the place was run, largely not bothered about by British governments until the Troubles broke out in the 1960s. But, yes, there is an aspiration, a hope, on their side that one day what they did not achieve in 1921 might be achieved in the future. That is all true, but I do not think that when it comes down to haggling over texts there is that much difference. Perhaps one could be critical of the unionists for not attending to some of these things as tightly as they might have, especially with the business of decommissioning. The linkage with the side letter that Tony Blair gave David Trimble was obviously born of need and expediency in the process when it was beyond the point of further negotiation. But perhaps David Trimble would have had fewer problems if he had identified his red line earlier and more clearly when the text of the Agreement was being settled. Having said that, it may be that if he had been tougher the Agreement simply would not have happened; it was all so finely balanced. Instead, there was the side letter, and the consequence was all the twists and turns of several years trying to ensure that the PIRA was really standing down. In that process decommissioning gave the republicans a lot of negotiating leverage. The reason they were able to get a lot of things out of the British Government over that period was because David Trimble badly needed movement on decommissioning and that meant that the republicans were able to extract quite a high price. Now, you could say that it was precisely because the unionists had not been tough enough and literal enough on texts earlier on that this happened, but I think the analysis is perhaps a bit more subtle than your question.

GS: Nevertheless, Sinn Féin are good at understanding symbolism and unionists are bad at understanding symbolism. Sinn Féin sold the Good Friday Agreement as a success and the unionists sold it as a failure. In your view, did the unionists approach text grudgingly, feeling they were forced into it?

WF: What the unionists wanted by 2000 was not text, but the PIRA to destroy weapons and to make it clear they were not going to go back to war. That was the issue, so the texts were not really being negotiated at that point and this caused a lot of difficulties subsequently. By this point the key talks were essentially between the British Government and Sinn Féin and the Irish Government. Now obviously there had to be conversations with others, not least David Trimble and his allies, because you had to do things that genuinely did help rather than do things that created a price you could not bear. But unionists were beyond texts, what they wanted was actions, and the big problem all along was whether the PIRA had given up for good. You could not insist on words like 'permanence' because what is permanent in this world? But you wanted satisfaction that this was not a tactic and that this was a definite crossing of the bridge. Ministers recognised and, even in reflective moments, unionists recognised that Gerry Adams and Martin McGuinness had pulled off an extraordinarily difficult achievement in securing the agreement of the PIRA to stop the violence. Also, it was in no one's interest for there to be a deep and wide split in the PIRA, so it was important that the leadership in the republican movement brought as many as possible, all but a few, across the bridge. Therefore, there was no point in demanding things they could not deliver. But what they could deliver was extremely difficult to assess because of the secrecy of the movement. Despite all the indicators that the authorities had, it was very difficult to judge and you know the history. The ceasefire broke down in 1996 with Canary Wharf, violence restarted, but it restarted in a fairly controlled form and one of the surprises of that period in 1996–7 was how tightly the PIRA leadership kept the violence under control. It was still wholly unacceptable, but it did not run out of control and it was very carefully calculated, so when the election came and everybody expected a change of government, which is indeed what happened when New Labour got a huge majority, it did not take very long for the republicans to be able to go back to a ceasefire and get back into the process. I also think that the effect of the attacks in America in 2001, and a hardening of attitudes on the part of the British and Irish governments, had a big part to play. I can remember in June 2001, just after elections in the United Kingdom when Tony Blair had won a second term, there was a meeting of the heads of government in Gothenburg in Sweden where it was arranged that Tony Blair and Bertie Ahern would have a bilateral in the margins of the meeting to take stock of the process, which was in rocky days at that time, with David Trimble teetering on the edge. There were serious questions about whether he could stay with devolution, and I went with Jonathan Powell to a meeting where a very candid exchange took place between the two prime ministers as they reflected on the fact that the PIRA had been involved in a robbery and had stolen tobacco etc. from a warehouse in Belfast worth several million pounds in the run-up to the British general election. I recall both prime ministers being very clear that if Sinn Féin wanted to be taken seriously as politicians they could not be part of a movement that dealt with cash flow problems by organising robberies. When the Labour Party or Fianna Fáil had a funding problem they did not send the boys out to commit robberies to procure funds. There was a fresh determination on the part of the prime ministers to get the republicans to make the decisive break from criminality in favour of politics.

GS: But at what point would there have been serious consideration about closing the process down because of such bad faith and the potential discrediting of the two governments. Was it a matter of the two governments keeping the process going regardless?

WF: I think that in the peace process, as so often in grown-up politics, you have to take a cool view of 'If not this then what is the alternative?'. And by 2000–2, and given the huge mandate that the 1998 Agreement had, anything that deliberately collapsed the peace process was obviously anathema, and rightly so. No sensible person wanted a return to widespread violence in Northern Ireland, and no one wanted to dash the hope of proper institutional arrangements surviving. But everyone knew it was unfinished business and that what had been achieved in 1998 was incomplete, because, first of all, it had carried the assent of only about half of the unionist community, who were becoming increasingly fed up because they saw Sinn Féin getting ever more goodies. So there was an understanding that this had to be more securely based across the unionist community. There was clearly unfinished business here because, despite the ceasefires and the much lower level of violence, the PIRA had not disbanded. On top of this, you had the Colombia arrests, the Special Branch offices at Castlereagh being broken into in March 2002, and then in the autumn the revelation of the intelligence-gathering at Stormont. As I was leaving at the end of 2002, devolution was on the edge of collapse and, indeed, did collapse shortly afterwards and did not come back for a long time. So you had to be prepared to take significant setbacks in this process, but that was different from saying, 'Well it's all up'. There was a real dynamic right through from the early 1990s that we had to try to secure peace if we could, that it might just be possible after all the wasted years, and that we had to try to have stable institutions of government. In the long run our analysis was that you were not going to sustain one without the other, and, if you are going to achieve some sort of normal society, you had to have stable institutions that commanded wide cross-community consent, and you had to disband private armies. You can say it took more than a decade after the GFA, but to think of stopping it all would have been mistaken because you would have had to re-start it at some point. You had to try to keep the momentum going, and I think underneath it all the prime minister and Jonathan Powell, and a good many in the NIO, did believe that Gerry Adams and Martin McGuinness had taken the decision that they wanted to be politicians, and thought that the republican movement strategically needed to invest in politics and that the military phase they had been through was over. That was the view, but, nevertheless, people like to have the best of both worlds, and it was a process of making clear that this could not last forever.

GS: In a process like this is there a danger of having too much text?

WF: Texts are only a means to an end.

GS: Can they prolong the end?

WF: At the end of the day, peace-making is about willpower and trust. As said, the NIO did all the analysis in the 1970s, and its basic assessment was sound as to what the elements of a lasting deal might be. But there was not the will. Or, to be more precise, there was the will among some, as with Sunningdale, but it did not hold. Circumstances conspired against success. Texts are only tools to help build trust in a context where there is sufficient will. Now, obviously, there are some things on which you need clarity. If you are drawing up how an Assembly is going to work, you have to establish the ground rules. If you are devising how an early release of prisoners scheme is going to work, you have to write it down as to whether people will serve two years or one year. Where you get into difficulties is when people either have not thought something through or have miscalculated the consequences. Everyone knew that if you were going to get a deal that enabled the republican movement to stay in a process, then they had to get their boys out of prison, and the loyalists wanted their boys out as well. And although nobody much liked it, people knew it was going to be necessary and the question in 1998 was what was the line going to be? As it turned out, the decision was two years. But people had not thought through what the consequence was of not having any other sort of mechanism for dealing with the past. And that is an issue that is still alive today. When I got back in August 2000, it was already looming quite large because Sinn Féin pointed to the cases of people, particularly someone who was very prominent for them politically in America and in the Republic, but who had escaped the jurisdiction in the early 1970s, who they wanted back in Northern Ireland. She was not convicted, she was not a prisoner and she had not done two years, so how could she come back given that she was wanted in relation to crimes that had been committed, but for which there had been no prosecution? One could see this was a problem.

GS: Was that when the OTR issue surfaced?

WF: That was in the beginning and they had been talking about this person even in Mo Mowlam's time, but they had other people as well. They portrayed it as an anomaly. There were some anomalies, but at root it was not so much an anomaly as consequence of going for an early release scheme rather than an amnesty or some mechanism by which, as in South Africa, you could wipe the slate clean. I would not say that was because of a shortage of text in 1998. It was partly because people thought that was all the market would bear and partly because people had not thought through all the potential difficulties that would arise. The government was not initially willing to consider a process that would enable the slate to be wiped clean, but they agreed that if people wanted to come back a mechanism would be in place whereby they could seek to ascertain whether they were still wanted. It was done entirely within the law, so it was a question of looking again at evidence that, in many cases, was twenty, thirty or more years old, and given that prosecutors bring prosecutions only if there is a better than 50 per cent chance of conviction, would they still do that?

GS: What debate did the OTR issue create at the time?

WF: It was in the public domain that this was an issue and it is in the Jonathan Powell book. I think the claim that Peter Robinson and others have made is that they did not know that there was a 'scheme' whereby names could be provided, that there would be a check and, in some cases, people might get a letter saying on the basis of the information at that moment, they would not be arrested and prosecuted. There were some parliamentary questions asked about it too. My own take is that it was one of those things that suited everybody not to probe that much. So, you come back to constructive ambiguity. It was one of those subjects that for a period everyone was content not to press too hard on for information. The early release scheme for prisoners, which was part of the Agreement, had been entirely above board and legislation had been passed, but even that still, understandably, left most pretty queasy. It was part of the deal, but people did not feel very proud about it and here you have other stuff that all feels a bit unsatisfactory. Underneath there is something more fundamental, which is that, depending on what question you ask, people would say 'Yes, of course we have to move on to a new chapter and draw a line under this because just raking up the past is not very constructive'. But if you ask the question in a different way, they would say 'It is completely unacceptable to the families of victims that people should get off free'. Even those who were released after two years had at least been convicted and there had been some reparation by being in prison for a while, but people were deeply torn on the subject. We knew in the NIO that this was an immensely sensitive subject. We knew because a number of us had worked in and around the criminal justice system and the Home Office, and that there were severe limits on what you could secure if you were just going to stay within the present law. If the prosecutors could see that the evidence was enough to sustain prosecutions, then, okay, people could come back. In addition, there were some cases where people technically did not qualify for the early release scheme because of the mix of offences for which they had been charged, which could only be applied as 'scheduled offences'.

GS: What was the discussion around possibly wiping the slate clean?

WF: The issue of moving from early release to some wider process for wiping the slate clean was exceptionally difficult, not least because of whether any such arrangement should extend to soldiers and police officers. There was a perfectly coherent intellectual argument under international law that the forces of the state should be treated differently from others since more was expected of the Army and the police. There was an argument that we had to be above reproach on this. But I have to say that those of us involved in the NIO always thought that politically the chances of getting a unilateral amnesty through Parliament, which benefited only the 'men of violence' and not people who had loyally served the Crown, but might have done something they should not have done, was just fanciful, and so it proved. The idea that you could have got a unilateral amnesty through would not run, and would be repugnant to a lot of ordinary public opinion in the United Kingdom. On most issues my experience was that people on this side of the water in London were prepared to cut quite a lot of slack as to what happened in relation to Northern Ireland, and Parliament accepted all sorts of legislation because it had been part of a deal and they did not want to unsettle that. But I think that on this issue of members of the British Army being potentially vulnerable to prosecution when people who had tried to blow them up were to be left off – no, that would have been too difficult for public opinion.

GS: One of the things I have asked others is about the relationship between principle and pragmatism. If you have a principle and it shifts does this not undermine the principle, as with say decommissioning?

WF: Well you get into difficulty when you are not sufficiently clear what the principles are. The real principle is that in a democracy people have to observe the rules of the game, so they must not behave fraudulently at elections, they must not break the law; so there are basic rules that people have to observe. Equally, principles of fair treatment are important, so in a divided community like Northern Ireland you do not have the power of the majority oppressing the minority in a way that happened between the 1920s and 1960s. There may be disputes over how bad that was, but the fact is that some did not get a fair deal. There are certain points of principle, but when you start from a deeply imperfect situation you have to be prepared to be pragmatic over the speed at which you move and the direction you take to get to where you want to be. To take an example, we have not talked about some of the governance arrangements built into the 1998 Agreement. They are very odd by the standards of normal society – all these safeguards about cross-community agreements and mandatory coalitions. In democracies you usually have elections and the people speak, and then you either have a majority for someone or they have to negotiate some sort of coalition. Now, the 1998 Agreement does not provide for that at all. It has all sorts of safeguards built in, and you could say, pragmatically really, that in a divided society it is not adequate to rely on simple majority rule because the majority will tend to oppress the minority unless you build in some safeguards. But, in terms of decommissioning, it was always a proxy for abandoning the armed struggle and being prepared to live by the rules of the democratic game. It was a symbol of that and you have to be careful with symbols that they do not come to assume disproportionate significance. As has often been said, no one was stupid enough to believe that if the PIRA got rid of weapons they would not be able to get more, so what mattered was that they stood down and stopped. In the end, they did come up with moves that were more radical than people might have thought possible only a few years before. But there is no textbook answer on principle or pragmatism because you have to apply both.

GS: Do you recall discussion about language and what words, like decommissioning, parity of esteem and consent, etc., might mean?

WF: I do remember some discussion and an official suggesting in 1992 that 50 per cent plus 1 would not be enough to secure democratic legitimacy for Northern Ireland leaving the United Kingdom. But that line of argument was fairly briskly choked off on the basis that in a democracy that is how it works. On that issue the terms were very clear and non-negotiable. With a lot of other language, never underestimate the extent to which stuff is made up on the hoof and then subsequently acquires a currency. I cannot remember where the word decommissioning came from, but certainly if you tracked back to the first time it was used I suspect that nobody expected it to acquire the totemic status that it did.

GS: Republicans called it 'putting arms beyond use' because of the connotations of surrender, and to accept a British word was always going to be a problem for them was it not?

WF: I can remember that the clash was on what we called 'security normalisation' and what they called 'demilitarisation', so when there were negotiations about which watchtowers in South Armagh were going to come down and which barracks would close, they demanded all sorts of discussion, but we used different language and tried to avoid what we saw as contentious terms.

GS: Was it important to have separations around language so you could mark out a British position that was different or were you seeking a mutually agreed language?

WF: Both sides conducted the discussions with eyes wide open and so you did not play games on these things. Agreement was in relation to some particular next step and this would be on the substance of what could be done. The British Government had to reach its own judgement in relation to troop levels or which watchtowers were needed at any particular point. Obviously, you had to attend to what the other side said, but the issue at stake was not so much the use of language but whether it would get the PIRA to move and to decommission; to make it clearer that the armed struggle had finished. That was naturally very difficult for them and you had to create the conditions in which that might happen, so the question was about how attractive was this set of proposals that the British Government could put. The two would have to move together. It was not the language in the sense of getting the register right or using our words or their words particularly. It was usually about whether there were enough goodies in the bag, that was the issue and they were always chiselling for a few more.

GS: Was it the case that text was the prime mover, creating a dialectical process of exchange etc.?

WF: If you are looking at the process from 1990 to 2010, I think it does turn quite a lot on what was going on and what was the nature of the haggle at any particular time. There were moments when we used to go for what were called 'soft landings', so in early 2001 we knew we were coming up to a general election. President Clinton had just been over to do a 'lap of honour', and there had been a hope that there was going to be a big shift on decommissioning and that there would be a big deal. Some of us doubted that it would happen, and the doubters were right because republicans had taken the view that

David Trimble was very rocky anyway. Who could be sure what might come after that? Real business was not going to be done until what turned out to be the June 2001 general election, so in March we secured a 'soft landing' to get the process to 'rest' for the moment in the hope that it would take it off again a couple of months later. In that situation words were quite important because you were not actually talking about the package, but mood and tone and trying to create a sense of trust, and that is where the nature of the words is very important.

GS: So, tone was important to these soft landings. Can you highlight this or give examples?

WF: Around March 2001 we had a full day's meeting in Hillsborough and, if I remember rightly, the PIRA put out a statement just before the meeting making it clear that they were not going to shift and do anything significant. But what everybody said at that point sort of 'drew stumps', to use a cricket phrase. It was not about calling the match off, more of a 'bad light stopped play' approach and that we would resume next morning. That was the hope anyway.

GS: When you produced a piece of text and you had meetings with secretaries of state how did it work? Would the secretary of state tell you what he or she wanted, or was there a consensus that evolved from the team?

WF: You have two sorts of document. Your internal communication with the secretary of state where, in a policy paper or submission, you analyse the questions and look at options, and come up with some pros and cons of what to do, how to communicate it and all the rest. Then, you have documents that are designed for sharing with others as part of the process, and as a civil servant you spend quite a bit of time in face-to-face discussions with secretaries of state. On tricky issues, such as OTRs and when David Trimble threatened to pull out of the Assembly, we effectively agreed to suspend devolution for twenty-four hours and then the six-week clock started ticking again so they could re-elect the first and deputy first minister. All those sort of things created quite a lot of complications, which you had to analyse and work through and take legal advice on, and you set that out in text for the secretary of state. You would then probably have a meeting to discuss it, because it might be tricky and he or she would want to make sure he or she understood it. One sort of document is about fuelling the private thinking within government, for example, about what needed doing the following week if David Trimble walked out etc. There might be a submission and a number of letters for the secretary of state to write to people or, more likely, speaking notes for him or her to have conversations with people. It would depend on what the nature of the problem was at that point. Or you would write a note reporting back about how you had got on in negotiation and what you might do next, which meant producing some fresh text to share and that was how business was done. Obviously, when you were really busy you did it all in real time and face-to-face.

GS: Sinn Féin would write everything down, was that your perception?

WF: They were very cautious, very disciplined, very meticulous, and they did not take chances. Things were carefully written down, yes. They had an enormous collective memory and they were hugely focused because this was their life, and there were those of them who had been involved in violence and had been in prison for some years. If you were talking to people like Gerry Kelly, the Old Bailey bomber, you were dealing with people who, years previously, had done dreadful things, but had also sacrificed and devoted their whole life to the cause. So they were completely focused.

GS: Did they try to draw out inconsistencies between what one person was saying and another was saying?

WF: Always, and they were in tight formation. They loved dealing with Number 10, partly because of the status and going to the top, but they had access at a lot of levels and all this would be testing. They were ruthlessly focused throughout and the advantage they had with Number 10, as opposed to the NIO (and Jonathan Powell acknowledges this in his book), was that the prime minister and Jonathan, because they had so many other things to attend to, were inclined to cut to the chase. As chief of staff Jonathan had so many other things on his plate that he could be switched into something intensively for thirty minutes, or an hour or maybe a day's talks before then having to go off and sort out something else, and that gives a bit of advantage to the person who is completely focused on this as their life's cause. The point of having a governmental system is making sure that you have discipline and coherence and you do not give things away. The process had its own self-correcting mechanisms and, since the British Government's role was essentially facilitative, there was not a serious risk that we were going to go off on a frolic with one side and give them all they wanted because that would have been a ridiculous thing to do. But it did mean that sometimes on the details in the negotiations, the republicans would remorselessly keep chiselling away and would get more than perhaps they should. It is my own belief, as with the OTR's issue, that dealing with the past was unfinished business. On this Number 10 were absolutely right. But some of the promises given in those negotiations were given without the full dimensions of the issue being properly scoped out. That was pragmatism based on having to get some movement.

GS: Is there a danger of over-analysis in a situation like this, where you can find things wrong with everything?

WF: There is that danger, and that is why the strategic insight that Jonathan Powell and Tony Blair brought to it, and indeed John Major and John Holmes beforehand, were important because they did cling on to the great simplicities that we had to sustain the peace and prevent it sliding back. The key is to try to hold the big picture and the details together in a synthesis and proper tension and not let one or the other get out of balance.

GS: Do you know what the big picture looks like? You have an end goal, but is it a tentative perception?

WF: I think the end goal was always clearly pictured as being the establishment of durable institutions of government in Northern Ireland that commanded cross-community consent in a society where the rule of law applied and where those who could not accept the framework were a minority pushed to the outside. In all societies you get some people who refuse to accept the rules of the game, but you contain them. That is what we were seeking to achieve and that is pretty much what was achieved.

12 The nature of dialogue: an interview with Sir Jonathan Phillips

Interview

GS: You came into the peace process just before the collapse of the institutions in 2002. Can you give me an overview of the frantic activity that took place to try to get the institutions up and running again? How did you re-build?

JP: Although the collapse of the Executive and the institutions happened very quickly, it had also been widely predicted for many months. The initial approach was to make sure that all the parties to the process remained engaged in the search for a solution. Of course, they were principally the people who most obviously had fallen out, the Ulster Unionist Party (UUP) and Sinn Féin. There was much private dialogue in the weeks immediately following. That period also included a change of secretary of state. John Reid was moved in an unexpected Cabinet reshuffle and replaced by Paul Murphy. This was less of a dislocation than might sometimes be the case because Paul arrived with earlier experience from the Good Friday Agreement (GFA) negotiations in 1997–8. This meant that he was able to hit the ground running, engaging quickly in political discussions that necessarily had a strong Number 10 lead.

GS: In what way does private dialogue work, and does it work better than public more open dialogue?

JP: In my experience private dialogue is the context in which real progress is generally made. There are, of course, exceptions, but in general that is the case. In the autumn of 2002, in a situation in which the PIRA had not come forward with language that confirmed that the conflict was at an end and trust had broken down, the fear of many was that the whole GFA structure would unravel. So, the immediate objective was to try to find a way of restoring the political institutions, but that was not going to happen without significant progress being made on the underlying issues, such as the PIRA's continuing activity, the need for clear evidence that the conflict was being brought to an end, action on decommissioning and, from the other side, progress on the

Sinn Féin agenda, which contained many elements, from 'demilitarisation' to aspects of human rights and so on. All those topics were much better suited to private dialogue in preparation for a later public phase, which took place in the context of the Joint Declaration negotiations of 2003.

GS: How did you view Sinn Féin's negotiating strategy over the time you were dealing with then?

JP: My encounters began in 2002 shortly before the collapse of the institutions. Unsurprisingly, perhaps, their strategy seemed to be a determination to extract every possible concession out of, on the one hand, unionism and, on the other, the British Government, before making long drawn out final moves on their side to do the deal. The question might well be asked, were they engaged in a serious attempt to reach a deal with David Trimble or was there a different strategy? I found this a very difficult question to answer. I had some colleagues and people in Northern Ireland who offered a variety of different answers. However, my presumption was that in any negotiating situation you have to start by believing that at least an element of your interlocutor's real position is the explicit one and that there is an intention to try to do a deal. But the question was always lurking in the 2002–3 period of whether expressions of frustration on their part about David Trimble's leadership of the UUP was actually a long game designed to ensure that any deal they did embraced the Democratic Unionist Party (DUP)?

GS: Would you have said that they were pursuing a twin strategy of disorientating unionism as well as promoting their own position?

JP: I have no doubt whatsoever that an element of their negotiating tactics was to seek to disorientate elements within unionism, and elements within the British and Irish governments too. You see in some sense a mirror-image approach when the DUP began to get into serious negotiations with Sinn Féin and the two governments in 2004. The DUP had learned a great deal by observing Sinn Féin and used similar tactics.

GS: For republicans was this partly about moving as they went along, but within a framework of knowing where they wanted to get to?

JP: You do not need to observe, let alone be involved in, the Northern Ireland peace process for very long to realise that there was a long-term strategy. However, no set of negotiations is predictable and in terms of their response to the unpredictable, I think they reacted as almost any party in a negotiation would, sometimes opportunistically seeking advantage and taking it, and on other occasions being knocked back, or surprised or discombobulated and at a slight loss. It is impossible to fit the whole narrative into an entirely preordained framework.

GS: Were they still saying from 2002 onwards that we run the risk of being isolated from our own people if you push too fast, too soon?

JP: They were certainly saying that if we pushed too far too fast, then we increased the risk of a substantial breakaway. While that was a credible position, they were also, in my view, trying to maximise what they could get out of the other players and test how much they could use that particular lever. To take one specific example, using that argument it was clearly an objective for them to see how much they could quicken and make more substantial the process of removing British military assets from Northern Ireland and so move along the process of, in their terms, 'demilitarisation'.

GS: How did Adams and McGuinness operate as a duo?

JP: My first observation, having met each of them separately when I started working on the process and then seeing them in many, many meetings as a team, would be to focus on precisely that word – team. It seemed to me that there was rarely an opportunity to put the metaphorical cigarette paper between them. They were always very well prepared in a team sense, sometimes one playing, if you like, good cop and the other bad cop, but not always predictably in either role. So, in that sense I think they were extremely skilled and subtle negotiators who left much scope for subsequent analysis as to where perhaps there might be differences between them. But, in reality, this almost always failed to provide evidence to their interlocutors on which to base strong conclusions as to who was perhaps taking a harder line or who was willing to be more flexible in a particular circumstance.

GS: Were they quite confrontational with you, or were they considerate or did they alternate?

JP: I saw them in a variety of contexts, in a succession of private meetings with Jonathan Powell, in a set of meetings with Irish officials, in meetings with secretaries of state for NI, in meetings with prime ministers and taoiseachs, so again you are asking for an impossible generalisation. In what I would call private dialogue, in general, unless there had been a particular event that called for a statement to be made – let us say, for example, that there had been an action on the part of the Police Service of Northern Ireland (PSNI) that they regarded as unhelpful in terms of its impact on their community and that required a pretty hard-line statement of how unacceptable that behaviour was from their perspective – then, by and large, you faced people who behaved entirely professionally in terms of their dialogue in a negotiating context. Of course, if they were interacting with politicians, some of that rather more formal, what I could call grandstanding, did inevitably occur from time to time – if you went on to ask about negotiating styles, it seems to me that they had the full repertoire of techniques, sometimes hard-line, sometimes seeking to engage sympathy, sometimes condescending and so on. At the end of the day, these guys were very skilled at doing the business they had to do.

GS: Would you say that private dialogue was important in the negotiation setting in that it may have helped to build trust or assist the accommodation process?

JP: I think that was true on all sides because it allowed for explanation and exploration of where the real boundaries of difference were and the build-up of trust, and because we could be more open in private about the limits of what we could achieve from our perspective.

GS: That is very interesting because that suggests that there are almost two negotiation processes going on at once, the formal setting, but then the informal private dialogue setting where you tell people what you are really up against. Did republicans use those private moments as negotiating opportunities in that sense?

JP: Certainly there were negotiating opportunities, but I do not see them as separate, I see them as distinctly related. If you take, for example, the period in early 2003, or if you take the period in the autumn of 2004, or if you take the period following the PIRA statement on decommissioning in 2005, what I am calling the private dialogue would all be preparatory to more formal negotiating encounters. Now, it may be that while private dialogue was going on, more public political encounters would have been necessary, but not really as vital aspects of the negotiating process. Most of the process then took place in private dialogue, whether with senior officials, the prime minister, the secretary of state or our equivalents on the Irish side.

GS: Is this to do with the fact, generally speaking, that in private dialogue you do not have a team of people, but more two-on-two working, which creates intimacy and is more conducive for progress?

JP: I dare say that the small numbers involved were a positive factor. But it is also partly to do with the question of private space, in terms of sensitive discussions not being exposed to media scrutiny. That is not to cast the media in an entirely negative light in the process. From time to time, the media were helpful either by providing information, because some people used the media in that way, or because, as we both know in the Northern Ireland process, there were some very informed and skilful commentators around who were able to draw out inferences that we had not necessarily perceived. But for making progress, by and large, we were very anxious to keep the private dialogue private. After all, it was not a dialogue with one side. There were conversations with at least two sides that we hoped eventually to bring together.

GS: Does that mean then that in aiming to bring everyone together you need to use a language that is along the lines of what has been called 'constructive ambiguity', or do you use the language of the 'specific community' with the people you are talking to at that point?

JP: In private dialogue, of course, with one side you are more inclined to use language that appeals to that community. To state the blindingly obvious, you did not have a conversation with republicans and bang on about the Belfast Agreement. Conversely, if you wanted to make progress with the DUP you probably did not mention the Belfast Agreement at all. However, more significantly, when it comes to the substance of any negotiation, there is almost always an essential requirement for some degree of constructive ambiguity as you test the water and try to stretch the boundaries of established negotiating positions.

GS: Is it the case that republicans were better at thinking of terms of process and a broader framework because they saw each agreement as a stepping-stone to a bigger goal, whereas the unionists were more concerned about the literal meaning of moments?

JP: I have absolutely no doubt that republicans, for quite a long time in this process, did take a long view and, therefore, as you say, saw any particular development as a stepping-stone. Whereas for unionists, and this is necessarily a contestable generalisation, such was the insecurity and scepticism among many of them that the emphasis was very much on the particular moment and what threat or threats were posed, rather than on what opportunity for the future might be on offer. Therein lay much of David Trimble's problem. He was handicapped by voices on his own side that were not as capable of identifying or articulating a long view. I do think that the DUP leadership, with the ability to more tightly control their spokesmen (and they were, overwhelmingly, men) found that easier, and it was reflected in its negotiating approach.

GS: I am interested as to whether in Catholic/republican/nationalist thinking there is the tendency to try not to adopt hard-line rigid either/or positions in relation to moral problems, and how often moral problems are seen to be connected to a bigger notion of the community or a bigger reality. And, in contrast, whether in Protestantism the emphasis is on right or wrong, you are in or you are out, very black and white. Is there anything in these generalisations?

JP: The story has been told in print of Ian Paisley, in 2004, saying at Leeds Castle when asked by Tony Blair whether he was serious about trying to do a deal with Sinn Féin that, yes, he was, because he wanted to see Northern Ireland at peace before he met his Maker. That was very clearly in my view a reference to a personal religious positioning on the part of someone who at the time thought himself to be seriously ill and perhaps closer to the end of his life than turned out to be the case. Looked at more generally, I have little doubt that a sceptical cast of mind among unionists derived in part, at least at a broad cultural level, from religious influences and an inherited tradition of thought. That is the way I think it works, and on the unionist side it led to a greater unwillingness to accept ambiguity, though I should say that David Trimble and his closest advisers were highly sophisticated in their understanding of drafting devices. On the republican/Catholic side, I think there is also some substance in your observation. For example, when, in the autumn of 2002, Tony Blair made his famous Belfast Harbour speech and said that the time had come when ambiguity was no longer right as a matter of principle, that it was not workable and that there was a need to move beyond ambiguity into precision about whether the PIRA was inside or outside this process, it was in part a response to republicans not having faced up to the need for a real change of mindset.

GS: Traditionally, there is a powerful religious underpinning to the republican impulse, and so I am interested as to whether for republicans the peace process was as much a religious journey as a political one?

JP: On the republican side I cannot think of an occasion on which the religious dimension played out in any way explicitly in a negotiating conversation. That is not to deny your underlying thesis, but in terms of presentation the objectives and the tactics towards achieving those objectives were always, in my experience, political. Clearly, as with the 'Armalite and the ballot box', the republican leadership had lived with ambiguity for years.

GS: I remember at Hillsborough, in 2010, when Gordon Brown and Brian Cowen came out of the building and Gordon Brown said, 'we have got the detail of the agreement right', and Brian Cowen said 'we have got the spirit of the agreement right'. I thought this was an interesting difference between the Scottish Presbyterian emphasis on the literal and the Irish Catholic notion of context or framework.

JP: They were both into the detail as I recall, though it is perfectly reasonable to observe that they were different personalities and Gordon Brown absorbed detail like a sponge. The truth is that in the course of negotiations of that kind there has to be a huge focus on the detail, whether or not the intention is to be as clear as possible or to paper over differences with the constructive ambiguity to which you have referred. Detail is important in other ways. In 2003, for example, Sinn Féin came up with a very long negotiating agenda on many aspects of which we had not previously developed positions. While one might see that as a negotiating device, rather than necessarily a long list of firm negotiating demands, the fact is that once something is on the table it actually becomes quite difficult to withdraw it, even if at a later stage you think that it is not needed because the main prize has been secured. If there is a person in the team who needs to be kept on board, but who is attached to an outcome in relation to what may be a trivial issue in the grand scheme of things, then that trivial outcome has to be delivered. That, of course, applies to all parties. You can see that I am being very cautious about giving examples!

GS: Can you take me through the reaction to the Northern Bank robbery and the murder of Robert McCartney and how Sinn Féin tried to explain their way out of those events?

JP: Jonathan Powell's book (2008) talks about how he and I were travelling to a private meeting with Gerry Adams and Martin McGuinness at Clonard, the monastery in West Belfast, and I received a phone call telling us that the chief constable was attributing this massive bank robbery to the PIRA. We were horrified because, potentially, it called into question a great deal of the trust that had been built up on our side as to the good intentions of the senior Sinn Féin negotiators. But, as Jonathan's book records, we continued with the meeting as arranged. Gerry Adams and Martin McGuinness were in complete denial about responsibility and, in a certain sense, one would have expected nothing else. My own view is that they remained in a certain amount of denial about the impact of that event despite its remaining pretty high in terms of public profile. Apart from anything else, the actions taken to withdraw the Northern Bank notes from circulation meant that this was not an issue that was quickly submerged by other stories. The McCartney murder and the subsequent clean-up operation, which most media commentators attributed to members of the PIRA, was, I think, still more powerful in its impact. A key moment was the refusal of senator Ted Kennedy to see the republican leadership during the St Patrick's Day celebrations in Washington. That signalled a very strong message to republicans in Ireland that a degree of ambiguity, which had been accepted by some of their supporters in Irish America, even after 9/11, had now disappeared. There are two other things to be said about that period. The first is that it was not one in which significant negotiating progress was being made. The second, a related point, is that the process of private dialogue was pretty thin in the early part of 2005. But the messages were very clear from the prime minister, the taoiseach, the secretary of state, the Irish foreign minister, officials, etc., that there had to be a final transition to exclusively peaceful means, because, without it, there was no possibility of a dialogue with unionism.

GS: Looking back on it, do you regret that after the bank robbery you went to meet them? Why did you not refuse to meet them and let them wait on that?

JP: Jonathan Powell and I were in agreement that it was the right thing to do because, first, although we had that preliminary assessment from the chief constable, we had no information that morning as to the particular involvement of the Sinn Féin leadership. Moreover, we had judged that the progress that we had made in negotiations during the autumn of 2004 needed somehow to be protected and sustained for the future, and that was certainly not going to be assisted by keeping away. It was conceivable to us that the shutters might come down in terms of contact for a period if there was a very clear attribution of responsibility to very senior republicans, but we still had the same task we had before the robbery, which was how on earth devolution might be brought back to Northern Ireland on a stable basis. That challenge remained.

GS: So that was partly driven by what has been referred to as the 'bicycle theory', which is where you have to keep the thing moving and that it is actually counter-productive to stop because at that stage things were quite far advanced?

JP: Yes, the 'bicycle theory' was a factor. And, again, as in past episodes of the peace process, we might have had to deal with the possibility of any acknowledged public dialogue being suspended while some private contact remained.

GS: Do you think that for Adams and McGuinness the Northern Bank robbery and the murder of McCartney enabled them to make the case even more strongly, given the public reaction, for decommissioning?

JP: The counter-factual stuff is all very difficult. What would have happened if ... ? How much longer could this have dragged on? We could speculate endlessly on that. Certainly, the combination of those two events was cathartic, and, certainly, as it had become clear from the negotiations in the autumn of 2004, real and substantial decommissioning was a prerequisite of progress from a DUP point of view. How long would it have taken to get to that point if there had not been a sequence of cathartic events? Almost certainly, quite a bit longer.

GS: Can you expand on the shift in American thinking after 9/11?

JP: It is generally acknowledged that 9/11 did see a shift in American thinking, and particularly Irish-American thinking, about the Northern Ireland conflict. During my time there was no doubt whatsoever that the US Government had reached a very clear position that the ongoing levels of paramilitary activity in Northern Ireland were unacceptable and had to stop as an essential precondition to making political progress. As presidential envoy, Richard Haass made very clear that was his government's view. My own observation remains that the Northern Bank robbery and the McCartney murder had an impact in the wider Irish-American community that was very important in influencing significant individuals like senator Kennedy to catch up with the notion that ambiguity was no longer tolerable, and that real pressure had to be exerted on republicans to make the final transition.

GS: How does one apply leverage in these situations? Is it through persuasion or mild threat as well?

JP: Do you mean from the perspectives of the governments?

GS: Yes, particularly after the Northern Bank robbery and the McCartney murder.

JP: First, I do not look at the negotiating process as a sequence of threats being made by or on behalf of the government. It is a process, of course, in which one tries to influence, tries to seize opportunities and tries to give incentive to movement, and creating incentives may, of course, contain negative as well as positive elements. What do I mean by that? If we take the key issue of decommissioning, it is abundantly clear to me that this had to be accompanied on the British Government side by movement to reduce the military presence. The pace and scope of that process was clearly a negotiating lever, linked to progress being made towards reducing the level of paramilitary activity. And, the greater the commitment to the reduction of the military presence, arguably the greater the chance that this would happen.

GS: And yet it is difficult to ascertain, is it not, why decommissioning took place at the time it did. And that if there had not been a bank robbery and a murder Sinn Féin might have dragged it out even longer?

JP: It is very difficult to say. My guess is that without the really profound effect of those two incidents in combination on external opinion, and not least Irish-American opinion, the process would have taken longer. Whether that would have been months or years longer I do not know, but certainly significantly longer than it did.

GS: When did you first hear that decommissioning was going to happen?

JP: It was part of the package when the PIRA made their statement about bringing the conflict to an end in 2005. When that statement was made, and when the British and Irish governments responded very positively to it, it was clearly part of our expectation, not in the form of a written agreement, but in the form of oral exchanges with Sinn Féin, that decommissioning would follow. We were unable to put a precise timescale on that and we were not told that it would happen by date x, but there was a clear expectation that it would happen in a short timescale, and then, of course, immediately after the statement from the PIRA, contacts were intensified between representatives of the PIRA and the Independent International Commission on Decommissioning (IICD), which began to set what became the September timetable.

GS: Choreography was obviously a crucial part of the peace process, but what about when choreography goes wrong, such as when John de Chastelain did not quite make the case for decommissioning and David Trimble said I cannot accept this? How do you deal with that and how did Sinn Féin react to it?

JP: You have chosen a good example of the choreography breaking down. A pretty immediate consequence of the failed Hillsborough press conference was an election in Northern Ireland, in November 2003. The outcome of that election, as it turned out, was that David Trimble no longer had a majority among unionists. We thought as the parties went into the election that was a plausible outcome, but it was not a certainty by any means. From a republican perspective, you could see it as an opportunity to ensure that the unionists who had so far stayed outside the 1998 framework were drawn into negotiation on the basis that, without their participation, there could be no certainty that the devolution to which they were committing would be stable. That is, as I said earlier, a perfectly plausible interpretation. And the British Government responded by dealing with the reality and working hard to establish effective relationships with the DUP leadership that would pave the way for their entry into negotiations. The emollience of the secretary of state of the time, Paul Murphy, was very helpful in that particular regard.

GS: Sinn Féin always seemed more considered on the symbolism of reaction. I recall the ceasefire of 1994 where the first thing they did was to make sure that the cavalcade of cars, the celebration of horns, made the ceasefire look a success. I recall, too, when the media were outside castle buildings during the build-up to the GFA and the unionists were coming in front of the cameras and saying how badly things were going, essentially giving their own community the impression that they were losing control. Sinn Féin did not really do that, they walked around the car park smiling and the cameras picked that up, and the message was that they were in control. I suppose that shows quite a considerable difference of sophistication in terms of knowing how to use the media and not revealing negatives. Did Sinn Féin maintain this ethos of control under questioning as well?

JP: Most conversations in the room were not conversations that were being rehearsed for the media. So I think one can say that in most cases, the simple answer to that question is, no. On the other hand, Sinn Féin were very well controlled as negotiators. The subtlety in the question is, perhaps, that Sinn Féin did, because of their history going back almost to the beginning of the Troubles, but certainly from the early 1980s, have a sophistication in terms of their handling of the media that unionists have developed only very recently and by close observation of Sinn Féin in the political world. And I think it has to be said that they have learned very, very effectively, and one has seen some significant unionist successes in media relations in the last few years.

GS: Did they reveal to you the problems they were having with the Army Council or the PIRA body?

JP: Therein lies one of the biggest questions for self-examination on the part of anyone who has been involved at the heart of the peace process. The best answer I can give you is that on some occasions there is no doubt whatsoever that this external authority was being used in textbook negotiating style; the reference point that could usefully be hinted at to indicate that something could not or would not be done. On other occasions, I think it was a genuine reflection of the reality. A good example of that is the discussions that took place in the autumn of 2004 around decommissioning. There was a demand from Ian Paisley and the DUP for the act of decommissioning, or the completion of the process of decommissioning, to be the subject of photographic evidence, physical proof if you like. Some of us might have wondered, in terms of modern technology, what the value of the photograph was, but that was the demand. And I can well remember Jonathan Powell in private conversations talking to Gerry Adams and Martin McGuinness about the need for a photograph and observing huge scepticism on their part about the deliverability. It would be perfectly possible to interpret that as a negotiating response, but I think it actually reflected the real position. Hence, eventually, the agreement that there should be two witnesses, one chosen by each side, to accompany the IICD.

GS: Do you think that republicans are better at dealing with defeat because of the sacrifice and martyrdom philosophy that is built into their tradition, which seems to find glory in defeat and uses it as a part of an impetus to drive on? As well as viewing defeat in a context that is always part of a much bigger context and reality?

JP: At a general level there is some truth in the notion that a particular defeat at a point in time, whether on the military level or the political level, can be absorbed, since it is a stage in a longer process and that goes back to your earlier question. Unreasonable and unacceptable though it is, that is actually part of the language that so-called 'dissident' republicans have continued to use. So I think there is some substance in your analytical point. My perception of the way Gerry Adams and Martin McGuinness negotiated was, as I said earlier, that they used a whole variety of techniques. Those techniques certainly encompassed the long history, the 800-year history, as well as the more immediate history of the process. That history was engaged in many circumstances, even to grind the other side into submission. But, then, for either side it was perfectly reasonable to want to ensure that those like me and my colleagues who were outsiders actually had a decent understanding of the respective cultures, traditions and aspirations. Occasionally, that could become patronising. I recall one occasion in a conversation about a parade that Gerry Adams immediately seized on my use of the term 'the Ardoyne' as opposed to 'Ardoyne', and cited it as a significant indicator of my uninformed British standpoint. Candidly, my linguistic ignorance made not a jot of difference to my desire to see a resolution to the regular conflicts in that particular neighbourhood. It is a trivial example that illustrates the bigger point.

GS: Can you elaborate how you thought Sinn Féin operated at a strategic level?

JP: Slowly, carefully and taking care to ensure that relevant internal constituencies moved with the leadership might be one answer to a question that raises many issues. Decommissioning, one of the biggest strategic issues in the process, may help to illustrate my answer. The history of the various decommissioning events, including the one to which you referred earlier in 2003, is well known. It was obviously a difficult issue for both Sinn Féin and the PIRA. It was also an issue that was highly significant tactically for them in terms of the moment they would choose in order to allow the process, and therefore the broader political process, to be completed. The actual endgame in relation to decommissioning took the better part of a year, between the negotiations that took place in the autumn of 2004 and the final and complete act of decommissioning, which took place in September 2005. As I mentioned earlier, during that 2004 negotiating season, the DUP, and Ian Paisley in particular, articulated very clearly their position that there had to be photographs of the eventual decommissioning act, perhaps even a video, in order to provide, from their perspective, credible evidence, even beyond the IICD, that it had actually happened. It took a long time for republicans to internalise that this was an issue that would not go away and to find a compromise in the form of two independent witnesses, one Protestant churchman and one Catholic priest attending alongside the de Chastelain team. The external influences brought to bear in this are pretty obvious: the DUP's oft-repeated position and the British Government's equally often stated view that at least a photograph would be required, because our judgement was that that was going to be the minimum requirement of the DUP. I cannot describe in detail the internal processes of the republican movement, but I am reasonably sure that careful consultation was a key part of the approach.

GS: To what extent was your own judgement of decommissioning shaped by what Adams and McGuinness were saying to you, and to what extent was it shaped by the security feedback you were getting?

JP: We had the statement about bringing the conflict to an end, and then, of course, it was a relatively short period until the September 2005 final act of decommissioning. It was not so much a question of keeping in touch or having security input, since we had a clear expectation following the PIRA statement that made clear that the conflict was at an end, that it would happen. It was obvious to Sinn Féin that it had to happen before really serious negotiations got under way with the DUP, and so I do not think that in that period the answer to your question is especially illuminating.

GS: Would it be fair to say that if you had not had the decommissioning problem to deal with you could have got a lot further and a lot quicker?

JP: It is perfectly plausible to say, with the benefit of hindsight, that if the decommissioning issue had been dealt with upfront in 1998, then a whole host of the problems that occurred subsequently could have been dealt with more easily. But you would have to make the even larger assumption that the GFA could actually have been achieved with none of the ambiguity that we both know surrounded its references to decommissioning.

GS: In the end was it a question of building the expectation that is what was going to happen and then it happened quickly?

JP: I think in the end that is right. If you take a comparative period in 2003 covering the negotiations and discussions around the Joint Declaration, it was a firm expectation that decommissioning would have to accompany any PIRA statement about the conflict (in some choreographed form), but in the absence of achieving an adequate formula from the PIRA signalling the end of the conflict, we did not get into the further discussions at that stage of how decommissioning might follow.

GS: I suppose one of the things is that once they have made a decision to decommission they need to do it fast because the longer it is dragged out the greater the risk of internal friction?

JP: I think that could have been a factor in 2005.

GS: Were Sinn Féin saying such things?

JP: I do not recall them saying that, but if I had been in their shoes it would not have been a comment I would have made in the context of negotiations. You would want to keep the whole issue as mysterious and apparently difficult as possible. But I think what you say is probably right.

GS: Yes, but you did not keep it as mysterious as possible with them did you?

JP: They needed clarity and, as I implied earlier, the prime minister's Belfast Harbour speech in the autumn of 2002 was very telling in that regard. The message was that ambiguity was no longer acceptable, not just because it was not right, but because it simply would not work anymore. So, whatever ambiguities there had been in the government's position before then, and there certainly had been some, I think that in the period afterwards and for most of the time I was engaged we were trying to make sure that we were clear as to what the bottom lines were. That does not mean, of course, that you do not continue to strive to find a formula that brings different positions closer together. Inevitably, there is an element of ambiguity in that kind of drafting, but in terms of the expression of positions, privately I think that we were making it pretty clear as to what the requirements were.

GS: Principle or pragmatism?

JP: It is a mixture of both. There are some givens, so if you say in a peace process a principle is the assertion of the rule of law, then that principle stands, notwithstanding all the history that is now being drawn to our attention about alleged acts of collusion. On the other hand, you have to have willing partners in order to take the process forward, and identifying willing partners will not be successful unless you are pragmatic.

GS: Would you say that the principle of a commitment to exclusively peaceful means was applied to punishment beatings as much as it was to weaponry? In other words, was there a difference in attitude to some forms of violence compared with others?

JP: Decommissioning needs to be looked at separately and, as you have suggested, it is an underlying theme. In my view, it was a great pity that it took on the prominence that it did. To make a point made over and over again by many commentators on the peace process, what was the significance of decommissioning? It was a signal of intention. That is to say, an intention not to engage in further acts of violence. But the reality was that if that intention changed it would be pretty easy to go and re-acquire weaponry. So, logic suggests to me that the real emphasis should have been more firmly on activity and punishment beatings, and so on. I think it is fair to say that by 2002 there was a very strong unionist focus on activity, because when I came to the role there was very considerable pressure to establish what I think was first called a 'peace monitor', but that, by the end of the negotiations around the Joint Declaration, became the Independent Monitoring Commission (IMC). And once that was established by legislation and got into its stride by 2004, the focus of its work was a comprehensive review of all the categories of violent activity. That did reflect a real level of anxiety in the unionist community, as well as an occasional and convenient tactical judgement on their part that it was helpful to draw attention to violence that was, in many in cases, intra-community as a reason for delaying political progress.

GS: On the point of exclusively peaceful means, did Sinn Féin try to take that apart and reconstruct what 'exclusively' might mean and what 'peaceful' might mean?

JP: I do not recall conversations of a semantic kind about what exclusively and peaceful meant. I recall lots of conversations around the fact that there was ongoing violence, some of which Sinn Féin would contest in terms of the attribution of responsibility and the distinction between paramilitary and criminal activity. And then there was a significant conversation related to that distinction in terms of our view that Sinn Féin had to face up to the prospect of showing support for the normal processes of police investigation and judicial consideration. And that led into specific questions about when Sinn Féin would come on board the policing reforms and support the PSNI and the Policing Board.

GS: How much latitude did you have when talking to these people? Were you heavily constrained by policy objectives or were you allowed to 'freewheel' to some extent?

JP: I would not quite characterise it that way. I would say 'we' were constrained by a set of realistic judgements about what it was practicable to achieve and what it was likely that we could persuade the other side to accept. Those were the constraints and, of course, in any negotiation if you are operating in relation to the minister or prime minister, then you are obviously operating within a control framework. In relation to Tony Blair and Gordon Brown, this was a team effort in which those like me reporting up to the prime minister were conscious of what the approach was. As said, that approach was a necessary mixture of principle and pragmatism, and if you know your boss in any context his or her willingness to accommodate more or less radical ideas is something that just becomes part of your own application of judgement to a dialogue.

GS: If you have a big problem is the best way to deal with it to break it down into a number of smaller problems? Make progress on different areas and come back?

JP: To pick up one point before going back to the main question, I do think a distraction technique is often helpful if you are getting locked into fundamentally opposed positions. Then, leave it, try something else, and if you can get movement there then come back to the other thing. On the main question, it is a bit of both. You have to keep focused on a main objective, so if we go back to the autumn of 2002 and early 2003 we had critical and interlinked objectives to put pressure on to reduce the level of violent activity and to make progress on the restoration of the political institutions. And within those strategic objectives there were a myriad of things that required attention relating to the ongoing implementation of aspects of the GFA.

GS: If you get a big problem do you think it is useful to have the same conversation over and over again to make very marginal gains on dealing with it? And is it through an accumulation of those marginal gains that one is able to achieve some significant movement?

JP: I think that is at the core of it, which is why one of Tony Blair's great contributions to this process was the patience he brought to bear in seeking those small step-by-step shifts. Listen carefully, very subtly move the position being articulated by one or other party, and then perhaps have officials produce a written statement of where some middle ground might be identified, using that written statement to try to achieve a further shift. And the value of that approach was that if the immediate response from the parties was negative, the prime minister could say that maybe officials had not captured the positions quite correctly and that it would be as well to start again. And then, through patient persistence and possibly with the introduction of some external factor like a telephone call from Washington you could finally move from an original starting point to a final conclusion.

GS: Was it ever discussed in advance that however well or badly a meeting went you were going to drop in a particular point for the participants to ponder afterwards? Or was it more a case of seeing how it went and making as much progress as possible until the next time?

JP: I am sure that happened from time to time. Of course, we had conversations about how we would try to run a meeting but on most occasions predicting how a conversation would turn out was extremely difficult. For example, we might be very clear that we wanted to cover a, b and c in a particular session, but one party or another might come in with a completely different set of priorities and quite a large part of the conversation would become an attempt to reconcile those different agendas.

GS: When you were in dialogue was it sheets of paper everywhere, or was the engagement reasonably relaxed and actually quite informal?

JP: A lot of the dialogue was reasonably relaxed and free flowing. On other occasions we were necessarily considering texts. And then there were set-piece engagements, where both sides would bring in larger teams of people and, once you are in a forum where both the British and Irish governments are involved, then inevitably the conversations take on a slightly greater degree of formality. But certainly the conversations would have been taken on the basis of reasonable trust, and I must say that there was reasonable trust between most of the people with whom I was in dialogue during my period of involvement. And by reasonable trust, I mean their good faith as negotiators. It is important to draw a distinction here, in the sense that no Irish republican is going to trust a British official, as Martin McGuinness once memorably made clear to Peter Hain shortly after he became secretary of state, but good faith can still exist and is important in relationships with negotiating partners.

GS: With regard to the private dialogues, can you remember how they helped to alter text? Can you, to put it slightly differently, think of a direct shift to the formal process of text construction that came out of a private dialogue?

JP: The answer to that is, 'on many occasions'. To take a relatively straightforward example, when we were drafting the documents that set out the structure and objectives of the IMC that was something that the UUP wanted to see established with a certain framework and it was something to which, in principle, republicans were predictably very hostile. I do not think it needs much imagination to appreciate that as you have a conversation with one side you see the need to strengthen text in relation to the other and vice versa, if you are to get some kind of agreement.

GS: Can you tell me what difference it made both to the republicans and unionists to take them out of Northern Ireland to somewhere like Leeds Castle in 2004? Why did you take them there and what difference did such a location make?

JP: I suppose the view was that in getting them on to neutral territory no party would be able to claim some additional strength from feeling more at home than another. Then there was the classic away-day mindset; such locations might generate more flexible thinking and there was also an element of theatre, including a notional end to the particular performance. I must say that personally I began to wonder over time whether this was overly indulgent to individuals who sought to grandstand at and around events. However, that said, I would be hard pushed to argue that it was an ineffective approach given the progress made at, for example, St Andrews in 2006. I might then compare that with the two weeks that we spent in Hillsborough and Stormont in January/February 2010, that is, on home territory so to speak, to deal with what at the end of the day were rather less extensive issues concerned with the devolution of justice and policing. Three days against nearly fourteen. I have to admit that there may be more to be said in favour of taking negotiators away from their comfort zones than I like to admit. One of the strongest points in justification of St Andrews, or Weston Park, or Leeds Castle or, indeed, to a lesser extent Hillsborough, was the ability to get the parties in a location from which they could not 'escape'. And because they simply could not take time out to try to wriggle out of an emerging conclusion that they did not like.

GS: Did you have trouble getting them to such places?

JP: I do not think so. It may be that the DUP was less enthusiastic, but I do not recall a great deal of resistance to it.

GS: And did they behave differently in such places?

JP: What was important was to create a context that was apparently constrained by time and that kept people in the same location.

GS: There was no big strategic thinking behind such a move then, it was more of a case of trying out different places to see if they are advantageous or not?

JP: I would not call it strategic thinking. The whole history of this goes back to Sunningdale, and the idea of getting parties off-site is a tested device in many conflict zones across the world – to move people, as I have said, into a neutral space.

GS: How did Sinn Féin try to use timetables laid down by the two governments, and how did the DUP and unionists more generally react to the Army presence being wound down?

JP: Certainly, for Sinn Féin it was presented as an absolute requirement that the various elements of the Army presence, from watchtowers to bases, should be removed. Then, for us, there was a need to build into that consideration the remaining security requirements. One could proceed in that regard only in the light of advice from the general officer commanding (GOC) and the chief constable in relation to what the requirements were on the ground. So you have already, if you like, two dynamics going on: the direct negotiation with Sinn Féin about what their demands were and then the tension, on the one hand, the security requirements as presented by the chief constable and the GOC and, on the other, the need of those involved in the political negotiations to be able to show as much ankle as possible. That in practice had something of an air of negotiation about it, too. Then there is the other dimension that you mention, the impact, in terms of their confidence, on unionists realising that the security presence is being wound down. And that, too, takes on an element of negotiation with the UUP or the DUP. Unsurprisingly, representations were made to the effect that if you proposed to do such and such at that speed before there was clear evidence of a real commitment to the ending of the conflict and/or decommissioning, then you had a third strand to the negotiation which was quite tricky to handle.

GS: Were you always willing to talk about anything or were you receptive to the possibility that sometimes talking could make the process of negotiation more ambiguous than it should be by complicating the mix, stalling or holding positions?

JP: In general, and always under instruction ultimately from the prime minister, we were prepared to carry on talking about anything for as long as it took. As in any such conversation, there were points at which it was quite clear neither side was prepared, at least in a particular time window, to make any shift. So someone might say, well I think we have exhausted that so there is no point in carrying on the conversation, and as in any context you have to acknowledge that.

GS: One of the things, if you think about the process in terms of the GFA being somewhat ambiguous, was that as the process went on it became apparent that more detail and clarity would be needed. Did that shift suit the unionists more than the republicans?

JP: There is more in the unionist Presbyterian, non-conformist mindset that prefers clarity rather than ambiguity, as you suggested earlier. And history suggests that republicans in particular used the GFA's ambiguities for all they were worth for a number of years, but, overall, I do not think that I would characterise a shift away from ambiguity as being more beneficial to one side than the other. As I said earlier, one observation that can be made about the DUP's approach to negotiating with Sinn Féin, indirectly in the first instance, is that they had observed from the outside over a number of years a different style of negotiating and they came into the process in 2004 determined not to make concessions unless they were satisfied that there was sufficient clarity from their perspective. I suppose that at a conceptual level you can describe that as squeezing ambiguity out of the system.

GS: Sinn Féin was able to sell the GFA as a gain and the unionists presented it as a loss. How often did you find yourself having to deal with these psychological differences over what agreement meant?

JP: There were quite a number of occasions when, whether in negotiations or in presenting the outcome of the negotiations to their respective community, unionists were less secure in their own identity, and that is a well-recognised phenomenon at the heart of the problems in the division of Ireland. An aspect of the British Government's role, and indeed the Irish Government's too, was to offer reassurance around the areas of ambiguity and the nervousness that existed in both communities about the good faith of their opponents.

GS: Were the British inclined to prefer clarity in their negotiating style, and was that style built more on a desire for outcomes in truth?

JP: I certainly would not like to attempt a conversation about the British negotiators in my period or in other periods in terms of their religious commitment or values if that is what you are focusing on. During my time members of the team were from several faith backgrounds and none. People in the British team came at it bringing their own very different experiences to bear. In the years before I came to these negotiations, I had been very focused on organisational change within the public sector, the privatisation and the restructuring of state activities. That had required a project-based approach: what is the objective?; what is the timescale?; what are the risks?; how are we measuring up to our timetable and the achievement of particular objectives? In other words, an approach less prone to ambiguity. My earlier immersion in Irish history did give me a very considerable sense of why we were where we were, and why we were not dealing with a forty-year period of violence, but a much longer history – Gerry Adams and I agreed on one particular occasion that we, 'the Brits', were being blamed for 800 years of history on the island of Ireland, and that, of course, was a serious point.

GS: Did Sinn Féin talk to you about a socialist united Ireland?

JP: No, is the simple answer to that. There were occasions when you could infer a socialist agenda, but most of our constitutional discussions did not stray into policy territory of that kind.

GS: Did they keep talking about a united Ireland?

JP: In the period in which I was involved, in private discussion no, but, of course, everybody knew that that was the underlying long-term goal. By that time they had accepted that the framework in which we were negotiating was the GFA, so a lot of the broader constitutional stuff was taken for granted. Towards the end of the time that I was involved, the language was switching to a formula that I still see being used and perhaps being used with the intention that it should become more part of the standard script, which is that in Sinn Féin's perception the British Government should become persuaders in favour of Irish unity. I do not see that happening!

GS: In 2003, Blair is said to have put three questions: Does the PIRA intend to end all its activities? Will the PIRA put all arms beyond use? And will the PIRA state final closure of the conflict? How did Sinn Féin handle those three points in the sense of did they ignore them, or did they handle them individually, or did they handle them collectively or did they try to blur them?

JP: There was a tendency to treat decommissioning as a separate issue, but, as far as the other two are concerned, they did tend to get wrapped up together and blurred. The period from the Joint Declaration at the beginning of April to the early summer of 2003 was dominated by a succession of attempts to get the language right. We did talk then about squeezing ambiguity and getting commitments into a form that would be acceptable to the two governments, unionists and also the Americans, who were quite heavily involved. They, of course, said in relation to any of the issues you raised and others that it would be difficult or impossible to achieve x, y or z, but I never saw that as a refusal to engage.

GS: Are there any examples where a relatively hard-line position at some point then became malleable, and, if so, what enabled it to become malleable?

JP: I think an interesting example of that comes right at the end of the process, that is to say, the negotiations surrounding the devolution of justice and policing. One issue that was seriously difficult at the late stage, the end of 2009 and early 2010, was the regulatory framework surrounding parading. Indeed, it has remained so subsequently and despite substantial earlier, private discussions following on from the review Peter Hain initiated by bringing in Lord Ashdown which suggested otherwise. Sinn Féin's position when we engaged at Hillsborough at the end of January 2010 was that it would be impossible for them to adopt any position that involved the abolition of the Parades Commission. It was only in the middle of the negotiations at Hillsborough Castle that they were manoeuvred into adopting a more flexible stance. They made a significant concession and, within the space of a fortnight, the overall deal was done so that there was agreement on the substance and timing of the devolution of justice and policing. But the implementation of the element covering parades required legislation to be taken through the Northern Ireland Assembly after the devolution of justice and policing powers had taken place. At that point, the Agreement at Hillsborough about parading unravelled and at the date of this interview in 2013 there remains no agreement, though we might hope that the American diplomat Richard Haass will find one. That episode is interesting because Sinn Féin and the SDLP regarded the Parades Commission as a very important part of the framework and were not prepared to see it sacrificed. On the other side, for the DUP, reflecting in its position the strong view of the Orange Order, the abolition of the Parades Commission and its replacement by a different framework was a key requirement without which they could not possibly do a wider deal. And yet they did reach what turned out to be a temporary agreement enabling the negotiations to reach a successful conclusion. What was going on? One interpretation might be that in reality both the DUP and Sinn Féin actually wanted the devolution of justice and policing to be agreed before the forthcoming British general election on the financially advantageous terms that had been agreed with the Treasury and, with that larger objective in view, were willing to accept the risk that the parading element of the Agreement would unravel.

GS: So it was not a situation or a moment where Sinn Féin, for example, if they wanted to bend on an issue or move, would use someone like Mitchel McLaughlin to say something marginally different from Adams and McGuinness in order to explore a possibility and then kind of retreat back after?

JP: I think Sinn Féin did play slightly different tunes, on different instruments, at different hours of the day or night, in order to confuse or try to elicit reactions that would illuminate their understanding of their opponents' positions. That is a negotiating skill that is widely deployed. We did spend much time pondering whether what we had heard from Gerry Kelly, for example, was precisely what we had heard from Martin McGuinness or Gerry Adams, and whether there was any significance to be attached to the difference. The same would be true in relation to our discussions with members of other parties. As I have said before, however, one of the most striking elements of the Adams and McGuinness approach, and all those who were part of their top team, was the extent to which there was usually a clear script that everyone was not only signed up to, but well rehearsed in and able to articulate. Over time, the DUP became practised at doing the same thing. The UUP and the SDLP, in my experience, found it much harder to achieve the same consistency.

GS: One of the things that I have heard said is that the peace process was over in 2010. But if that is so, then perhaps the question is who won or lost? But both parties continue to talk about the peace process as if it is still in motion. What is your view on that?

JP: First of all, with any peace process one of the objectives has to be achieving reconciliation across divided communities. In Northern Ireland that is very, very far from over despite progress at the political level in terms of people working together. There are many signs of communities remaining divided, segregated. It would also have been desirable for the two dominant parties to adopt and then implement a strategy for a shared future. One recognises that there are some very difficult issues to be grappled with in this context, which include trying to find common ground on dealing with the legacy of the conflict, and, in my view, taking bold steps to bring divided communities together through much more integrated education. That's one dimension. Second, is the ideological conflict over? I do not think it is for many republicans because the ambition to achieve a united Ireland remains. And if it is not over for republicans, then it is not over for unionists either since at a certain level their insecurity remains. Then there is a third element, which is at what point will it be necessary to make changes to the political structures around power-sharing? As we know, to use a term not widely used outside academia, the consociational model is designed for circumstances in which you are trying to bring divided communities together, but it is hardly a perfect form of democratic engagement. I would not like to predict a timescale in which there will be significant changes in the constitutional framework in Northern Ireland, but, since some of the parties and the British Government have already raised the possibility, I think the likelihood is that at some point there will be an engagement that will be described as a continuation of the process. Put simply, however much we might wish it were otherwise, the ending of a conflict always leaves hanging threads of greater or lesser significance. In Northern Ireland, they are of huge significance.

GS: On the one hand, you could say that the Sinn Féin project could always keep rolling on because the utopia of a united Ireland is always out of reach. On the other hand, if they do not make political progress or they come up against serious political obstruction, they are going to run into some serious problems because how can you maintain the illusion or the image of political progress when more than 30 per cent of Catholics now want Northern Ireland's status to stay as it is?

JP: Sinn Féin's position in the North and its need to articulate very loudly an ideology objective around unification depends, to a certain extent, on what progress it makes in the South. If it could achieve a position in which it was in coalition in both parts of Ireland that would make for a compelling narrative. I do not want to speculate on the longer term, not least because I think there is a range of other factors that need to be borne in mind: the relationship of the United Kingdom with the European Union; Scotland's relationship with the rest of the United Kingdom; the economy and so on.

GS: Clearly, the conflict had come to a stalemated situation where the British could not defeat the PIRA and the PIRA could not defeat the British. One could ask how this was known, but I am more interested in the idea of the stalemate in the context of negotiations and how you moved the protagonists away from that position.

JP: I would first of all begin by saying that from the perspectives of the governments it was always a central motivating factor that the conflict had to be brought to a resolution in order to save lives. That was the fundamental and it was a powerful motivator. Did we ever reach stalemate or, if I can use a different word, did we reach an impasse that looked as though it was insurmountable? Actually, I would say, yes. In the autumn of 2002 the institutions collapsed and on the day that happened the future looked very bleak indeed. Likewise, around the period of the Northern Bank robbery and the McCartney murder, it was not instantly obvious that this was going to have the transformative effect about which I have spoken before. That became clear only with hindsight. But, if I may relate the 'bicycle theory' to the impasse, the point is that it is vitally important in the perception of the parties in a conflict that there seems to be a prospect of some progress. In 2002 and late 2004, it looked as if Sinn Féin's commitment to the ongoing political dialogue would weaken and that, I think, would have been catastrophic. Those who have been combatants need to be continually encouraged to believe that there is a prospect of real political progress that might take them towards their goals and see that it is the path of negotiations that can facilitate such progress.

GS: Presumably, though, a lot of people have to lose their lives on both sides before dialogue begins, because if one side thinks it can defeat the other why would it want dialogue? Unpalatable though this may sound, is it not the case that to reach a stalemate there has to be a lot of suffering first in order to make people see that they cannot win and that the most they can expect is to go into negotiations as equal partners on that basis?

JP: Your observations bring to my mind a real hesitation I have about the transferability of lessons from one conflict zone to another. If we just focus on Northern Ireland, the sad fact is, to recall Seamus Mallon, that the GFA was 'Sunningdale for slow learners', and I think that is one of the most insightful observations made throughout the period of the Troubles.

GS: But there is a key difference, which is in 1972–4 the PIRA thought they could win. Of course, Sunningdale should have been the beginning of the end, but it was not because the circumstances and conditions were not right at that point.

JP: You are certainly right to point out the importance of context and conditions, but, without going into a debate with you about that earlier history, the PIRA were only one of the players in that period. So you have to consider what may have happened if unionists and moderate nationalists had actually come together then and formed a power-sharing government, which might have been more advantageous to unionists than the GFA.

GS: Are you are in agreement with Jonathan Powell that one must always talk with terrorists?

JP: I certainly hold that view in the context of Northern Ireland – and other conflict zones – where there is a clear set of objectives expressed by the combatants, since that provides the basis for a dialogue. My slight hesitation is in relation to conflicts where it is far from clear that there are objectives that can be reduced to meaningful political aspirations to which it is possible to offer any rational response.

GS: There has been some recent speculation that the peace process has started to run out of process and that the parties are getting stuck. Do you think the two governments left the stage too soon? And do you think that dealing with the legacy of conflict requires a sense of process that should be externally driven rather than left to the main parties in Northern Ireland?

JP: I do not think the governments left the stage too soon because the fact is there was no prospect of real political progress in Northern Ireland until powers were devolved back to Northern Ireland's politicians, and that applies both to devolution in 2007 and the devolution of justice and policing powers in 2010. However, I think you can question whether either government has stayed close enough in the period since. I am going to use the theatre as a metaphor, so if the criticism is that the governments left the stage too soon as actors in 2007 or 2010, I do not accept that. They had to, as I have just indicated. The governments needed to get off the stage. But, since you are fond of counter-factuals, I do wonder whether in a drama with inexperienced actors the presence of stronger promptings from off-stage might have helped to ease the way. In fairness, there has been a good deal of that kind of intervention and it is obvious that promptings are of little use if the actors pay insufficient attention to them!

GS: Talk now is about a peace and reconciliation, or truth and reconciliation, process. What are the problems attached to such ideas, and do you think either is going to happen?

JP: I would like to hope that there could be an agreed way forward, but I think it remains very hard to imagine because the generations involved in the conflict will find it immensely difficult to agree the terms. Part of the explanation is the perceived problem of inequality in any process, with certainly some of the state actors subjected to rather more scrutiny than at least one of the non-state actors, namely, the PIRA, and I think that is a major stumbling block to any overarching approach to the past. I also happen to think that huge damage to the process of reconciliation occurs when you constantly unearth the past. I have long been attracted to the Spanish approach in the transition from the former republican dictatorship to monarchy and democracy. In simple terms a pact of forgetfulness was adopted, which, if applied in Northern Ireland, would require people to say that while they recognised the pain and difficulty in past events (for all sides), there was a single imperative for the current generation to build a new society and economy, leaving the detail of what happened to be reviewed with greater historical perspective and less personal animus in years to come. I know that is a very hard thing to suggest when people have suffered great loss, and it is particularly hard to say when you see something like the Bloody Sunday Inquiry reaching conclusions that are so clearly and fundamentally at odds with the earlier judgements on those events. But I do see a vital need for people on all sides to remember, but with forgiveness, and to concentrate on building a better future.

Reference

Powell, J. (2008). *Great Hatred, Little Room*. London: Bodley Head.

13 Managing the tensions of difference: an interview with Jonathan Powell

Interview

GS: You have stated how it is important to talk or communicate with your enemies. Are there moments when it is a good idea not to talk?

JP: It may not always be the right time to negotiate with your enemies, but it is always the right time to talk. On whether there are also moments when it is a good idea not to talk, I do not think so. I cannot think of any circumstances when you would not want to talk with your enemy, or have some way of communicating with them. There may be very little you can do, but it is always worth having that channel. If you look at the channel we had to the PIRA from 1972 on, it only really sprung into life for useful purposes in 1973–4, in 1980 over the hunger strike and then crucially with the John Major correspondence from 1991 to 1993. But having that channel there, having the ability to talk, was absolutely crucial because without it we would not have been able to get to the Downing Street Declaration and to the ceasefire.

GS: How do you gauge the relationship between the informal and the formal, and do you have to make the distinction between the dangers of possible overlap or do you see them as conjoined?

JP: I think that the chances of making progress across the table are not high. People rarely want to make concessions in a public setting, and by public setting I mean even twenty people around the table, because people hate to make concessions in those circumstances. They are far more likely to explore something when you are talking privately to them. I used to find that Gerry Adams was much more inclined to look very tentatively at the ways forward when I went for a walk with him round the garden at the Clonard Monastery than he would even in the room with his closest colleagues. The formal aspects are crucial, and the danger of overlap comes if you have lots and lots of negotiating channels because then things can get very muddled. In contrast, if you have one person that is handling negotiations, or one team that is handling negotiations on each side, that should not happen. When we were negotiating with the Democratic Unionist Party (DUP) we were shuttling backwards and forward between them and Sinn Féin, and both had a back channel at the same time. I suppose we could have got confused by that, but actually the DUP and Sinn Féin were pretty clear with us what they were discussing, so we did not have a big problem with them. The possibility of confusion exists, but as long as you have a fairly clear negotiating team and a fairly clear channel, that should not be a problem.

GS: How important was momentum to the peace process?

JP: Our analysis was that John Major had run into trouble because he had let it drag out too long. Because it was so difficult to solve, he had let it go on and on and on, and the republicans had begun to believe that he was not serious about it at all, that he was just trying to string them along, which is why they went and did Canary Wharf. We were very keen that you could not have that problem; that we would try to use the momentum of the election victory to get straight into it and to set a deadline for when the Agreement would be reached. The republican feeling was that the British Government would not let them into the talks, that we would string them out and out, and, even if we did let them into the talks, they would go on forever rather than having a date by which they would be resolved, which is why we adopted that approach.

GS: Were you always thinking about the endpoint in the negotiations or were you more concerned with reaching interim positions first?

JP: If negotiations of this sort are going to be successful you have to keep your eye on the strategic goal in the end. You have to know what you are working for. If you ever lose sight of that you get tied up in the tactics and the games and you never get there. So you have to do that, but you have to be ready to get there in a very oblique sort of way. When you think about it from the point of view of Adams and McGuinness, had they set out their aims of what they were going to settle for in the Good Friday Agreement (GFA) and afterwards at any time in the 1980s or 1993 or 1994 when the ceasefire happened, they would never have got support from the republican movement. They had to get there crab-like through a series of tactical moves. Likewise for us, trying to get through decommissioning, we had to find a series of crab-like moves. We tried to break it down into little steps to allow us to get there bit by bit.

GS: Was it a 'carrot and stick' approach to the parties?

JP: I think there was a problem from that point of view, from 1998 to 2003, when we kind of thought we could keep both sides on board, where, like a see-saw, we would rush down one end and offer them a carrot and then the see-saw would go swinging the other way and we would have to rush down there and give them a carrot, so it did feel like that and I think we undermined our own credibility by doing too much of that. Our justification was that we had to keep this thing going, if we allowed it to fall over, it would have been impossible to pick it up again. So we had to keep both sides on board by offering them small concessions, signs that they could achieve something that they wanted to achieve, on policing or whatever it might be. But I think part of the way that the credibility of the process was undermined was through too much giving a little bit here and a little bit there. Both sides felt they were terribly badly treated and that we had given everything to the other side, but they were a kind of reflection of each other from that point of view.

GS: In your book, *Great Hatred, Little Room* (2008), the importance of choreography is clear. How much a part of the process was dependent on choreography?

JP: Almost all of it was about choreography rather than the substance, if you like. Almost all of it was trying to find ways of convincing both sides that the other would move if they moved, because there was a huge gap of trust in that the republicans simply felt the unionists were not serious about sharing power with Catholics, that they were never going to set up the administration in a lasting way. The unionists were convinced that republicans were never going to give up the weapons, they were always going to keep this secret army behind them, and they wanted to trick them into government and then they would just leave that army in place to try to use it as a threat over them. Because both sides had this great gap of trust nearly everything was about choreography, to find small steps that both sides could take to reassure the other that things would happen. So, for example, at the time of the de Chastelain press conference we had a whole series of complex steps worked out that they would announce; the republicans would do the act of decommissioning, the British Government would announce that an election was going to happen, de Chastelain would have his press conference, the unionists would respond; a whole series of steps. Again, in 2004, with the DUP agreement, there were a whole series of steps that were supposed to happen one after another, so each side could see that the other had made a concession, because neither side was prepared to move first. From 1999 onwards, it was largely about choreography.

GS: What other factors would you say are essential for a successful negotiation process?

JP: There is a general rule in negotiations that the more people in the room, the harder it is and the less serious negotiations will be. In serious negotiations people do not like to give away their true positions unless they are in a very private context and believe they can trust the people they are talking to not to spread it around. On the occasions where we got flexibility in the negotiations there tended to be small numbers of people in the room. Anyone who brings a delegation of ten into a room is not serious about negotiating. Sometimes you did not answer the question on the table, but a different question and, by answering that different question, find a way round the problem. Relaying messages literally could be counter-productive, so you have to temper the message from one side to the other. You have to explain what you think they mean and what you think might be on offer, as well as suggest a way of meeting the points. In effect, you are bending the message, but if you change the message totally then you destroy the usefulness of the go-between position. At that point people will no longer trust you and things close down. Personally, I was trying to keep my eye on the strategic goal and asking what are we trying to achieve here? But above all else you have to try to keep the thing going. You cannot get too preoccupied with the details, which can be worked out, but you must keep the endpoint in mind. This was important if you were to prevent people walking out of the room.

GS: What role does the informal have to play in a negotiation process like this?

JP: It is the crucial part of negotiations. When you are actually exploring very informally what people think you can make some progress, but when you are stuck and beating each other back and forth over the head you are very much less likely to be making progress. Any real breakthroughs tend to happen in those circumstances, whether when Gerry Adams and Martin McGuinness came to Chequers to see Tony Blair, or I would go to a safe house in West Belfast. At those times you would get some inkling of what the way forward might be.

GS: Did republicans use history as a negotiating context?

JP: There was often a sense of victimhood, which was very much a part of their identity, and there would be a need for them to get that off their chest when talking to you. They spent a lot of time doing that. I used to joke that when there was a break after half an hour they would have only got to 1689, and that there would be another 200 years of grievances to get off their chest before they started to talk about what was happening now. They would particularly emphasise the unfairness and being done down, and they used that approach when something happened in negotiations they did not like. They would also refer to Bloody Sunday, Castlereagh, internment, unemployment, lack of housing, the civil rights movement, and those kinds of things too. The emphasis was that Northern Ireland had been created by the British, who had forced the conflict on them. It was very much to do with the British plot of wanting to hang on to territory, so it was a combination of myth and actual realities about contemporary life and the quite recent past.

When we met for the first time in Downing Street in the Cabinet Room, Martin McGuiness wanted to break the ice and said, 'So this was where all the damage was done?' I thought he was referring to when the PIRA bombed

Downing Street in 1991where they nearly wiped out the War Cabinet who were meeting to discuss the Iraq War. But McGuinness was referring to where the treaty was signed by Michael Collins and Lloyd George, so he was thinking about a completely different timescale. For republicans history is very important and it was a salutary lesson to us about just how important history and myth was to them. Once you hear this a few times you begin to understand more where they are coming from and what they are trying to say, and it becomes less of a problem in negotiation. I think they were stuck in history because they were constantly looking back instead of looking forward. They wanted to focus on past unfairness, deaths, murders and mistreatment. In a sense, we got to an agreement because they started looking forward at how they were going to share power and reform the police force, and this required more and more looking at the future rather than the past.

GS: But you were clear that they were serious about wanting to end violence?

JP: I think they had made the decision in the late 1980s that they wanted peace, and they knew approximately the terms they would have to settle on in the end and that would include the Union going on. If they had said that to the movement in the 1980s they would have been rejected, so they had to lead the movement crab-like to a peace process. They had a broad notion of the terms without telling others what they were doing. That was done step-by-step. They would never say we are having severe problems with the Army Council or sort of implicate themselves as being members of the PIRA, which Adams always denied, because you could bang them up for that. But they would say we have got a real problem, can you help us? Or that you need to do this or we are not going to be able sell this. The reason they used for over-negotiating was that they had to carry the movement with them. Adams was very explicit at the first meeting that we had in Downing Street when he took Tony and me to a part of the room where the pillars separated people off and said he could deliver the PIRA, but that it would be better to do it with the whole movement rather than just reaching agreement with some of them. He argued that it was important to win the movement over, and we accepted that and we kept to that because we thought it better to try to do this all at once rather than try to make peace lots of times in lots of different rooms with different factions. That would complicate things and make the whole thing much harder to deal with.

GS: How much do you think the peace process for republicans was about a united Ireland and how much was it about addressing issues within Northern Ireland?

JP: The peace process was about getting to a fundamental fairness that they felt had been denied. Eventually they came to the conclusion that they did not just want to have their grievances heard, but to change things and get a practical approach for going forward. Occasionally, you would get a bit of pseudo-Marxism, but not actually with the key figures, more from others and especially when you were negotiating on social issues. A number of times they had to go off, disappear for twenty-four hours, then come back looking like they had been dragged through a hedge backwards. They would have gone and consulted with the Army Council and we were fairly certain about that. Sometimes they would be turned over for having agreed to things in the room, and would then come back to say, 'Sorry we can't do that'. Some of it would have been Adams and McGuinness just playing us off by pretending that 'her indoors' was making it very difficult for negotiations. They left most of the creativity to the two governments, and we had to be the ones who came up with ideas to resolve problems because they rarely made any sort of constructive proposal themselves. They would tend to work out a piece of strategy for the next three months, and when it came to the end of it they had little idea and would look for someone else to come up with ideas for the next phase, and it tended to be us who did that. I think republicans had a long-term goal of getting to an agreement and Adams and McGuinness clearly wanted to do that. I am not sure whether they had a very clear plan about how to do it though. They tried lots of different routes such as reaching out to John Hume, the Irish Government through Martin Mansergh and Father Alec Reid, and then through the Irish Government to the British Government. Then they got into negotiations and had to deal with the DUP. What struck me was that they had an overall goal and they had a series of strategies that ran out of road. They had a strategy that would be used for a period of time and then it would fail for some reason and they did not then have a new idea to replace it, so we had to come up with that idea to keep it going. In negotiations, it is often the third party or governments, because they have more resources and people to come up with the bright ideas rather than the armed group. They tended to have set-piece strategies that got to a certain point, which came to an end, whereupon someone else had to help them construct a new one.

GS: So Sinn Féin tended to work to a long-term view and their short-term view was much weaker?

JP: I totally understand why they only had that long-term strategy, because it was a very difficult thing to lead the movement from its original aims to where it needed to end up, where there was a settlement to be had. They could not set out a detailed route map to where they wanted to be because they would have lost their membership if they had done so. It was important for them not to have that kind of strategy. The problem though was that we would get to the end of a particular piece of work, where they would work out a specific tactic with a very short-term goal, such as with decommissioning or the Irish language, and then you would get to the end of that particular piece of road and they would be out of ideas and it would then be thrown back on us to have ideas.

GS: Did they make it known what their 'bottom line' in negotiations would be?

JP: We had to guess their bottom line and their relationship with the organisation. They would say things like 'If you do not remove the towers along the border we are going to have trouble with the South Armagh brigade because nothing has changed in their lives', so 'as long as you have a tower outside Murphy's house he is not going to think much has changed', and 'if you want to stop dissidents they are the people who are going to have to help us'. We saw the value of that argument and the importance of carrying that constituency with them. Also, if you want a lasting agreement, they had to feel that they, as well as the other side, had won and so there had to be no winners and losers from that point of view. Adams did say to me that Tony Blair wanted to meet the Army Council, but that these people are military men and not interested in politics so it might make things worse rather than better. It was not going to be a meeting of minds, so it was probably the right decision that he did not meet them. It was also in their interest not to let this happen because they could continue to say, 'Look these people are difficult', and we might have questioned why we were trying to convince people like that, which could have been counter-productive. It was probably in both our interests that we did not meet them. Mo Mowlam used to joke that when Gerry Adams and Martin McGuinness left the room to consult the Army Council they were in fact going to look in the mirror and then coming back in again! I do not think it was actually quite like that, however. I think the Army Council had different views and different factions, and they probably had to go away and argue those points out with the people from the Army Council, many of whom were barrack-room lawyers with strong views and who would often insert phrases into the language that we were then faced with.

GS: How effective were they tactically?

JP: I think the republicans were too tactical in their approach to negotiations because they over-negotiated. If they had settled five years earlier, they would have got a better deal than they did in the end. They actually undermined their position by negotiating, and although they knew when to hold they did not know when to fold. They would say that they could not carry the movement at that moment and that the unionists were not helping by being difficult, etc. A lot of this was of their own making and they would have been better if they had been more strategic. Things like the PIRA refusing to let de Chastelain say anything about what sort of weapons had been decommissioned reduced the press conference where he was supposed to announce what had happened to a farce. It was a tactical move just to spite the unionists and it screwed the whole thing. That collapsed and it was really the end of Trimble. It was only when Adams came to understand in the end that he needed to think about the constituency on the other side as well as his own in selling an agreement that we got a lasting peace. Sinn Féin had a long-term game plan and that did not involve walking out of the negotiations, but they would prefer the unionists to walk out.

They could be very aggressive, but that tended to be more of a good cop/bad cop scenario. They could shout and threaten at times, but the only way to deal with that was to ignore it and carry on. It was not a cultural thing, more a tactical device they used. One should also remember that they were very defensive and had been hemmed in by their ghetto for a long time. Gradually, as they got a bit of international respectability by going to Washington etc., they became more statesmanlike and this was reflected in their language. They also had to be careful that in the eyes of their community they were not being seen as too big for their boots.

The military organisation helped them a lot in terms of negotiating leverage, but, apart from Adams and McGuinness, I do not think the military organisation had many sophisticated political minds. They had been leaders for decades, unlike most political leaders, and this meant that they had to separate the paramilitary mind from the political mind. But Adams and McGuinness were better at thinking about how something would be received by the constituency, how to sell what was agreed, what would look best for their side, and what things would look like if they were forced to surrender and then go on television to defend it. Part of the leadership art for them was staying in sync with history because history is so important to the movement; the idea that you cannot betray your history and that you do not mention physical security. They would quite often talk to me about threats to their lives, about the risks they were taking, the graffiti at the end of McGuinness' street saying 'We will get you' from dissidents, or the danger of a seventeen-year-old being given a gun and told to go and kill him. They were very conscious of their own security and the risks they were taking. It was not just normal political interplay. If they took a wrong step they could quite easily have been bumped off, and this concentrated their minds in terms of thinking about the negotiations.

GS: Did you tend to go to places that suited them more than you?

JP: A lot of the meetings took place on their turf and we decided that would be better than them coming to us. So, I did quite a lot of meetings with them in safe houses in West Belfast or Derry. On the point of where meetings took place, we decided it was the right thing to go to their turf instead of demanding that they came to Downing Street or the grand rooms of Stormont, a symbol of repression. To go to a place where they felt they were not being bugged was important because they would then feel better about what was happening. I think it was a good idea to go to their turf, where they were more relaxed and willing to give you a little more about what their position was. You want to suggest things to people, but not to insist on ownership. This is important in order to give space to think about things and to allow ideas to be kicked back and forth. So it is a process of feeling things out in those terms and this worked better on their turf.

GS: Is it more of a philosophical exercise being involved in a negotiation like that and more about twisting inside the logic and trying to win your argument?

JP: No. The mistake people make is to think that negotiation is a debate, and negotiation is not a debate. Negotiation is about words on paper, and if you are negotiating an agreement what you are trying to do is get to a signed agreement. If you spend so much time trying to convince the other side that you are reasonable or that your argument is right you are wasting time, because in the end you are not going to convince the other side that you are right and they are wrong, and the conflict between you will go on. In the end, the GFA was an agreement to disagree. The unionists still wanted to be part of the United Kingdom, the republicans still wanted to be part of a united Ireland. They just agreed to carry on the conflict by political means rather than by armed force, and that is usually the case in other such agreements round the world. You do not actually solve the argument and trying to get that across the negotiating table is actually a waste of time. What you are trying to do is build enough trust to get to a piece of paper that has words on it, that is an agreement that you will implement on both sides, and that will influence further building of trust.

GS: Do you think it is important to have empathy with people that you are negotiating with?

JP: Having spoken to other people who have been in this situation, I think it is important that you can empathise, that you can understand the point of view of the other side, that you can put yourself inside their heads and see the demands being made on them, what the pressures are and what they need to demonstrate by way of success to their constituency. There are others who argue that you need to go beyond that and that you need to become friends with the people on the other side, whereas others argue that you should not become friends. But it is important that you stick to your word and that if you make a promise you have to stick to that promise or else you undermine all the credibility you may have established. So there are different points of view on that.

GS: So becoming friends actually risks creating all sorts of problems?

JP: I am not sure that it is quite as clear as that because I have talked to very successful negotiators, experienced negotiators, who take different views. Some say it is actually important to be a friend, because sometimes you need to ask others to do things that they do not want to do, and if you have a bit of friendship with them they can maybe bring themselves to do it more and it certainly makes the meetings more pleasant. Others say, no, being a friend may even be a danger, like the Stockholm Syndrome, that it really is thinking like your opponents rather than just understanding where they are, that you are sympathising with their position and almost joining their position. I think there is a line before you get to the Stockholm Syndrome, but I think it is possible to be friends with the people you are negotiating with without crossing that line and becoming so relativistic that you actually believe their position.

GS: How vital then are personal relationships?

JP: I think it is absolutely crucial to negotiations, not just Northern Ireland, but anywhere I have been involved in negotiations that you have to build up personal trust. You are not going to get anywhere if people completely doubt your good intentions. I think Tony and Bertie Ahern in particular did an amazing job of building up trust on both sides. It took time, we were very suspicious of Sinn Féin, they were very suspicious of us when we first met them in 1997, and, likewise, the unionists were pretty suspicious of us largely because the Tory Government had been on their side since the creation of the state. But if you had not established those kinds of personal relationship you could not have concluded a deal. And if later on Tony had not established a relationship with Ian Paisley, it is very hard to see how you would have got to a deal. So it is absolutely fundamental, and not just, as I say, in Northern Ireland, but in any political negotiation of that sort, that you have an element of trust and that you build trust into negotiations. The trouble can come if you build trust by joking etc. and then someone lets you down and fails to do what they promised to do. That can blow the whole thing.

GS: How did you gauge the line between giving people enough space to make the right decision, but also applying the right amount of pressure so that you got movement and not collapse?

JP: At the very beginning when Gerry Adams took Tony Blair to the end of the Cabinet Room in a meeting near Christmas in 1997, saying he needed to deliver as much of the organisation as possible and that he would need time and space to do it, we made a conscious decision to give that time and space. In other words, we did not try to force the issue, because we wanted to make peace once rather than lots of times with lots of different groups. Working out how long that length of time should be and working out how insistent you should be on the deadlines you set was a difficult thing, because we never really knew quite what was the bottom line for the republicans and we did not know quite how many concessions to make. David Trimble argues that we should have pushed them much harder after 9/11 because they had no choice, that they had to sign up for a peace agreement, and we should have just forced the issue and given an ultimatum. I do not think you can know the bottom line of a covert organisation like you can if you are negotiating with a more conventional group on the other side of the table and you do not want to take the risk of pushing them into violence. It is not like trying to buy a car at the lowest price. You want them to go away feeling like they are winners, and you want the people on the other side of the table to go away feeling like they are winners too. So it is a difficult line to tread, but I think you need to be patient and give time and space, and you do need to get a balance of carrots and sticks. We started off with the analogy of the train leaving the station when we did negotiations with Sinn Féin and that if they did not get on board, we would go without them. In fact, it was pretty unconvincing because the Social Democratic and Labour Party (SDLP) were clear that they would not move ahead without Sinn Féin, and we could not go ahead without any Catholic parties in the negotiations at all. So despite talking about the train leaving the station, we were really pretty stuck.

GS: Is a negotiation process like this about mobility, forging positions and blurring edges where possible?

JP: It is very helpful if you can make negotiations seem and feel like a joint exercise. If you talk to people who work in a negotiation setting, many will see it as a joint-task, trying to find a common solution and working together towards that. This, it seems to me, is a more helpful way of thinking about a negotiation rather than an antagonistic relationship which is more about tit for tat and trading things off against each other. I think blurring the edges comes with ambiguity and any agreement is going to be ambiguous unless it is two million pages long. It is not ever going to be precise and there will be ambiguity in it. What you are trying to do is find language that both sides can live with. There is a danger if you go too far in terms of ambiguity though. When I talk about constructive ambiguity, it is more in relation to how that can get you out of a jam, but if there is too much ambiguity it can come back to haunt you later on when both sides complain that what they expected to happen has not happened.

GS: How did you determine when ambiguity would be more useful than clarity?

JP: I do not think that we had a sort of cleverly worked out tactic on this, but I think that Tony was very clear from early on that we were not going to be able to bridge the gap on decommissioning. Major had tried and got completely stuck in a cleft stick on the subject and we had to find a way of getting through it, not just letting it block the whole process, so it was absolutely clear in these conversations with the unionists, through 1997 and into 1998, that he was trying to get them off decommissioning and onto the far more important issue of consent, which needed to be their victory out of the GFA – the acceptance of a separate Northern Ireland as part of the United Kingdom, on the basis of the consensus of the people in Northern Ireland, that was what they needed to have rather than decommissioning, that was their victory. I think it was clear that we had to be ambiguous about decommissioning in the GFA, or else we would not have got an agreement. That is why we had this last-minute blip with David Trimble trying to get clarity on something that was not going to be resolvable in that negotiation, and then we had the side-letter and the mess that that caused in subsequent years.

GS: As time goes on the ambiguity has to be replaced by more and more detail. Can you say something about that shift?

JP: It is about the implementation because an agreement is just a bunch of words and an agreement does not build trust. Having an agreement does not make two sides trust each other. The only thing that makes people trust each other is when both sides actually start doing what they promised to do. So it is the implementation phase that builds trust. Even if there is ambiguity in the agreement, it is when people come to do what they said they were going to do, when people do not do what they said they were going to do, or do not do what the other side thinks they said they were going to do, that increases the chances of collapse.

GS: Constructive ambiguity, then, was obviously an important factor. Were republicans more comfortable with this?

JP: You are certainly right in assuming that republicans are more comfortable with ambiguity in general. Although both sides spoke the same language, English, they actually meant very different things by the English language. The language deployed by republicans would be very florid, very, as you say, ambiguous, full of sub-clauses, whereas the unionists would speak a language that was much more sort of Doubting Thomas, very sort of plain and very direct. One of our jobs was to try to interpret between the two sides and explain what they really meant. So, if a republican said something, what they were actually saying was this, and if unionists were saying something, this is what they meant. It was a very different sort of language, so, yes, ambiguity was much more in the mindset of the republicans, but that was actually also very damaging in the long run, because they tried to get away with that ambiguity for too long – the ambiguity of the Armalite in one hand and the ballot box in the other. They thought they could keep on getting away with it much longer than they should have done from their own point of view, and we had to put an end to it with the Belfast Harbour speech where they had to choose between one or the other. But it is true, we built constructive ambiguity into the GFA about decommissioning. I am not quite sure how conscious we were in doing it, but it was certainly there, and then we tried to live with it right through to 2003 before we had to drive it out of the system from the Belfast Harbour speech onwards. A key question for us was how far were republicans deliberately avoiding being clear? One has to say that because, in the end, when they unilaterally decided to decommission and give up all paramilitary activity the thing that struck me was the clarity of what they were saying. After all, this sort of fencing around about is it over or isn't it over, they said it is not going to happen any more in an incredibly clear way. So when they wanted to be clear they could be clear. The key question put to them was whether they would say the war was over as a result of the GFA or when the conditions were met. So there were questions about whether the war was conditionally over or whether it would not be over until there is a united Ireland. Obviously, they did not want to say the war was over because their constitution would not let them say that until there was a united Ireland, and yet, since they had signed up for a peace agreement with the GFA, this was clearly the case. That is why I think we ended up with ambiguity. They would not be clear about their conditions because, given their constitution, they could not be. They could not face up to this question that there could and would be peace without a united Ireland.

GS: Is it true that the unionists thought successful negotiations were about 'going down to the wire'? That the final moments were the most important?

JP: The republican criticism of the unionist position would very much be that and that they never went about preparing their base for any agreement they came to, but I think it was just a lack of political ability to communicate, they were not out there selling an agreement before they reached it. To be fair, Trimble's criticism of the republicans was that they were not preparing their base either. He thought, correctly, I guess, that if the republicans were going to deliver on decommissioning, they should have been selling that to their base at the time of the GFA, which they were not. So I think both sides can be accused of being guilty of not preparing their base for the agreements that were going to happen. However, when the republicans wanted to do a deal, they did go out and systematically prepare their base. They would go and brief volunteers in the PIRA, and the whole way down a chain everyone would get briefed before it was announced, so they were quite sophisticated in doing that when they wanted to do so. The Ulster Unionist Party (UUP) had no mechanism for doing the same and no sophisticated political leadership that thought about doing that either.

GS: Just to develop this point a bit further, you intimate in your book that whereas Sinn Féin were always off talking to their people David Trimble was not talking to his people enough. Can you elaborate on this?

JP: Sinn Féin and the PIRA have a very detailed system of briefing their volunteers. They had a tree of briefings where some people were briefing others, and Adams and McGuinness would be travelling all over Ireland meeting republicans and telling them what their position was, so they had a very elaborate method of taking everyone with them. However, it was briefing, not discussion. In other words, once it had been agreed by the central leadership of the republican movement, it was a kind of Stalinist party and they all went along with it. They were not asking people what they thought, they were briefing them on where they were so that it did not come as a surprise to them when something was announced, which was a good way to carry them. The problem with David Trimble was because he became increasingly isolated from his party he never really discussed with his fellow leaders the compromises he had agreed to and he constantly found himself being caught out as a result. He would agree to something as on the eve of the GFA, but when the others saw it they would not agree to it, which made negotiating with him very complicated. At Hillsborough, in 2003, after the failure of the de Chastelain press conference we had a last go at negotiating before the elections, and it felt like negotiating with a focus group where every single member of the delegation from the UUP had a different bottom line. There was no combined bottom line but eight bottom lines, and trying to meet a negotiation from this position was hopeless. This partly explains why Trimble did not want to discuss it with his colleagues because they could never come to a common position. The DUP, by contrast were very disciplined about things. Every time they made a move in negotiation they would discuss it with quite a wide group of the party leadership, including all the MPs, and although that made it quite slow to negotiate with them they could at least carry everyone with them.

GS: Did republicans talk to you about British withdrawal?

JP: No, that had gone, and it is an interesting question as to when that finally went out of their lexicon. Presumably, it went after the ceasefire in 1994, because there would have been no point in turning up for meetings with Quentin Thomas in 1994–5 at Stormont without having dropped that from the things they were demanding. There would have been no point in sitting down with Quentin and saying this is when the British forces are going to leave. I suppose somewhere between the Downing Street Declaration and the ceasefire they dropped that demand.

GS: Is it important not to have surprises in a process like this? I am thinking of the Northern Bank robbery as an example.

JP: Yes, well there were spoilers, both deliberate and unintended, accidents if you want to call them that, that could derail a negotiation. The most obvious was the Omagh bomb in August 1998, which in a normal peace process would have derailed the whole thing because the unionists in normal circumstances would have gone out and said 'We do not care what sort of republicans these are, this bomb was from the republicans and we are not in a peace process if the republicans are going to carry on blowing things up'. Equally, if Adams and McGuinness had refused to condemn the attack as being the traditional position of the PIRA, never to condemn another republican attack, if they had stuck to that it would have been very hard to hold the unionists on board, and McGuinness did, after a slight hesitation, go out and condemn it, so we were saved from that spoiler pushing things off track. The Northern Bank robbery was certainly very disconcerting for me personally, since I had just arrived and was told about the robbery by a Northern Ireland Office official as I came off the plane. I felt betrayed by that because I was the only person negotiating as at that stage the Irish had given up. It was after the breakdown of the Leeds Castle talks. So, yes, there were spoilers, but I do not think the PIRA intended to knock the talks off balance, they just thought, 'Well we are in a hiatus anyway since the Leeds Castle talks have broken, so we have this opportunity, so let's make as much money as we can'.

GS: The relationship between planning and spontaneity is interesting. I assume that the real test for you was in dealing with spontaneous moments more than planned ones. Was that the case?

JP: You had to be incredibly careful that you did not concede something that your masters, like Tony, were going to say no way to because then your credibility is gone. You are overruled and are no longer going to be a useful negotiating partner to the other side. So you have to be very clear about what is acceptable and what is not, but only up to a point because you are negotiating a referendum, you are going to go away and consult others about it, so you do not have to be pitch perfect, but obviously it is better if you do not concede anything unless you are sure it is going to be fine. So, yes, there is quite a lot of tension, quite a lot of pressure on you to make sure you do not go too far, but, equally, if you are too cautious and do not agree anything, then, again, you are not a very useful negotiating partner either. So it is a bit like skiing, you want to be confident, but not over-confident.

GS: So how important is improvisation in negotiations of this nature?

JP: Very important. And in a negotiation like this, it is crucial to have people who can think on their feet, who can adapt their positions on their feet and have the authority to do that, because otherwise if everyone has to go back and refer every time, you will not get very far. In Weston Park, we were sort of starting from the wrong place. We had misinterpreted what the republican position was. We had a hugely worked-out position with the Irish, we had twelve working papers, lots of work had been done before, but it was as if we just sort of turned up and said let's hope for the best. We had actually misjudged where the republicans were, and we had to twist our negotiating position right round 180 degrees to a different position in order to get them to where we needed them to be. So, you can have all the worked-out positions you want when you go into negotiation, but you also have to be ready to twist the thing around in order to get to where you need to be. One of the examples that stick in my mind came right at the end of the process in March 2007, when we had Ian Paisley and his team come in to see us to say that they were not going to agree to go into government. They had had an executive meeting where it was unanimously decided that they would not go into government until May, and the whole thing was in tatters. We did not know what to do, and Tony and I went out of the room and walked around outside in the outer private office, trying to work out what to do, and we came up on the spur of the moment with the idea of suggesting that Adams and Paisley meet to agree this. So we conceded what the DUP wanted, but they had to meet face-to-face with Adams for the first time ever. We had no idea if it would work, it was just something that we thought of in five minutes. We went back in and proposed it, and to our slight surprise they did not just reject it out of hand and although Ian Paisley Junior asked some pretty difficult questions, Dodds and Robinson were clearly pretty much in favour. They went away, said they would think about it, and then they called us from the airport and said that they had decided to do it, so we managed to find a way through. In that case, it was completely spontaneous, but if you do no preparation then that is completely hopeless as well, so one needs to be able to adjust from one position to the other.

GS: Did you side-line problems in order to change tack and work on others? Change direction and emphasis in other words.

JP: No, you constantly try to work round things. More than sort of leaving it on one side, what you try to do is enlarge the context so if you come to a complete blockage on something specific, you try to widen the focus, to try to find a way round it, to try to think of other solutions that might make it palatable to both sides. For example, we could see that we were going to get nowhere with the actual act of decommissioning, so we thought laterally about what would work and I went away and talked to a number of generals, and they had the idea of what had happened in Bosnia and Kosovo, where dumps had been sealed and inspected by NATO troops regularly. There, weapons had not been given up, but they had been inspected, and then we applied this different solution to the problem and found a way through for setting up the administration with a gesture by republicans towards decommissioning, without decommissioning actually happening. It was that sort of lateral thinking, broadening the context that works, and we tried some of those things later on in the last bit of negotiations with Trimble, just before the 2003 elections as well. After the debacle of the de Chastelain press conference, we tried to find ways of looking at a percentage of weapons decommissioning rather than being specific about weapons; we looked at timetables of decommissioning instead of lists of weapons as ways round it. So, as in this case, you can often try to find different solutions to things that are not actually directly addressing the point of conflict between the two sides, but that enable the sides to unlock horns.

GS: You mention in your book that on occasions the negotiations were run on a sense of feel for what was going on rather than knowing what was going on. How much was instinct being used?

JP: It happened much more in the earlier days, because there was no way of knowing what was the real bottom line for Sinn Féin, or indeed for the unionists, or how far they knew themselves what their bottom lines were, so we had to explore it by feel and Tony was just sort of brilliant at that. We had an endless session with the unionists at Number 10, all sorts of configurations over dinner, in the garden and over lunch, trying to feel out and explore with them, to get them to articulate what their bottom line was, think through what their bottom line was, and that was crucial on one side. On the other side were Adams and McGuinness. Because of the secrecy of the PIRA and the republican movement it was pretty much impossible to know what their bottom line was and to a certain extent we had to take their word for it. The way I thought about it is this, that it is not like buying a car – we were not there to haggle down to the best price, we did not care if we were paying an extra thousand quid to get the car, if we could get a car that was going to carry on working forever, in other words a lasting peace process. So you had to have a certain leeway for both sides when they said this is really serious for us.

GS: How did you try to stay ahead of developments and pre-empt consequences?

JP: It tended to be more like driving straight at the wall and then hitting it rather than being able to avoid hitting it. The occasion when we tried to pre-empt was on demilitarisation. Tony and I were convinced that if you could move on demilitarisation you would be able to persuade republicans that they should make the gestures they needed to the unionists on decommissioning, so we tried to get ahead of the curve, but we never quite succeeded because of the resistance from the Army and to a lesser extent the police, who were worried about the effects of demilitarisation on managing the dissidents. We were caught in this conundrum where Adams and McGuinness were saying to us that the best way to combat the dissidents was to show them that you could change life in South Armagh, but the military were saying that we could not risk taking away the towers because we had to monitor them, so we got caught in this Catch 22 situation from that point of view. Another aspect was 'On the Runs', trying to solve the problem of terrorists on the run. You had the prisoners who had been released, the existing prisoners of 1997 who had been released one or two years after the Agreement, then there were a whole bunch of people in an anomalous situation because they had not been in prison and could not come back to Northern Ireland because they were on the run for offences. We wanted to try to sort that out, but we could never persuade the attorney general that it would be right legally to pardon them. We legislated, but then we could not get the legislation through Parliament, so on the occasions we did try to pre-empt we did not really succeed.

GS: How much attention did you give to what was not said as well as what was said?

JP: You are always listening, and there is a real difference between listening and hearing. Quite a lot of people say they are listening, but they are not really hearing what people are saying and you have to be very, very nuanced in listening for the way they change their language, how something they have always stressed in the past is not being stressed now, and then you are looking for gaps and if that means that they have really dropped such and such a point, then maybe we could go in a different direction with a different point. So you want to be listening very carefully and actually hearing what they say and what they mean.

GS: So how did the meetings tend to work? Was there a clear attempt by the parties to try to set the agenda, or was it more relaxed and interchangeable than that?

JP: It was a bit more mechanical than that depending on who had gone away to think about things and come back to the next meeting, because normally at the end of a meeting one side went away to consult so they tended to come back and say we can agree to this but we cannot agree to that. We would go to a meeting and would usually come up with the idea for either side and we would then put the ideas on the table to the Irish Government, and then they, or Sinn Féin, or the DUP or the UUP, would say, right okay maybe it is this or that, and we would pull together a text and they would go off and consult on that and come back to us. And when met, we would listen to what they said and try to amend it. So we would go away, change it and come back with a new text, which we might send to them in advance to discuss at the next meeting. So it is literally a process. I do not think it is important who started the meetings, because they were not a debate, they were actually working meetings where we would try to get things agreed on paper, so they were much more about whose turn it was to take the next steps.

GS: And did you find that in those meetings people were thinking the same way as you in terms of ideally needing to move from here to there by the next meeting, or were meetings often the same meeting over and over again?

JP: In many ways it was the same meeting over and over again. I am trying to think on your point of different expectations. I do not think there were probably expectations to start with but they soon caught on to the game, and I think that after ten years with particular people they and you get the expectations and you tend to form a certain pattern and stick to it. Maybe at the beginning the expectations were a bit different, and I think that Adams and McGuinness thought that a certain amount of play-acting helped to set the mood to convince us that they were serious about a particular point or not serious about a particular point. You would get quite emotive speeches, particularly from Martin McGuinness, which Adams would occasionally interrupt or make fun of, but they were trying to indicate what was important.

GS: Coming back to reactions to language, is it the case that unionists preferred precise wording, whereas republicans were more worried that they were going to be 'boxed in' by such wording?

JP: One of the things that is attractive about the unionist tradition is the literalness of it and the honesty. When I was negotiating with the Orangemen, their idea of a negotiating position was to come in and say 'Here is our position', and we would come back and say 'the other side want...', and they would say, 'well sorry, we told you our position, that is our position and it would be immoral to change it'. One of the attractive aspects of the unionists is that they are very much people of their word. If they say something they expect other people to stick to it as well as themselves. Republicans were slightly more disingenuous. If you look at all the PIRA statements, and this is what got us into terrible trouble over the years, they constantly made the statements ambiguous, and that was one of the reasons that the unionists came to doubt them and not to trust them, because they never appeared to be prepared to say something clearly and absolutely.

GS: There is a perception that republicans tended to think in terms of frameworks whilst looking way down the road and using the Agreement as a stepping-stone to the next phase, whereas for unionists, it was about damage limitation and trying to stop things there. Is there substance in this?

JP: I think it is a very important point about change and stopping change. In the end, the GFA, and what happened subsequently, does not actually resolve the issue of Northern Ireland. Republicans and nationalists still want a united Ireland and the unionists still want a United Kingdom, so we never resolved the political issue. Most of the negotiating processes around the world try to resolve the issues at the centre of conflict, but we did not try to do that. You might ask what did republicans gain out of this, why did they have the war if they ended up simply saying, 'Okay we will live in the United Kingdom'? The answer is, and I think this is very important to understand, that what republicans were really demanding was change and the ability to bring about change without the unionists being able to veto it. The issue was the unionists always being able to block change – first, the creation of the Republic, then the separation of the North, then any change within the North and then the civil rights movements. Every time Catholics tried to emancipate themselves, it was blocked by unionist veto. Really what the republicans were asking for was not a united Ireland, although, of course, that is their aspiration and their aim, but to be able to do something on the Irish language, human rights, unemployment, law and so on without unionist boycotts. This competition between keeping things the same and change was really what it was all about underneath the actual negotiations themselves.

GS: You cite a few examples in your book of where you thought things are finalised with Sinn Féin and then they would find a problem and stop proceedings. Was this a deliberate control strategy employed by them to dictate the pace?

JP: As an example, in 1998 there were a series of meetings where we got to an agreement with Sinn Féin and where they said they had agreement as well. Adams and McGuinness then went off to consult their people and announced that they did not have an agreement, that they could not sign up for it. Sometimes they went out to try to sell something to their membership, the Army Council and other people, and then they were not actually able to sell it. In other words, they went along, had an argument and lost. Other times, they got into a sort of false position, where they would be negotiating on something not because they thought they could not say no, but because the other side, the unionists, would never agree to it. Then that position was exposed because we would get to that point and the unionists would agree to their side of the bargain and then the Shinners [Sinn Féin] would not be able to match it. This happened on demilitarisation. We had finally managed to persuade the military and the police that we could do the demilitarisation that Sinn Féin wanted and then they were unable to deliver on their side of the bargain. So, really, they had been negotiating from a false basis, and they were caught out by that and had to have a lot of bluster and try to pretend that it was our fault rather than theirs.

GS: How did you determine when things were being strung out to such an extent that they had to be confronted?

JP: It was very difficult, but we eventually decided that we had had enough by the beginning of 2003. That was largely because we were just haemorrhaging support on the unionist side of the Agreement and were down to about

30 per cent support in the opinion polls amongst the unionist population. We could not sustain it any longer, the thing had been discredited and the government had been discredited because we were letting our wishful thinking substitute for reality. Punishment beatings were still going on, the PIRA were not decommissioning and the problem was not being solved. So we had to confront it and say right, enough is enough, we have to face up to this issue now, get rid of the ambiguity, get rid of the Armalite altogether and move to an exclusively political way forward. I remember that we agonised quite hard about it at the time, because we were afraid that in doing that we might push the republicans over the edge and find ourselves alienating them totally from the process, because this was pressure we were putting on them, rather than on the unionist side. But as a matter of fact, Adams' response was a positive one, which was engaging, and that, in the end, enabled us to find the way through.

GS: What do you understand by the 'mechanics of negotiation'?

JP: Again, words on paper: Are you using square brackets? Are you going to agree the text? Are you going to have a single-text negotiation or are you going to have different text presented backward and forward from the two sides? You know, if you are a mediator who puts text down on the table, are you using text at all or are you just going to read pieces out to people and then go away and change it and do the negotiations orally? Those kind of questions.

GS: What is the difference between reading it out rather than showing people what you think?

JP: It is very hard for them to amend it when it is read out because they have to keep it in their heads and amend it in their heads.

GS: Did that happen?

JP: We mainly used the single text method, which means you have a text that you take backward and forward between two sides, and it is what we and the Irish Government basically accepted as the method of the process. It was not entirely like that, however, because we did not get the PIRA presenting us with a new or different text. Rather, we would give them a draft statement and they would send one back that was completely different, so it was not always single text, but it started on the same basis. Sometimes, you had to do it orally because it would be too offensive to put something on paper and if they took it away it would offend all their supporters, so you had to do it orally to get a sense of whether it was even in the ball park.

GS: Presumably on a piece of text if you write too much you get potential problems and if you do not write enough you still get potential problems, so how do you gauge exactly what is enough?

JP: That is very hard. At one end, too much ambiguity means it will unravel when you come to implement it because people have not really agreed. At the other end, too much detail and you get tangled in detail that has not really taken into account the flexibility that you really need for implementing an agreement. If you look at the Philippines Agreement in 2008, that fell down in part because it was too detailed and the supreme court turned it over because it breached the constitutional provisions. Or if you think of the agreement in Cyprus in Kofi Annan's time, it was much too detailed, there were thousands of pages, including whole draft bills, and if you get into that much detail you are bound to have something that people will complain about. So it is a difficult balance.

GS: So the more you have in it the more people can pull it apart?

JP: That is exactly it, but equally the more detailed it is the more chance you are agreeing things and therefore implementation ought to be easier.

GS: When the unionists came out of the GFA they seemed to sell it as a disaster, whereas the republicans seemed to sell it as a victory, would you agree with that?

JP: Well, of course, the republicans did not sign up to the GFA and were the only ones who left saying they had not agreed it. So I am not sure I would agree about that, but in general negotiations over the next nine years there was a problem in that the republicans were much cleverer at leaving a meeting as if they had won, where they would leave smiling, regardless of the substance, and where the unionists would all believe they had lost because Gerry Adams was smiling regardless of what they had got on a piece of paper. That was the problem, but it was actually a problem not just for unionists but also for Gerry Adams too because then he could not get a balanced agreement. I think he finally got that and realised that he had to appeal, or rather had to sell the Agreement, to both the unionist side and the republican side. He could not just sell it to his own constituency, both constituencies needed to see it as a fair deal in which both sides were winners.

GS: As you intimate, Sinn Féin used non-verbal communication techniques quite a bit at that time, smiling to give the impression of success rather than talking, which might give a different impression. Was this important?

JP: Well, not for us because we regarded ourselves as the referee in this rather than on either team. We were conscious of how cleverly the republicans in particular were playing this zero-sum politics, and actually I think they came to realise over time that they could be too clever by half on this stuff, that if they went out and claimed victory, they were actually making life more difficult for Trimble and therefore less likely that Trimble would live by his agreement. Towards the last stages I was very impressed by Adams' and McGuinness' ability to swallow some pain on their own side in order to make it easier for Trimble, and for Paisley and others, to say that they had won, they had succeeded, so that they could get the Agreement. The trouble with zero-sum politics is that you are never going to get a lasting agreement if you go out and say that you have won and the other side has lost. Similarly, they were not going to get an agreement if Paisley came out and said the PIRA have surrendered because they have given photographs of decommissioning. So you had to have a deal that was sellable to both sides.

GS: What was your feeling about the possibility of dissidents and elements fracturing away from the PIRA? Did you think that was their problem not ours?

JP: God, no, we were very conscious of this. As I said at the beginning of the meeting with Adams in the Cabinet Room, we wanted to get as much of the movement into peace as possible, not just a bit of it. Traditionally, the British Government had tried to split the PIRA in any way it could, whether it be the Officials, the Provos, the Irish National Liberation Army (INLA) or others. And governments liked the idea of splitting because that is a good way to reduce its strength. We took the opposite point of view. We wanted to get the whole movement to move as one into peace, but we were conscious that was not going to be everyone, that some people would hold out, and we wanted for that to be as small a group as possible. I am not quite sure how quickly we realised the danger, but obviously it hit us by the time we got to Omagh and thereafter. I still do not think that the Real IRA or the Continuity IRA have political significance. They have military significance in terms that they can kill people, and that is a personal tragedy for the people killed and it is an enduring job for the security forces, but they have so little political support that they do not really pose a significant threat to the system in Northern Ireland in a way that the PIRA did because, even at the worst of times, they had a third of the Catholic vote. So, really, in the end we talked to the PIRA and Sinn Féin not because they had guns, though that was part of it, but mainly because they had political support. If they had just had guns and no political support, there would have been no need to talk to them, but because they had both we had to.

GS: Who wrote the speeches?

JP: It varied from speech to speech, but the important ones were all written by Tony Blair himself. If you take the Balmoral speech, which was the important speech he made in 1997, the first visit he made outside London after becoming prime minister, John Holmes, who was the private secretary and had been John Major's private secretary for Foreign Affairs and Northern Ireland and Security, wrote the first draft, but Tony changed it substantially himself. He re-wrote it and made it very unionist-friendly. He put in remarks like, 'I don't expect to see a united Ireland in my lifetime'. Those kind of key phrases were all from him. Another speech that was important was the Belfast Harbour speech. Tom Kelly, our press spokesman, who had been the press spokesman in the Northern Ireland Office before as well as political editor of the BBC in Northern Ireland, had a go at the first draft of that speech to set out what he thought would be appealing to the unionists – he was a unionist and so wrote in the terms he though would appeal. But again, Tony sat down on a flight from Moscow back to London, the day before he delivered the speech, and wrote it out again in longhand. The key speeches were all written by Tony himself. All those sort of speeches were cleared with the Northern Ireland Office (NIO) and in the case of Balmoral we cleared it with the Irish Government too. Belfast Harbour would have been cleared with the NIO and those that affected the Ministry of Defence would all go through a bureaucratic process after they had been written. But it tended to be a short bureaucratic process because Tony would tend to write them at the last minute, so there was not a lot of time for changes.

GS: Was the context in which the speech was delivered almost as important as the speech itself?

JP: I would say that we thought quite hard about the environment in which the speeches were given before we wrote the speech. With Balmoral we were very conscious that this was the bastion of unionism. It was a very conscious decision to make this Tony's first visit outside London. Likewise, with the Belfast Harbour speech we thought quite hard about it. We made it different from other visits to Northern Ireland – we did not meet the parties or see anyone else. We just flew in, made the speech and flew out again. It was very clear that this was not part of a negotiation, but an ultimatum, if you like, saying to the PIRA that it is either the ballot box or the Armalite, but not both. We thought hard about that context. If you want to get a message across from a speech, the context is as important as the speech itself.

GS: In your book you say that at times you would write a speech for Gerry Adams to deliver. Did Sinn Féin write paragraphs for you to include in speeches?

JP: Yes, they did. Maybe once a year they would say to us, 'Look, here's a paragraph of things it would be really helpful to say for our community, who are getting worried, who we're losing support for this negotiation and this Agreement from, could you say something like this?' The trouble was that it was always drafted in over-the-top republican terms and it was very hard to ever deliver anything even approximating that. A number of times I would send paragraphs to them with speech suggestions, but again their comments were very maximalist and very hard to meet, so they never drafted a speech as delivered. However, we tried to meet their concerns by putting the key points they wanted to get across into speeches, and likewise for unionists.

GS: How important was the media to what you were doing and what impact did it have?

JP: Well, it was different from the impact of the media on domestic politics in London. In London an awful lot of politics was about the media and how you got your story out and how you communicated all that, and it was very integral to the survival of the government and the popularity of the government. What was happening in Northern Ireland was not like that and we did not think of it in those terms. In Northern Ireland we thought more about where we were trying to get to, and the handling of the media was a tool for getting to that end rather than almost the essence of it, as politics in London was. So it was a slightly different nature. We spent a lot of time thinking about the press handling of it though. The press conferences that Bertie Ahern and Tony Blair did on a series of occasions, often halfway through negotiations, as in the Hillsborough meeting in 1998, and President Clinton's visits, were used to try to present the idea that the process was still ongoing rather than being dead, and a lot of time was spent talking to journalists for that purpose. Tom Kelly's role as the press spokesman was crucial to managing the mood.

GS: Did you try to camouflage some things with the media?

JP: If you start from the position of misleading the press you get yourself into terrible trouble on these things, so you could not do that. I would say it was more a matter of trying to conduct the negotiations in private and not to let people know what was going on, because that would be a betrayal of trust which would disrupt the talks. Mo Mowlam had a sense sometimes that it would be much more democratic to conduct the negotiations in the full glare of publicity, with all the parties participating equally, but the trouble with that is that neither side is going to be prepared to reveal its bottom line, to show its hand in the full glare of publicity and in particular its own side, because they do not want their own side to know what they are prepared to concede. So that made it essential to conduct the negotiations in private. To that extent you are keeping things away from the press. Negotiations are going on in private that they did not know about and that you did not want them to know about, but you could not actually mislead the press. One thing that struck me about the negotiations and the press all the way through was how often when it looked absolutely terrible in the press and that everyone had given up and all was hopeless, I knew that things were going on in private that might lead to a settlement. And at other times when things looked wonderful in the press, they were often absolutely and totally dead. In December 2004, which was when we were going over to try to launch the Agreement between the DUP and Sinn Féin, I knew it was dead, but everyone in London was coming up and congratulating me, saying how wonderful it was that we had the Agreement, when I knew perfectly well that there was no way we were going to get it off the ground. It is true that the press were not aware of what happened, and it was important that they were not, but we did not have a deliberate policy of trying to mislead them.

GS: In those final hours in Castle Buildings before the GFA, were you and Tony Blair watching TV and seeing people who were in the talks then going outside and saying we cannot accept this or that?

JP: We did not have a TV in the main room, and Tony is pretty allergic to watching TV anyway on these sort of things, but Alastair [Campbell] was certainly watching it and keeping an eye on it. He would come in and tell us what was being said, or he would go out to do a briefing that tried to balance up the mood. When the Shinners deliberately went out and said it was all dead, he then tried to go out to remedy it the other way, and so on. So we tried to keep it on an even keel from that point of view. But Tony was not monitoring it, sort of moment-to-moment, no.

GS: You mention in your book that once the Agreement was basically agreed, you needed to get out your emphasis before anyone else did in case they put a spin on it. This indicates the importance of determining the media agenda.

JP: Well, the reason for that is because of the zero-sum politics in Northern Ireland. If you think about the first ceasefire in 1994, because it was the republican supporters who were going around waving flags out of their cars and hooting the horns, unionists thought they had lost and you had these bizarre statements from Molyneaux and Paisley suggesting that unionists had somehow lost because the PIRA had stopped fighting. It was very difficult for a Brit to understand. With this problem of zero-sum politics we had to get out our interpretation before either side tried to claim it as their success. If it had been the unionists out first saying they had won that would have been a problem for republicans, and if republicans had gone out there first saying it was their triumph that would have been a problem for unionists, so we needed to get out there with the Irish Government to give a balanced picture of it, before both sides tried to interpret it and present it for themselves.

GS: In your view why did decommissioning become such a dominant issue?

JP: You have to remember the history of decommissioning. What happened was that when John Major initially had the ceasefire he tried to get the ceasefire declared as permanent; to get the PIRA to say it was permanent. When he could not get this, he then moved on to decommissioning as a surrogate to show that it was permanent, and you can see why his reasoning went down that line. Interestingly, the issue of the permanent ceasefire comes up again and again in terrorist disputes around the world where they do not want a temporary ceasefire, they want a permanent ceasefire, because otherwise the threat of violence is always there when you are negotiating with them. And yet for terrorist movements, because of their very nature, it is almost impossible for them to say that it is permanent, because if the causes of the conflict are not resolved, they want to keep the struggle going, so it is a very difficult issue. I think the mistake that John Major made was that he allowed the issue of decommissioning to become a complete hurdle they had to cross, when there was no way that republicans were going to cross it. They would not have gone on the ceasefire if they knew that this was going to be required of them right up front in the process. Decommissioning is something that happens right at the end of the process not at the beginning. I think that the trouble was that Major made it a precondition. He said that we could not come into talks until this had happened. At first he said complete decommissioning, and then backed down from that and said majority decommissioning, and then backed down from that and said some decommissioning, and then backed down from that and said token decommissioning. If you looked at it from the republican side you would think well, they are going to back down all the way, so I am not going to give on this and, anyway, I am not going to give in because they are asking me to surrender, so I am not going to agree to it. It was a terrible mistake to allow decommissioning to become this blockage and it should never have been put up front as a precondition. It was an important issue and in terms of the substance the unionists were quite right, why on earth should they go into government with a private army behind the other party that they are sharing power with? In the Republic, Bertie Ahern made it clear that he would not go into government with Sinn Féin until the PIRA was disbanded, so why should they? In logic, it is perfectly sensible and a perfectly reasonable position to take. The trouble was, from the other point of view, it was surrender and therefore it was not going to happen. We did spend an awful long time having to work our way round it, but in the end, I mean I know this is a slightly funny thing to say, I do not think it was about decommissioning, but about trust. Decommissioning just became the vehicle for expressing lack of trust on both sides, and if it had not been decommissioning it would have been something else. You need to have a period where the thing is pushed through, where the trust is built before it is really implemented in full and both sides are reconciled, and I think that is really what was happening from the GFA in 1998 onwards. That long period was trying to build trust, even if it was actually going backwards some of that time. After the initial act of decommissioning in 2003, then full unilateral decommissioning in 2005, trust was gradually built.

GS: Were you surprised about the things that people were concerned or angry about?

JP: In particular, what both Tony and I and the Brits in general misunderstood was the importance of symbols, because in British life symbols are just not that significant, whereas in Northern Ireland they really are. So on things like the badge for the reform of the Police Service of Northern Ireland (PSNI), it is hard to believe, but it seemed to Trimble that whether or not the badge for the PSNI had a crown on it was more important than decommissioning. For us that was a sort of a puzzling thing. Or, for republicans, the importance of different aspects of the Irish language, which was largely symbolic rather than real. Then we had the issue on the unionist side of the Scottish/Irish dialect that they wanted to have preserved at the same time. So the importance of symbols completely side-swiped us often and was something that we had a tin ear towards.

GS: How important was the European context?

JP: The European context was important as a background rather than as a sort of motivating factor. John Hume thought the European context enormously important and it changed the way the Irish thought about themselves. They were no longer obsessed with their bigger neighbour and much more interested in the role they could play in the broader entity of Europe. It also made the issue of the border less significant, since we were both inside the EU. I think that the fact of the EU, the fact that Ireland and Britain both joined and were members of it, and the fact that Ireland joined the Euro made a big difference to the relationship between Britain and Ireland and made it easier to have the sort of discussions we needed to have in the peace process. There were also specific measures like the financial grants that the EU gave to the border areas etc., which helped, but I do not think that any of this was really instrumental in the particular aspects of the talks. They were much more important as a background.

Reference

Powell, J. (2008). *Great Hatred, Little Room*. London: Bodley Head.

Conclusion

The contributions in this book indicate not just interpretations about the relationship between text and context, the significance of key principles, or the dynamic that exists between the generalities and specificities of negotiation and dialogue, but, more importantly, *pragmatism*. That is, where approaches to policy and principle are based on the practical consequences of twists and turns which invariably emerge with changing conditions and circumstances rather than because of adherence to some fixed or absolute concept. The peace process was to a large extent built on the nuances of ambiguity, yet the logic and application of pragmatism played a bigger role. Through pragmatism key principles were perceived more in relative terms, where conceding to the truth of principle was far less important than conceding to its value. The pragmatic approach can also be observed throughout this book, where principles were reviewed and revisited as part of a shifting process that required meanings to be adjusted and adapted accordingly. Obviously, the realities of engagement framed expectations about principles and core positions, but it is apparent that, important though this was, commitment to the process was more significant. As with the decommissioning issue, although recognition of its importance was integral for demonstrating an exclusively peaceful approach to political engagement, it is also apparent that judgements about when and how this should be done changed, and that this change was a result of the governments responding to contestations about the form and impact of delivery. Managing those contestations was more vital than merely seeking to impose such principles as demands. And, even though that may have been the initial position, it soon became clear that such rigidity would make decommissioning less rather than more likely.

Along with the pragmatic approach, what also comes across from the chapters is the hard graft of negotiation to create subtle movements that, over time, would accumulate into edging the parties away from intransigent positions. The presentation of these shifts was of particular importance since participants would be scrutinising recommendations not only for signs of how they might be advantaged or disadvantaged, but how their opponents would be advantaged or disadvantaged too. The reciprocity of effect that this created was, of course, integral to choreography and movement, but movement in one direction was often met by a resistance to movement in another. Within this narrowly contested space, creativity and pragmatism proved vital, but the intensity of the process and the contestations within it also pulled the participants towards similar terrain and so linked interests. Contestations over meanings and how things were communicated and stated created a dialectical arrangement that had movement at the core and, unlike the conventional win/lose outcomes that tend to be associated with war, the peace process depended on the symmetry of win/win or lose/lose scenarios. This required tensions to be both managed and used to generate momentum so as to try to bind the parties further into the process and pull those connected with paramilitary groups deeper into negotiations.

Early attempts to bring about an end to the conflict before the peace process developed obviously failed and, as indicated, there are a number of reasons for this (not least of which is timing), but the peace process succeeded where other efforts did not largely because the emphasis was not only on pragmatic thinking, but *inclusiveness*. Throughout the individually authored and interview-based contributions in this book it is apparent that the inclusive approach meant that all parties could seek to exert influence and so claim some ownership of responsibility towards peace. The eventual result of this was to move the extreme parties (Sinn Féin and the Democratic Unionist Party (DUP)) towards the centre of power and so effectively isolate the threat of large-scale opposition outflanking those parties. As we have seen, since the Good Friday Agreement 'dissident' republican factions have arisen in response to Sinn Féin sharing power and supporting policing and justice structures short of the longed for united Ireland, and these factions are seeking to destabilise the Sinn Féin project by killing those working for the police and justice system. At this time, however, such is the support for Sinn Féin that the activities of 'dissidents' have some way to go before establishing a serious alternative, currently lacking popular support and offering little beyond the standard articulations of using armed force to get the British to withdraw.

But, along with pragmatism, inclusivity and the hard grind of initiating dialogue and producing text, there is another factor that explains the success of the peace process and that is the *cohesion* that developed not only within but between the two governments. All the civil servants in this book confirmed that there was a very strong working relationship across the team, but that this was also translated into positive working relations with their Irish counterparts. A consensual approach to the peace process helped to develop closeness between the governments, which not only increased the chances of success, but also restricted the possibility of the Northern Ireland parties trying to exploit any potential divergence of interest that may have arisen between them. Further, although it has been acknowledged in various accounts (both in political memoir and documentary form) that there were differences and even heated exchanges between both governments on a range of issues, the chances of those differences derailing the peace process were considerably minimised by the sense of common purpose that prevailed. A commitment from each government to bring the conflict to an end and secure a peace agreement meant that each was envisaging compromise as necessary in order to realise those goals.

At the end of the period of British involvement in Northern Ireland that this book covers, the Hillsborough Castle Agreement of February 2010 gave formal recognition that the parties in Northern Ireland would move towards devolved policing and justice effective from April 2010, and set out the operational responsibilities needed for the successful transference of policing and justice powers, including an independent judiciary and chief constable responsible for the Police Service of Northern Ireland. A key part of the Agreement was on how to deal with parades, and on this the Agreement stressed that it is best for local people to seek local solutions with regard to parading issues. These solutions would need to take account of 'competing rights', but should be seen in relation to a universal right 'to be free from sectarian harassment'. The Agreement was an attempt to forge consensus in its expression of 'working together in a spirit of partnership to deliver success for the entire community' and to help to ensure a 'spirit of partnership, mutual respect and equality', as well as making the Executive work towards the promotion of 'greater inclusiveness'. But since that time there have been growing strains on the power-sharing arrangement that have required further 'external' help in order to try to address the unsettling effect that this is having on political and social progress.

In the final months of 2013, the American diplomat Richard Haass was called to Northern Ireland to act as chair of a Panel of Parties in the Northern Ireland Executive. His role, along with vice-chair Meghan O'Sullivan, was to try to produce a template that the parties would accept on the contentious areas of parades and protests, flags and emblems, and dealing with the legacy of conflict. In doing this Haass would be working to try to facilitate moves towards a society that, he stressed, should strive to be 'compassionate', 'shared' and 'open', rather than divided, tense, antagonistic and oppositional, which was the reason Haass was called in the first place. A series of riots and protests developed in late 2012 after a vote was taken amongst the Northern Ireland parties to stop the Union Jack flag from flying over City Hall in Belfast every day of the year. An attempted compromise to fly the flag on designated days was not enough to curb serious dissent and animosity amongst unionists and loyalists, who saw the gesture as a diminution of their identity. This tension and anger then fed into other expressions of cultural identity such as parades and protests, compounding fears of loss and associated expectations of resistance and obstruction. A need to 'deliver success for the entire community', as stressed in the Hillsborough Agreement, led to Haass' recommendations referring not just to 'the community', but to 'communities' in order to get a framework accepted that would ease

Northern Ireland through a contentious phase of social and communal relations. The use of the word 'communities' alongside 'community' casts an interesting light on perceptual management of relations in the peace process at the start of 2014, since as the perceptive Glenn Patterson observed in an article after the publication of the Haass recommendations, '"Community" is a word of aggregation, "communities" is a word that rather than multiplying, as plurals ought, actually divides' (Patterson also noted how the Haass report uses the word 'community' twelve times and 'communities' nine times) (Patterson 2014).

The Haass recommendations outlined new arrangements, including an Office for Parades, Select Commemorations and Related Protests (designed to resolve disputes about the above by using an adjudication process); a Commission on Identity, Culture and Tradition (to 'sustain a conversation' about these areas); a body to deal with Contending with the Past (with the formation of a new body – the Historical Investigations Unit – to work on past injustices and victims issues); and an Implementation and Reconciliation Group (to monitor the implementation and function of the other bodies above and to 'consider other initiatives that could contribute to reconciliation, a better understanding of the past, and a reduction in sectarianism'). The range of the recommendations indicates how much work is still to be done in addressing the legacy of conflict in Northern Ireland. Important, too, is that although the recommendations are wide-ranging they lack detail and tend to frame the new arrangements in general terms. This, to some extent, returns us to one of the key factors used to develop the peace process in Northern Ireland – ambiguity. What strikes one when reading the *Proposed Agreement* by Haass (released 31 December 2013) is that it provides more questions than answers, and in doing so recognises that in a divided society, such as Northern Ireland, answers can be highly problematic because they can fix positions that make parties more vulnerable in what is still a shifting 'post-conflict' environment. The *Proposed Agreement*, in many ways like the agreements of the British and Irish governments, is an example of movement by questions, rather than creating a potential logjam by laying out answers.

At the time of writing, the Haass recommendations have not been accepted by the DUP or the UUP. Each appears to be watching the other, still fearful of the dreaded 'sell-out' accusation in the run-up to various elections taking place across the next three years. There is also the expected reaction within unionism and loyalism that if republicans and nationalists agree to run with the recommendations then this can only be because it suits their agenda and so therefore must be to the detriment of unionism and loyalism. In many ways this demonstrates how much important work still needs to be done in Northern Ireland and that general rather than specific discussion and debate on the most divisive issues remains key to keeping the parties constructively engaged with those issues. It also continues to show how the two political communities tend to depict themselves in binary opposition.

The question as to whether the British and Irish reduced their involvement in the peace process too early is a matter of conjecture (the work of Haass makes it apparent that the 'external' third party may be needed for some time yet), but it does seem that without the formal structures and efforts of the two governments to help to create movement as before, the parties in Northern Ireland are struggling to find an agreed approach to political change. That change, until 2010, as detailed in this book, encompassed a wide range of complex and interlocking approaches that created momentum and direction. But the peace process has been largely successful (whilst acknowledging the problem of dissident groups and the fragility of relations when confronted with seriously divisive concerns) because it has functioned primarily as a *process*. In so doing, it has reoriented the parties away from the fixations of conflict to the fluidity of peace, thereby adjusting static concerns to become dynamic concerns (even if they are connected). In such a new landscape traditional positions are less likely to be effective for maintaining security and that landscape will be increasingly shaped by forces and tensions that will depend more on the reflexivity of political skill and decision-making if Northern Ireland is to succeed in unbinding itself from the restraints of conflict. Of course, the British and Irish governments were dealing with established positions all the time with the parties in negotiations, but they slowly and incrementally were able to help to move those positions and get the parties to look forward rather than backward and outward rather than inward. A successful and positive Northern Ireland will depend on constantly looking forward and outward because the dangers of looking backward and inward are self-evident. It will depend, to put it another way, on the continuation of process and pragmatism if the hard ties of division are to become loosened. Or, as the historian Linda Colley put it when commenting on acts of union and disunion in the United Kingdom, 'Only in recent decades has it come to be more widely accepted that acts of union of any kind may be too crude instruments in regard to Ireland, and that what is needed are messier, more variegated and more pragmatic political solutions. The work of compromise remains in progress' (Colley 2013: 103).

References

Colley, L. (2013). *Acts of Union and Disunion*. London: Profile Books.
Haass, R. (2013). *An Agreement Among the Parties of the Northern Ireland Executive on Parades, Select Commemorations, and Related Protests; Flags and Emblems; and Contending with the Past*. Belfast: Northern Ireland Executive.
Patterson, Glen (2014). 'Don't Mention the C-Word', *The Irish Times*, 4 January.

Index

9/11. *See* Al Qaeda attacks on US
10 Downing Street. *See* Prime Minister's Office

'acts of completion'
  issues relating to, 152–3
  Joint Declaration (2003), 166
  talks on, 149
  Tony Blair calls for, 149, 296
  see also cessation of conflict; decommissioning
Adams, Gerry
  and Albert Reynolds, 210–11
  assessment of, 144, 197, 242–3
  and ceasefire, 256, 267–8
  choice of political solution, 269–70
  and David Trimble, 148–9, 169, 197–8
  and decommissioning, 233, 238, 242, 284, 287, 288–9, 321–2
  desire for peace, 191–2
  and Good Friday Agreement, 232
  'Groundhog Day' reference, 229–30, 260
  and IRA, 306, 308–9
  and John Hume, 30–1, 129, 184, 210–11, 245, 254–5
  and Joint Declaration, 158, 164, 167
  Jonathan Powell writes speeches for, 325–6
  leadership abilities, 87, 94–5, 171–2, 309, 315
  and Martin McGuinness, 279–80
  meeting with DUP, 316–17
  on negotiating with British, 90
  negotiational approach, 92, 99, 110, 154, 242–3, 287–8, 297–8, 302–3, 305, 306–7, 318, 320, 321, 323
  and Northern Bank robbery, 283, 315–16
  on reduction of British Army presence, 318–19
  sense of history, 295–6
  and Tony Blair, 311–12
  US visit, 130–1, 139–40, 210–11

Ahern, Patrick (Bertie)
  aspiration to rejoin Commonwealth, 100
  on government with Sinn Féin, 328
  involvement in negotiations, 167, 195–6
  and John Major, 74
  and Tony Blair, 146, 150, 187, 246–7, 262–3, 311, 326
Al Qaeda attacks on US (9/11), impact of, 238, 283, 311–12
Alliance Party, 58, 74, 141, 150, 265
ambiguity
  abandonment of, 289–90
  Anglo-Irish Agreement, 48–9
  clarity and, 88, 263–4, 295, 312–13, 320
  'constructive ambiguity', 22, 263–4, 281, 313–14
  Good Friday Agreement, 295
  importance of, 3, 14–15, 93
  religion and, 282
  Sinn Féin and, 205
  specificity in relation to, 281
  talking as source of, 294
  as theme, 14
  understanding of, 82
  unionist parties and, 205
  see also pragmatism and principle, balancing of
Anglo-Irish Agreement (1985)
  ambiguity, 48–9
  breakdown of negotiations, possibility of, 47–9
  British approach, key factors, 35–6, 38–9
  collaboration and cooperation, emphasis on, 33
  communiqué post-conclusion, 51
  comparison of British and Irish approaches, 43
  consent principle, 1–6, 44, 111
  'constitutional status', use of term, 49
  devolution, 65
  early British proposals, Irish response to, 42

335

Anglo-Irish Agreement (1985) (*cont.*)
  final draft, 45, 49–50
  Garret FitzGerald, and *see* FitzGerald, Garret
  historical continuity within, 98–9
  Intergovernmental Conference. *See* Intergovernmental Conference
  Irish constitutional claims, 63–8
  Irish Government's consultative role, 48, 51–2
  Irish note, British response to, 43
  Margaret Thatcher, and *see* Thatcher, Margaret
  meetings, 44–5
  negotiational process, 45
  negotiations, 29–30, 33–8, 39–40, 41–52
  Northern Ireland Civil Service and, 29
  operation of. *See* Intergovernmental Conference
  opposition to, 63
  order of construction, 44
  origins of peace process, 1–2, 6
  peace process after, 51–2, 114
  preliminary discussions, 40–1
  presentation post-conclusion, 51
  Provisional IRA (PIRA) attacks, effect on negotiations, 52
  security cooperation, British focus on, 64
  significance of, 37–8
  Sinn Féin, aim of marginalising, 116
  success of, 36
  Sunningdale Agreement contrasted, 48
  timescale of negotiations, 44–5
  unionist opposition, 46–7, 50, 52–3, 64–5, 68
Anglo-Irish relations
  background to, 9
  cohesion, 331–2
  consultation and cooperation
    emphasis on, 33
    proposals for, 27–8
  dialogue, contrasting approaches, 257–8
  and European Union, 51–2
  Falklands War, 38–40, 41
  joint authority. *See* joint authority
  Joint Declaration. *See* Joint Declaration (2003)
  see also Anglo-Irish Agreement; negotiations
Armstrong of Ilminster, Robert Armstrong, Lord
  on Anglo-Irish Agreement, 9, 33–53
  involvement in negotiations, 1–6, 98–9

attacks by paramilitary groups. *See* loyalist organisations; Provisional Irish Republican Army (PIRA)

Belfast Agreement. *See* Good Friday Agreement (1998)
Belfast Harbourmaster's speech (October 2002). *See* Blair, Tony
Blair, Tony
  achievement summarised, 199–200
  and Bertie Ahern, 146, 150, 187, 246–7, 262–3, 311, 326
  calls for 'acts of completion', 238–9, 296
  charisma, 228
  commitment to peace process, 187
  and decommissioning, 190–1
  emphasis on maintaining momentum, 188–9, 192, 227
  and Good Friday Agreement, 192–9, 233
  Harbourmaster's speech (October 2002), 149, 281–2, 289–90
  Hillsborough talks (April 2003), 149
  and Ian Paisley, 281–2
  John Major compared, 187–8, 192–3, 197, 199–200, 227, 275–6
  and Mo Mowlam, 97
  and multiparty negotiations, 75
  negotiational style, 187–8
  'peace train' metaphor, 221
  Royal Agricultural Society speech (May 1997), 188–91
  and Sinn Féin, 189, 190
  speechwriting, 324–5
  strength of mandate, 188
  transition from Major Government. *See* transition between governments
  and unionists, 189–90
Bloody Friday and origins of peace process, 4–5
Bloody Sunday and origins of peace process, 4–5
Bloomfield, Sir Kenneth
  on drafting of documents and speeches, 9, 17–32
  involvement in peace process, 66, 151
bombings. *See* loyalist organisations; Provisional Irish Republican Army (PIRA)
British Army, reduction of presence, 294, 318–19
British Commonwealth. *See* Commonwealth of Nations (Commonwealth)
British Government
  acknowledges stalemate situation, 299–300

Index

belief in military victory, 87–8, 109–10, 256
clarity in negotiations, preference for, 295–6
consent to international involvement in peace process, 225–6
constitutional issue, perspective on, 57–8
contact with PIRA. *See* 'link, the'
cost of conflict, 109
drafting of documents and speeches. *See* drafting of documents and speeches
Government of Ireland Act 1920. *See* Government of Ireland Act 1920
imbalanced relationship with nationalists and unionists, 206–7
'no selfish strategic or economic interest' statement. *See* 'Whitbread' speech
objectives for peace, 151–2
policy shortcomings, 1922–72, 209
relations with Irish Government. *See* Anglo-Irish relations
transition between governments. *See* transition between governments
see also Northern Ireland Office (NIO); United Kingdom
'British presence' speech. *See* 'Whitbread' speech
British withdrawal
  Harold Wilson considers, 4
  talks about, 315
Brooke, Peter
  'British presence' speech. *See* 'Whitbread' speech
  commitment to political settlement, 68, 69, 102, 112–13, 114, 260–1
  secretary of state, 13–14, 22–3, 24, 30, 67, 83, 114, 122, 202, 209, 255
  see also Brooke/Mayhew talks
Brooke/Mayhew talks (1991–3)
  commencement, 124
  Dublin meeting (September 1992), 125–6
  leaks to media, 125
  progression, 125
  three-strand structure, 124–5
Brown, Gordon
  and Brian Cowen, 282–3
  and Mo Mowlam, 97
Bush, George W.
  Hillsborough talks (April 2003), 149
  involvement in peace process, 152

Cabinet Official Committee on Northern Ireland, establishment of, 66
Cahill, Joe, allowed US visa, 85
Callaghan, James (Jim), contingency planning for intervention, 79
Campbell, Alastair, *Irish Diaries*, 212
Catholic community. *See* nationalist community; republican movement
ceasefires. *See* loyalist organisations; Provisional Irish Republican Army (PIRA)
cessation of conflict
  acknowledgement of stalemate situation, 299–300
  IRA acknowledges, 153–4
  verification as issue, 152–3
Chastelain, General John de
  British consent to appointment, 225
  IICD chairman, 95–6, 144–5, 288
  influence, 225–6
  press conference, 149–50, 169, 218, 286, 304, 308, 315, 317–18
  reports on decommissioning, 149–50
'Chiffon'. *See* 'link, the'
Chilcot, Sir John
  drafting of text, 265
  on negotiational approach, 10, 79–100
  permanent secretary, 66, 101, 128–9, 154
Chile, parallels with Northern Ireland, 148
civil rights campaign, student marches, 121
civil servants
  analytical approach, 258–9
  dialogue between, British and Irish contrasted, 257–8
  educational background, influence of, 96
  importance of role, 6–7
  Martin McGuinness on trusting, 292
  trust-building, 258
  see also drafting of documents and speeches; Northern Ireland Civil Service
civil unrest pre-1969, 120–1
Clinton, Bill
  hosts Irish investment conference, 139
  and Tony Blair, 188–9, 195–6
  US president, 134–5
  visits Northern Ireland, 140, 273–4
collusion by security forces. *See* Cory Collusion Inquiry
Combined Loyalist Military Command (CLMC). *See* loyalist organisations
commemorations, Haass recommendations, 332–3
Commonwealth of Nations (Commonwealth), Bertie Ahern aspires to rejoin, 100
communities, conflicts within. *See* intercommunal conflicts
conflict, end. *See* 'acts of completion'; cessation of conflict

consent principle
  Anglo-Irish Agreement, 1–6, 44, 111
  centrality of, 26, 27–8
  'constitutional guarantee', 57, 58, 68, 69–70, 72, 77
  Downing Street Declaration, 111
  Dublin Summit agreement on, 60–2
  emphasis on, 14–15, 110–11
  Frameworks for the Future, 111–12
  Good Friday Agreement, 112, 230
  importance, 214–15
  Irish acceptance, 57
  Joint Declaration, 153
  republicans and, 215
  Sunningdale Agreement, 2–3
  Whitbread speech, 70–1
Constitution. *See* Irish constitutional claims; Northern Ireland Constitution Act 1973
Constitutional Convention (1974), drafting of documents and speeches, 28
'constitutional guarantee'. *See* consent principle
'constitutional imperative'. *See* Irish constitutional claims
constitutional status, change in
  Anglo-Irish Agreement, 49
  British position, 41–2
  consent principle. *See* consent principle
  see also sovereignty, transfer of
consultation and cooperation
  Anglo-Irish. *See* Anglo-Irish relations
  Northern Irish, unionist opposition, 60
Cooke, David
  on drafting of Joint Declaration, 12, 147–74
  involvement in peace process, 66, 83, 101
Cory Collusion Inquiry, Weston Park proposals and, 162–3
Council of Ireland
  establishment of, 1–2
  opposition to, 3
counter-terrorism. *See* security
courts
  Anglo-Irish Agreement and 'Diplock' courts, 63–4
  devolution, 152–3, 164, 165, 166, 167, 168–9, 170, 209, 293, 296–7, 300–1, 332
Cowen, Brian
  and decommissioning, 167–8
  and Gordon Brown, 282–3
  involvement in peace process, 167
  Weston Park proposals, 161–2
'Crossroads' speech, drafting of, 23–4

Darlington conference (1972), drafting of documents and speeches, 27–8
decommissioning
  'collective act of reconciliation' proposal, 232–3
  creative problem-solving, 95–6
  devolution and, 195, 196–7, 244–5
  difficulties, 180–3, 218
  Downing Street talks and proposals (1999), 233–4
  first act of, 144–5
  Good Friday Agreement, 116–17, 230, 289
  Hillsborough Castle talks and declaration (1999), 232–3
  importance of, 327–8
  International Independent Commission on Decommissioning (IICD). *See* Chastelain, General John de
  Irish Government's negotiational stance, 90
  issue of, 152–3
  Joint Declaration, 167–8, 169–70
  language differences as to, 273
  Mitchell Principles, 182
  Mitchell Report (1996), 180–1, 182
  murder of Robert McCartney, effect of, 284
  Northern Bank robbery, effect of, 284
  PIRA commitment, 285
  progress, 149–50
  progress reports, 234
  significance of, 290
  strategic approach to negotiations, 288–90
  talks, 140
  unfulfilled promises, 220
  Washington Three conditions, 180–1, 182
  Weston Park proposals (July 2001), 237
'demilitarisation'. *See* 'normalisation'
Democratic Unionist Party (DUP)
  boycotting of talks, 71, 141
  and decommissioning, 284, 287, 288
  and devolution of justice and policing, 296–7
  district councils, 126, 127, 128, 142
  electoral support, 141, 149–50, 243
  End to Drift, An, 52–3
  and Good Friday Agreement, 76, 149, 153, 198, 205, 240–1, 281
  and Irish Government, 265
  and Joint Declaration, 150, 170
  meeting with Bill Clinton, 140
  multiparty negotiations, 74–5, 76–7, 252–3
  negotiational approach, 281, 315, 319
  negotiational strength, 172–3, 281, 297–8
  negotiational tactics, 278
  and Northern Ireland Executive (1998), 192–3, 197–8

Index

power-sharing, 87
and reduction of British Army presence, 294
relations with, 286, 293, 302–3, 304
returns to talks, 125–6, 174
and Sinn Féin, 278, 306–7, 316–17, 326–7
and UUP, 87, 150
withdraws from talks, 75, 125, 141, 248
see also Paisley, Ian; Robinson, Peter
Devlin, Patrick (Paddy), 2–3, 4
devolution
  Anglo-Irish Agreement, 53, 65
  Constitutional Convention (1974), 28
  deadlock as to, 197–8, 229–30, 233, 239–40
  decommissioning and, 195, 196–7, 244–5
  devolved government. *See* Northern Ireland Executive
  DUP and, 296–7
  Framework for Accountable Government in Northern Ireland, A, 138
  integration and, 60
  Irish Government and, 33–4, 36, 65
  Joint Declaration, 166
  justice and policing, 152–3, 164, 165, 167, 168–9, 170, 209, 293, 296–7, 300–1, 332
  Mitchell Review and, 247–8
  as objective, 66–7, 283–4
  power-sharing and, 126–7, 209–10
  'rolling devolution', failure of, 38–40
  SDLP and, 57
  suspension. *See* direct rule
  unionist support, 29–30, 60
  see also new institutional framework
d'Hondt procedure, use of, 234–5
dialogue
  alteration of text, 292–3
  ambiguity and clarity in relation, 281
  background to role of, 14
  between civil servants, British and Irish contrasted, 257–8
  collapse of the Executive, after, 277
  with PIRA. *See* 'link, the'
  private dialogue, 277–8, 280–1, 292–3
  text in relation, 216–17, 259
  see also exploratory dialogue; negotiations
'Diplock' courts, Anglo-Irish Agreement and, 63–4
direct rule
  commencement, 27
  reintroduction, 138, 148–9, 235–6, 258–9, 268, 274–5
district councils
  Sir Patrick Mayhew visits, 128
  views on British Government intentions, 126

Divis Street Riots (1964), Ian Paisley and, 120–1
documents
  dialogue in relation, 216–17, 259
  drafting of. *See* drafting of documents and speeches
  in negotiations, 216–17, 322–3
  see also single text negotiation
  peace process as text-driven process, 224
Downing Street. *See* Prime Minister's Office
Downing Street Declaration (1993)
  consent principle, 111
  exchange of letters, 130–1
  Irish constitutional claims, 71–3
  and Joint Declaration, 159–60
  loyalist paramilitary response, 131
  publication, 130
drafting of documents and speeches
  ambiguity, 22
  anticipating responses to texts, 86, 261–2
  background to, 9, 12, 13–14
  civil servants' role, 22
  civil servants' role in speech-writing, 21
  clarity as to likely effect, 93–4
  concealment and transparency in relation, 260–1
  Constitutional Convention (1974), 28
  constitutional White Paper (24 March 1972), 26–7
  continuity and change, balancing of emphases, 262
  contribution to peace process, 32
  'Crossroads' speech, 23–4
  dialogue and text in relation, 216–17, 259
  difference between draft and final text, 223–4
  equivalence in responding to texts, 255
  exchange of views, facilitation by text, 273–4
  expression, limits of, 94
  fiftieth anniversary speech, 25–6
  Future Development of the Parliament and Government of Northern Ireland, The (consultative document) (1 January 1971), 26
  Future of Northern Ireland, The (discussion document) (November 1972), 27–8
  inclusiveness and, 254–5
  interpretation by British and Irish contrasted, 256–8
  interpretation by republicans and unionists contrasted, 265–8
  introduction, 17–18
  Joint Declaration, 153–67
  language and meaning, 272–3

drafting of documents and speeches (*cont.*)
  language tone, 274
  language, use of, 160, 272–3
  length of text, 93
  meaning of words, 272–3
  means to end, texts as, 269–70
  Northern Ireland Civil Service, 18, 19
  Northern Ireland Government, 19–20
  Northern Ireland Office, 22–3
  'On the Runs' (OTRs) issue, 270–1
  O'Neill/Lamass meeting communiqué, 21–2
  persuasiveness, 262
  political analysis and, 253–4
  political developments and, 254
  'Pottinger' speech, 20
  pragmatism and principle, balancing of, 262, 271–2
  private agreements, 259–60
  private dialogue and, 292–3
  process, 252–3
  Queen's Speeches, 20–1
  reform declaration (1968), 24–5
  secretary of state's input, 274–5
  speeches
    context of, 325
    cooperation in writing, 325–6
    value of, 261, 305
  speechwriters, 324–5
  strategic approach, 93
  tactical approach, 93
  during talks, 265
  tone of language, 274
  too much text, 269
  transparency and concealment in relation, 260–1
  videoconferencing, 30
  'Whitbread' speech, 30–1
Dublin Summit (1980), agreement on consent principle, 60–2
Dungannon, Sir Patrick Mayhew visits, 127

economy
  Census 2001, 151
  'peace dividend' from Good Friday Agreement, 78
  unionist concerns, 59
elections for representation at multiparty negotiations (1996). *See* multiparty negotiations
Elizabeth II, Queen, Martin McGuinness toasts, 263
End to Drift, An (1987), 52–3, 64–5
European Union
  Anglo-Irish relations and, 51–2
  and Good Friday Agreement, 329
  support for peace process, 113
exclusively peaceful means, principle of and decommissioning, 290
  Sinn Féin and, 290–1
Executive. *See* Northern Ireland Executive
exploratory dialogue
  announcement of, 134
  conditions for, 133–4
  loyalist organisations, 136–9
  Sinn Féin, 135, 137–8, 139–40, 141
  timing of commencement, 135

Falklands War and Anglo-Irish relations, 38–40, 41
Faulkner, Brian
  fiftieth anniversary speech, 25–6
  leads Northern Ireland Executive (1974), 121
  on Sunningdale Agreement, 1–3
Fianna Fáil
  and Anglo-Irish Agreement, 68
  and constitutional claims amendment, 69–70
  foundation, 56
  opposition to consent principle, 60
  opposition to partition, 56–7
Fine Gael
  and constitutional claims, 57
  foundation of, 56
Fitt, Gerard (Gerry), 24–5, 26–7, 121
Fittall, William
  on drafting of documents, 13–14, 252–76
  principal private secretary, 161, 162–3
FitzGerald, Garret
  Anglo-Irish Agreement, 29–30, 33–5, 36, 37–8, 40–1, 46, 47–8, 98–9, 116
  constitutional reform attempts, 62
  and Margaret Thatcher, 34–5, 39, 40, 41, 43, 45–6, 50
  New Ireland Forum. *See* New Ireland Forum
forgiveness. *See* reconciliation
Framework for Accountable Government in Northern Ireland, A (1995), 138–9, 179–80
Frameworks for the Future (1985), 111–12
fugitives. *See* 'On the Runs' (OTRs)
Future Development of the Parliament and Government of Northern Ireland, The (consultative document) (1 January 1971), drafting of, 26
Future of Northern Ireland, The (discussion document) (November 1972), drafting of, 27–8

Index 341

Good Friday Agreement (1998)
  ambiguity, 295
  background to negotiational challenges, 14
  Brooke/Mayhew talks. *See* Brooke/Mayhew talks
  comprehensiveness, 230
  consent principle, 112, 230
  decommissioning. *See* decommissioning
  difference between draft and final text, 223–4
  'double referendum', 76, 77, 142–3
  Downing Street Declaration. *See* Downing Street Declaration
  early talks, 69–71
  effects of, 76–8
  and European Union, 329
  framework text for negotiations, 114, 118–19
  implementation difficulties. *See* implementation of Good Friday Agreement
  implementation proposals. *See* Weston Park proposals
  interpretational differences between parties, 295
  key agreements, 75–6, 142–3
  multiparty negotiations. *See* multiparty negotiations 1996–8
  naming of, 223
  negotiations process. *See* negotiations
  new institutional framework. *See* new institutional framework
  Northern Ireland ministers, provision for removal, 231
  policing, 76, 230
  preliminary developments, 63–8
  prisoner releases, 76, 230
  responses to, 55, 76, 149, 295, 323
  and Sunningdale Agreement, 3, 209–10, 221
  three-strand structure, 67, 74–5, 89, 115
  transition between governments, 192–9
  see also implementation of Good Friday Agreement
Goodall, Sir David
  on Anglo-Irish Agreement, 9, 33–53
  British negotiator at Intergovernmental Conference, 40
Government of Ireland Act 1920, Irish unity provisions, 57
Gow, Ian, 49
Great Hatred, Little Room (Jonathan Powell), 258, 270–1, 275, 304
Greysteele massacre (1993), effect on peace process, 129–30

Guzmán, Patricio, *Nostalgia for the Light* (film), 147

Haass, Richard, recommendations on parades, symbols and commemorations, 332–3
Harbourmaster's speech (October 2002). *See* Blair, Tony
Haughey, Charles
  and consent principle, 60–1, 62, 63
  and constitutional claims amendment, 69–70
  and Margaret Thatcher, 38–40, 60–1
  and New Ireland Forum, 62–3
Heath, Edward, and Sunningdale Agreement, 2–3, 47
Hill, David, on 'constitutional issue', 10, 55–78
Hillsborough talks (April 2003), and Joint Declaration, 149
history
  Haass recommendations on parades, symbols and commemorations, 332–3
  high politics approach to peace process, 147
  and memory, parallels with Chilean 'Disappeared', 148
  peace process as historical narrative, 90–1
  sense of, 287–8, 305
Holmes, Sir John
  private secretary, 275–6, 324–5
  on transition between governments, 12, 177–200
Hume, John
  on Europe, 329
  and Gerry Adams, 30–1, 86, 129, 139–40, 184, 210–11, 245, 253, 306–7
  and Irish Government, 29–30, 34, 191, 254
  and John Major, 254–5
  negotiational role, 92
  and New Ireland Forum, 62–3
  Nobel Peace Prize, 108
  and power-sharing, 26
  and SDLP, 87
  sense of identity, 96
  strategic approach, 25–6, 87
  and US involvement, 85
  willingness to compromise, 87
hunger strikes and origins of peace process, 5

implementation of Good Friday Agreement
  alternative approaches, possibilities for, 244–8
  background, 13

implementation of Good Friday
    Agreement (*cont.*)
  bilateral negotiations (April 2000), 236–7
  Civil Service perspective, 250–1
  and continuation of PIRA activity, 238–9
  and continuation of violence and disorder,
    243–4
  decommissioning. *See* decommissioning
  Downing Street talks and proposals (1999),
    233–4
  'Groundhog Day', description as, 229–30
  Hillsborough Castle talks and declaration
    (March 1999), 232–3
  introduction, 229–30
  lack of comprehensiveness, 239–40
  language sensitivities, 231–2
  lessons from, 248–50
  literal approach, 231–2
  Mitchell Review (September 1999), 235–6
  public statements, use of, 232
  Sinn Féin's approach, 242
  unionist opposition, 240–2
  Way Forward, The, 233
  Weston Park proposals (July 2001), 237
  willing participation, need for, 231
inclusiveness
  author's early political experience, 120–1
  background to, 11
  Brooke/Mayhew talks. *See* Brooke/Mayhew
    talks
  contacts with paramilitary organisations,
    128–33, 143–4, 145–6
  see also 'link, the'
  and convergence of differences, 262–3
  district councils, visits to, 126–8, 142
  exploratory dialogue. *See* exploratory
    dialogue
  importance of, 331
  introduction, 120
  multiparty negotiations. *See* multiparty
    negotiations
  Northern Ireland Executive as model, 121
  Northern Ireland Office, work of. *See*
    Northern Ireland Office
  Political Affairs Division, work of. *See*
    Northern Ireland Office
  prison regime reforms, 122
  US involvement, 134–5, 139–40
Independent Monitoring Commission (IMC)
  establishment, 290
  proposal for, 152–3
institutional reform. *See* new institutional
    framework
integration with United Kingdom, unionist
    support for, 60

intercommunal conflicts
  challengers' objectives, 105–6
  differences between incumbents and
    challengers, 106
  features of, 103–4
  incumbents' objectives, 105
  introduction, 101–3
  preconditions to settlement
    all-party confidence in peace process,
      108–9, 112–13, 114
    conflict not best chance of achieving
      goals, 107, 109–10, 113
    cost of continuing conflict is
      unacceptable, 106–7, 109, 113
    external stakeholders' support, 109, 113,
      114
    grievances capable of peaceful resolution,
      107–8, 110, 113
    meeting of in Israeli–Palestinian dispute,
      113–14
    meeting of in Northern Ireland, 109–13
    prospective all-party acceptance of deal,
      108, 110–12, 114
  process of settlement, importance of, 114
  settlement of, 10–11
  threat of violence, leverage from, 116–17
Intergovernmental Conference
  establishment of, 40
  meetings, 43–4
  operation of, 64
intergovernmental relations. *See* Anglo-Irish
    relations
International Independent Commission on
    Decommissioning (IICD). *See*
    decommissioning
international involvement in peace process
  British Government's consent to, 225–6
  scope post-Joint Declaration, 152
  see also European Union; United States
Irish-Americans
  fact-finding group visit, 129–30
  shift in thinking after 9/11, 284–5
  support for Anglo-Irish Agreement, 48
  withdrawal of support for PIRA, 283
Irish Civil War, political consequences, 56–7
Irish constitutional claims
  amendment
    achievement of, 77
    initiatives for, 62, 69–70
    offers of, 40–1, 71
    support for, 69–70
  Anglo-Irish Agreement, 63–8
  background to 'constitutional issue', 10, 55
  Belfast Agreement. *See* Good Friday
    Agreement (1998)

Index

British objective of amendment, 41–2, 46
British perspective, 57–8
'constitutional imperative', 31–2, 69, 110–11
Downing Street Declaration, 71–3
drafting of constitution of 1937, 56–7
Frameworks for the Future, 111–12
multiparty negotiations 1996–8, 74–6
nationalist perspective, 56–7
negotiations during 1980s, 60–3
negotiations during 1990–2, 69–71
Sunningdale Agreement, 3, 31–2
Supreme Court ruling, 69
unionist perspectives, 58–60
Irish Diaries (Alastair Campbell), 212
Irish Free State
  accepts partition, 56–7
  creation, 56–7
Irish Government
  contact with loyalist organisations, 146
  and decommissioning, 90
  and DUP, 265
  opposition to consent principle, 60
  relations with British Government. *See* Anglo-Irish relations
  relationship with nationalists and unionists, compared with British Government's, 206–7
Irish Labour Party, 57, 60, 62, 63, 68
Irish National Liberation Army (INLA)
  ceasefire, 144–5
  ceasefire talks, 143–4
  contact with, 146
  and Joint Declaration, 150–1
Irish Republic
  Constitution. *See* Irish constitutional claims
  cost of conflict, 109
  see also Irish Free State; Irish Government
Irish Republican Socialist Party (IRSP). *See* Irish National Liberation Army (INLA)
Irish Supreme Court, constitutional claims ruling, 69
Irish unity
  nationalist support for, 58
  see also Irish constitutional claims
Israeli–Palestinian conflict, preconditions for settlement of, 113–14

Jeffrey, Sir William (Bill)
  on implementing Good Friday Agreement, 13, 229–51
  involvement in peace process, 161, 162–3
joint authority
  'consultative structures' agreement, 36
  Irish proposals, 34–5, 36

Joint Declaration (2003)
  achievement in international context, 174
  acts of completion, 166
  aims, 147, 167
  assessment of, 170–1
  background, 12, 148–53
  British negotiation critiqued, 169–74
  chronology, 174–5
  consent principle, 153
  devolution, 166
  and Downing Street Declaration, 159–60
  drafting of, 153–67
  hypothetical impact of, 170
  introduction, 147–8
  key issues, 152–3
  key personalities, 167
  lessons learned, 169
  negotiation with Sinn Féin, 173
  Northern Ireland Office and, 153–7
  other issues, 153
  phases in negotiations, 168–9
  place within peace process, 148–9
  political manoeuvrings, 150
  publication, 149
  revision of draft, 163
  single text negotiation, 166–7
  sufficient consensus principle, 173
  varied approach to issues, 167–8
  and Weston Park proposals (July 2001), 161–3
justice system. *See* courts; policing

King, Tom, 22–3, 24, 30

language
  drafting of documents and speeches, 160
  in negotiations, 90
leaks to media, use of, 125, 129–30
'link, the'
  breaking news of secret exchanges, 130
  'Chiffon', code name, 129
  existence, 80, 128–9, 218, 253
  intelligence assessment, 80
  reliability, 80
Loyalist Commission, establishment, 145
loyalist organisations
  ceasefire (October 1994), 73, 133–4
  Combined Loyalist Military Command (CLMC), 130–1, 133, 134, 140–1, 145
  contact with, 130–3, 144, 145–6
  cost of conflict, 109
  decommissioning of weapons. *See* decommissioning

loyalist organisations (*cont.*)
  and Downing Street Declaration, 131
  exploratory dialogue, 135
  fugitives. *See* 'On the Runs' (OTRs)
  Greysteele massacre (1993), 129–30
  and Joint Declaration, 150–1
  reactive nature of violence, 109
  response to PIRA ending of ceasefire, 140–1
  US funding for peace projects, 145–6

Maccabe, Chris
  on inclusiveness in peace process, 11, 120–46
  involvement in peace process, 66, 101, 155, 156, 172–3
Maginess, Brian, 18–19
Major, John
  and Albert Reynolds, 92–3
  announces exploratory dialogues, 135, 136–7
  calls 1997 general election, 142
  and decommissioning, 180–3, 312–13, 327–8
  defeat in 1992 general election expected, 253–4, 264
  Downing Street Declaration, 130–1
  end of Government, 179–87
  and Gerry Adams, 130–1
  and Hugh Smyth, 133, 134
  and Joe Cahill visa, 85
  and John Hume, 254–5
  momentum of peace talks, 303
  and multiparty negotiations, 74
  and PIRA, 302
  on talking with PIRA, 130
  Tony Blair compared, 187–8, 192–3, 197, 199–200, 227, 275–6
  and Tory right wing, 87–8
  transition to Blair Government. *See* transition between governments
  and unionists, 179–80
Mallon, Seamus
  critiques British Government policy, 170–1, 172
  elected MP, 65
  on Good Friday Agreement, 1–2
  resigns as deputy first minister-designate, 234–5
  on Sunningdale Agreement, 221
Mandelson, Peter
  secretary of state, 250
  suspends Northern Ireland Executive, 236
Mason, Roy, 79
Mayhew, Sir Patrick
  announces exploratory dialogues, 136–7
  district councils visits, 128, 142
  Orange Order meeting visit, 131
  Washington Three conditions as to decommissioning, 180–1, 182
  see also Brooke/Mayhew talks
McGuinness, Martin
  and ceasefire, 256, 267–8
  choice of political solution, 269–70
  and decommissioning, 167–8, 242, 287, 288–9
  deputy first minister, 146, 192–3
  desire for peace, 191–2
  exploratory dialogue, 137–8
  and Gerry Adams, 279–80
  and Good Friday Agreement, 303
  'Groundhog Day' reference, 260
  and Ian Paisley, 198
  leadership abilities, 94–5, 171–2, 309
  meetings with, 92, 137–8, 162–3
  negotiational approach, 99, 154, 242–3, 287–8, 297–8, 306–7, 318, 320, 323–4
  and Northern Bank robbery, 283, 284, 315–16
  on peace negotiations, 141
  and PIRA, 308, 315, 321
  on reduction of British Army presence, 318–19
  on self-determination, 129
  sense of history, 305
  toasts queen, 263
  and Tony Blair, 197, 305
  on trusting civil servants, 292
  verbal abilities, 163
McMichael, Gary, unofficial talks with British Government, 131–3
media
  leaks. *See* leaks to media
  negotiations and, 286–7, 326–7
minorities, conflicts involving. *See* intercommunal conflicts
minority participation in government
  Good Friday Agreement, 78
  Parliamentary Committees proposals, 25–6
  see also power-sharing
Misunderstanding Ulster (David Trimble), 170–1
Mitchell, George
  chairs multiparty negotiations, 74, 141, 142–3, 221
  consent to appointment, 225
  decommissioning principles, 182
  decommissioning report (1996), 180–1, 182
  influence, 225–6
  Review on implementation of Good Friday Agreement, 235–6

Index 345

Molyneaux, James
  and 1994 ceasefire, 327
  and Anglo-Irish Agreement, 47–8
  and Frameworks Document, 179–80
  and Irish Government, 265
  and Margaret Thatcher, 47–8
  meetings with, 29–30
  sense of identity, 96
  and Sir Patrick Mayhew, 124–5
Mowlam, Marjorie (Mo)
  and Gerry Adams, 308
  and Martin McGuinness, 308
  Maze Prison visit, 142–3
  negotiational approach, 326
  secretary of state, 83, 97, 102, 142, 187, 250
multiparty negotiations (1996–8)
  Belfast Agreement. *See* Good Friday Agreement (1998)
  Blair Government and, 75
  commencement, 184
  elections for representation, 74, 140–1, 184
  preparatory talks, 141
  progress, 75
  Sinn Féin and, 184–7
  'strands' of negotiations, 74–5
  sufficient consensus principle, 74
Murphy, Paul
  Joint Declaration, 158
  negotiational skill, 286
  secretary of state, 149, 153–4
  verbal abilities, 163

narrative. *See* historical narrative
nationalist community
  British Government's relationship with, compared with Irish Government's, 206–7
  'Catholic' analysis of peace process, 225
  constitutional issue, perspective on, 56–7
  language sensitivities, 231–2
  participation in government. *See* minority participation in government
  sense of identity, 96
  support for Irish unity, 58
  see also nationalist parties
nationalist parties
  moral stance, 281–2
  negotiational stance, 90–1
  participation in government. *See* minority participation in government
negotiations
  acknowledgement of issues, 96
  ambiguity. *See* ambiguity
  analytical approach, 258–9
  as argument-winning, 310

  background to British approach, 10, 12–13, 14
  'bicycle theory'. *See* momentum *below*
  'big picture'. *See* strategic approach *below*
  big problems, dealing with, 291–2
  body language, 323–4
  'bottom line', 226–7, 308
  breaking point, judging of, 215–16
  bureaucratic process, 83
  'carrot and stick' approach, 303–4
  catastrophic events, effect of, 99
  'Catholic' analysis, 225
  change, attitudes to, 320–1
  change in political context, 264–5
  changes in direction and emphasis, 317–18
  charisma, 228
  choreographing of, 217–18, 286
  clarity
    preference for, 295–6
    shift to, 295
  clear objectives
    adjustment of, 226
    advantages of, 98
    keeping in view, 303
  cohesion, 331–2
  'common ground', 224–5
  competitiveness, 219–20
  comprehensiveness and convergence in relation, 262–3
  concessions, use of, 220–1
  confidentiality, tactical use of, 94
  contextual understanding, importance of, 96
  controlling pace of, 321–2
  as cooperative task, 312
  deciding to continue, 84
  detail, importance of, 282–3
  differences in approach, 82–3
  different types of talks, strategy across, 89–90, 125
  discipline, 212
  disorientation as tactic, 278
  dissident factions, danger of, 324
  distraction, use of, 291
  drafting of text. *See* drafting of documents and speeches
  egotism, 219–20
  embassies, role of, 85
  empathy, 310
  end planning, 209
  end point, keeping in view, 303
  facilitating of, 86
  familiarity with opponents, 219
  final moments, importance of, 314
  firmness, 205–6

negotiations (*cont.*)
  flexibility
    conditions for, 296–8
    need for, 98
  formality, degree of, 292, 302–3, 319
  friendship, 310–11
  goals, importance of clear, 84
  'going down to the wire', 314
  hearing and listening, difference between, 319
  historical understanding, advantages of, 99
  history, sense of, 287–8, 305
  humour, use of, 221–2
  imbalance between nationalists and unionists, 206–7
  improvisation, 316–17
  inclusiveness. *See* inclusiveness
  independent chairs, 113
  informality
    degree of, 292, 302–3, 319
    role of, 305
  instinct, 318
  interim positions as objective, 303
  interpretative differences, 82
  as joint task, 312
  keeping ahead, 318–19
  language, skill in use of, 90
  latitude, 291
  leaks to media, 129–30
  listening, 208–9, 228
  listening and hearing, difference between, 319
  location, use of, 293–4, 309–10
  as logical exercise, 310
  long-term strategy, 307–8
  'mechanics of', 322
  media, use of, 286–7, 326–7
  metaphor, use of, 221
  minimum demands, adherence to, 227
  momentum, 83, 207–8, 284
  moral integrity, 83
  moral stance, 281–2
  neutral territory, use of, 293–4
  non-verbal communication, 323–4
  number of persons, 304
  observers, 208–9
  officials and politicians, relationship between, 92–3
  one-to-one conversations, 226
  organisations with paramilitary arm, difficulties with, 206
  outcome
    accuracy of predictions, 87
    long-term change, 86, 87
  over-analysis, dangers of, 275–6

over-negotiation, 308–9
pace, control of, 321–2
parties' priority points, 217
party discipline, 212
pausing, 84
personal relationships, 311
as philosophical exercise, 310
PIRA attacks, effect of, 283–5
planning and spontaneity in relation, 316
political thinking and party political thinking distinguished, 88
practical approach, 215
pragmatic approach, 215
pragmatism and principle, balancing of, 88, 212–13, 290, 330
pre-emption, 318–19
pre-meeting planning, 292
precise wording, 320
pressure, degree of, 311–12
private agreements, 259–60
process, importance of, 84, 114
process of talks, 125
  progressing of, 14
reconciliation
  meaning of, 83–4
  prospects for, 88
repetition, 320
reporting back, 315
responses, managing, 84–5
right amount of talking, gauging, 207
rightness to talk, 300, 302
shifts in position, 330–1
'single text negotiation', 115, 166–7, 322
skill, 210–11
speediness, 83, 207–8
spontaneity, 218–19, 228, 316
stalemate, 299
stalling tactics, 321–2
stereotypes, 91–2
strategic approach, 215, 275–6, 281
strategic use of statements, 87
strategy across different types of negotiations, 89–90, 125
strategy and tactics, confusion between, 98
sufficient consensus principle. *See* sufficient consensus principle
surprise, effect of, 315–16
suspension of, 125–6
switching between strands, 89
'symbolic leadership', 79–80
symbolism, understanding of, 267–8, 286–7, 328–9
symmetry, 217–18

Index

tactical approach, 308-9
talk and text in relation, 216-17, 259
text, use of, 322-3
'the link', 80
third party, role of, 91
time management, 99
toughness, 211-12
transition between ministers and governments, during, 97
trust, 82, 94
unfulfilled promises, 220
US involvement, 85
videoconferencing, 85
see also dialogue
New Framework for Agreement, A (1995), 139
new institutional framework
British Government objective, 151-2
Good Friday Agreement, 75, 76-7, 78, 230, 252-3
New Ireland Forum
establishment of, 33-4, 42
failure of, 62-3
proposals by, 50
new political institutions. *See* new institutional framework
'normalisation'
consent principle, 152-3
Good Friday Agreement, 76
Joint Declaration, 165
Northern Bank robbery, effect on peace process, 283-5, 315-16
Northern Ireland
Census 2001, 151
constitutional position. *See* consent principle; Irish constitutional claims
death toll, 151
institutional reform. *See* new institutional framework
local government. *See* district councils
post-conflict relationship with UK, 100
Northern Ireland Assembly (1998)
difficulties, 149
suspension (October 2002), 149
Northern Ireland Assembly (2003), elections, 149-50
Northern Ireland Assembly (2007), inauguration, 146
Northern Ireland Civil Service
and Anglo-Irish Agreement, 29
and direct rule, 27
drafting of documents and speeches, 18, 19
perspective on Good Friday Agreement implementation, 250-1
political discussions within, 28-9

Northern Ireland Constitution Act 1973, 'constitutional guarantee', 57
Northern Ireland Executive (1974)
appreciation of, 28, 121
compromise and decision-making, 2-3
failure of, 1-2, 3
as model of inclusiveness, 121
Northern Ireland Executive (1998)
d'Hondt procedure for nominating ministers, 234-5
dialogue after collapse of, 277
establishment, 234-5
removal of ministers, Good Friday Agreement provision, 231
restoration, 153, 236-7, 241, 300-1
suspension. *See* direct rule
Northern Ireland Government
constitutional White Paper (24 March 1972), 26-7
drafting of documents and speeches, 19-20
Queen's Speeches, 20-1
Northern Ireland ministers. *See* Northern Ireland Executive (1998)
Northern Ireland Office (NIO)
and Anglo-Irish Agreement, 63-4
approach to talks process, 66-7, 83
calibre of ministers, 102
consent principle, defence of, 61-2
contact with loyalist organisations, 130-3
contact with PIRA, 128
contacts within political parties, 128
cooperation with Irish officials, 101-2
drafting of documents and speeches. *See* drafting of documents and speeches
experience and expertise, 65-6, 101
initiative on political settlement, 65-7
and Joint Declaration, 153-7
ministerial longevity, advantages of, 97-8
negotiations. *See* negotiations
permanent secretary, 201
personnel changes, 161
Political Affairs Division, 122-4
political analysis by, 253-4
political discussions within, 22-3, 28-9
role in relation to Government policy, 201
'Stormontgate' (October 2002), 149
trust-building, 258
unionist suspicion of, 178
videoconferencing, 30
Northern Ireland Parliament, and partition, 57
Northern Ireland Prison Service, prison regime reforms, 122
Northern Ireland Women's Coalition (NIWC)
establishment, 141
and Joint Declaration, 150

Omagh bomb (August 1998), effect on peace process, 144–5, 315–16
'On the Runs' (OTRs)
  agreement on, 254–5
  drafting of documents, 164
  issue of, 259, 270–1, 274–5
  Joint Declaration, 152–3, 162
O'Neill, Terence
  'Crossroads' speech, 23–4
  meeting with Seán Lamass, 21–2
  Northern Ireland finance minister, 19
  Northern Ireland prime minister, 20–1
  'Pottinger' speech, 20
  as reformer, 24–5
  relations with ministers, 21
  resignation, 23–4
  speech-writing ability, 19–20
Orange Order
  Parades. *See* parades
  Sir Patrick Mayhew visits meeting, 131

Paisley, Ian
  and 1994 ceasefire, 327
  and decommissioning, 287, 288, 323–4
  desire for peace, 281–2
  Divis Street Riots, 120–1
  first minister, 146
  and Good Friday Agreement, 265
  humour, 154
  and Martin McGuinness, 198
  meetings with, 29–30, 316–17
  meets Bill Clinton, 140
  moves amendment of Northern Ireland Constitution Act 1973, 57
  and Paul Murphy, 155
  sense of identity, 96
  and Tony Blair, 170, 311
  verbal abilities, 163
  withdraws from talks, 125
Palestinian–Israeli conflict, preconditions for settlement of, 113–14
parades
  Haass recommendations, 332–3
  regulation of, 296–7
paramilitary activities
  ending of, Joint Declaration provision, 152–3, 164, 171
  organisations with paramilitary arm, difficulties negotiating with, 206
  punishment beatings, 214
  see also loyalist organisations; Provisional Irish Republican Army (PIRA)
Parliamentary Committees, minority participation in, 25–6

partition of Ireland
  nationalist perspective, 56–7
  political consequences, 56
  see also Irish constitutional claims
Patten Review. See policing
peace process
  ambiguity and, 3, 14–15
  approach by present study, 1, 7
  choreographing of, 286, 304
  chronology of, xiv–xxii
  closing down, possibility of, 268–9
  commitment to peaceful means, 214
  content and structure of present study, 7–15
  context and detail in relation, 204–5
  context and text in relation, 222
  continuation
    perception of, 298
    prospects for, 100
  continuing process, sense of, 300–1
  continuity, 95, 209–10
  control, degree of, 227
  creativity, 95–6, 204
  formal and informal mechanisms, timing of usage, 102–3
  'high politics' approach to history of, 147
  historical context, 1–2
  importance of process, 114
  inclusiveness. *See* inclusiveness
  international involvement, 152, 225–6
  interviews, author's approach to, 7–9
  key developments, 102
  key principles, importance of, 214–15
  as metaphorical process, 89
  momentum, 227, 303
  moral dimension, 203–4
  as narrative process, 90–1
  and political development, 203–4
  positional approach, 90–1
  and reconciliation, 301
  reduced Anglo-Irish involvement, 334
  religious influence, 282
  stalemate, 210
  studies of, 6
  success in political terms, 222
  surprise, effect of, 95
  text and context in relation, 222
  as text-driven process, 224
  turning points, identification of, 95
  use of term, 202
  see also Anglo-Irish relations; exclusively peaceful means, principle of; negotiations

Index

Phillips, Sir Jonathan
  drafting of documents, 159
  involvement in peace process, 153–4, 155, 157, 158, 161, 162–3, 167
  on role of dialogue, 14, 277–301
Pilling, Sir Joseph
  drafting of documents, 158
  involvement in peace process, 66, 157–8
  on negotiational approach, 12–13, 201–28
  permanent secretary, 101, 153–4
  political director, 156–7
  reference to, 249–50
policing
  devolution, 152–3, 164, 165, 166, 167, 168–9, 170, 209, 293, 296–7, 300–1, 332
  Good Friday Agreement, 76, 230
  Patten Review, 152–3, 162–3
political institutions, development of new. *See* new institutional framework
'Pottinger' speech, drafting of, 20
Powell, Enoch, 31–2, 49, 60
Powell, Jonathan
  anecdotes by, 229–30
  and Blair/Ahern meeting, 268
  chief of staff, 145–6, 153–4, 156–7, 158, 159, 167, 187, 227, 246–7, 275–6
  and 'creative ambiguity', 249
  and decommissioning, 287
  on dining at home, 174
  drafting of documents, 158, 160
  Great Hatred, Little Room, 258–9, 270–1, 275, 304
  Joint Declaration, 158, 162–3
  meetings with Sinn Féin, 162–3, 279–80, 283–4, 287
  on negotiating Good Friday Agreement, 14, 302–29
  negotiational strength, 169
  and Northern Bank robbery, 283–4
  and personnel continuity, 161–2
  speechwriting with Sinn Féin, 325–6
  on talks with terrorists, 300
power-sharing
  devolution and, 126–7, 209–10
  Executive. *See* Northern Ireland Executive (1974)
  local promotion of, 128
  negotiations, 87
  proposals for, 27–8
  unionist opposition, 60
pragmatism and principle, balancing of, 88, 212–13, 215, 262, 271–2, 290, 330
Prime Minister's Office
  and Irish Government, 178–9
  Overseas Adviser, 177–8
  unionist relations with, 178
Prior, James (Jim), 'rolling devolution', 38–40
prisoner releases
  agreement on, 167, 254–5
  drafting of documents, 164, 168–9
  Good Friday Agreement, 76, 230
  issue of, 152–3
prisons. *See* Northern Ireland Prison Service
Progressive Unionist Party (PUP)
  boycotting of talks, 141
  and Combined Loyalist Military Command, 130–1
  contact with, 136, 146
  electoral support, 74, 145
  exclusion from talks, 128
  inclusion in talks, 11, 74, 120, 136–7, 140–1, 142
  visit to US, 134–5
  see also Smyth, Hugh
Protestant community. *See* unionist community
Provisional Irish Republican Army (PIRA)
  abandonment of armed struggle, 210–11
  acknowledges end of conflict, 153–4
  acknowledges stalemate situation, 299–300
  and Anglo-Irish Agreement, 50–1, 52
  belief in military victory, 110
  Canary Wharf bomb (February 1996), 73, 140–1, 180, 183, 206–7
  ceasefire
    breaking of, 75
    declaration (August 1994), 73, 131
    ending (February 1996), 73, 140–1, 180, 183, 206–7
    renewal (July 1997), 75, 142–3
    unionist response, 327
  claims to governance of united Ireland, 56
  contact with British Government, 128
  cost of conflict, 109
  decommissioning of weapons. *See* decommissioning
  fugitives. *See* 'On the Runs' (OTRs)
  and Good Friday Agreement, 238–9
  and Joint Declaration, 150–1
  murder of Robert McCartney, 283
  negotiations ('the link'). *See* 'link, the'
  Northern Bank robbery, 283–5
  possibilities of defeating, 87–8
  secret meeting with British Government (1972), 4–5
  Shankill bomb (1993), 129–30
  and Sinn Féin, 287
  and Sunningdale Agreement, 4
  support for, 33–5
  suspension of operations, 129–30

Provisional Irish Republican Army (PIRA) (*cont.*)
  Teebane bomb (1991), 123
  Tony Blair challenges on 'acts of completion', 149
  and 'Whitbread' speech, 81
punishment beatings
  attitudes to, 290
  effect on peace process, 214

Real IRA
  and Joint Declaration, 150–1
  Omagh bomb (August 1998), 144–5, 315–16
reconciliation
  act of, proposal for, 232–3
  meaning of, 83–4
  process of, 301
  prospects for, 88
Rees, Merlyn
  secretary of state, 79
  on Sunningdale Agreement, 4
reform declaration (1968), drafting of, 24–5
Reid, John
  secretary of state, 149, 153–4, 250
  Weston Park proposals, 161–2
religion and ambiguity 282
republican movement
  ambiguity and clarity, 295, 313–14, 320
  'Catholic' analysis of peace process, 225
  change, attitude to, 320–1
  consent principle and, 215
  defeat, attitude to, 287–8
  desire for peace, 306
  interpretation by, 265–6
  language sensitivities, 266–7
  moral stance, 281–2
  religious influence, 282
  sense of history, 287–8, 305
  united Ireland, aspiration for, 306–7
  violence, attitude to, 91
  see also Irish National Liberation Army (INLA); Provisional Irish Republican Army (PIRA); Sinn Féin
Reynolds, Albert
  and Downing Street Declaration, 71
  and John Major, 92–3
Robinson, Mary
  and Anglo-Irish Agreement, 63
  proposes constitutional claims amendment, 69–70
Robinson, Peter
  DUP leader, 192–3
  first minister, 192–3

proposes elections to multiparty negotiations, 140
'rolling devolution', failure of, 38–40
Royal Agricultural Society speech (May 1997). *See* Blair, Tony
Royal Ulster Constabulary (RUC). *See* policing

sanctions
  drafting of documents, 168–9
  issue of, 152–3
Sands, Bobby, 5
secret exchanges. *See* 'link, the'
security
  British proposals, 39, 45–6, 64
  collusion by security forces. *See* Cory Collusion Inquiry
  improvement after Good Friday Agreement, 78
  Irish proposals, 34, 36, 40–1
  'normalisation'. *See* 'normalisation'
  unionist concerns, 58
Shankill bomb (1993), effect on peace process, 129–30
single text negotiation
  Good Friday Agreement, 115, 322
  Joint Declaration, 166–7
Sinn Féin
  and 'acts of completion', 296
  Adams and McGuinness as duo, 279–80
  and ambiguity, 205
  and Anglo-Irish Agreement, 1–6, 37–8, 50–1, 116
  ban on contact with, 127
  commitment to peaceful means, 214
  date of British withdrawal, adherence to demand for, 227
  and decommissioning, 220, 286, 288–90
  dialogue with, 202
  see also 'link, the'
  and Downing Street Declaration, 71
  and DUP, 278, 306–7, 316–17
  electoral support for, 29–30, 33–5, 40–1, 46, 184
  exclusion from peace talks, 74–5
  and exclusively peaceful means principle, 290–1
  exploratory dialogue, 135
  future progress, 298–9
  and Good Friday Agreement, 76, 77, 295, 323
  and hunger strikes, 5
  internal authority, 99–100
  and Joint Declaration, 150, 173
  long-term strategy, 307–8

media, skill in using, 286–7
and multiparty negotiations, 184–7
negotiational control, 321–2
negotiational discipline, 212
negotiational flexibility, 297–8
negotiational focus, 275
negotiational skill, 210–11, 308–9
negotiational stance, 90–1, 94–5, 278–80, 308
negotiational toughness, 211
non-verbal communication, 323–4
participation in peace talks, 73, 75
and PIRA, 287
power-sharing, 87
and reduction of British Army presence, 294
reporting back on negotiations, 315
respectability, growth in, 210–11
response to PIRA attacks, 283
and SDLP, 65, 68
secret contact with. *See* 'link, the'
socialist united Ireland, aspiration for, 296
speechwriting with Jonathan Powell, 325–6
'Stormontgate' (October 2002), 149
strategic approach to negotiations, 281, 288
symbolism, understanding of, 267–8, 286–7
united Ireland, aspiration for, 296
unofficial contact with, 123–4
written records of negotiations, 275
see also Adams, Gerry; McGuinness, Martin
Smyth, Hugh
meets John Major, 133, 134
unofficial talks with British Government, 131–3
Social Democratic and Labour Party (SDLP)
and Anglo-Irish Agreement, 37–8
and devolution, 57
and Downing Street Declaration, 71
and Joint Declaration, 150
and Sinn Féin, 65, 68
and Sunningdale Agreement, 1–2
and unionist parties, 65
see also Fitt, Gerard (Gerry); Hume, John
sovereignty, transfer of, British reservations as to, 41–2, 49
speeches, drafting of. *See* drafting of documents and speeches
Stormont. *See* Northern Ireland Parliament
'Stormontgate' (October 2002), effect on peace process, 149
'strategic or economic interest, no'. *See* 'Whitbread' speech
sufficient consensus principle
Joint Declaration, 173
multiparty negotiations, 74
Sunningdale Agreement (1973)

Anglo-Irish Agreement contrasted, 48
effect if had been successful, 47
failure of, 3, 4, 36
and Good Friday Agreement, 3, 209–10, 221
Irish constitutional claims, 31–2
opposition to, 2–3
origins of peace process, 1–2
symbols
Haass recommendations, 332–3
'symbolic leadership', 79–80
understanding of, 267–8, 286–7, 328–9

text. *See* documents; drafting of documents and speeches
Thatcher, Margaret
agrees to further talks with Irish Government, 67–8
Anglo-Irish Agreement, 35–7, 38–9, 41–3, 45–6, 47–9, 50, 51–2, 98–9
and Charles Haughey, 38–40
and consent principle, 63
and Garret FitzGerald, 34–5, 39, 40, 41, 43, 45–6, 50
and New Ireland Forum, 62–3
Thomas, Sir Quentin
drafting of documents, 99
involvement in peace process, 66, 83, 97, 123–4, 137–8, 141, 154, 315
on settlement of intercommunal conflicts, 10–11, 101–19
transition between governments
background to, 12
decommissioning, 180–3
Good Friday Agreement, 192–9
introduction, 177
Labour victory assumed, 179
Major's and Blair's achievement summarised, 199–200
and multiparty negotiations, 184–7
negotiations during, 97
Prime Minister's Office. *See* Prime Minister's Office
transition, 187–8
unionist influence at Westminster, 179
unionist 'veto' on Major's policy, 179–80
Trimble, David
clarity of vision, 212–13
commitment to peace process, 174
critiques British Government policy, 170–1, 172
and decommissioning, 149–50, 195, 218, 286
on dining at home, 174
first minister, 149

Trimble, David (*cont.*)
  and Gerry Adams, 86, 148–9, 164, 197–8
  and Good Friday Agreement, 232, 233, 236–7, 238–9
  and Joint Declaration, 159, 163
  and Loyalist Commission, 145
  Misunderstanding Ulster, 170–1
  and *Mitchell Review*, 236
  negotiational approach, 174, 217
  negotiational difficulties, 281
  negotiational skill, 281–2
  negotiational toughness, 211–12
  Nobel Peace Prize, 108
  and Paul Murphy, 163
  political cost of peace, 192–3
  reporting back on negotiations, 315
  resigns from Executive, 168
  and Sinn Féin, 278
  on sufficient consensus principle, 173
  on Sunningdale Agreement, 154
  on talks with terrorists, 171
  and UUP, 198, 205
  verbal abilities, 163
truth and reconciliation. *See* reconciliation

Ulster Defence Association (UDA). *See* loyalist organisations
Ulster Democratic Party (UDP)
  and Combined Loyalist Military Command, 130–1
  contact with, 130–2, 133–4, 136–9
  electoral support, 74–5, 120, 141, 145
  exclusion from talks, 75, 76, 128, 142–3
  inclusion in talks, 74, 120, 134, 140–1
  and Ulster Political Research Group, 145
Ulster Freedom Fighters. *See* loyalist organisations
Ulster Political Research Group (UPRG), establishment, 145
Ulster Unionist Party (UUP)
  boycotting of talks, 141
  decline, 87
  discussions with, 29–30
  Dublin visit (September 1992), 125–6
  and DUP, 87, 150
  and Irish Government, 265
  and Joint Declaration, 150
  political cost of peace, 192–3
  see also Molyneaux, James; Trimble, David
Ulster Volunteer Force (UVF). *See* loyalist organisations
Ulster Workers' Council strike and origins of peace process, 3
'Ulsterisation' policy, impact of, 4
unification of Ireland

Government of Ireland Act 1920, provisions of, 57
see also Irish constitutional claims
unionist community
  and Anglo-Irish Agreement, 64–5, 68
  British Government's relationship with, compared with Irish Government's, 206–7
  constitutional issue, perspective on, 55, 58–60
  cooperation with Ireland, opposition to, 60
  devolution, support for, 60
  economic concerns, 59
  and Good Friday Agreement, 55
  and Irish constitutional claims, 60
  literalness, 231–2
  Orange Order, 131
  political concerns, 59–60
  power-sharing, opposition to, 60
  Protestant identity, concerns as to, 58–9
  security concerns, 58
  sense of identity, 96
  support for Union, 55, 59
  United States and, 134–5, 225
  violence, attitude to, 91
unionist parties
  and ambiguity, 205
  ambiguity and clarity, 295, 320
  Anglo-Irish Agreement, 29–30, 37–8, 46–8, 50, 52–3, 64–5
  change, attitude to, 320–1
  End to Drift, An, 52–3, 64–5
  Good Friday Agreement, 76, 77, 295, 323
  interpretation by, 265–6
  and Joint Declaration, 150
  literalness, 266–7, 281, 320
  moral stance, 281–2
  negotiational approach, 90–1, 314
  negotiational discipline, 212
  negotiational toughness, 211–12
  and reduction of British Army presence, 294
  and SDLP, 65
  and Sinn Féin, 73
  and 'symbolic leadership', 79–80
  symbolism, understanding of, 267–8
  United States, and, 134–5
united Ireland. *See* Irish constitutional claims; Irish unity
United Kingdom
  general election 1974 and Sunningdale Agreement, 3
  general election 1997, 142

Index

see also transition between governments
government. *See* British Government
integration with. *See* integration with United Kingdom
Northern Ireland's post-conflict relationship with, 100
United States
 Al Qaeda attacks (9/11), impact of, 238, 283, 311–12
 Catholic bias, unionist perception of, 225
 consulate general's role in peace process, 134–5
 funding for loyalist projects, 145–6
 Gerry Adams visit, 130–1, 139–40
 Haass recommendations, 332–3
 independent chairs of 1996–8 talks, 113
 involvement in negotiations, 85, 225
 involvement post-Joint Declaration, 152
 Joe Cahill allowed visa, 85
 shift in thinking after 9/11, 284–5
 unionist relations with, 134–5, 225
 see also Bush, George W.; Clinton, Bill; Irish-Americans; Mitchell, George

videoconferencing, Northern Ireland Office use of, 30
violence
 attitudes to, 91, 290

paramilitary activities. *See* loyalist organisations; Provisional Irish Republican Army (PIRA)

Washington Three conditions. *See* decommissioning
Weston Park proposals (July 2001)
 implementation of Good Friday Agreement, 237
 and Joint Declaration, 161–3
'Whitbread' speech (9 November 1990)
 consent principle emphasised, 70–1
 context, 81–2
 drafting, 30–2
 non-inclusion of 'political', 81
 origin, 80–1
 purpose, 53
 renunciation of interest, 44
 timing, 81, 129–30
 unionist response, 68
Whitelaw, William (Willie)
 new proposals for talks (1991), 123
 secret meeting with PIRA (1972), 4–5
 secretary of state, 27
Wilson, Harold
 considers British withdrawal, 4
 and Sunningdale Agreement, 47
 'Ulsterisation' policy, 4